ALSO BY DAN ARIELY

Dollars and Sense

Payoff

Irrationally Yours

The (Honest) Truth About Dishonesty

The Upside of Irrationality

Predictably Irrational

AMAZING DECISIONS

AMAZING DECISIONS

THE ILLUSTRATED GUIDE TO IMPROVING
BUSINESS DEALS AND FAMILY MEALS

DAN ARIELY

ILLUSTRATED BY
MATT R. TROWER

A NOVEL GRAPHIC FROM HILL AND WANG
A DIVISION OF FARRAR, STRAUS AND GIROUX
NEW YORK

Hill and Wang

A division of Farrar, Straus and Giroux

120 Broadway, New York 10271

Printed in the United States of America

Published simultaneously in hardcover and paperback

First edition, 2019

Library of Congress Cataloging-in-Publication Data

Names: Ariely, Dan, author. | Trower, Matt R., author.

Title: Amazing decisions / Dan Ariely and Matt R. Trower.

Description: First Edition. | New York : Hill and Wang, A division of Farrar, Straus and Giroux, [2019]

Identifiers: LCCN 2018044060 | ISBN 9780374103767 (hardcover) | ISBN 9780374536749 (paperback)

Subjects: LCSH: Decision making.

Classification: LCC BF448 .A747 2019 | DDC 153.8/3—dc23

LC record available at https://lccn.loc.gov/2018044060

Our books may be purchased in bulk for promotional, educational, or business use. Please contact your local bookseller or the Macmillan Corporate and Premium Sales Department at 1-800-221-7945, extension 5442, or by e-mail at MacmillanSpecialMarkets@macmillan.com.

www.fsgbooks.com

www.twitter.com/fsgbooks • www.facebook.com/fsgbooks

1 3 5 7 9 10 8 6 4 2

CONTENTS

AMAZING DECISIONS

CHAPTER ONE

TWO DIFFERENT WORLDS

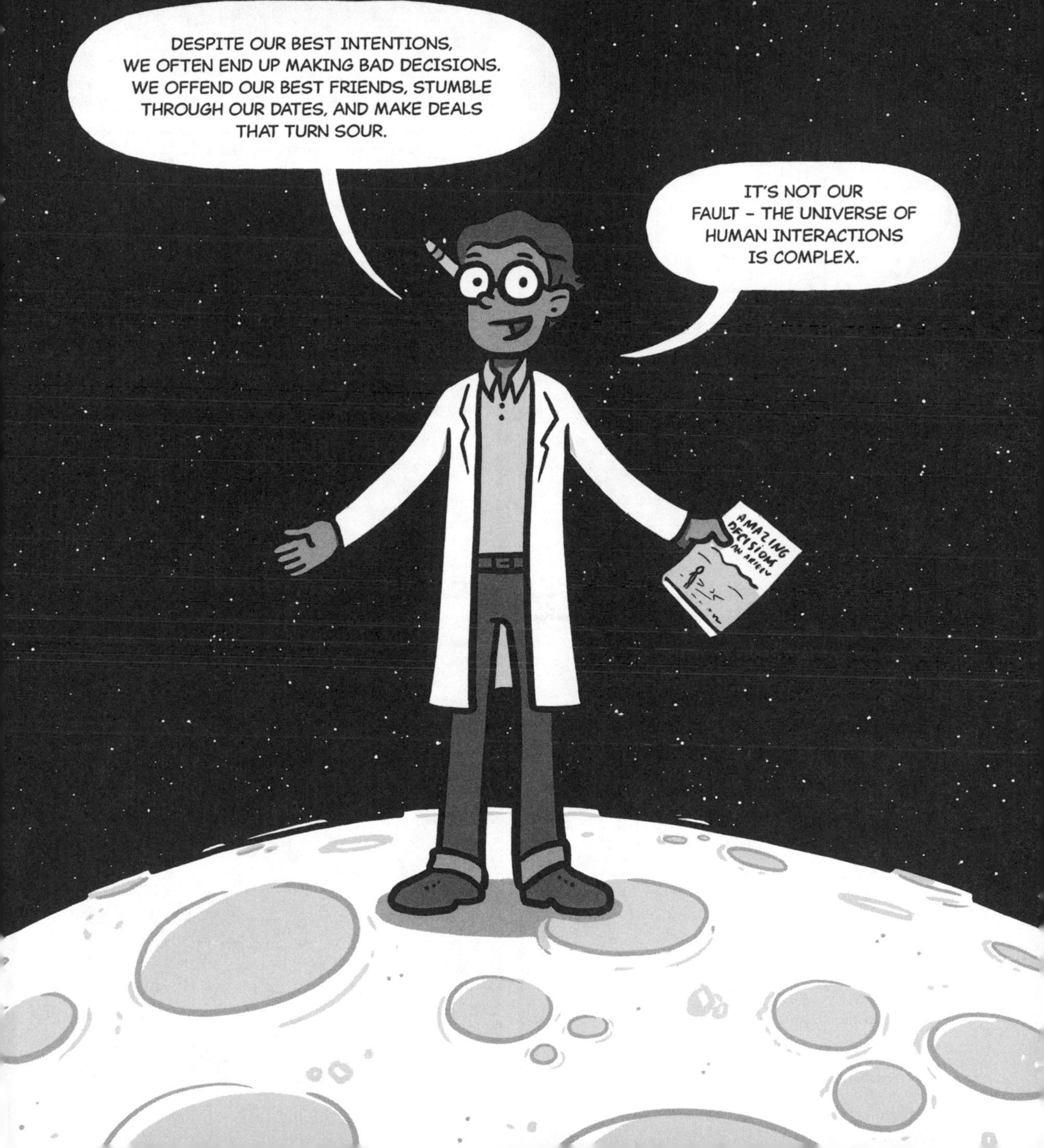
DESPITE OUR BEST INTENTIONS, WE OFTEN END UP MAKING BAD DECISIONS. WE OFFEND OUR BEST FRIENDS, STUMBLE THROUGH OUR DATES, AND MAKE DEALS THAT TURN SOUR.
IT'S NOT OUR FAULT – THE UNIVERSE OF HUMAN INTERACTIONS IS COMPLEX.

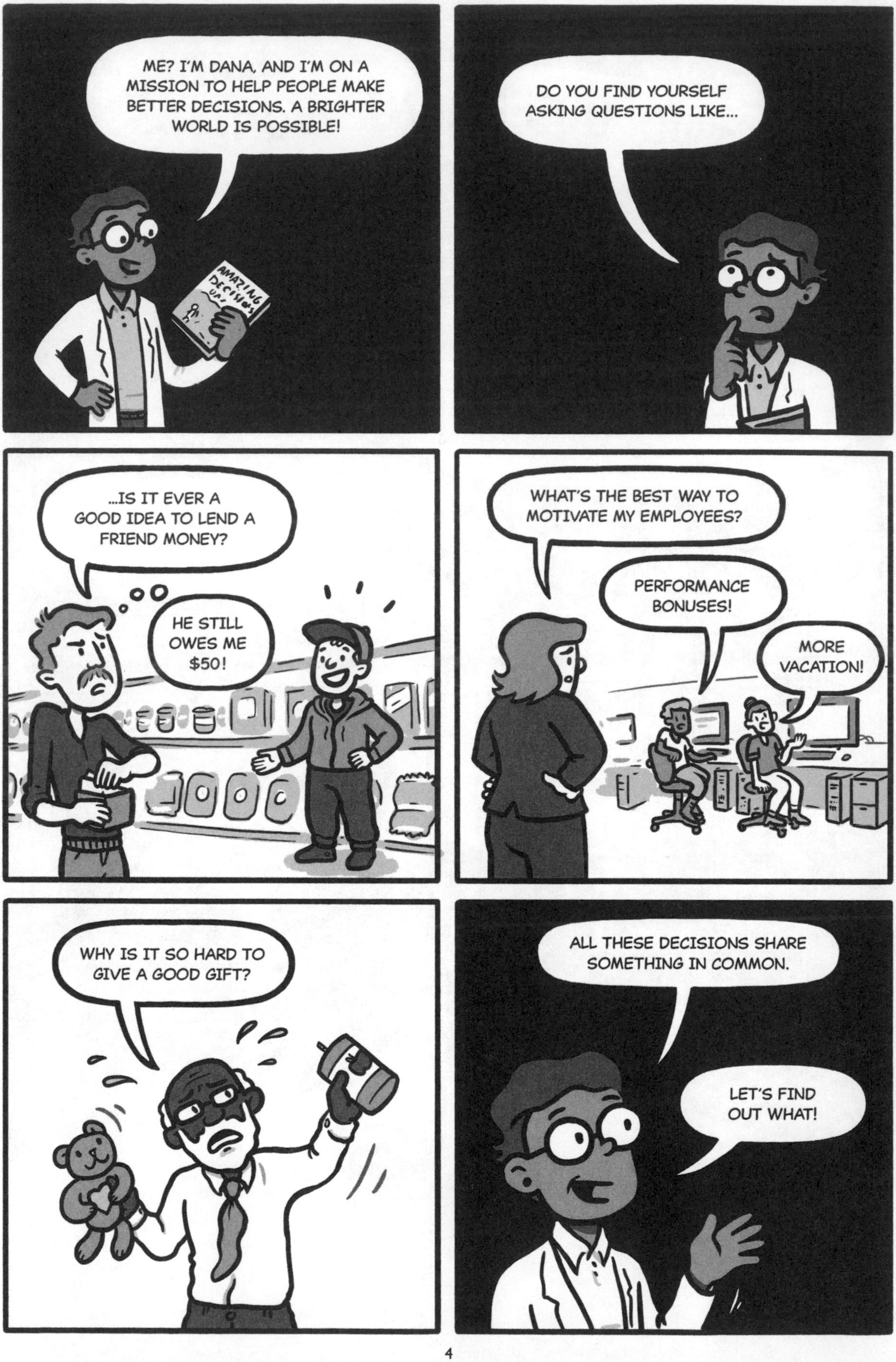
ME? I'M DANA, AND I'M ON A MISSION TO HELP PEOPLE MAKE BETTER DECISIONS. A BRIGHTER WORLD IS POSSIBLE!
AMAZING DECISIONS
DO YOU FIND YOURSELF ASKING QUESTIONS LIKE...
...IS IT EVER A GOOD IDEA TO LEND A FRIEND MONEY?
HE STILL OWES ME $50!
WHAT'S THE BEST WAY TO MOTIVATE MY EMPLOYEES?
PERFORMANCE BONUSES!
MORE VACATION!
WHY IS IT SO HARD TO GIVE A GOOD GIFT?
ALL THESE DECISIONS SHARE SOMETHING IN COMMON.
LET'S FIND OUT WHAT!

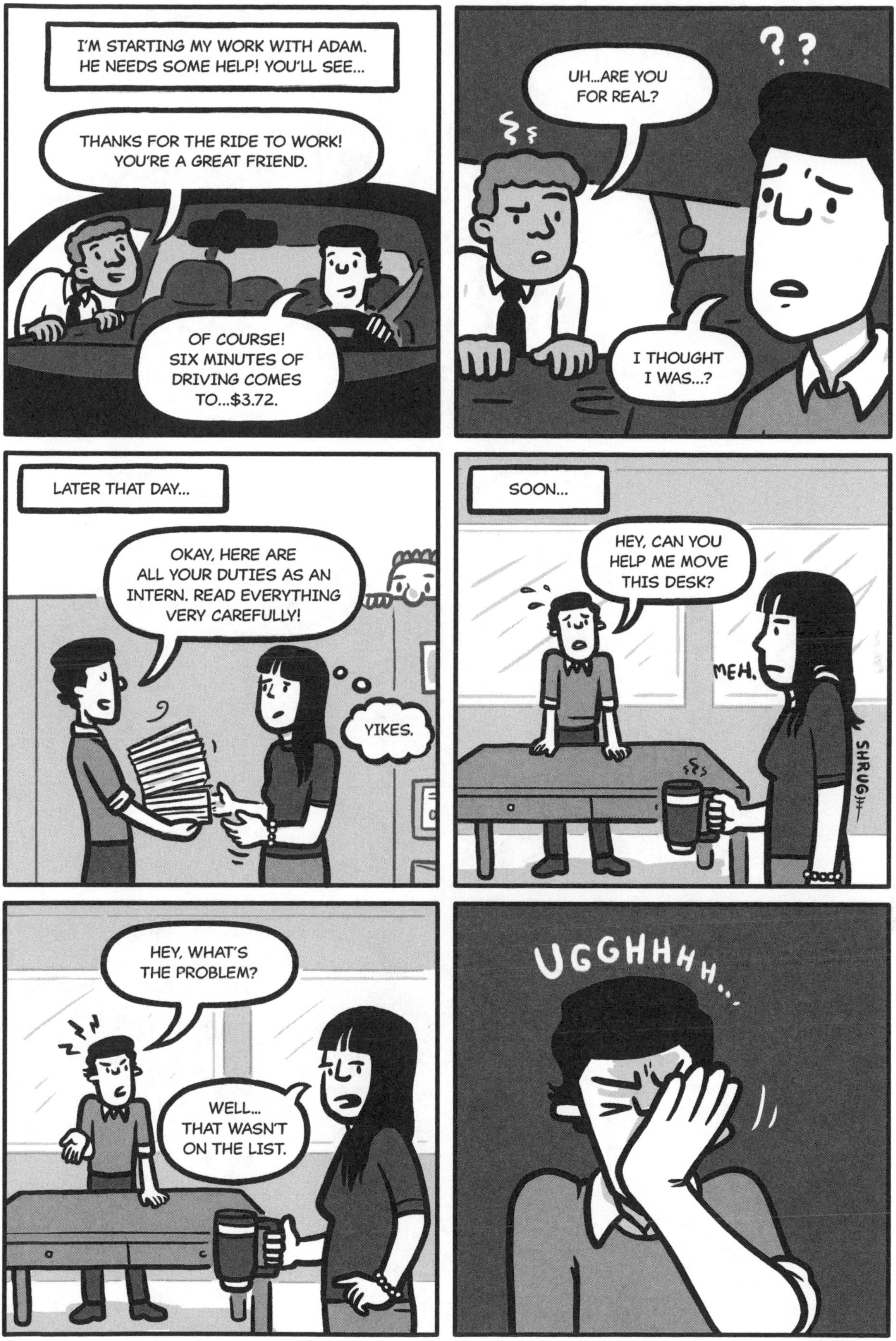
I'M STARTING MY WORK WITH ADAM. HE NEEDS SOME HELP! YOU'LL SEE...
THANKS FOR THE RIDE TO WORK! YOU'RE A GREAT FRIEND.
OF COURSE! SIX MINUTES OF DRIVING COMES TO...$3.72.
UH...ARE YOU FOR REAL?
I THOUGHT I WAS...?
LATER THAT DAY...
OKAY, HERE ARE ALL YOUR DUTIES AS AN INTERN. READ EVERYTHING VERY CAREFULLY!
YIKES.
SOON...
HEY, CAN YOU HELP ME MOVE THIS DESK?
MEH.
SHRUG
HEY, WHAT'S THE PROBLEM?
WELL... THAT WASN'T ON THE LIST.
UGGHHHH...

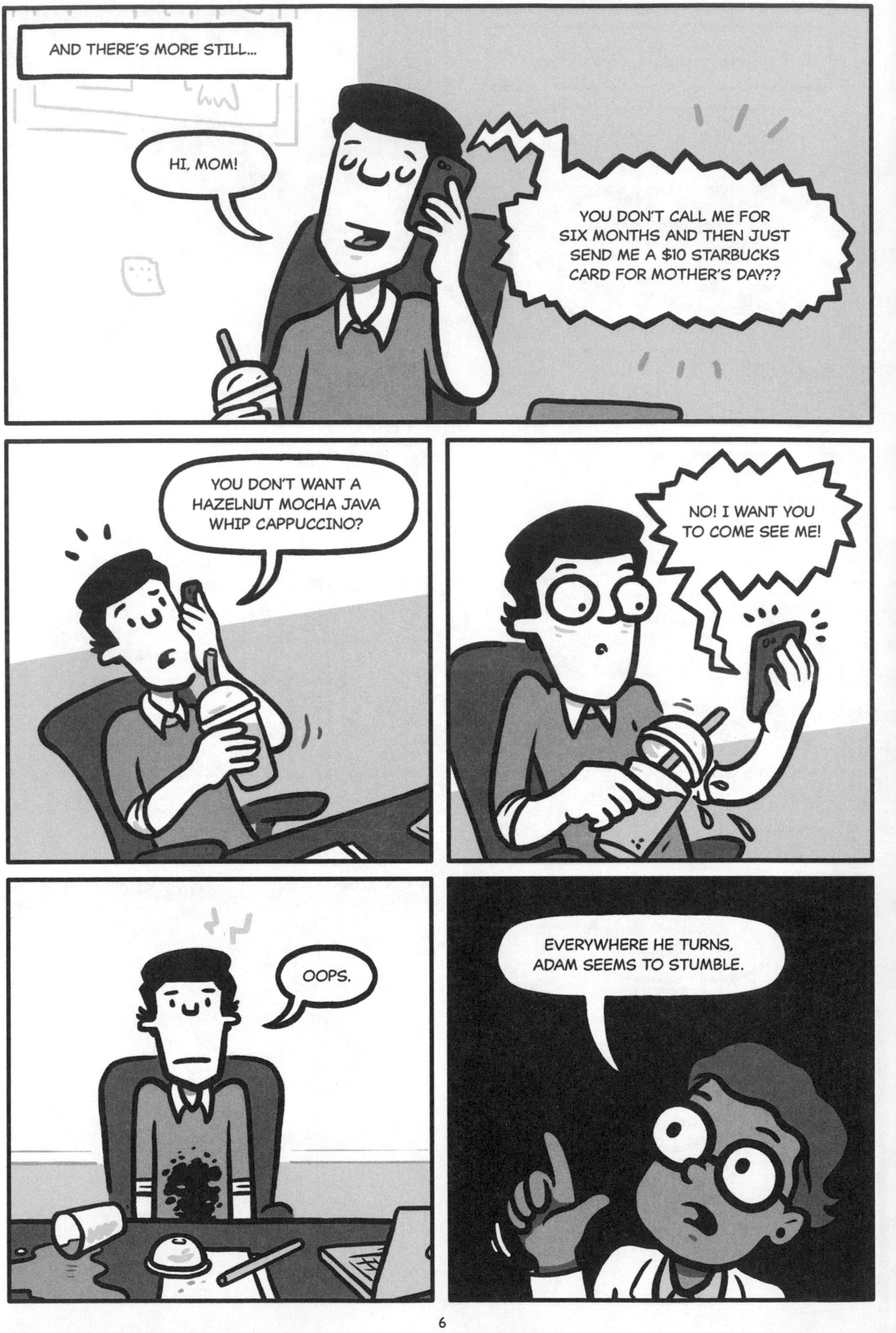
AND THERE'S MORE STILL...
HI, MOM!
YOU DON'T CALL ME FOR SIX MONTHS AND THEN JUST SEND ME A $10 STARBUCKS CARD FOR MOTHER'S DAY??
YOU DON'T WANT A HAZELNUT MOCHA JAVA WHIP CAPPUCCINO?
NO! I WANT YOU TO COME SEE ME!
OOPS.
EVERYWHERE HE TURNS, ADAM SEEMS TO STUMBLE.

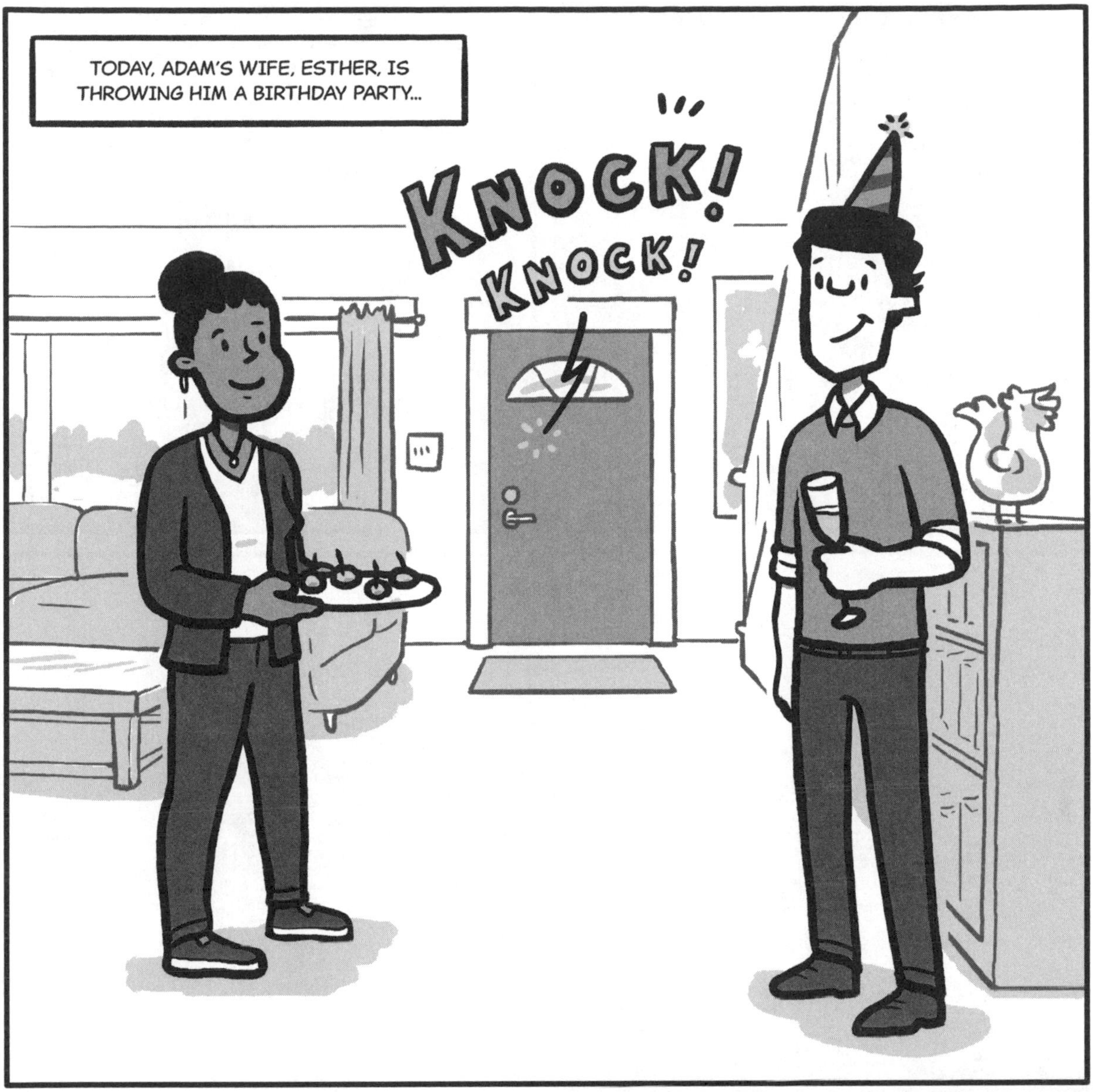
TODAY, ADAM'S WIFE, ESTHER, IS THROWING HIM A BIRTHDAY PARTY...
KNOCK!
KNOCK!

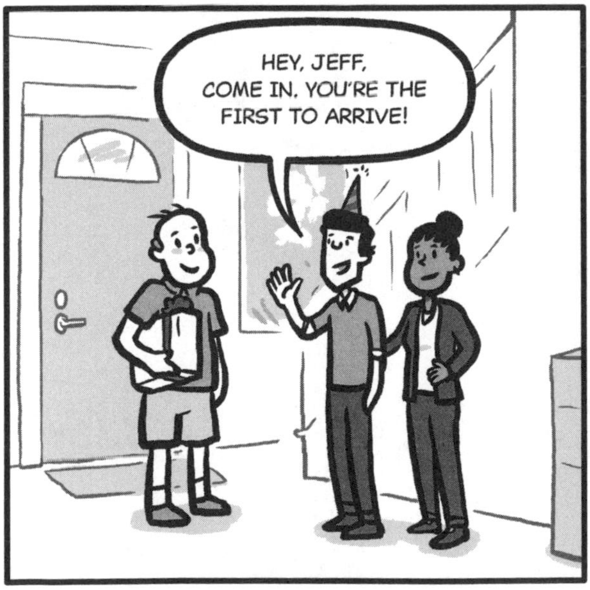
HEY, JEFF, COME IN. YOU'RE THE FIRST TO ARRIVE!

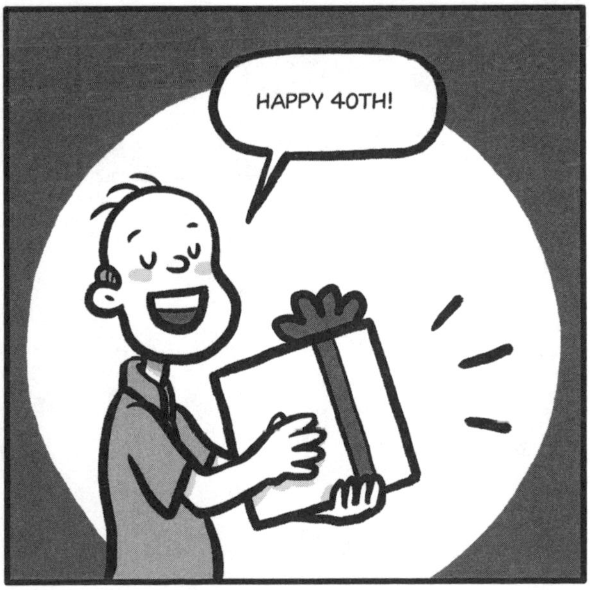
HAPPY 40TH!

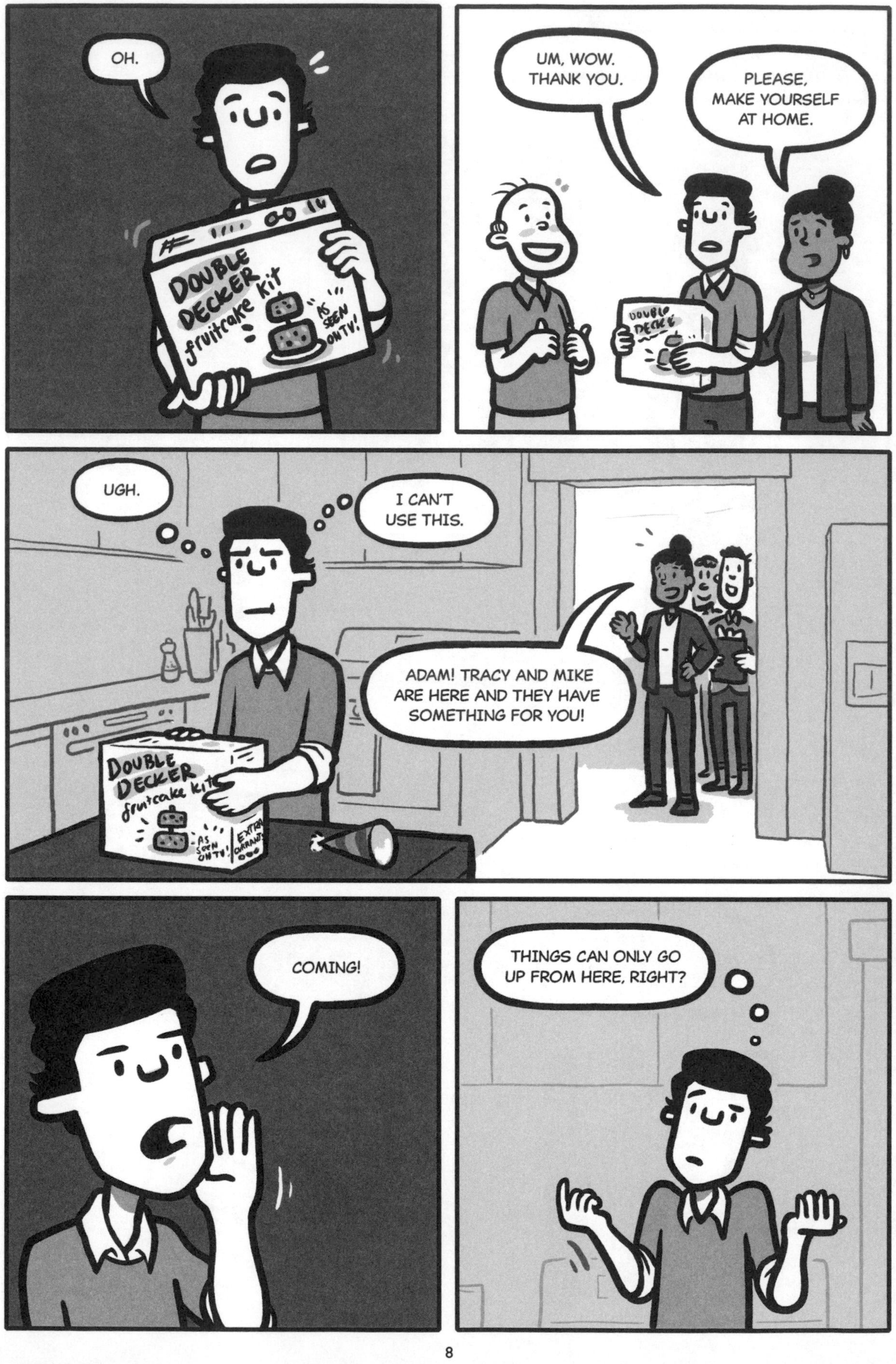
OH.
DOUBLE DECKER fruitcake kit
AS SEEN ON TV!
UM, WOW. THANK YOU.
PLEASE, MAKE YOURSELF AT HOME.
UGH.
I CAN'T USE THIS.
ADAM! TRACY AND MIKE ARE HERE AND THEY HAVE SOMETHING FOR YOU!
DOUBLE DECKER fruitcake kit
EXTRA CURRANTS
COMING!
THINGS CAN ONLY GO UP FROM HERE, RIGHT?

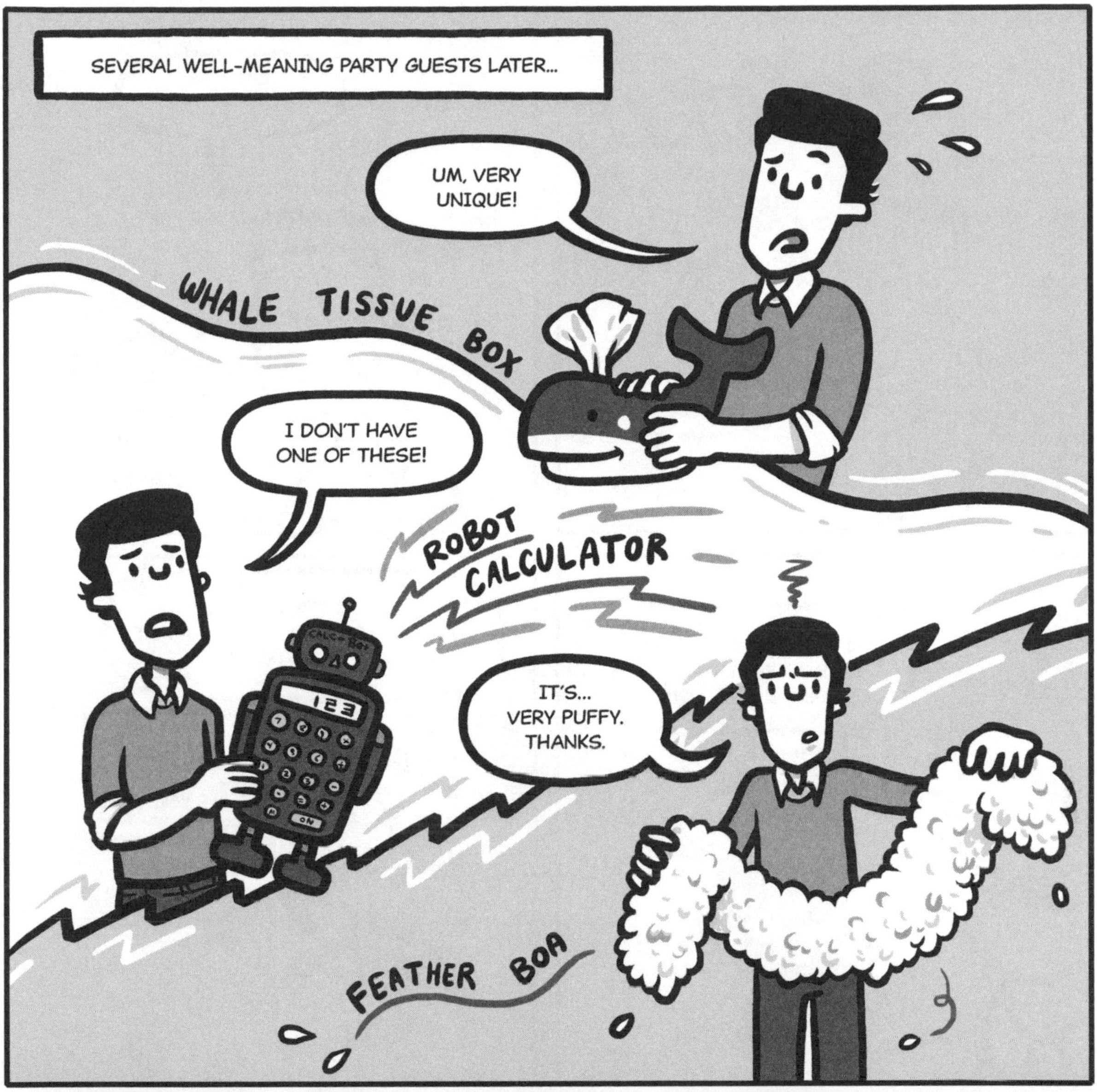
SEVERAL WELL-MEANING PARTY GUESTS LATER...
UM, VERY UNIQUE!
WHALE TISSUE BOX
I DON'T HAVE ONE OF THESE!
ROBOT CALCULATOR
123
ON
IT'S... VERY PUFFY. THANKS.
FEATHER BOA

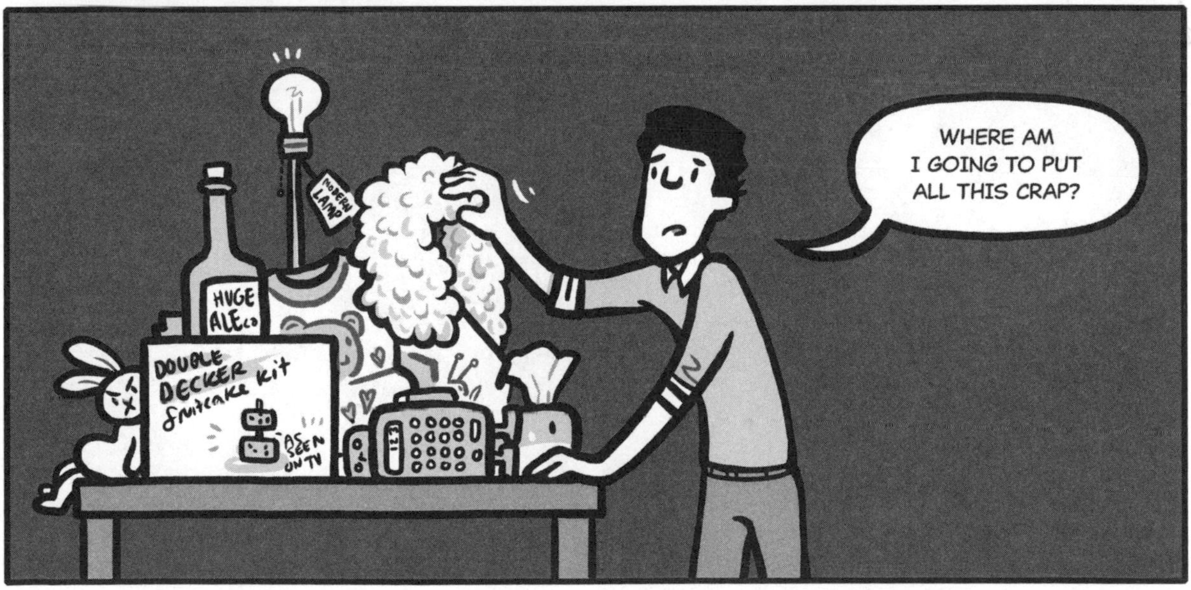
WHERE AM I GOING TO PUT ALL THIS CRAP?
MODERN LAMP
HUGE ALE Co
DOUBLE DECKER fruitcake kit
AS SEEN ON TV

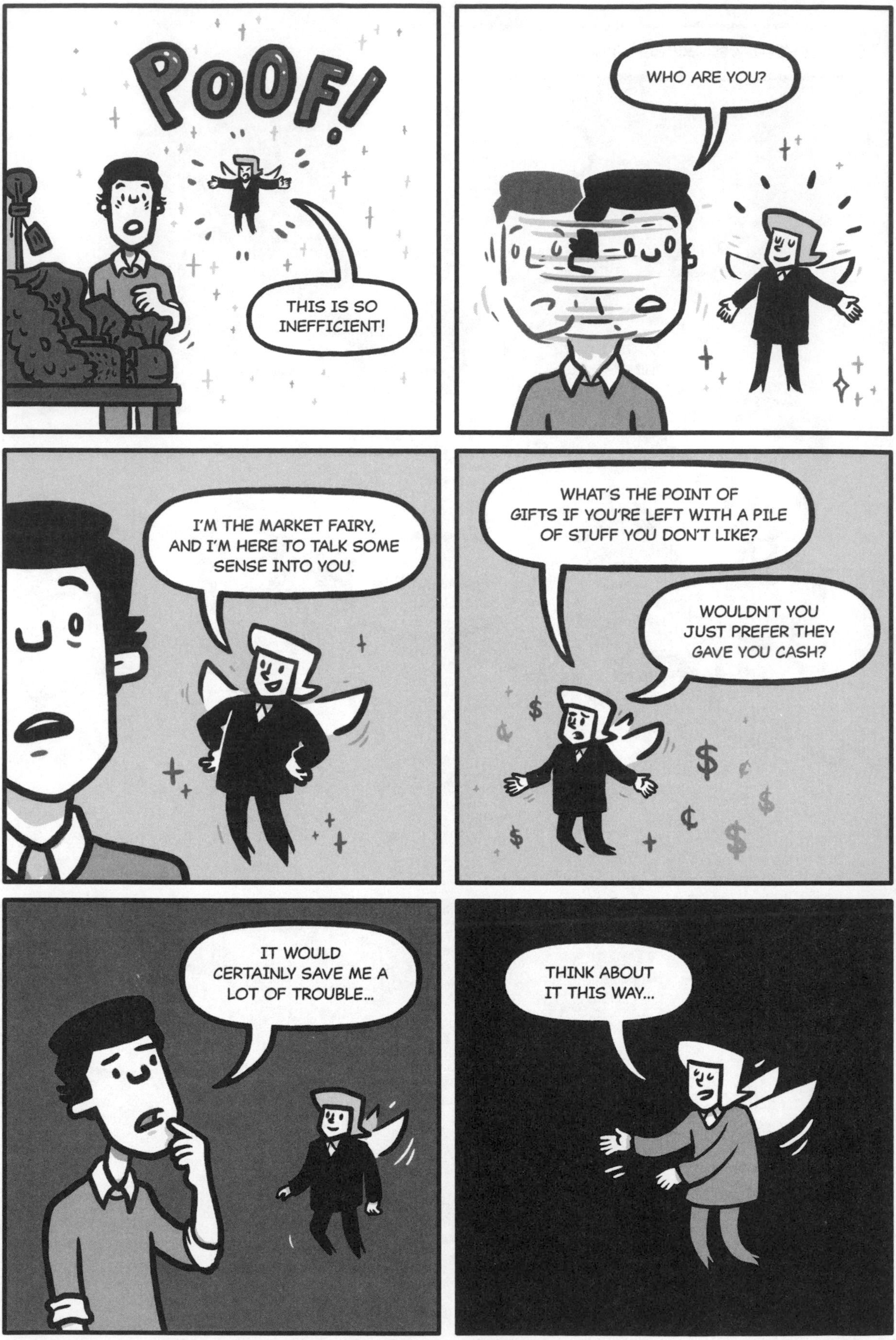
POOF!
THIS IS SO INEFFICIENT!
WHO ARE YOU?
I'M THE MARKET FAIRY, AND I'M HERE TO TALK SOME SENSE INTO YOU.
WHAT'S THE POINT OF GIFTS IF YOU'RE LEFT WITH A PILE OF STUFF YOU DON'T LIKE?
WOULDN'T YOU JUST PREFER THEY GAVE YOU CASH?
IT WOULD CERTAINLY SAVE ME A LOT OF TROUBLE...
THINK ABOUT IT THIS WAY...

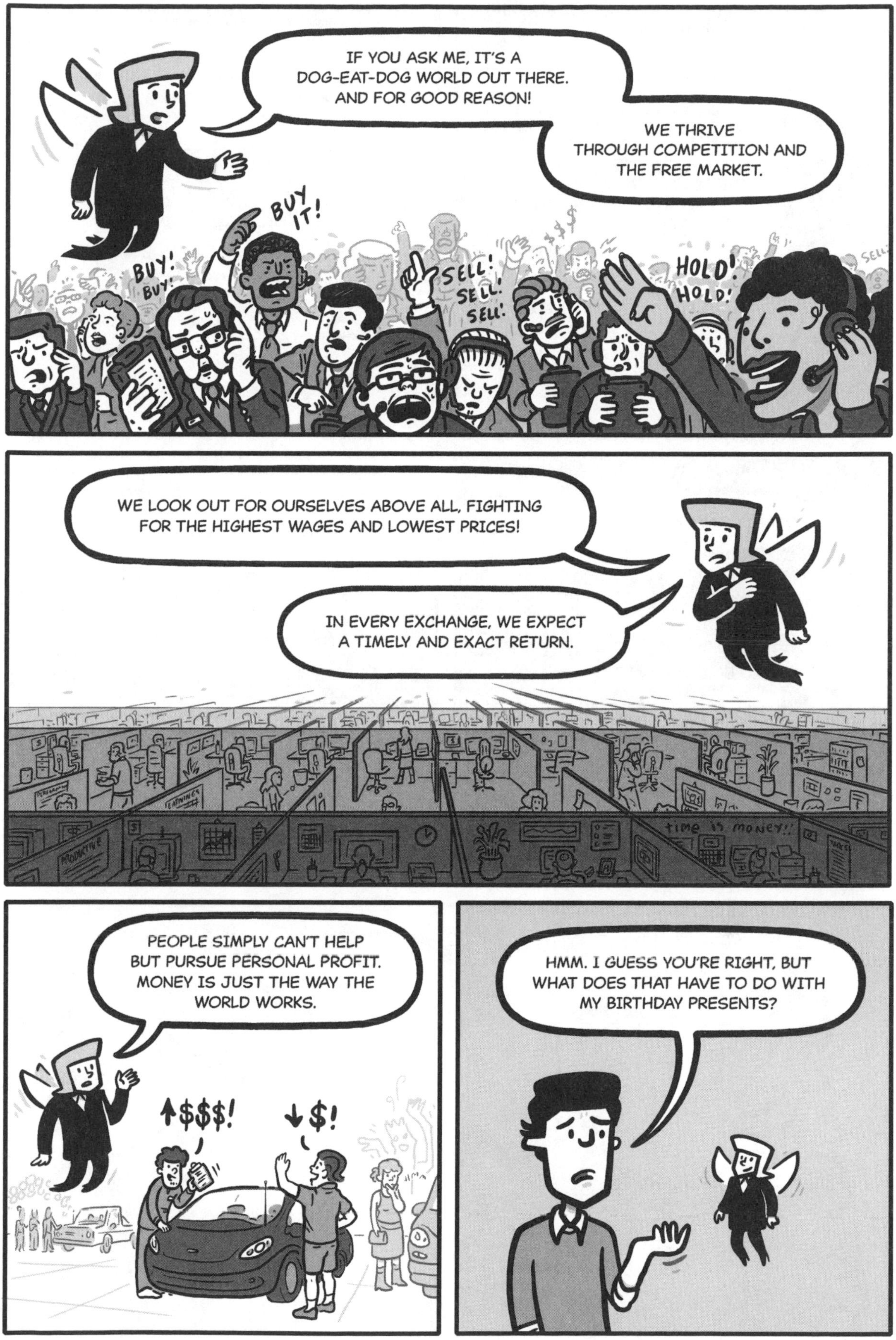
IF YOU ASK ME, IT'S A DOG-EAT-DOG WORLD OUT THERE. AND FOR GOOD REASON!
WE THRIVE THROUGH COMPETITION AND THE FREE MARKET.
BUY IT!
BUY! BUY!
SELL! SELL! SELL!
HOLD! HOLD!
WE LOOK OUT FOR OURSELVES ABOVE ALL, FIGHTING FOR THE HIGHEST WAGES AND LOWEST PRICES!
IN EVERY EXCHANGE, WE EXPECT A TIMELY AND EXACT RETURN.
time is money!!
PEOPLE SIMPLY CAN'T HELP BUT PURSUE PERSONAL PROFIT. MONEY IS JUST THE WAY THE WORLD WORKS.
↑$$$!
↓$!
HMM. I GUESS YOU'RE RIGHT, BUT WHAT DOES THAT HAVE TO DO WITH MY BIRTHDAY PRESENTS?

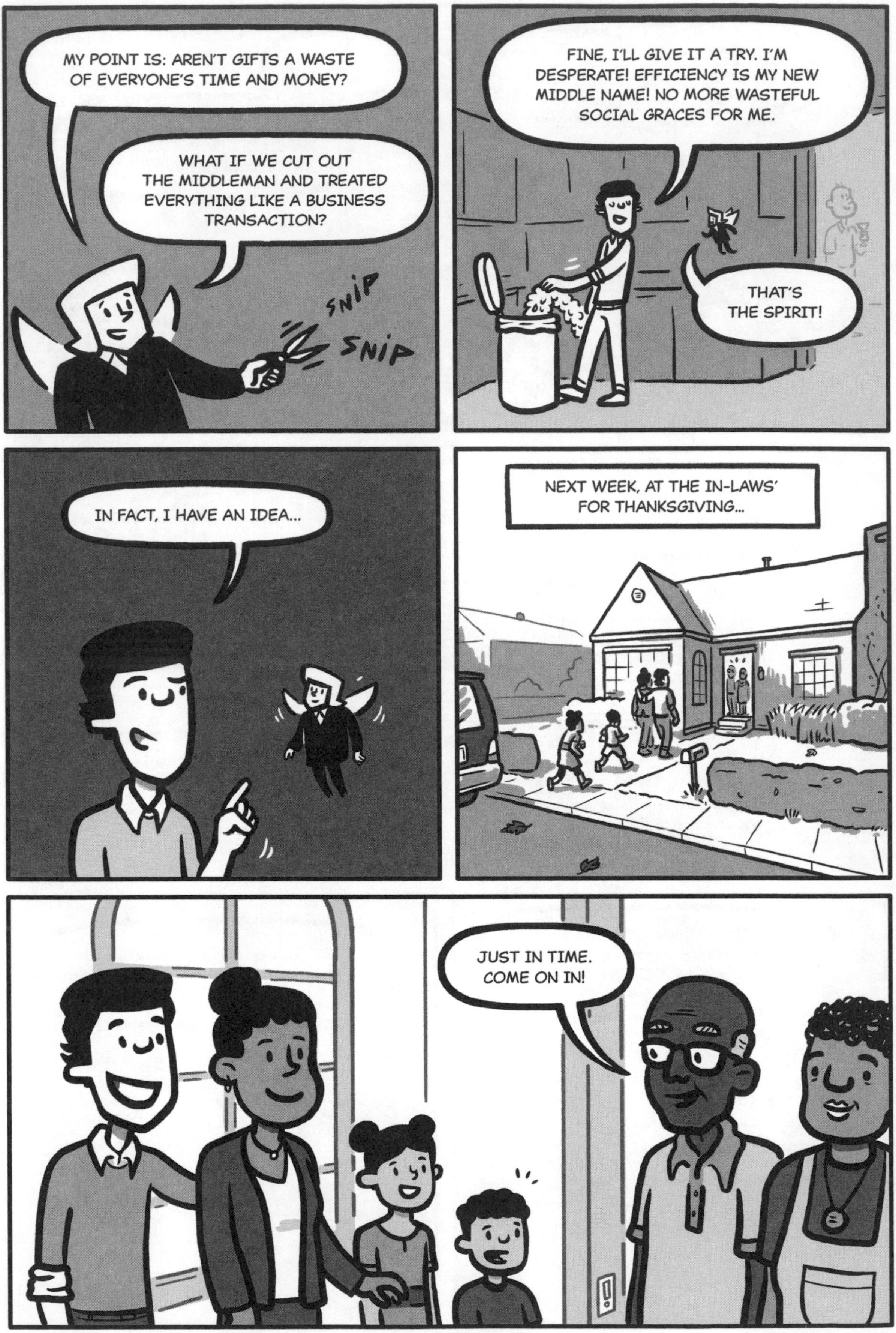
MY POINT IS: AREN'T GIFTS A WASTE OF EVERYONE'S TIME AND MONEY?
WHAT IF WE CUT OUT THE MIDDLEMAN AND TREATED EVERYTHING LIKE A BUSINESS TRANSACTION?
SNIP
SNIP
FINE, I'LL GIVE IT A TRY. I'M DESPERATE! EFFICIENCY IS MY NEW MIDDLE NAME! NO MORE WASTEFUL SOCIAL GRACES FOR ME.
THAT'S THE SPIRIT!
IN FACT, I HAVE AN IDEA...
NEXT WEEK, AT THE IN-LAWS' FOR THANKSGIVING...
JUST IN TIME. COME ON IN!

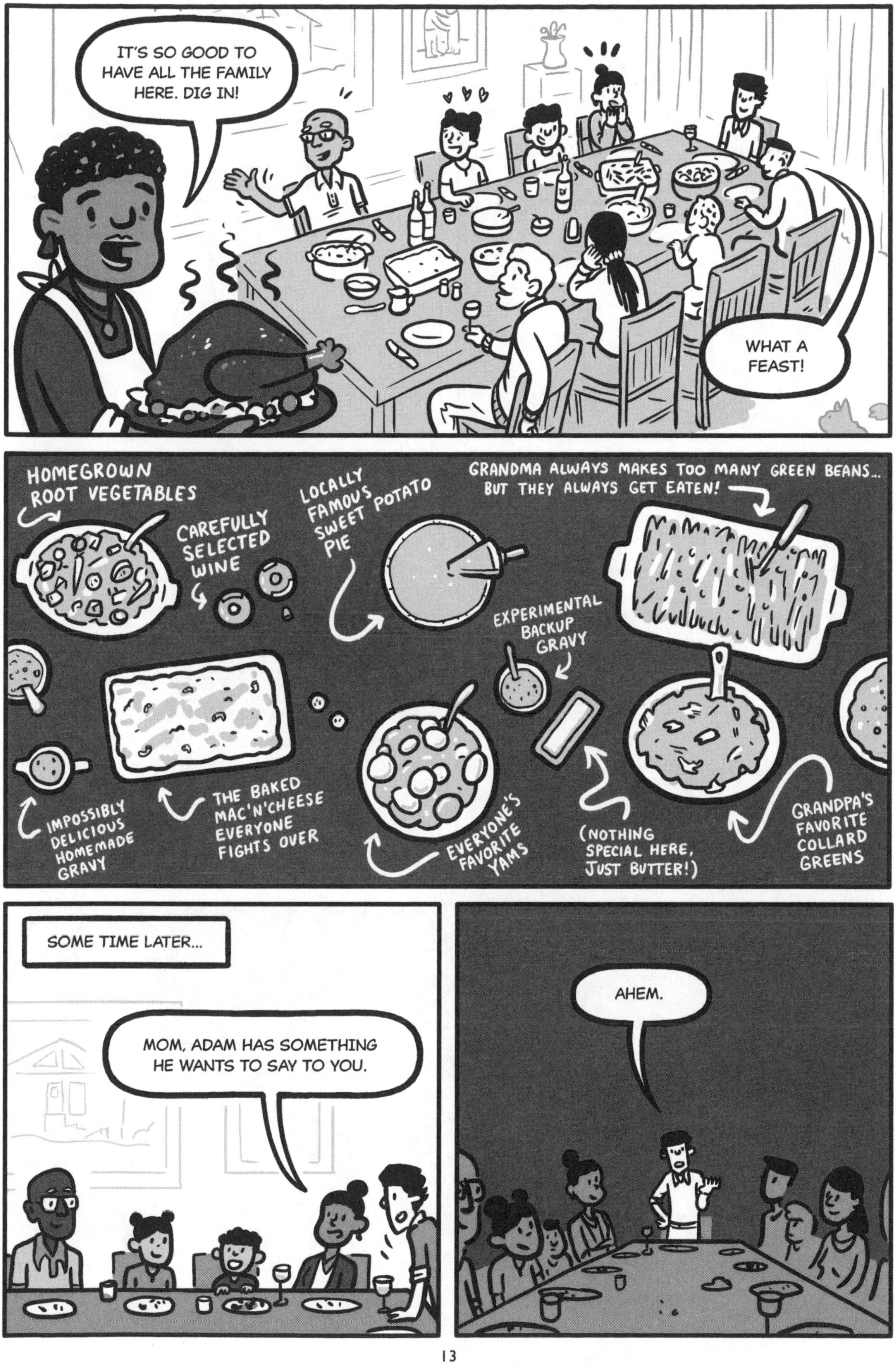
IT'S SO GOOD TO HAVE ALL THE FAMILY HERE. DIG IN!
WHAT A FEAST!
HOMEGROWN ROOT VEGETABLES
CAREFULLY SELECTED WINE
LOCALLY FAMOUS SWEET POTATO PIE
GRANDMA ALWAYS MAKES TOO MANY GREEN BEANS... BUT THEY ALWAYS GET EATEN!
EXPERIMENTAL BACKUP GRAVY
IMPOSSIBLY DELICIOUS HOMEMADE GRAVY
THE BAKED MAC'N'CHEESE EVERYONE FIGHTS OVER
EVERYONE'S FAVORITE YAMS
(NOTHING SPECIAL HERE, JUST BUTTER!)
GRANDPA'S FAVORITE COLLARD GREENS
SOME TIME LATER...
MOM, ADAM HAS SOMETHING HE WANTS TO SAY TO YOU.
AHEM.

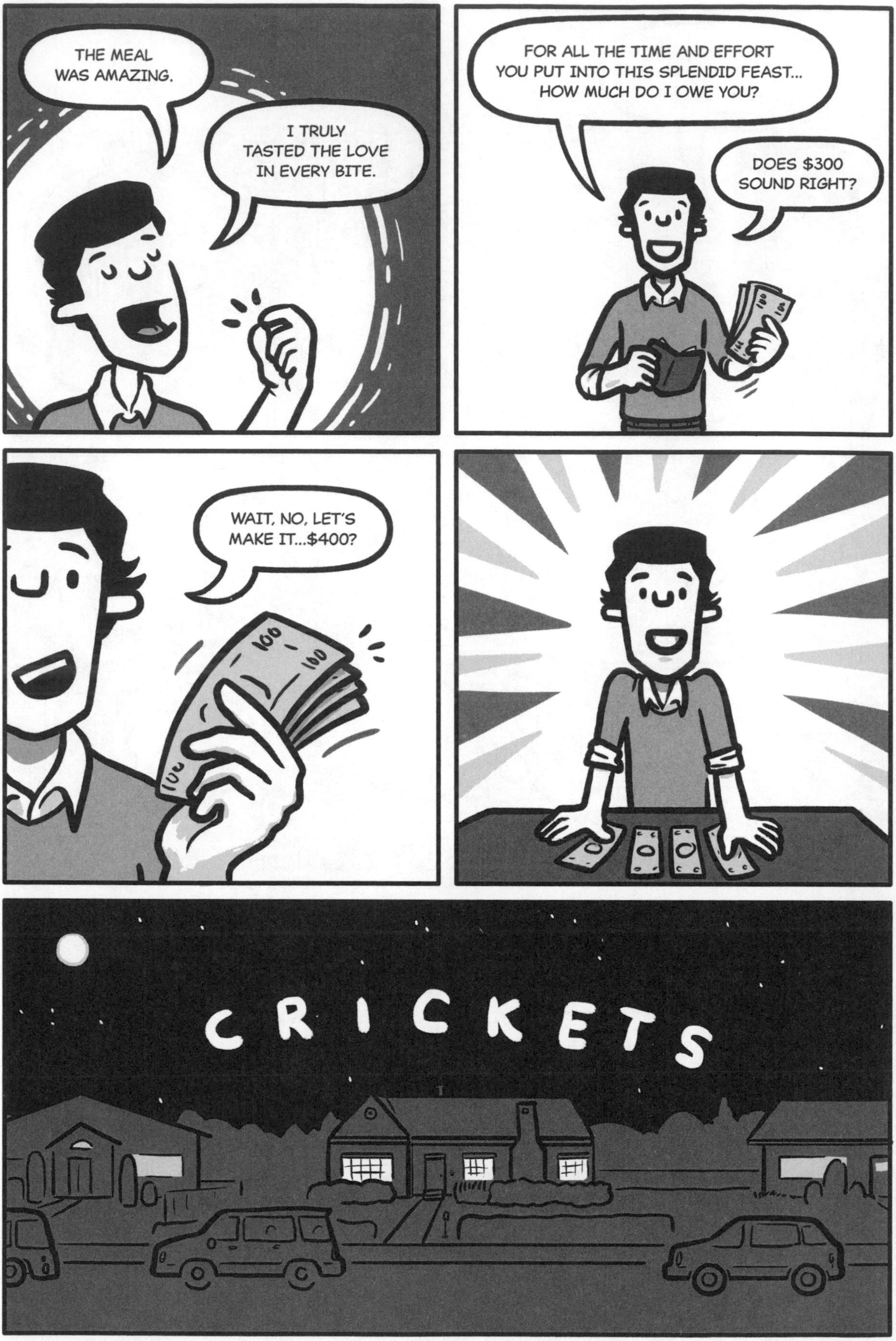
THE MEAL WAS AMAZING.
I TRULY TASTED THE LOVE IN EVERY BITE.
FOR ALL THE TIME AND EFFORT YOU PUT INTO THIS SPLENDID FEAST... HOW MUCH DO I OWE YOU?
DOES $300 SOUND RIGHT?
WAIT, NO, LET'S MAKE IT...$400?
CRICKETS

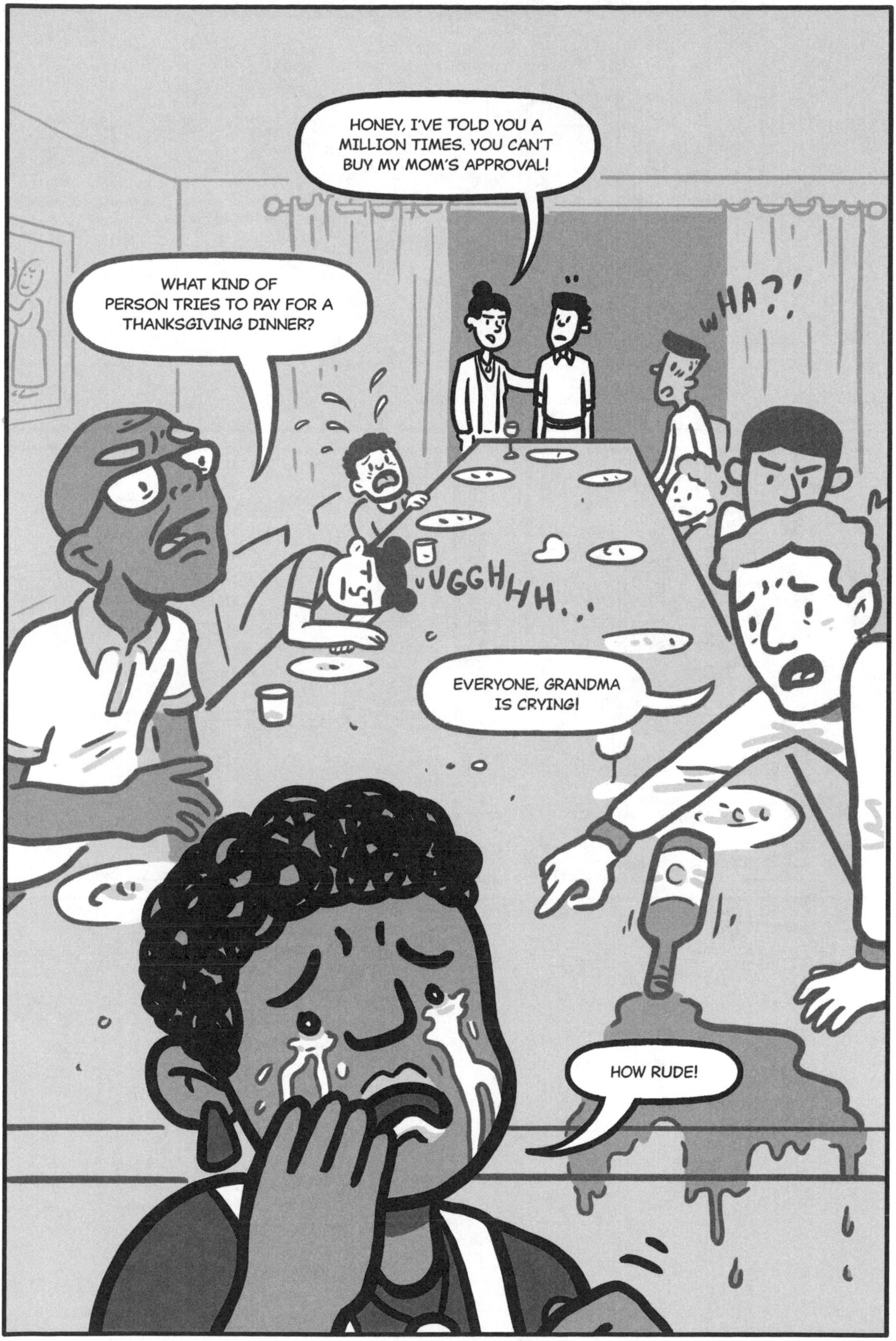
HONEY, I'VE TOLD YOU A MILLION TIMES. YOU CAN'T BUY MY MOM'S APPROVAL!
WHAT KIND OF PERSON TRIES TO PAY FOR A THANKSGIVING DINNER?
WHA?!
UGGHHHH...
EVERYONE, GRANDMA IS CRYING!
HOW RUDE!

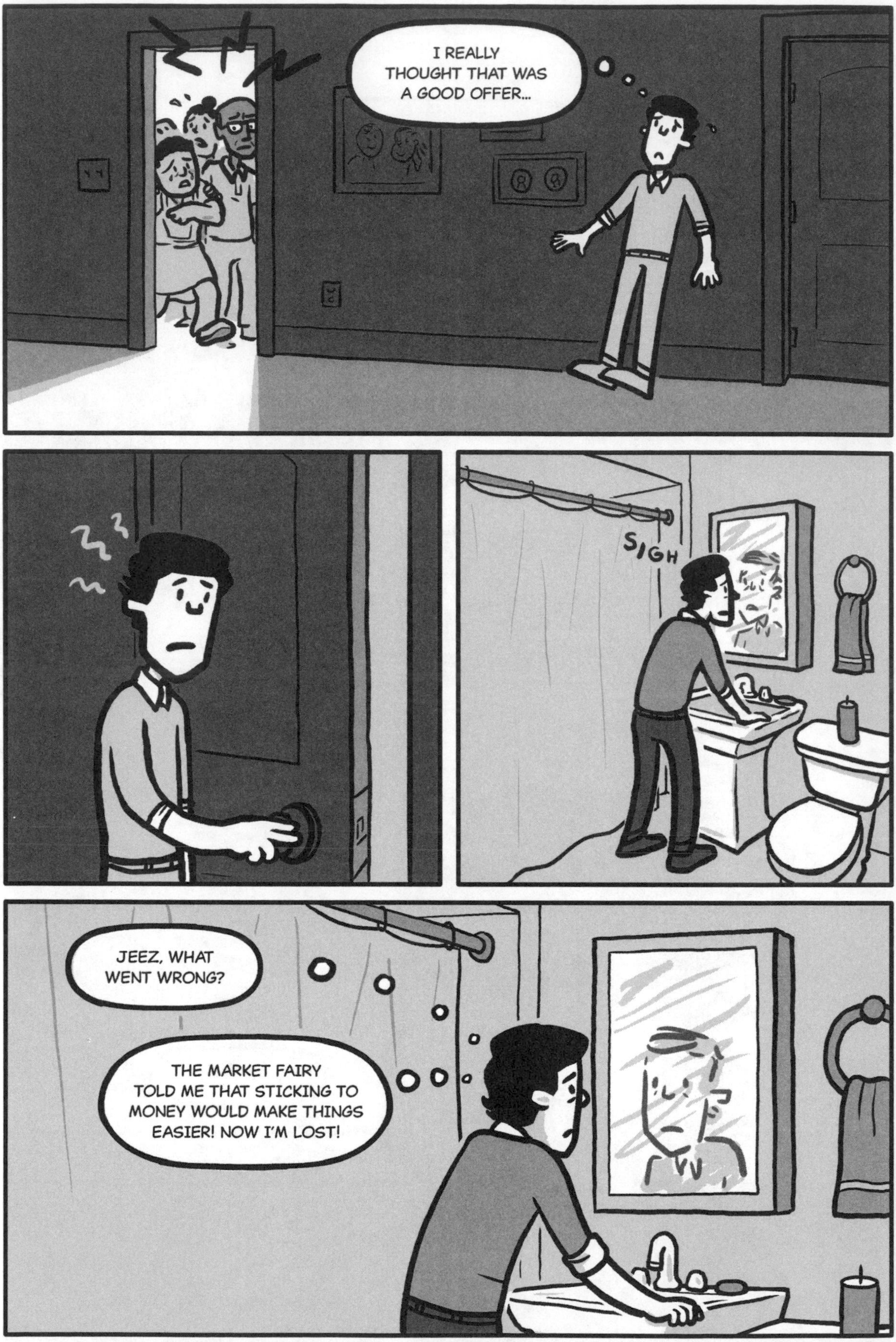
I REALLY THOUGHT THAT WAS A GOOD OFFER...
SIGH
JEEZ, WHAT WENT WRONG?
THE MARKET FAIRY TOLD ME THAT STICKING TO MONEY WOULD MAKE THINGS EASIER! NOW I'M LOST!

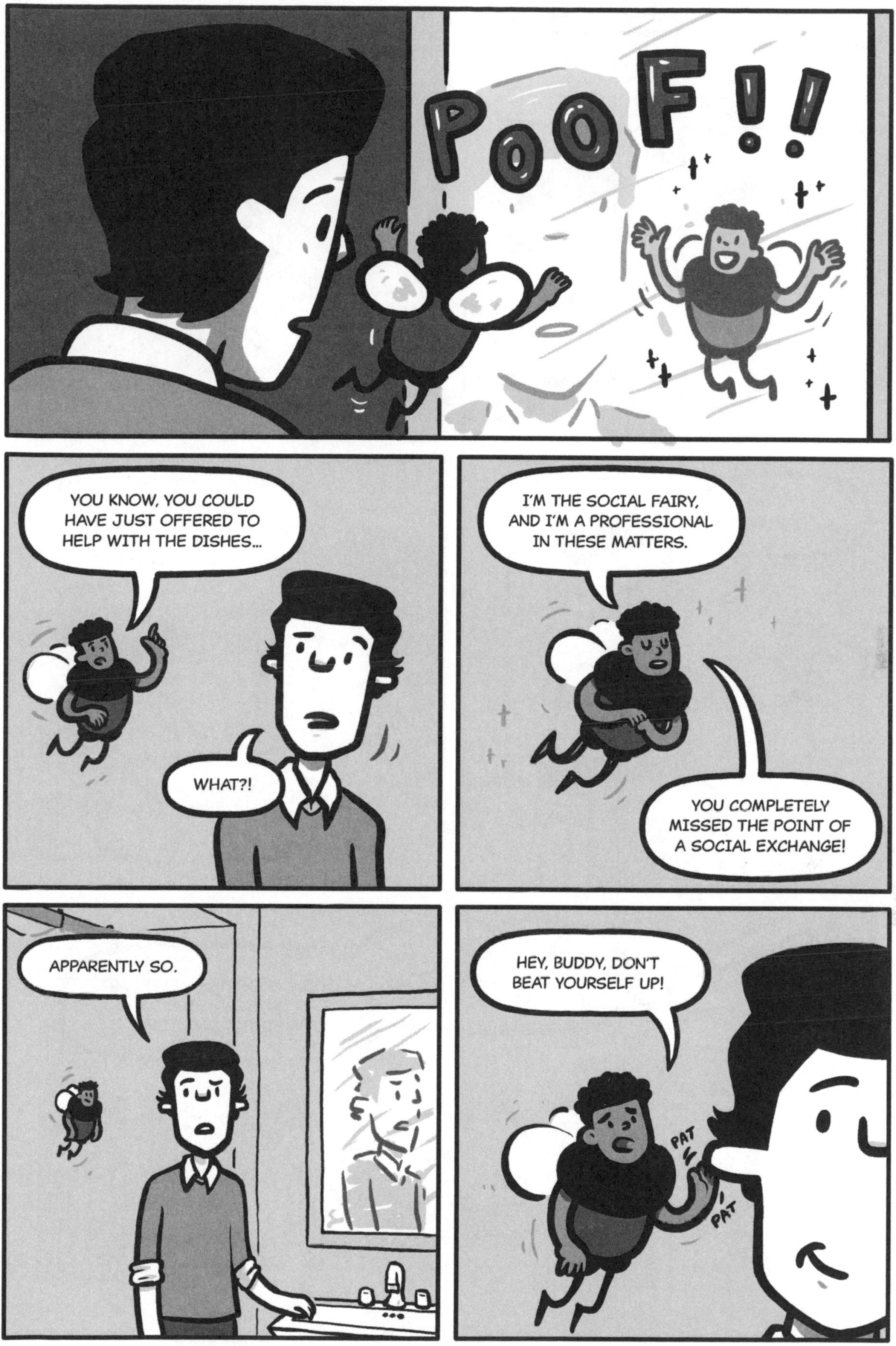
POOF!!
YOU KNOW, YOU COULD HAVE JUST OFFERED TO HELP WITH THE DISHES...
WHAT?!
I'M THE SOCIAL FAIRY, AND I'M A PROFESSIONAL IN THESE MATTERS.
YOU COMPLETELY MISSED THE POINT OF A SOCIAL EXCHANGE!
APPARENTLY SO.
HEY, BUDDY, DON'T BEAT YOURSELF UP!
PAT
PAT

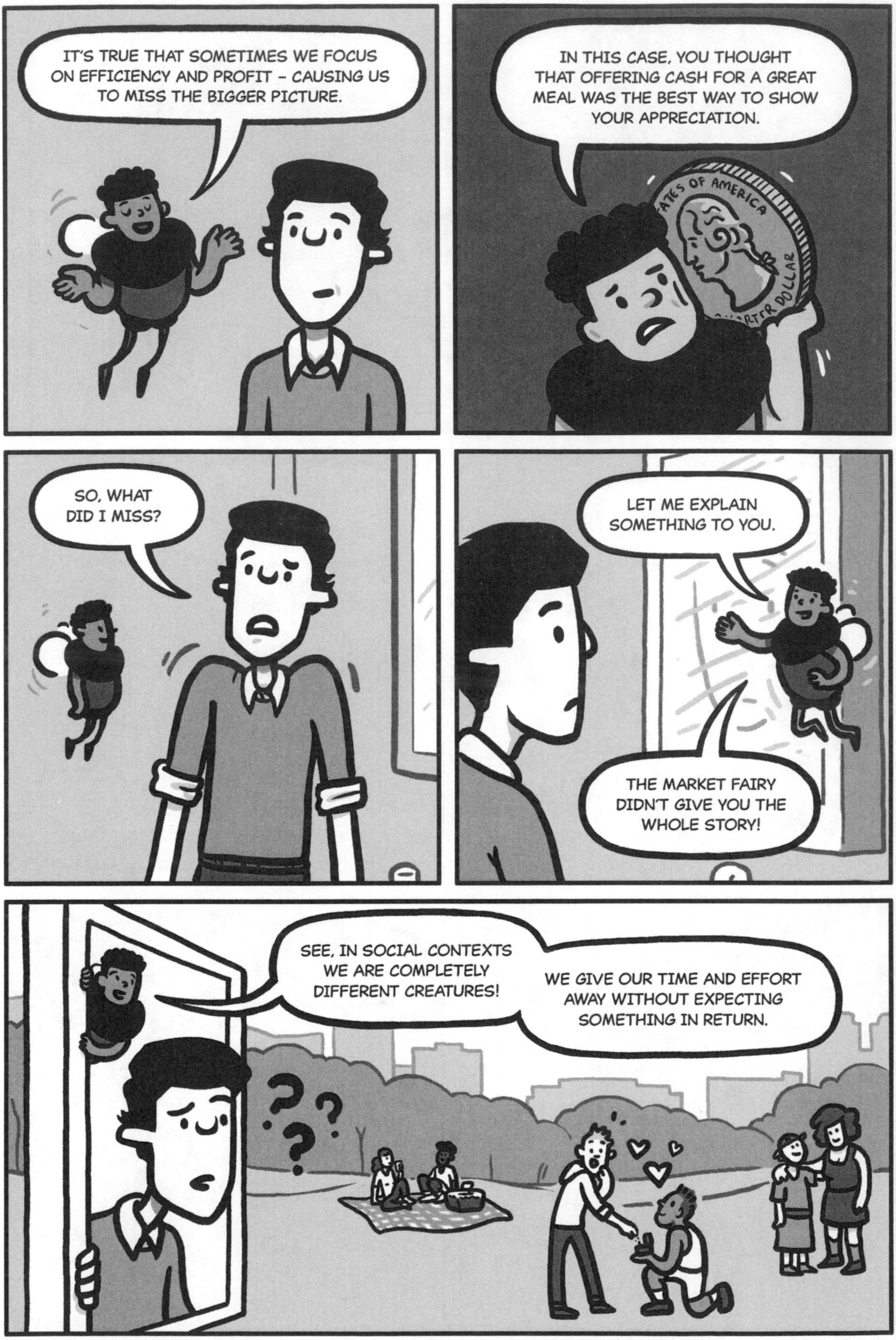
IT'S TRUE THAT SOMETIMES WE FOCUS ON EFFICIENCY AND PROFIT – CAUSING US TO MISS THE BIGGER PICTURE.
IN THIS CASE, YOU THOUGHT THAT OFFERING CASH FOR A GREAT MEAL WAS THE BEST WAY TO SHOW YOUR APPRECIATION.
SO, WHAT DID I MISS?
LET ME EXPLAIN SOMETHING TO YOU.
THE MARKET FAIRY DIDN'T GIVE YOU THE WHOLE STORY!
SEE, IN SOCIAL CONTEXTS WE ARE COMPLETELY DIFFERENT CREATURES!
WE GIVE OUR TIME AND EFFORT AWAY WITHOUT EXPECTING SOMETHING IN RETURN.

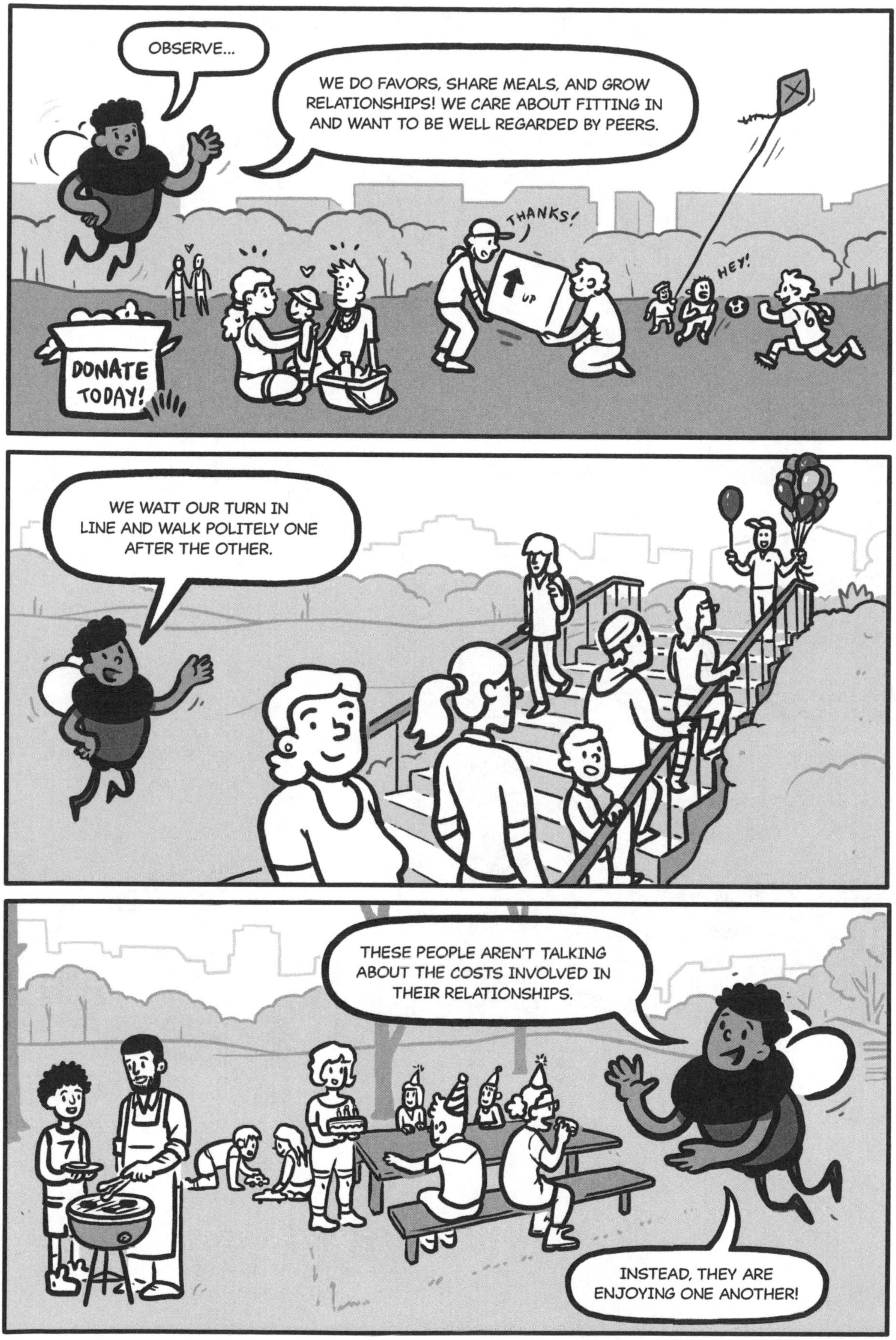
OBSERVE...
WE DO FAVORS, SHARE MEALS, AND GROW RELATIONSHIPS! WE CARE ABOUT FITTING IN AND WANT TO BE WELL REGARDED BY PEERS.
THANKS!
UP
HEY!
DONATE TODAY!
WE WAIT OUR TURN IN LINE AND WALK POLITELY ONE AFTER THE OTHER.
THESE PEOPLE AREN'T TALKING ABOUT THE COSTS INVOLVED IN THEIR RELATIONSHIPS.
INSTEAD, THEY ARE ENJOYING ONE ANOTHER!
7

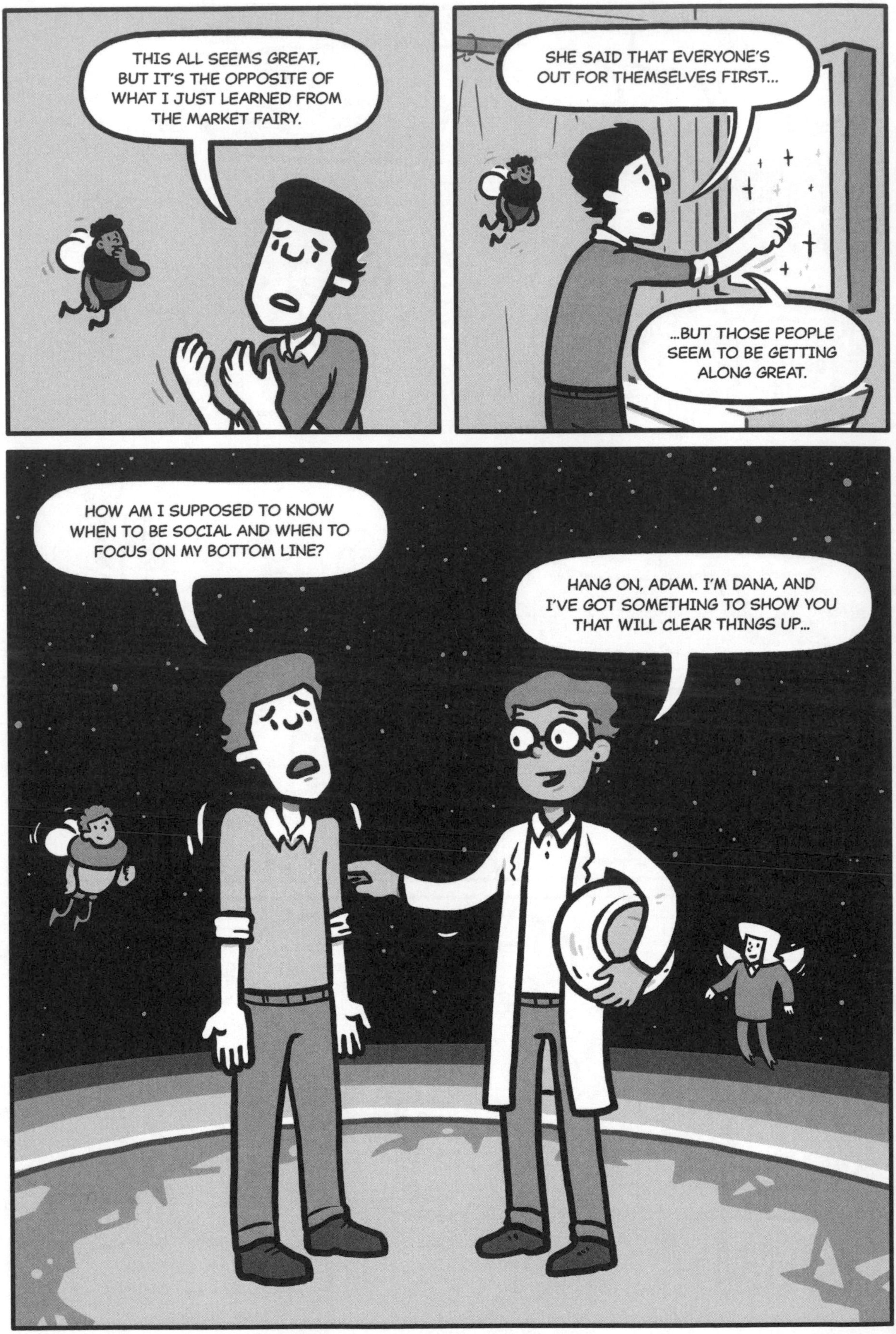
THIS ALL SEEMS GREAT, BUT IT'S THE OPPOSITE OF WHAT I JUST LEARNED FROM THE MARKET FAIRY.
SHE SAID THAT EVERYONE'S OUT FOR THEMSELVES FIRST...
...BUT THOSE PEOPLE SEEM TO BE GETTING ALONG GREAT.
HOW AM I SUPPOSED TO KNOW WHEN TO BE SOCIAL AND WHEN TO FOCUS ON MY BOTTOM LINE?
HANG ON, ADAM. I'M DANA, AND I'VE GOT SOMETHING TO SHOW YOU THAT WILL CLEAR THINGS UP...

HOW CAN WE SIMULTANEOUSLY HOLD SEEMINGLY OPPOSITE VALUES? WELL, I'M HERE TO TELL YOU THAT WE ACTUALLY LIVE STRADDLING TWO VERY DIFFERENT WORLDS.
MARKET NORMS RULE ONE WORLD...
...WHILE SOCIAL NORMS RULE THE OTHER.
"NORMS" ARE THE PRINCIPLES THAT GUIDE THE EXPECTED BEHAVIOR IN A GIVEN SITUATION.
LET'S LOOK AT THESE WORLDS ONE AT A TIME...

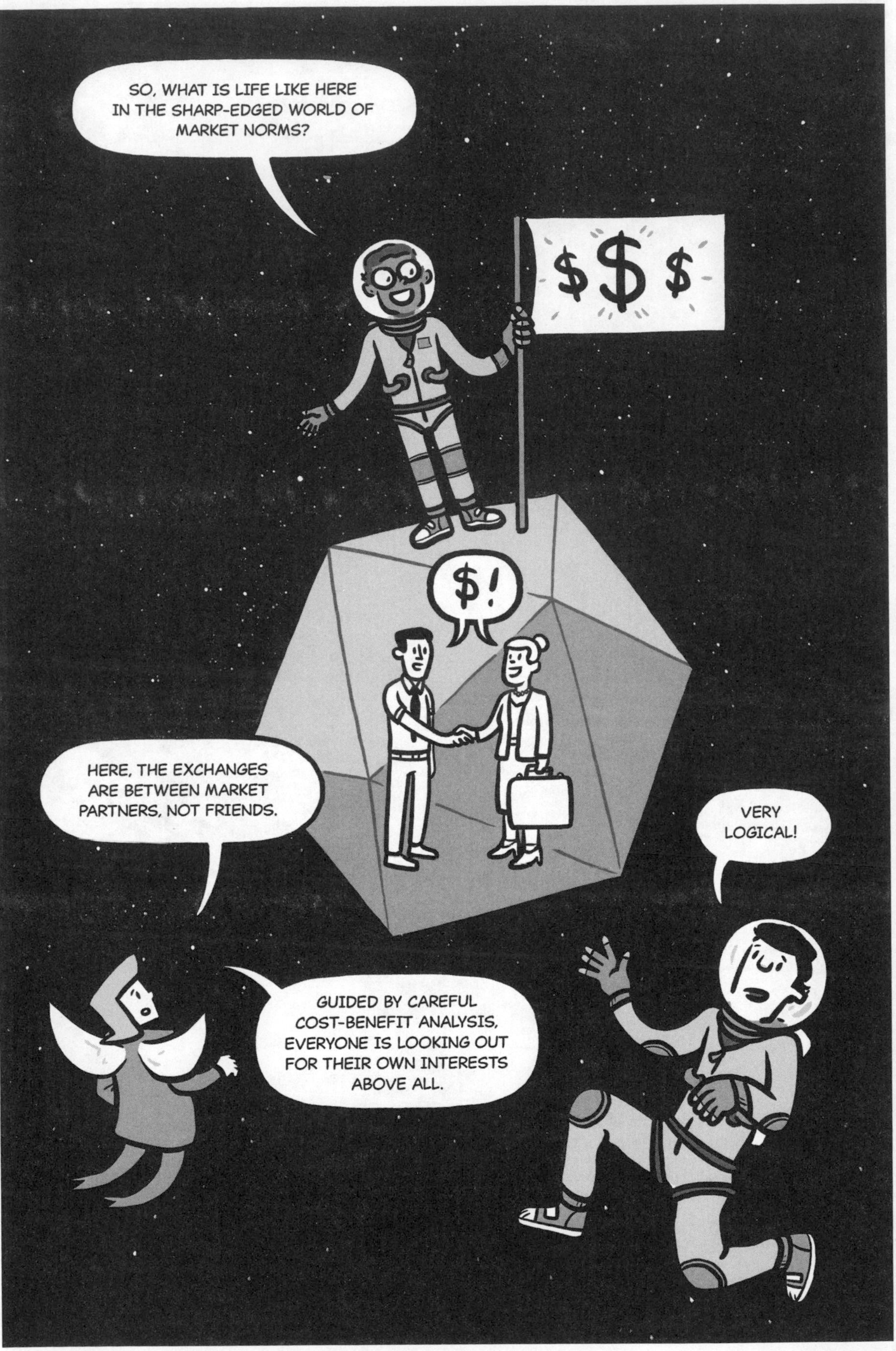
SO, WHAT IS LIFE LIKE HERE IN THE SHARP-EDGED WORLD OF MARKET NORMS?
$$$
$!
HERE, THE EXCHANGES ARE BETWEEN MARKET PARTNERS, NOT FRIENDS.
VERY LOGICAL!
GUIDED BY CAREFUL COST-BENEFIT ANALYSIS, EVERYONE IS LOOKING OUT FOR THEIR OWN INTERESTS ABOVE ALL.

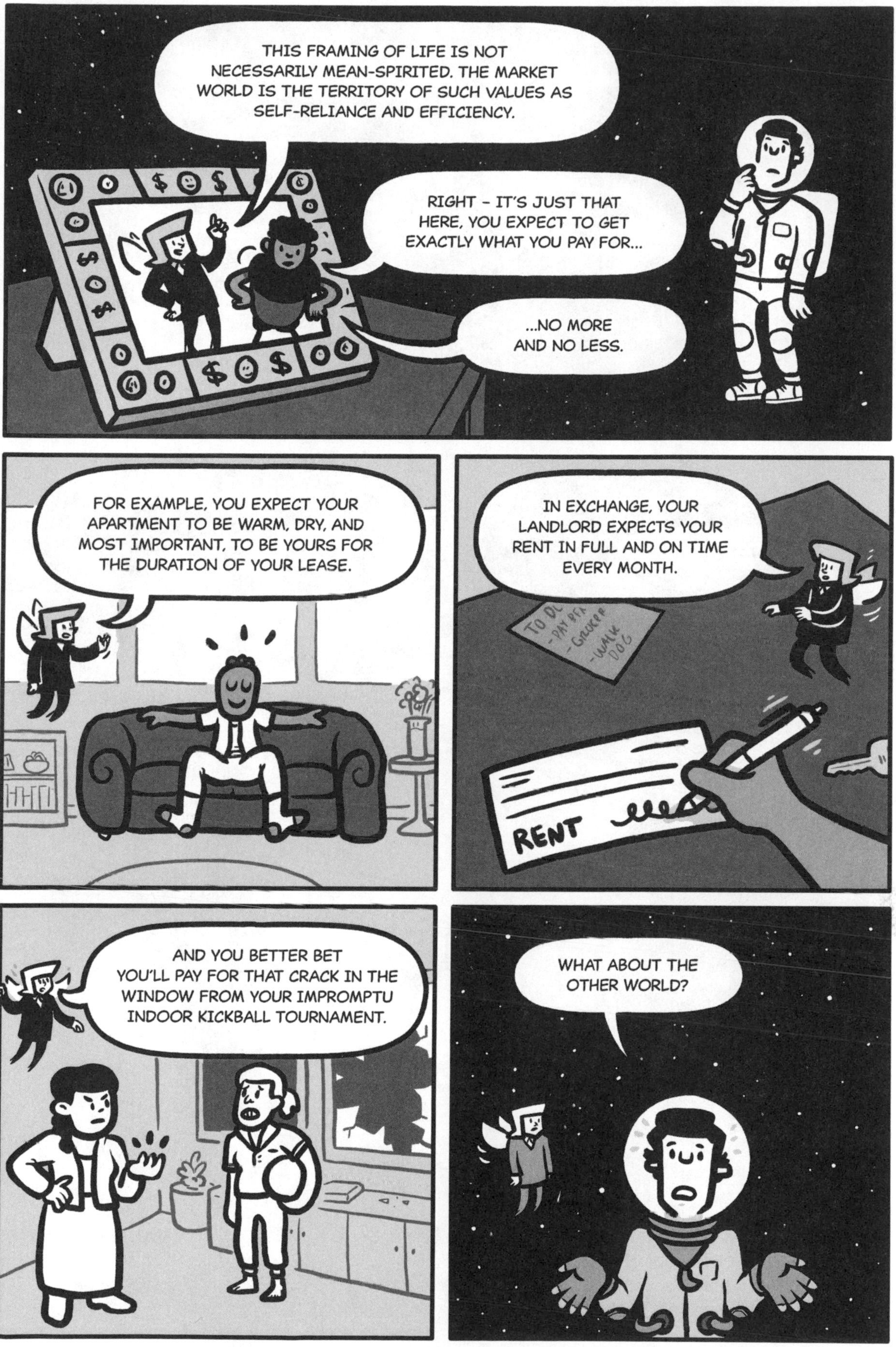
THIS FRAMING OF LIFE IS NOT NECESSARILY MEAN-SPIRITED. THE MARKET WORLD IS THE TERRITORY OF SUCH VALUES AS SELF-RELIANCE AND EFFICIENCY.
RIGHT – IT'S JUST THAT HERE, YOU EXPECT TO GET EXACTLY WHAT YOU PAY FOR...
...NO MORE AND NO LESS.
FOR EXAMPLE, YOU EXPECT YOUR APARTMENT TO BE WARM, DRY, AND MOST IMPORTANT, TO BE YOURS FOR THE DURATION OF YOUR LEASE.
IN EXCHANGE, YOUR LANDLORD EXPECTS YOUR RENT IN FULL AND ON TIME EVERY MONTH.
RENT
AND YOU BETTER BET YOU'LL PAY FOR THAT CRACK IN THE WINDOW FROM YOUR IMPROMPTU INDOOR KICKBALL TOURNAMENT.
WHAT ABOUT THE OTHER WORLD?

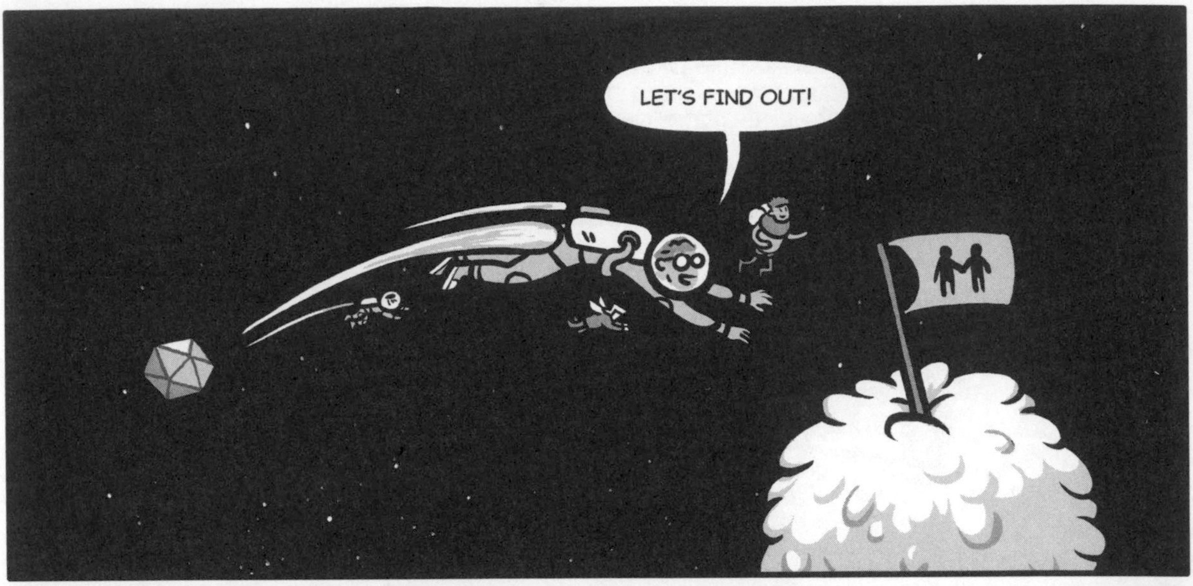
LET'S FIND OUT!

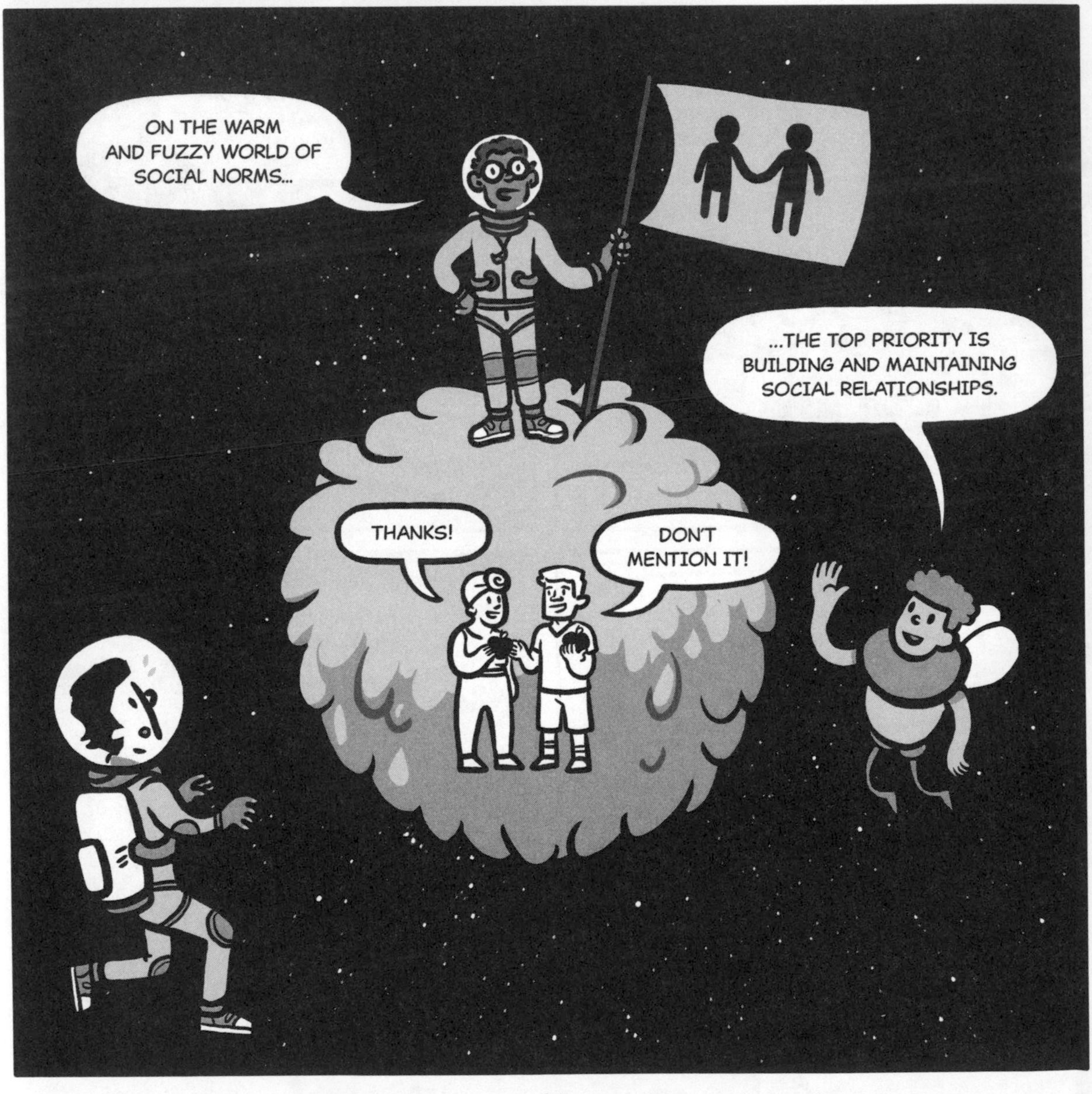
ON THE WARM AND FUZZY WORLD OF SOCIAL NORMS...
...THE TOP PRIORITY IS BUILDING AND MAINTAINING SOCIAL RELATIONSHIPS.
THANKS!
DON'T MENTION IT!

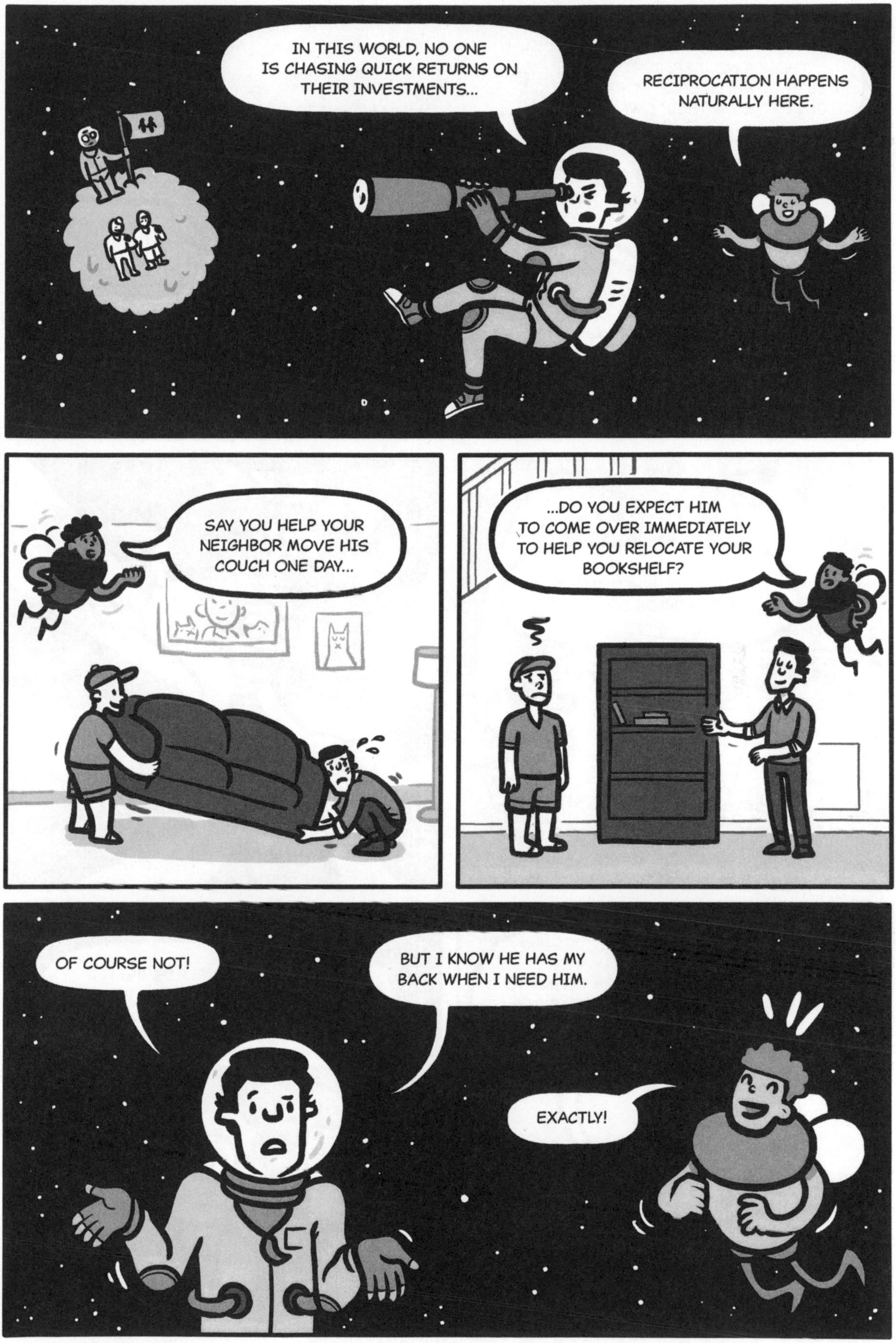
IN THIS WORLD, NO ONE IS CHASING QUICK RETURNS ON THEIR INVESTMENTS...
RECIPROCATION HAPPENS NATURALLY HERE.
SAY YOU HELP YOUR NEIGHBOR MOVE HIS COUCH ONE DAY...
...DO YOU EXPECT HIM TO COME OVER IMMEDIATELY TO HELP YOU RELOCATE YOUR BOOKSHELF?
OF COURSE NOT!
BUT I KNOW HE HAS MY BACK WHEN I NEED HIM.
EXACTLY!

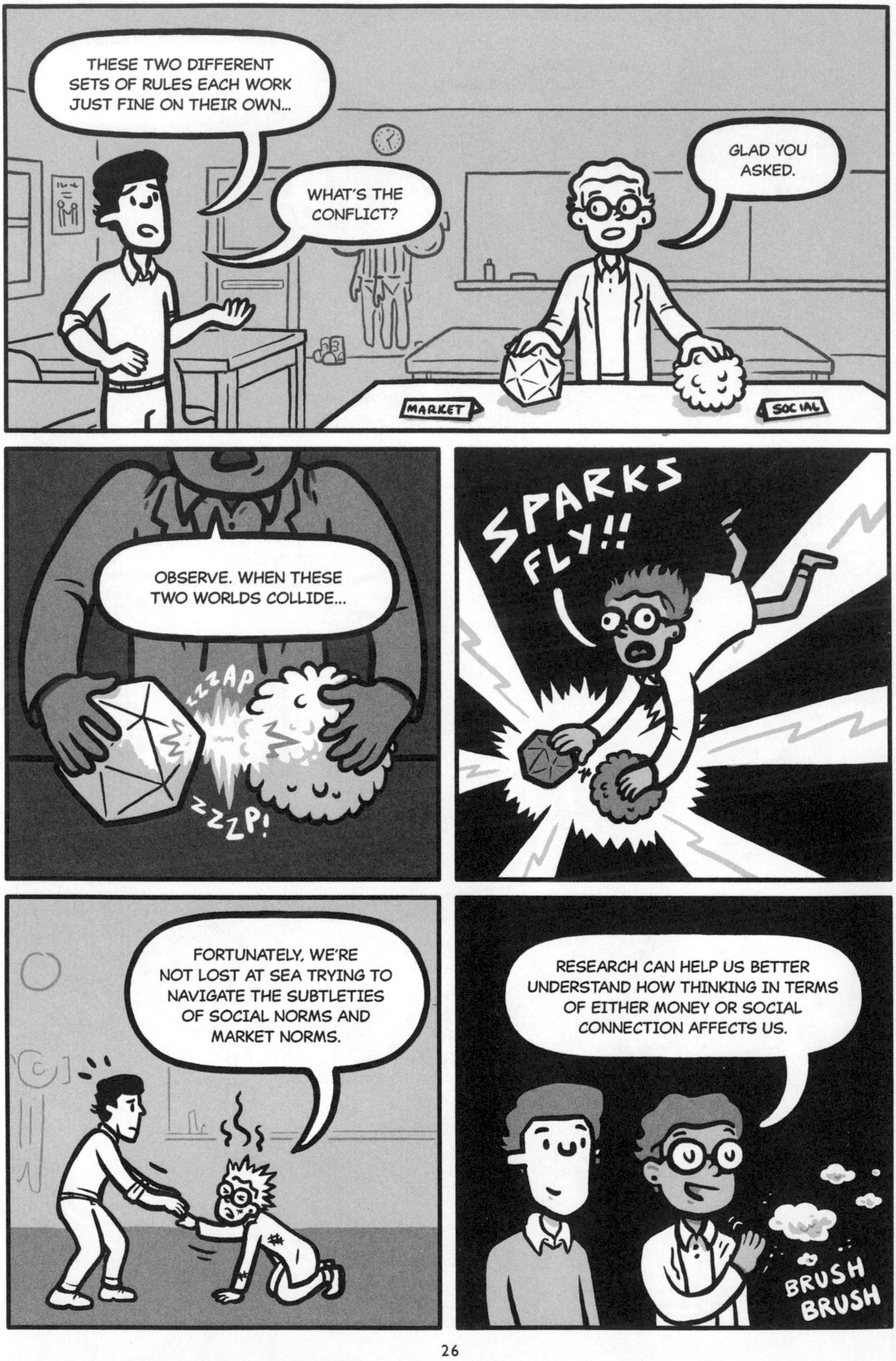
THESE TWO DIFFERENT SETS OF RULES EACH WORK JUST FINE ON THEIR OWN...
WHAT'S THE CONFLICT?
GLAD YOU ASKED.
MARKET
SOCIAL
OBSERVE. WHEN THESE TWO WORLDS COLLIDE...
ZZZAP
ZZZP!
SPARKS FLY!!
FORTUNATELY, WE'RE NOT LOST AT SEA TRYING TO NAVIGATE THE SUBTLETIES OF SOCIAL NORMS AND MARKET NORMS.
RESEARCH CAN HELP US BETTER UNDERSTAND HOW THINKING IN TERMS OF EITHER MONEY OR SOCIAL CONNECTION AFFECTS US.
BRUSH BRUSH

BEHAVIORAL ECONOMICS RESEARCHERS JAMES HEYMAN AND DAN ARIELY HAVE EXAMINED OUR SENSITIVITY TO SOCIAL AND MARKET NORMS.

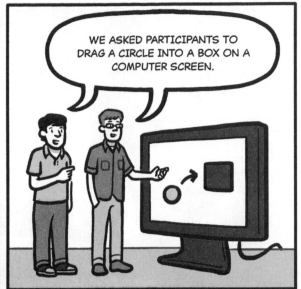
WE ASKED PARTICIPANTS TO DRAG A CIRCLE INTO A BOX ON A COMPUTER SCREEN.

EACH TIME A CIRCLE WAS SUCCESSFULLY DRAGGED INTO THE BOX...

PING!

...A NEW ONE APPEARED!

FOR THREE MINUTES, DRAG AS MANY CIRCLES INTO THE BOX AS YOU CAN. ONCE THE TIME IS UP, YOU CAN LEAVE.

3:00

IT'S AN EASY, IF VERY MONOTONOUS TASK. THE NUMBER OF CIRCLES PARTICIPANTS DRAGGED REPRESENTED HOW MUCH EFFORT THEY WERE WILLING TO PUT INTO THE TASK.

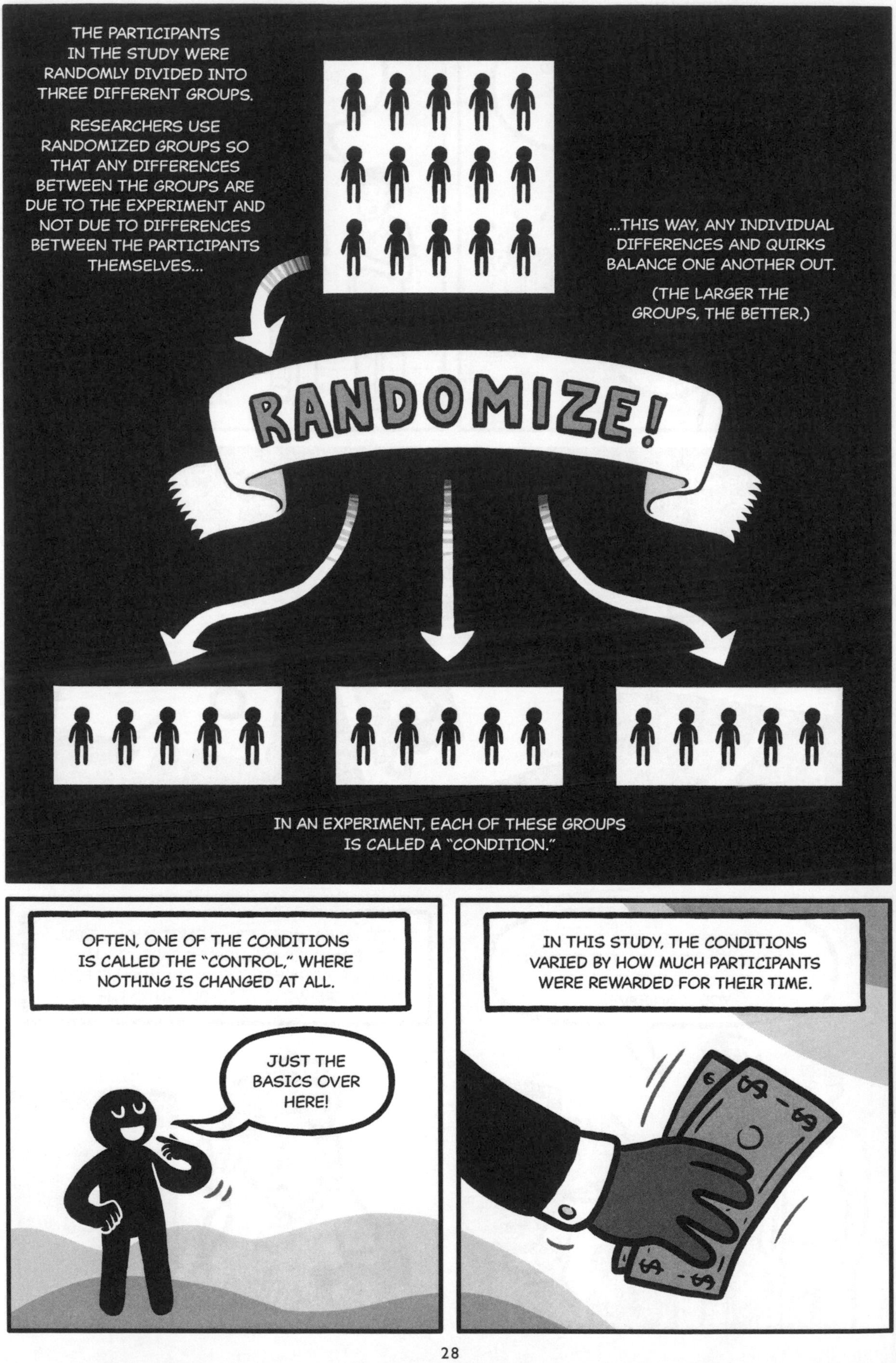
THE PARTICIPANTS IN THE STUDY WERE RANDOMLY DIVIDED INTO THREE DIFFERENT GROUPS.
RESEARCHERS USE RANDOMIZED GROUPS SO THAT ANY DIFFERENCES BETWEEN THE GROUPS ARE DUE TO THE EXPERIMENT AND NOT DUE TO DIFFERENCES BETWEEN THE PARTICIPANTS THEMSELVES...
...THIS WAY, ANY INDIVIDUAL DIFFERENCES AND QUIRKS BALANCE ONE ANOTHER OUT.
(THE LARGER THE GROUPS, THE BETTER.)
RANDOMIZE!
IN AN EXPERIMENT, EACH OF THESE GROUPS IS CALLED A "CONDITION."
OFTEN, ONE OF THE CONDITIONS IS CALLED THE "CONTROL," WHERE NOTHING IS CHANGED AT ALL.
JUST THE BASICS OVER HERE!
IN THIS STUDY, THE CONDITIONS VARIED BY HOW MUCH PARTICIPANTS WERE REWARDED FOR THEIR TIME.

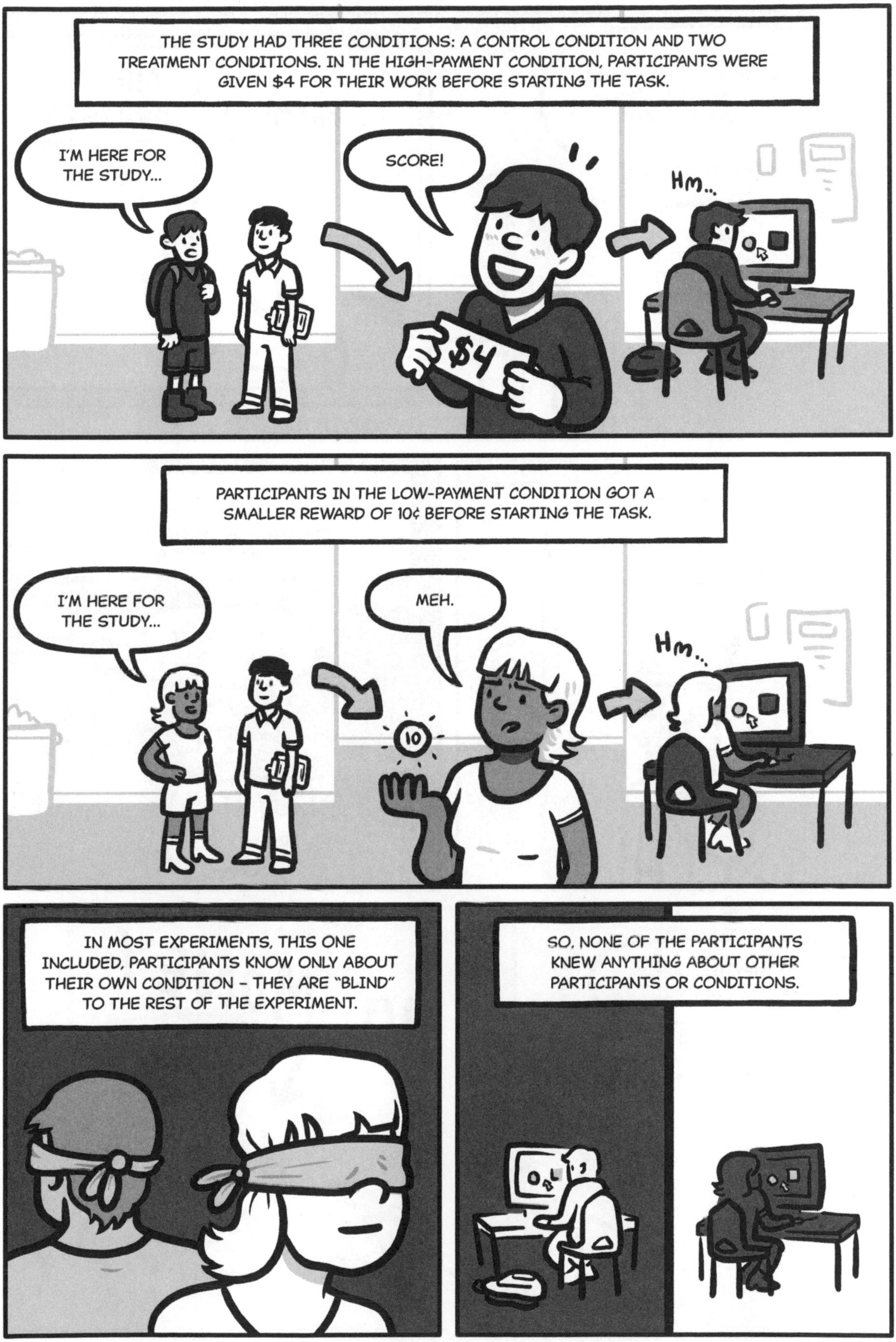
THE STUDY HAD THREE CONDITIONS: A CONTROL CONDITION AND TWO TREATMENT CONDITIONS. IN THE HIGH-PAYMENT CONDITION, PARTICIPANTS WERE GIVEN $4 FOR THEIR WORK BEFORE STARTING THE TASK.
I'M HERE FOR THE STUDY...
SCORE!
$4
Hm...
PARTICIPANTS IN THE LOW-PAYMENT CONDITION GOT A SMALLER REWARD OF 10¢ BEFORE STARTING THE TASK.
I'M HERE FOR THE STUDY...
MEH.
10
Hm...
IN MOST EXPERIMENTS, THIS ONE INCLUDED, PARTICIPANTS KNOW ONLY ABOUT THEIR OWN CONDITION – THEY ARE "BLIND" TO THE REST OF THE EXPERIMENT.
SO, NONE OF THE PARTICIPANTS KNEW ANYTHING ABOUT OTHER PARTICIPANTS OR CONDITIONS.

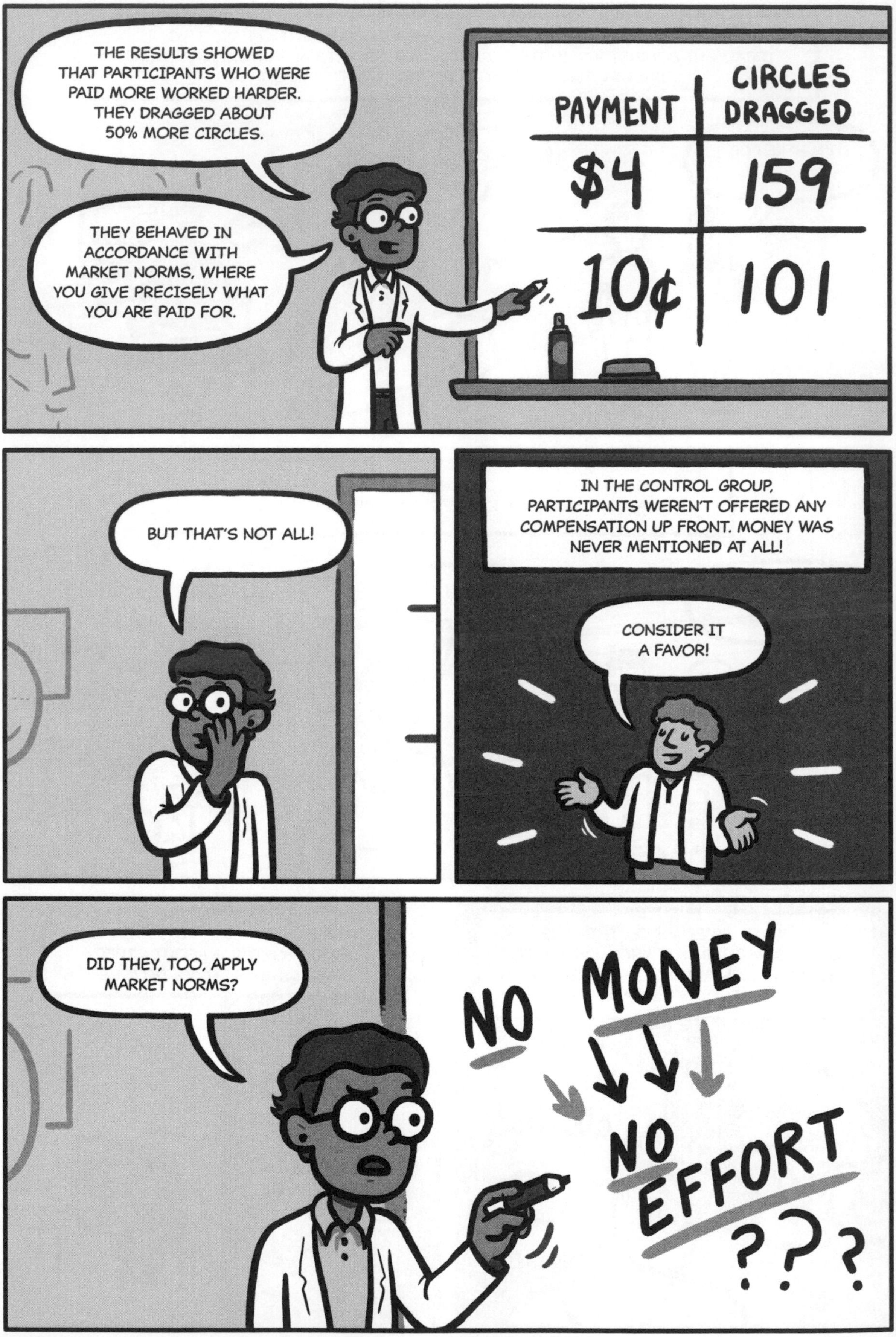
THE RESULTS SHOWED THAT PARTICIPANTS WHO WERE PAID MORE WORKED HARDER. THEY DRAGGED ABOUT 50% MORE CIRCLES.
PAYMENT
CIRCLES DRAGGED
$4
159
10¢
101
THEY BEHAVED IN ACCORDANCE WITH MARKET NORMS, WHERE YOU GIVE PRECISELY WHAT YOU ARE PAID FOR.
BUT THAT'S NOT ALL!
IN THE CONTROL GROUP, PARTICIPANTS WEREN'T OFFERED ANY COMPENSATION UP FRONT. MONEY WAS NEVER MENTIONED AT ALL!
CONSIDER IT A FAVOR!
DID THEY, TOO, APPLY MARKET NORMS?
NO MONEY
NO EFFORT
???

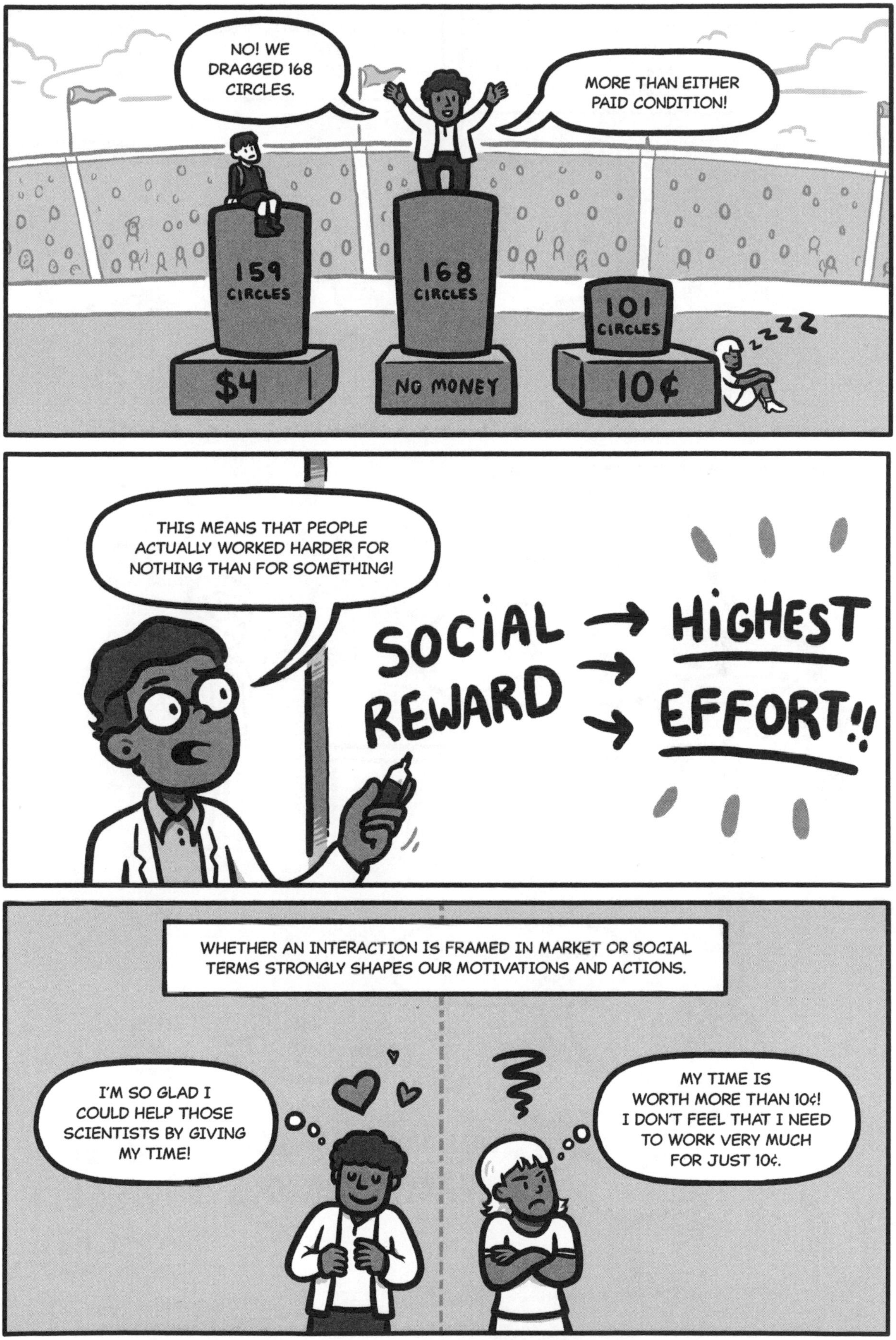
NO! WE DRAGGED 168 CIRCLES.
MORE THAN EITHER PAID CONDITION!
159 CIRCLES
168 CIRCLES
101 CIRCLES
$4
NO MONEY
10¢
ZZZZ
THIS MEANS THAT PEOPLE ACTUALLY WORKED HARDER FOR NOTHING THAN FOR SOMETHING!
SOCIAL REWARD → HIGHEST EFFORT!!
WHETHER AN INTERACTION IS FRAMED IN MARKET OR SOCIAL TERMS STRONGLY SHAPES OUR MOTIVATIONS AND ACTIONS.
I'M SO GLAD I COULD HELP THOSE SCIENTISTS BY GIVING MY TIME!
MY TIME IS WORTH MORE THAN 10¢! I DON'T FEEL THAT I NEED TO WORK VERY MUCH FOR JUST 10¢.

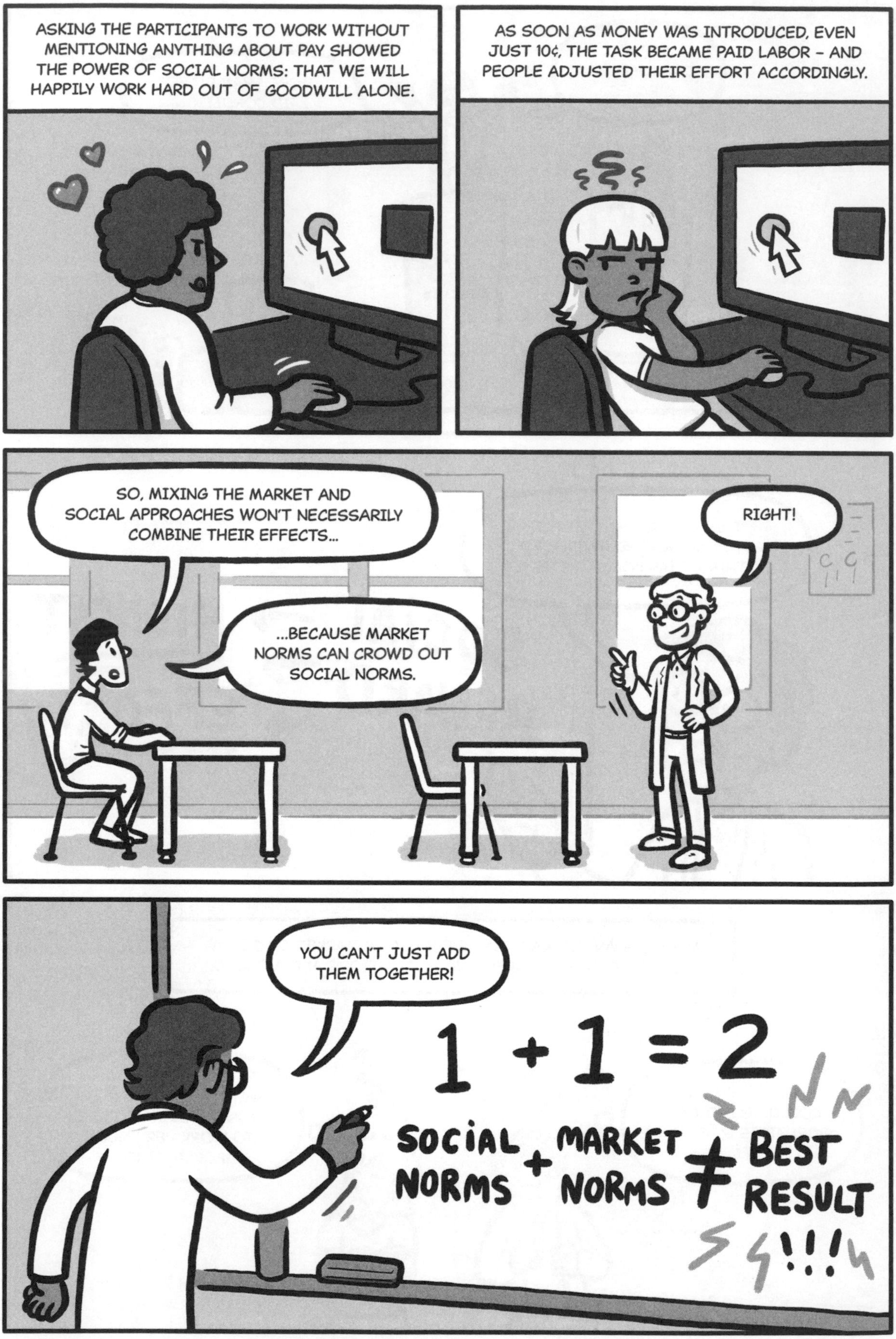
ASKING THE PARTICIPANTS TO WORK WITHOUT MENTIONING ANYTHING ABOUT PAY SHOWED THE POWER OF SOCIAL NORMS: THAT WE WILL HAPPILY WORK HARD OUT OF GOODWILL ALONE.
AS SOON AS MONEY WAS INTRODUCED, EVEN JUST 10¢, THE TASK BECAME PAID LABOR – AND PEOPLE ADJUSTED THEIR EFFORT ACCORDINGLY.
SO, MIXING THE MARKET AND SOCIAL APPROACHES WON'T NECESSARILY COMBINE THEIR EFFECTS...
...BECAUSE MARKET NORMS CAN CROWD OUT SOCIAL NORMS.
RIGHT!
YOU CAN'T JUST ADD THEM TOGETHER!
1 + 1 = 2
SOCIAL NORMS + MARKET NORMS ≠ BEST RESULT
!!!!

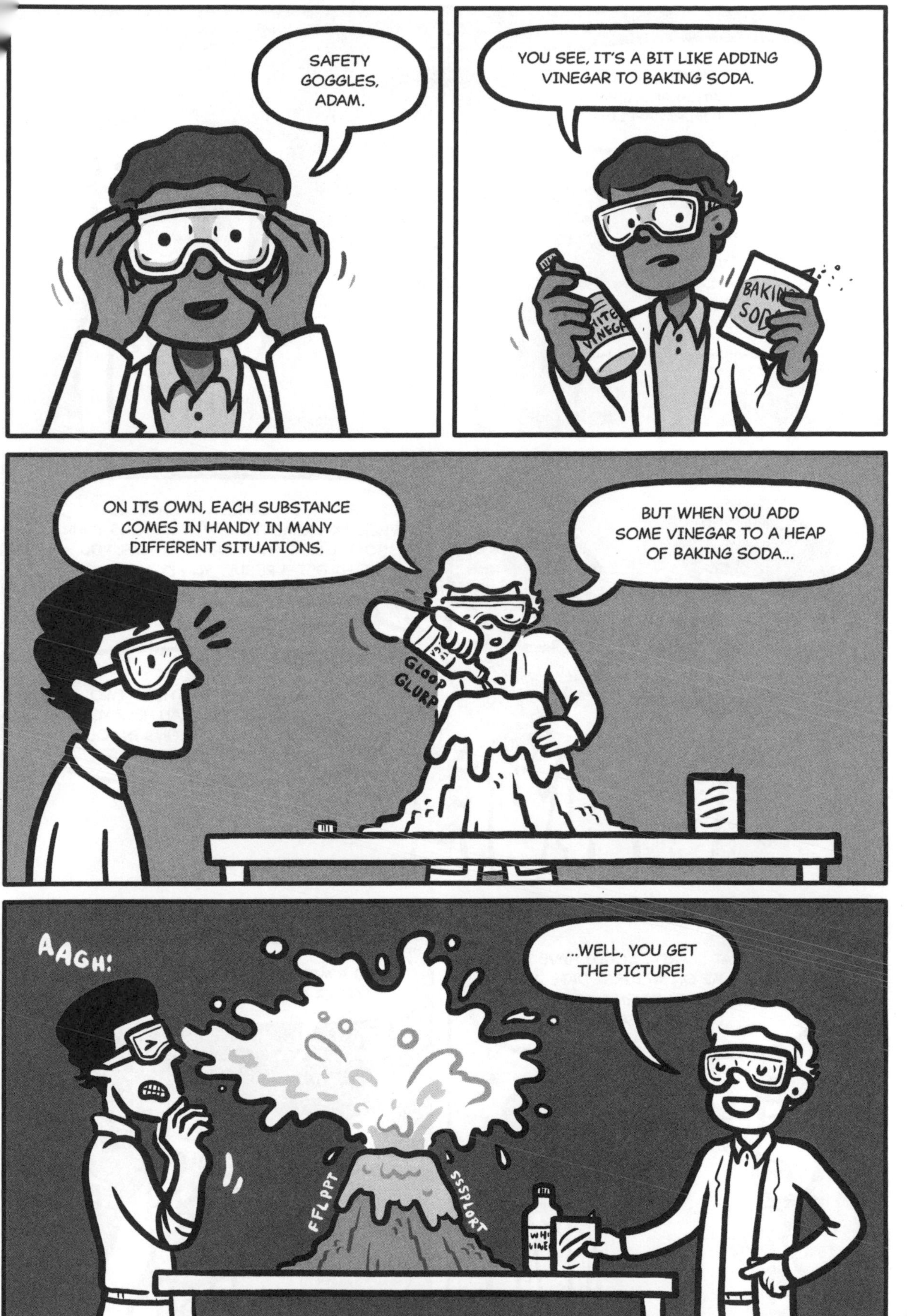
SAFETY GOGGLES, ADAM.
YOU SEE, IT'S A BIT LIKE ADDING VINEGAR TO BAKING SODA.
BAKING SODA
ON ITS OWN, EACH SUBSTANCE COMES IN HANDY IN MANY DIFFERENT SITUATIONS.
BUT WHEN YOU ADD SOME VINEGAR TO A HEAP OF BAKING SODA...
GLOOP
GLURP
AAGH!
...WELL, YOU GET THE PICTURE!
FFLPPT
SSSPLORT

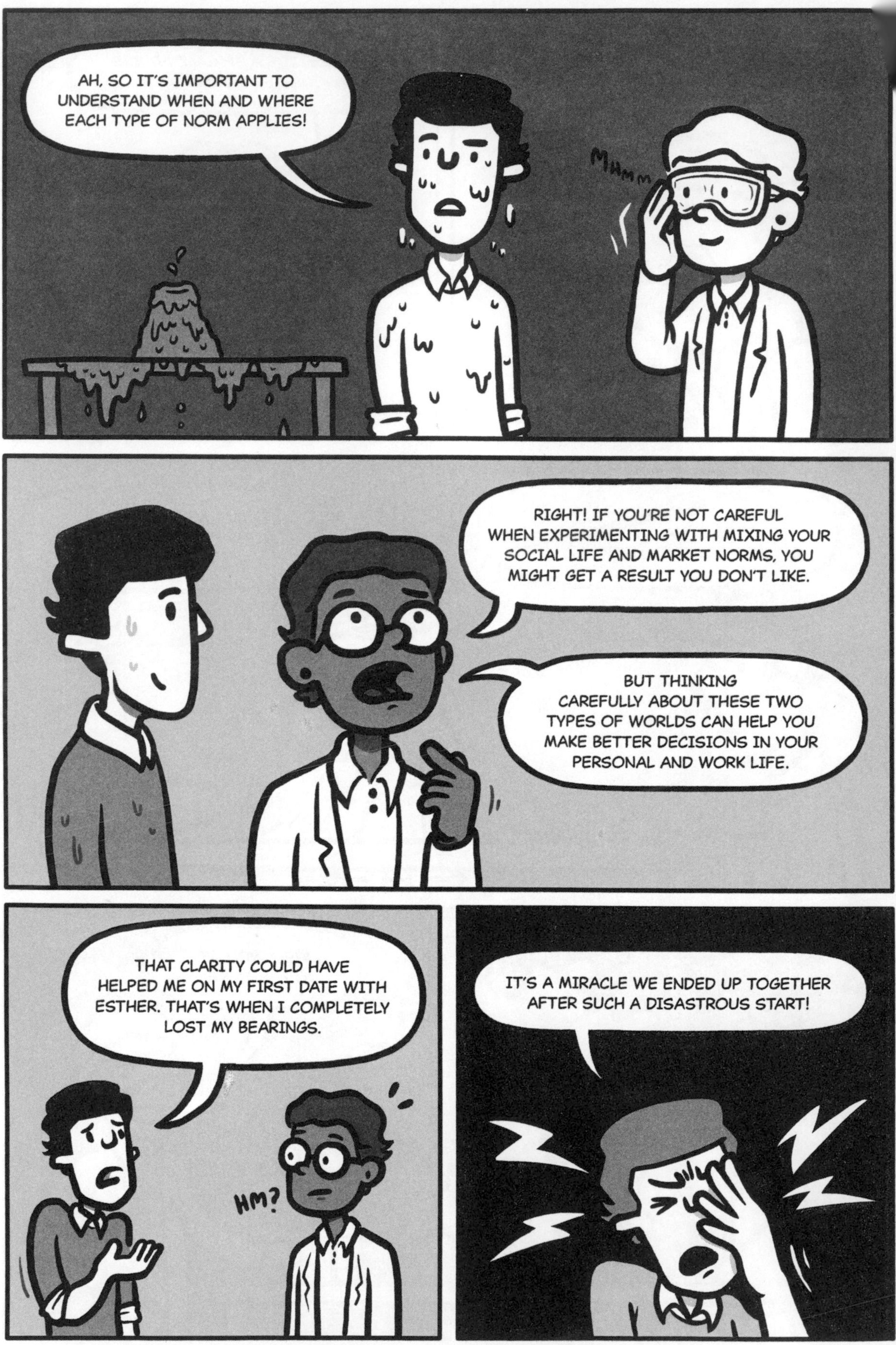
AH, SO IT'S IMPORTANT TO UNDERSTAND WHEN AND WHERE EACH TYPE OF NORM APPLIES!
MHMM
RIGHT! IF YOU'RE NOT CAREFUL WHEN EXPERIMENTING WITH MIXING YOUR SOCIAL LIFE AND MARKET NORMS, YOU MIGHT GET A RESULT YOU DON'T LIKE.
BUT THINKING CAREFULLY ABOUT THESE TWO TYPES OF WORLDS CAN HELP YOU MAKE BETTER DECISIONS IN YOUR PERSONAL AND WORK LIFE.
THAT CLARITY COULD HAVE HELPED ME ON MY FIRST DATE WITH ESTHER. THAT'S WHEN I COMPLETELY LOST MY BEARINGS.
HM?
IT'S A MIRACLE WE ENDED UP TOGETHER AFTER SUCH A DISASTROUS START!

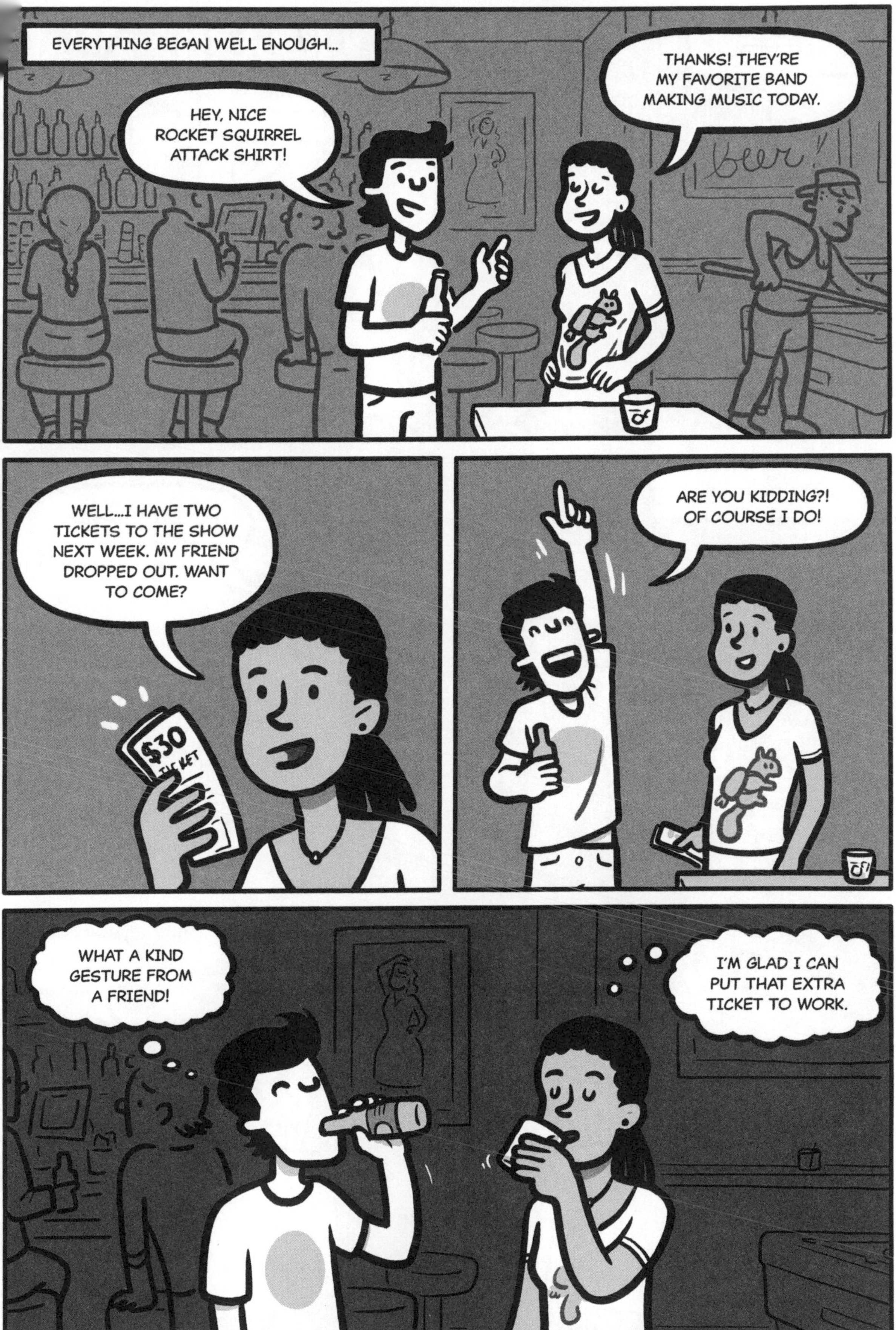
EVERYTHING BEGAN WELL ENOUGH...
HEY, NICE ROCKET SQUIRREL ATTACK SHIRT!
THANKS! THEY'RE MY FAVORITE BAND MAKING MUSIC TODAY.
beer!
WELL...I HAVE TWO TICKETS TO THE SHOW NEXT WEEK. MY FRIEND DROPPED OUT. WANT TO COME?
$30
ARE YOU KIDDING?! OF COURSE I DO!
WHAT A KIND GESTURE FROM A FRIEND!
I'M GLAD I CAN PUT THAT EXTRA TICKET TO WORK.

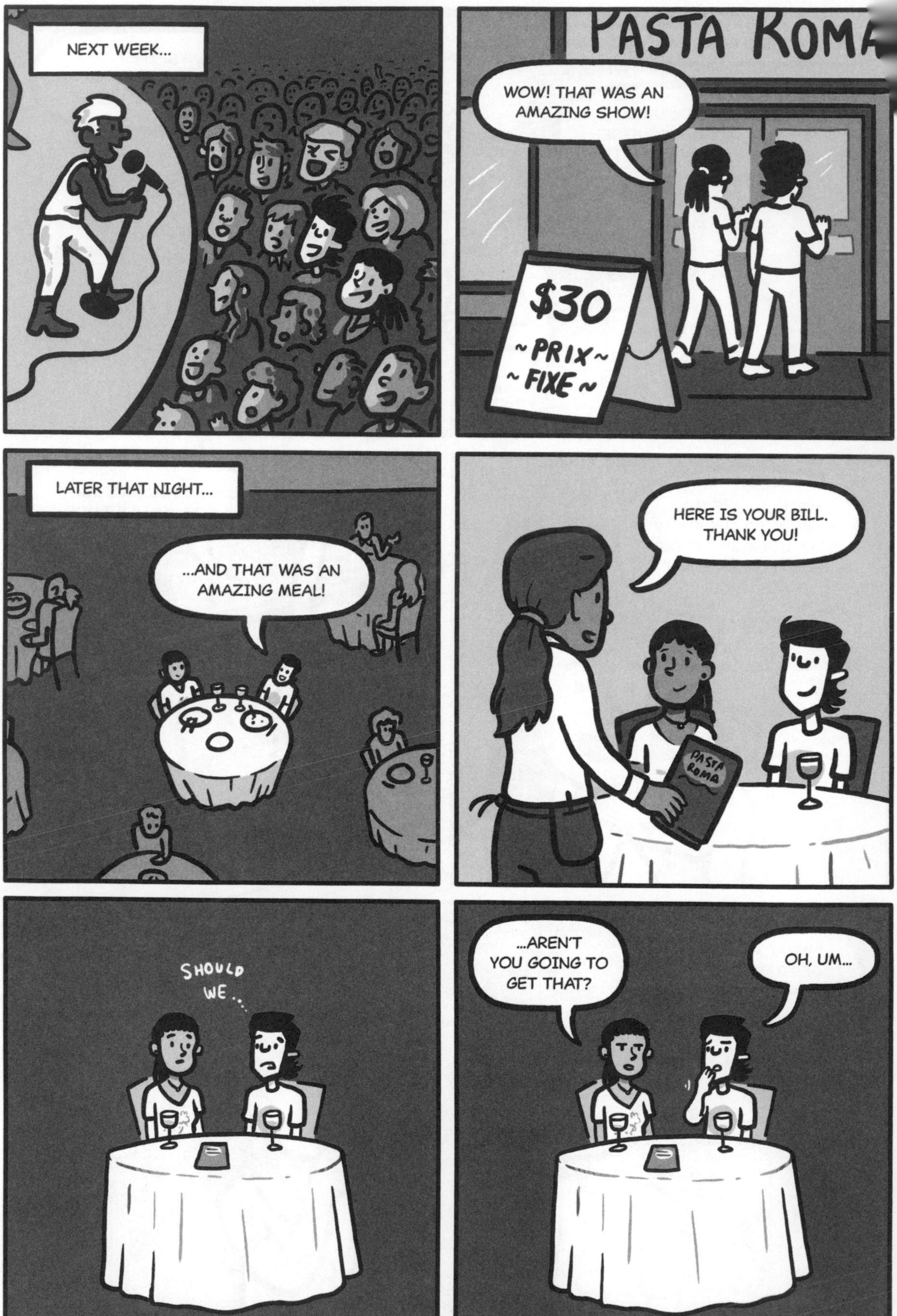
NEXT WEEK...
PASTA ROMA
WOW! THAT WAS AN AMAZING SHOW!
$30 ~PRIX~ ~FIXE~
LATER THAT NIGHT...
...AND THAT WAS AN AMAZING MEAL!
HERE IS YOUR BILL. THANK YOU!
PASTA ROMA
SHOULD WE....
...AREN'T YOU GOING TO GET THAT?
OH, UM...

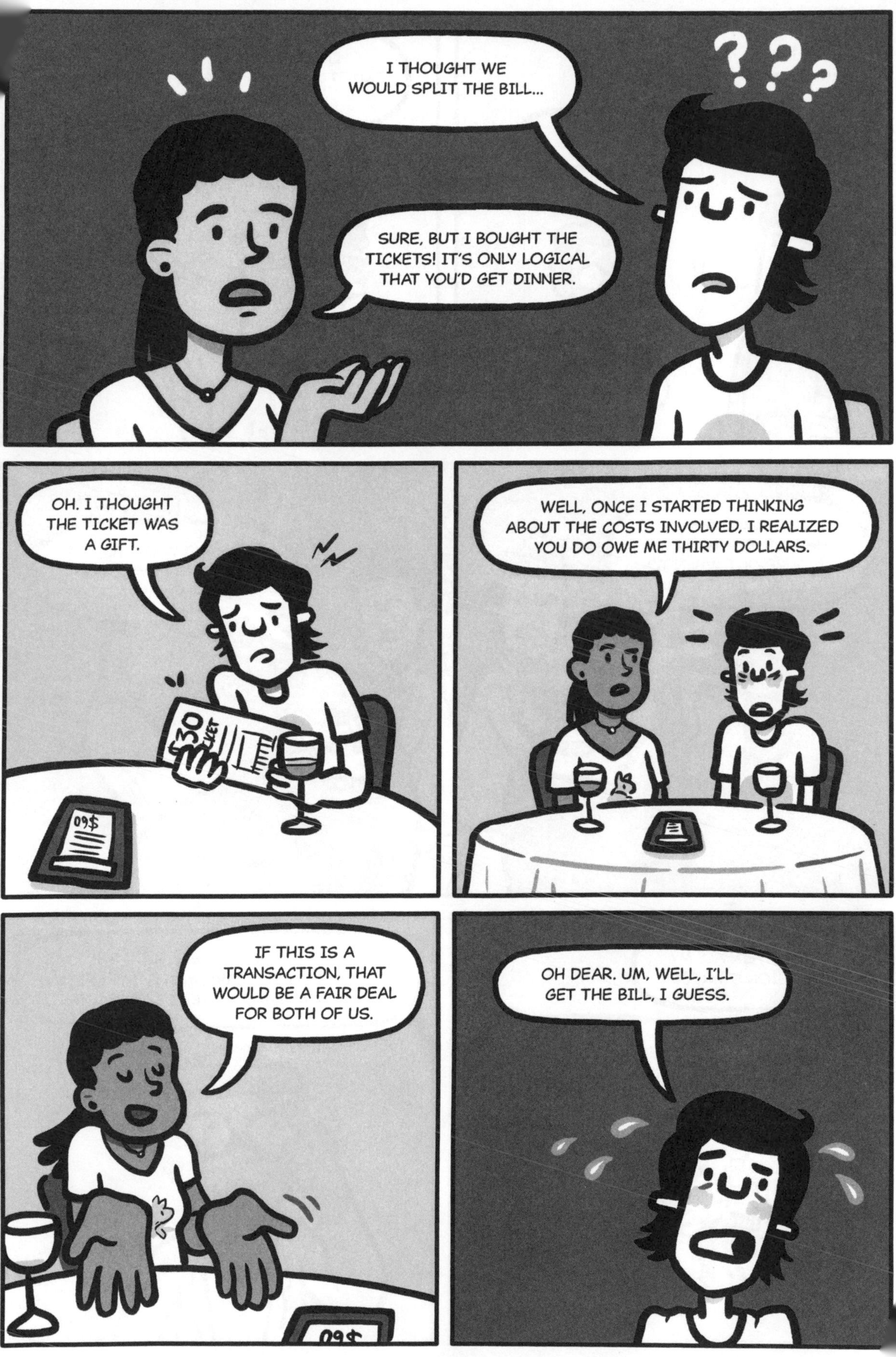
I THOUGHT WE WOULD SPLIT THE BILL...
SURE, BUT I BOUGHT THE TICKETS! IT'S ONLY LOGICAL THAT YOU'D GET DINNER.
OH. I THOUGHT THE TICKET WAS A GIFT.
$30
$60
WELL, ONCE I STARTED THINKING ABOUT THE COSTS INVOLVED, I REALIZED YOU DO OWE ME THIRTY DOLLARS.
IF THIS IS A TRANSACTION, THAT WOULD BE A FAIR DEAL FOR BOTH OF US.
$60
OH DEAR. UM, WELL, I'LL GET THE BILL, I GUESS.

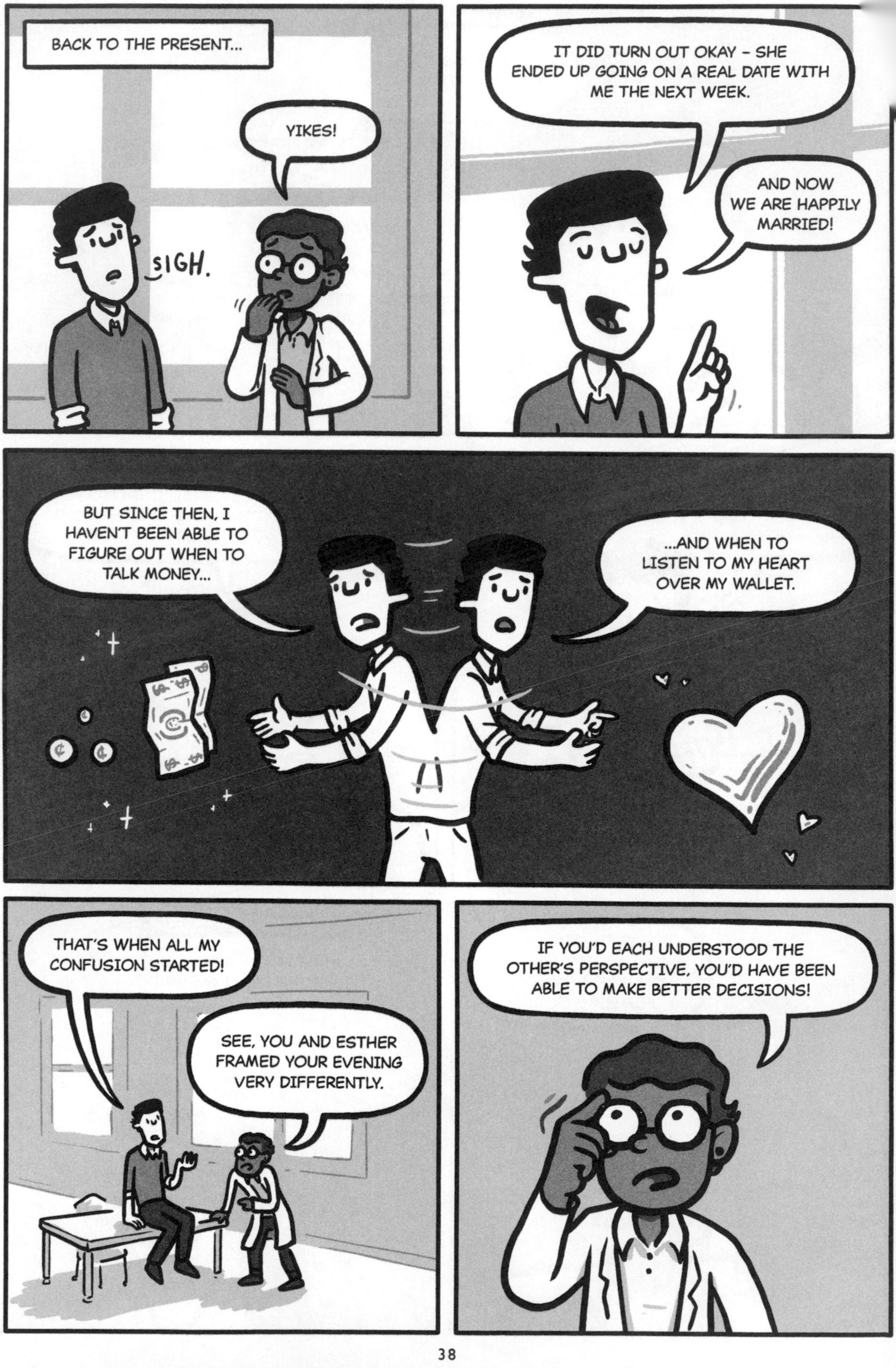
BACK TO THE PRESENT...
YIKES!
SIGH.
IT DID TURN OUT OKAY - SHE ENDED UP GOING ON A REAL DATE WITH ME THE NEXT WEEK.
AND NOW WE ARE HAPPILY MARRIED!
BUT SINCE THEN, I HAVEN'T BEEN ABLE TO FIGURE OUT WHEN TO TALK MONEY...
...AND WHEN TO LISTEN TO MY HEART OVER MY WALLET.
THAT'S WHEN ALL MY CONFUSION STARTED!
SEE, YOU AND ESTHER FRAMED YOUR EVENING VERY DIFFERENTLY.
IF YOU'D EACH UNDERSTOOD THE OTHER'S PERSPECTIVE, YOU'D HAVE BEEN ABLE TO MAKE BETTER DECISIONS!

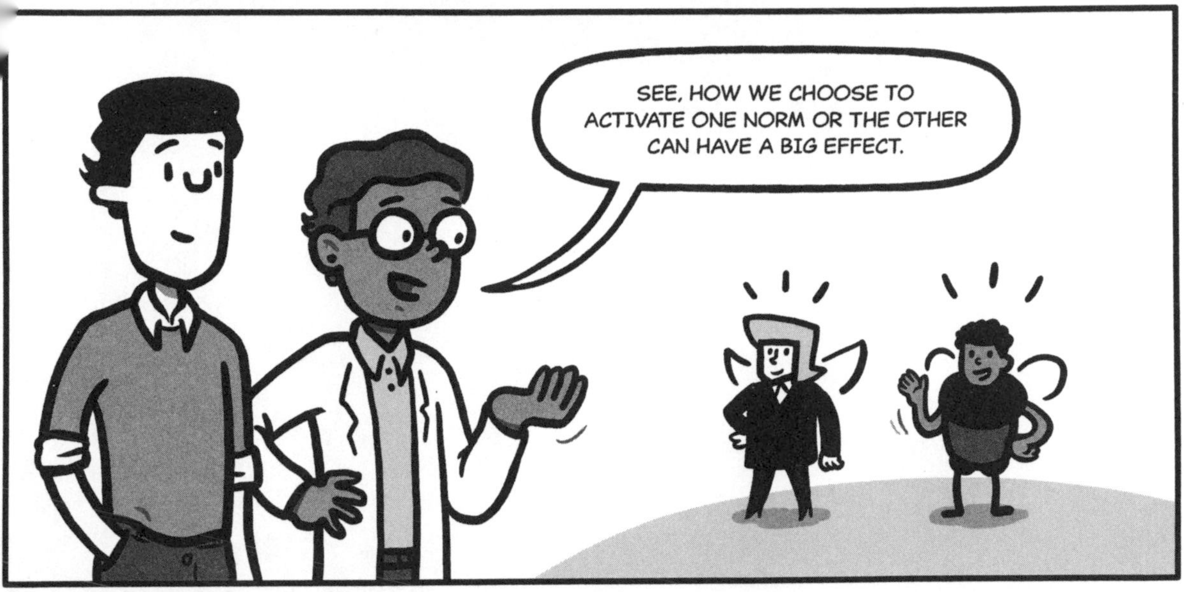
SEE, HOW WE CHOOSE TO ACTIVATE ONE NORM OR THE OTHER CAN HAVE A BIG EFFECT.

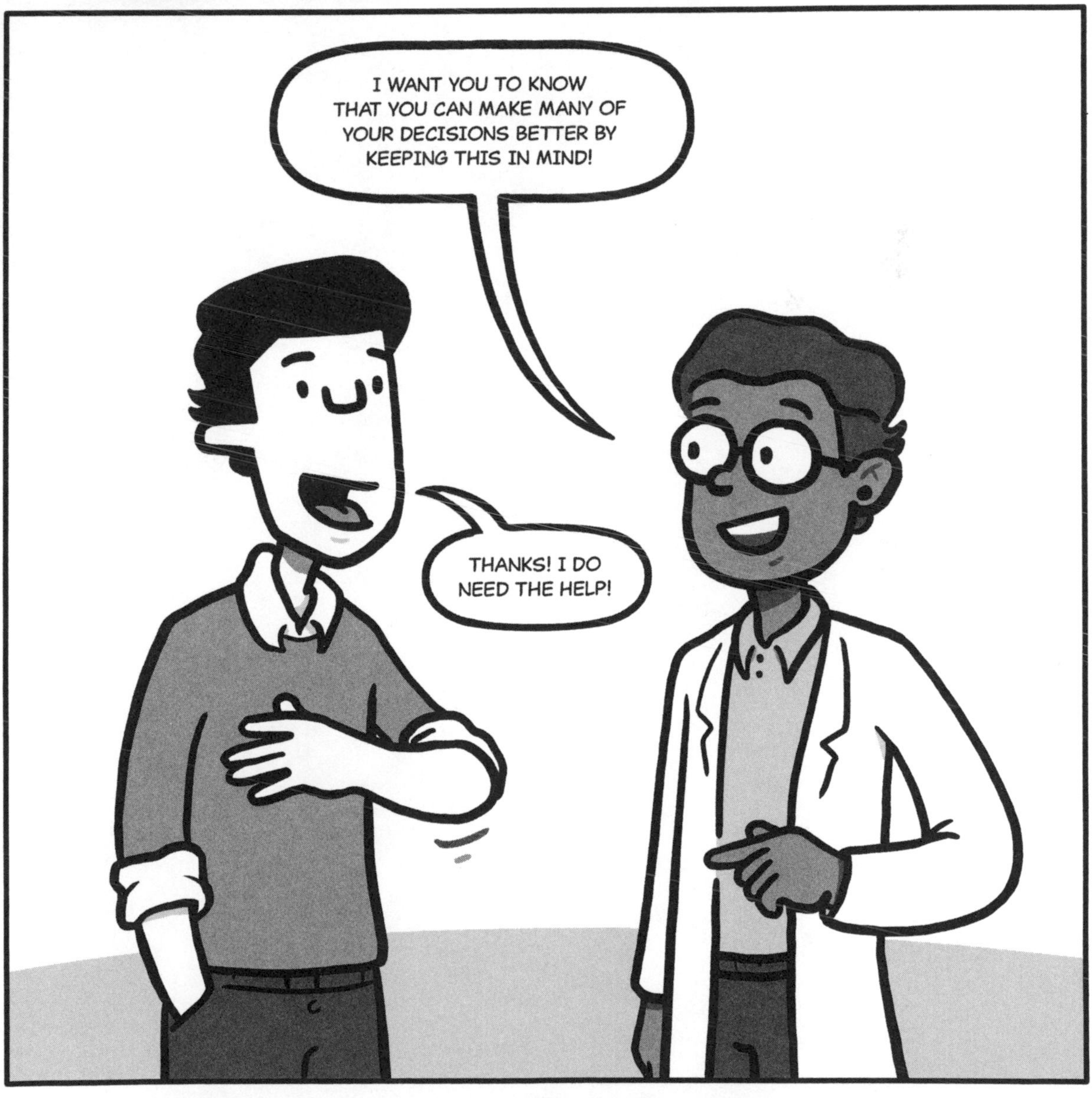
I WANT YOU TO KNOW THAT YOU CAN MAKE MANY OF YOUR DECISIONS BETTER BY KEEPING THIS IN MIND!
THANKS! I DO NEED THE HELP!

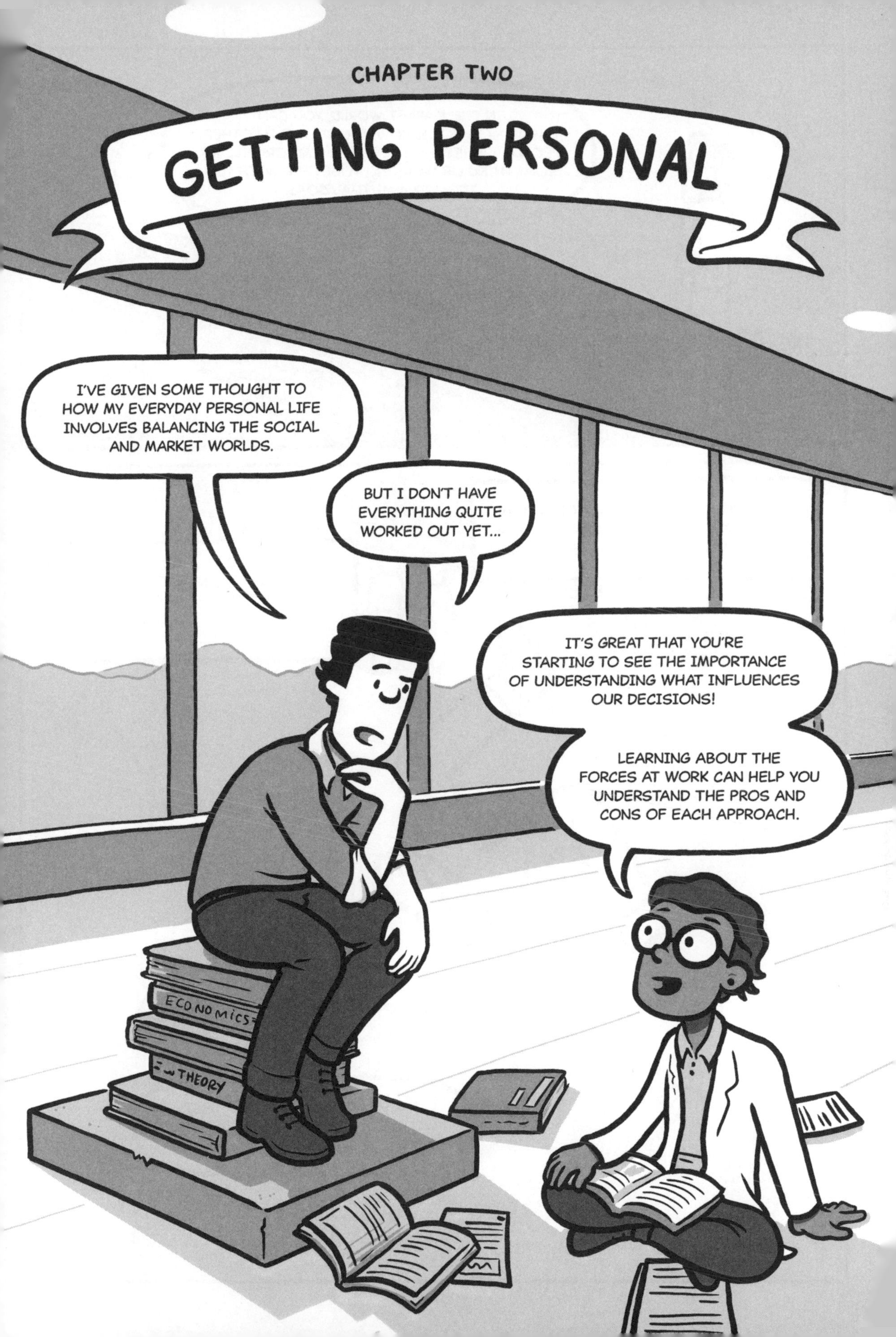
CHAPTER TWO
GETTING PERSONAL
I'VE GIVEN SOME THOUGHT TO HOW MY EVERYDAY PERSONAL LIFE INVOLVES BALANCING THE SOCIAL AND MARKET WORLDS.
BUT I DON'T HAVE EVERYTHING QUITE WORKED OUT YET...
IT'S GREAT THAT YOU'RE STARTING TO SEE THE IMPORTANCE OF UNDERSTANDING WHAT INFLUENCES OUR DECISIONS!
LEARNING ABOUT THE FORCES AT WORK CAN HELP YOU UNDERSTAND THE PROS AND CONS OF EACH APPROACH.
ECONOMICS
THEORY

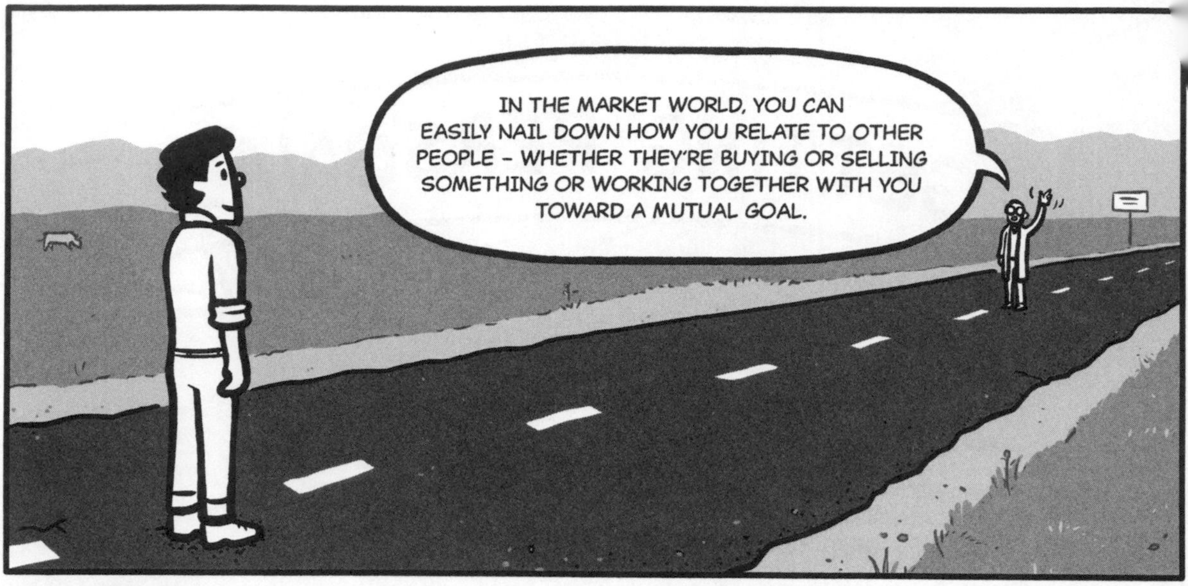
IN THE MARKET WORLD, YOU CAN EASILY NAIL DOWN HOW YOU RELATE TO OTHER PEOPLE – WHETHER THEY'RE BUYING OR SELLING SOMETHING OR WORKING TOGETHER WITH YOU TOWARD A MUTUAL GOAL.

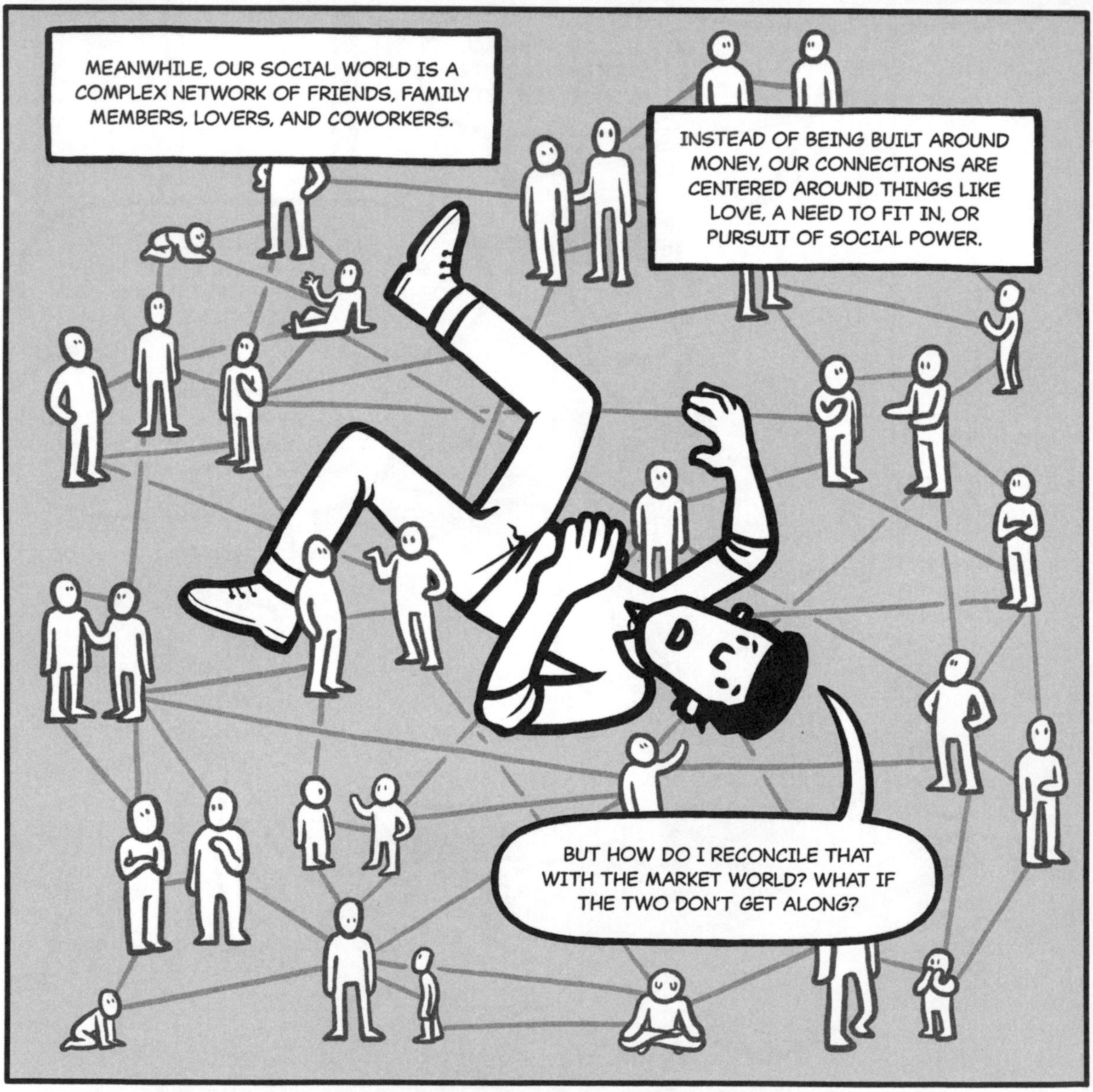
MEANWHILE, OUR SOCIAL WORLD IS A COMPLEX NETWORK OF FRIENDS, FAMILY MEMBERS, LOVERS, AND COWORKERS.
INSTEAD OF BEING BUILT AROUND MONEY, OUR CONNECTIONS ARE CENTERED AROUND THINGS LIKE LOVE, A NEED TO FIT IN, OR PURSUIT OF SOCIAL POWER.
BUT HOW DO I RECONCILE THAT WITH THE MARKET WORLD? WHAT IF THE TWO DON'T GET ALONG?

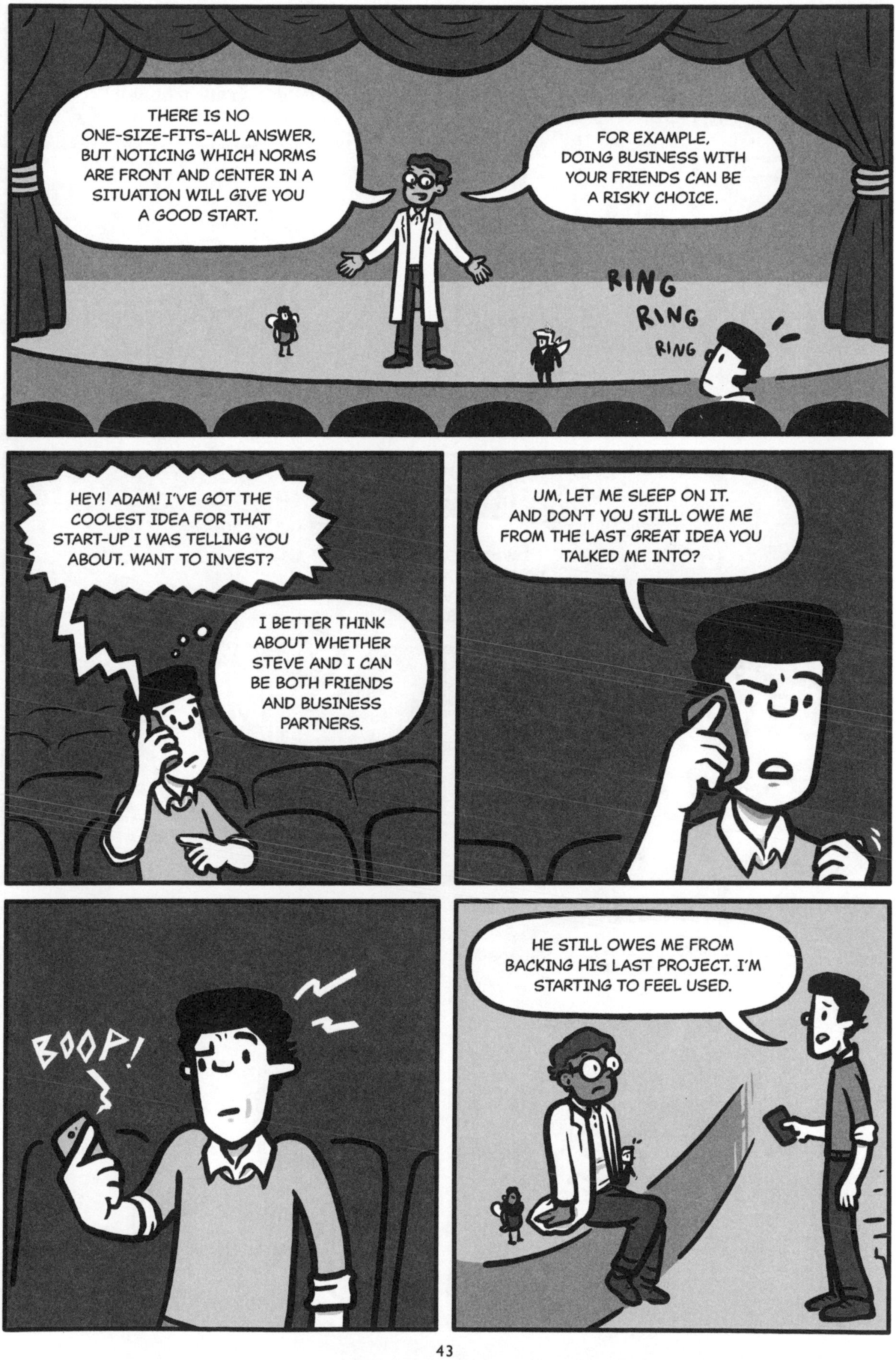
THERE IS NO ONE-SIZE-FITS-ALL ANSWER, BUT NOTICING WHICH NORMS ARE FRONT AND CENTER IN A SITUATION WILL GIVE YOU A GOOD START.
FOR EXAMPLE, DOING BUSINESS WITH YOUR FRIENDS CAN BE A RISKY CHOICE.
RING
RING
RING
HEY! ADAM! I'VE GOT THE COOLEST IDEA FOR THAT START-UP I WAS TELLING YOU ABOUT. WANT TO INVEST?
I BETTER THINK ABOUT WHETHER STEVE AND I CAN BE BOTH FRIENDS AND BUSINESS PARTNERS.
UM, LET ME SLEEP ON IT. AND DON'T YOU STILL OWE ME FROM THE LAST GREAT IDEA YOU TALKED ME INTO?
BOOP!
HE STILL OWES ME FROM BACKING HIS LAST PROJECT. I'M STARTING TO FEEL USED.

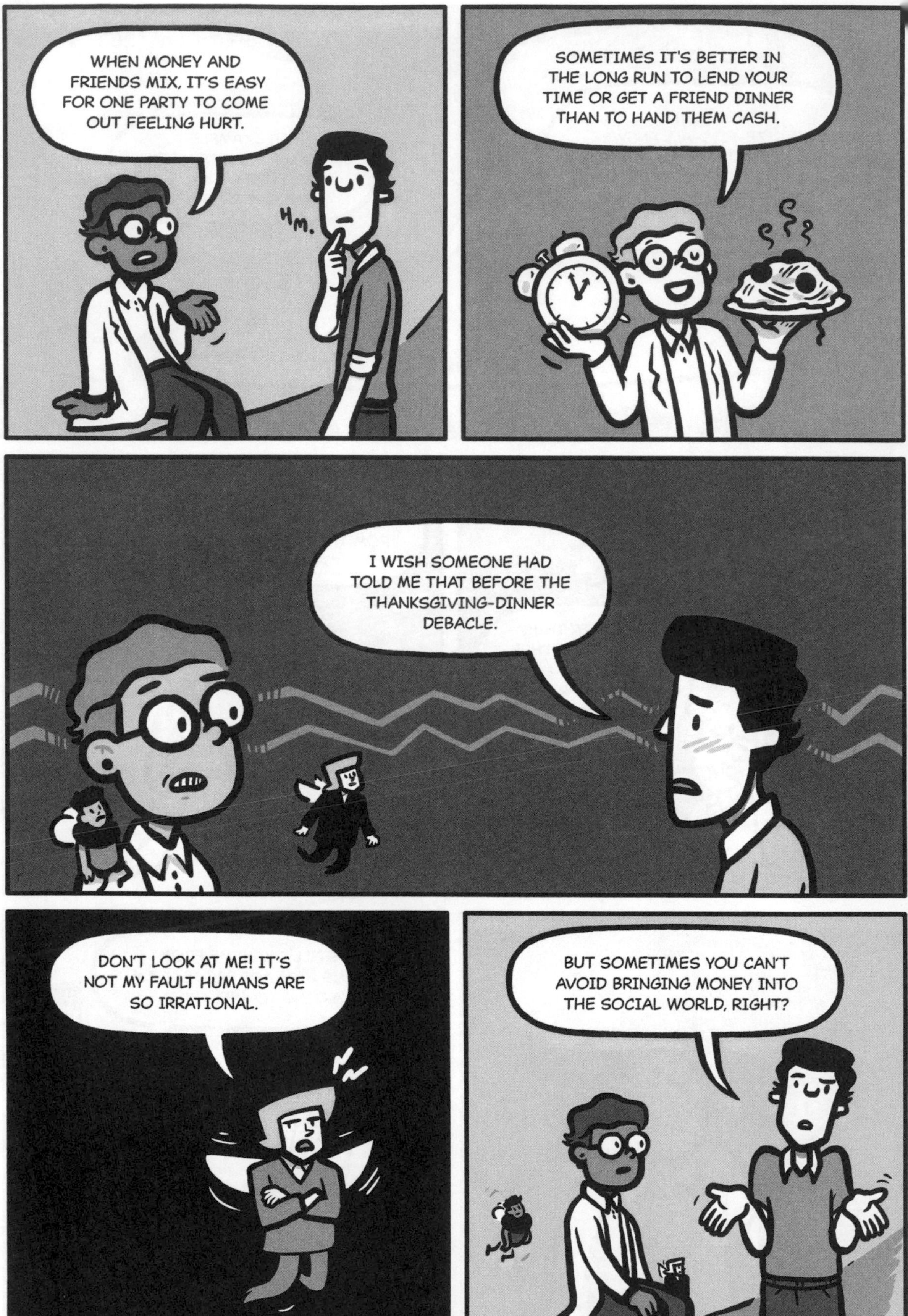
WHEN MONEY AND FRIENDS MIX, IT'S EASY FOR ONE PARTY TO COME OUT FEELING HURT.
HM.
SOMETIMES IT'S BETTER IN THE LONG RUN TO LEND YOUR TIME OR GET A FRIEND DINNER THAN TO HAND THEM CASH.
I WISH SOMEONE HAD TOLD ME THAT BEFORE THE THANKSGIVING-DINNER DEBACLE.
DON'T LOOK AT ME! IT'S NOT MY FAULT HUMANS ARE SO IRRATIONAL.
BUT SOMETIMES YOU CAN'T AVOID BRINGING MONEY INTO THE SOCIAL WORLD, RIGHT?

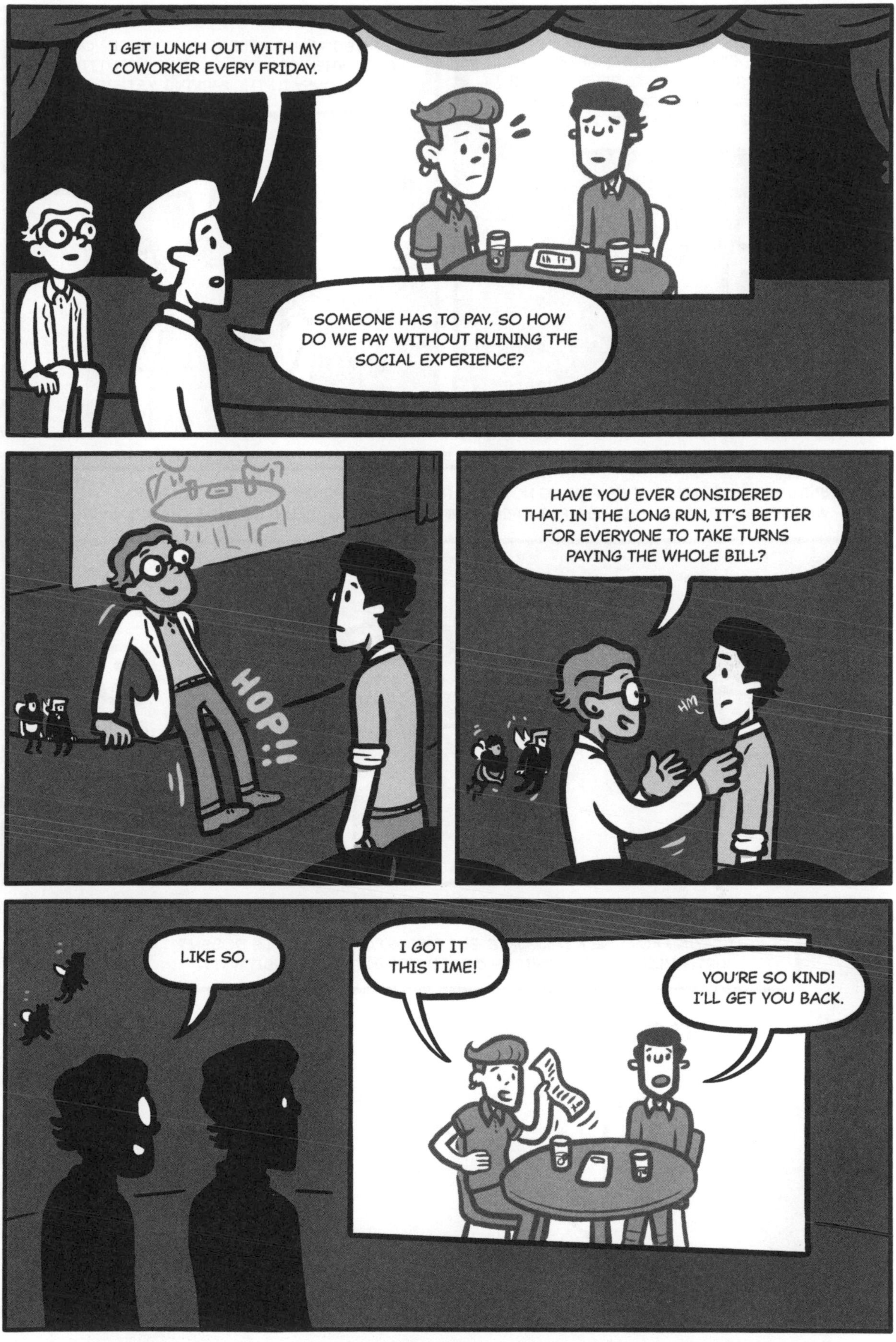
I GET LUNCH OUT WITH MY COWORKER EVERY FRIDAY.
SOMEONE HAS TO PAY, SO HOW DO WE PAY WITHOUT RUINING THE SOCIAL EXPERIENCE?
HOP!!
HAVE YOU EVER CONSIDERED THAT, IN THE LONG RUN, IT'S BETTER FOR EVERYONE TO TAKE TURNS PAYING THE WHOLE BILL?
HM
LIKE SO.
I GOT IT THIS TIME!
YOU'RE SO KIND! I'LL GET YOU BACK.

LET ME EXPLAIN WHY THIS APPROACH WORKS. PSYCHOLOGISTS REFER TO THE EMOTIONAL DISTRESS CAUSED BY SPENDING MONEY AS THE "PAIN OF PAYING."

THIS IS THE UNPLEASANT TWINGE YOU FEEL WHEN SIGNING A CHECK OR PUTTING MONEY IN THE PARKING METER.

OOF, I DEFINITELY KNOW THAT FEELING.

SURPRISINGLY, THE AMOUNT OF PAIN IS NOT VERY RESPONSIVE TO THE AMOUNT OF THE BILL. WE FEEL WORSE AS THE BILL INCREASES, BUT EACH ADDITIONAL DOLLAR PAINS US LESS THAN THE FIRST.

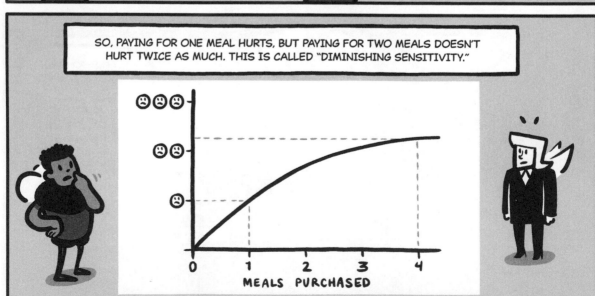

SO, PAYING FOR ONE MEAL HURTS, BUT PAYING FOR TWO MEALS DOESN'T HURT TWICE AS MUCH. THIS IS CALLED "DIMINISHING SENSITIVITY."

MEALS PURCHASED

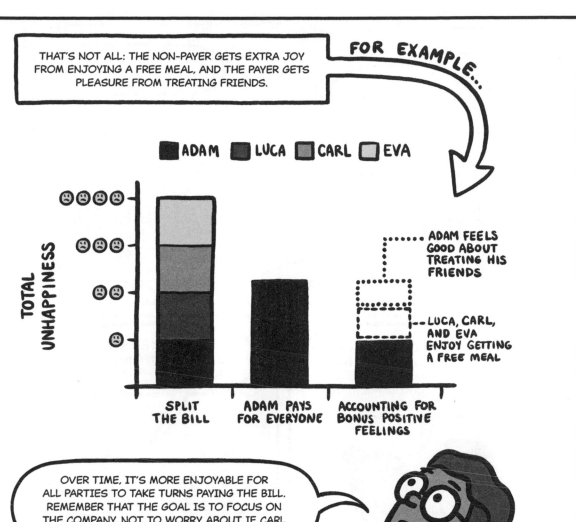

THAT'S NOT ALL: THE NON-PAYER GETS EXTRA JOY FROM ENJOYING A FREE MEAL, AND THE PAYER GETS PLEASURE FROM TREATING FRIENDS.

FOR EXAMPLE...

■ ADAM ■ LUCA ■ CARL □ EVA

TOTAL UNHAPPINESS

ADAM FEELS GOOD ABOUT TREATING HIS FRIENDS

LUCA, CARL, AND EVA ENJOY GETTING A FREE MEAL

SPLIT THE BILL

ADAM PAYS FOR EVERYONE

ACCOUNTING FOR BONUS POSITIVE FEELINGS

OVER TIME, IT'S MORE ENJOYABLE FOR ALL PARTIES TO TAKE TURNS PAYING THE BILL. REMEMBER THAT THE GOAL IS TO FOCUS ON THE COMPANY, NOT TO WORRY ABOUT IF CARL ORDERED AN EXTRA DESSERT.

I WILL GIVE IT A TRY. MAYBE YOU'VE SOLVED MY COWORKER CONUNDRUM.

WHATEVER YOU CHOOSE, FOCUSING ON THE MONEY WHEN SOCIALIZING WILL ONLY SET YOU UP FOR FAILURE. REMEMBER THAT FIRST DATE?

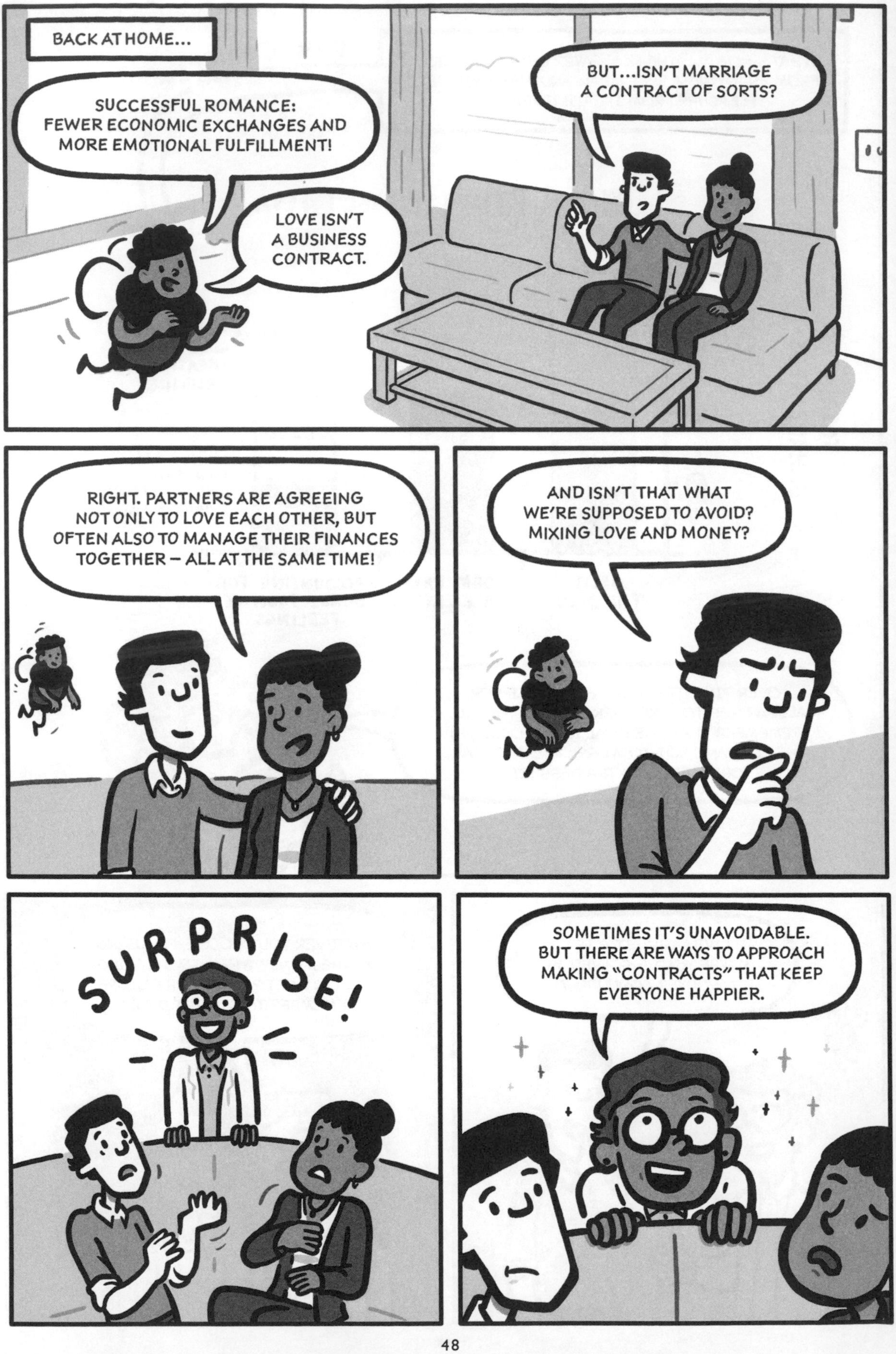
BACK AT HOME...
SUCCESSFUL ROMANCE: FEWER ECONOMIC EXCHANGES AND MORE EMOTIONAL FULFILLMENT!
LOVE ISN'T A BUSINESS CONTRACT.
BUT...ISN'T MARRIAGE A CONTRACT OF SORTS?
RIGHT. PARTNERS ARE AGREEING NOT ONLY TO LOVE EACH OTHER, BUT OFTEN ALSO TO MANAGE THEIR FINANCES TOGETHER – ALL AT THE SAME TIME!
AND ISN'T THAT WHAT WE'RE SUPPOSED TO AVOID? MIXING LOVE AND MONEY?
SURPRISE!
SOMETIMES IT'S UNAVOIDABLE. BUT THERE ARE WAYS TO APPROACH MAKING "CONTRACTS" THAT KEEP EVERYONE HAPPIER.

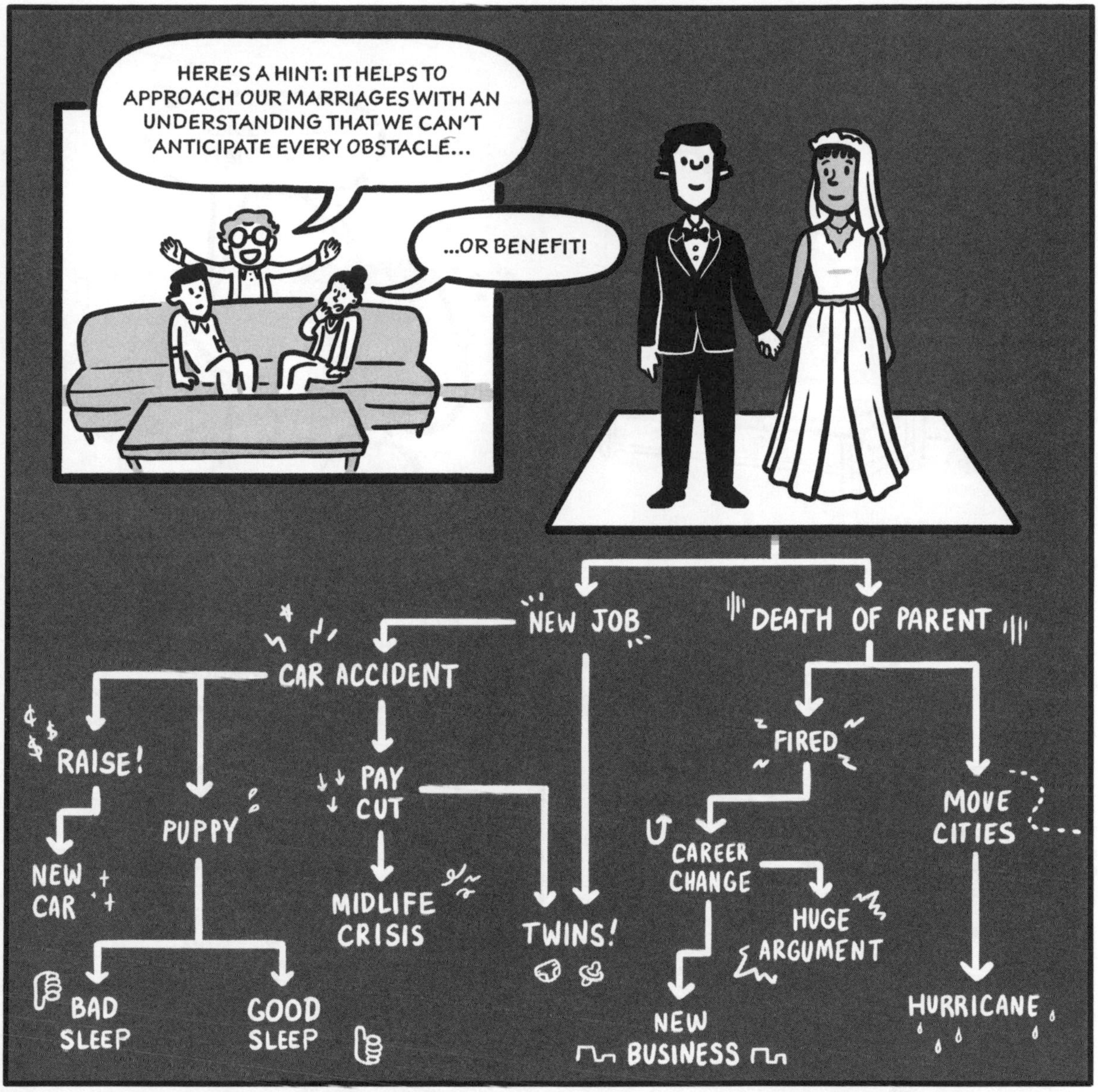
HERE'S A HINT: IT HELPS TO APPROACH OUR MARRIAGES WITH AN UNDERSTANDING THAT WE CAN'T ANTICIPATE EVERY OBSTACLE...
...OR BENEFIT!
NEW JOB
DEATH OF PARENT
CAR ACCIDENT
RAISE!
PUPPY
PAY CUT
NEW CAR
MIDLIFE CRISIS
TWINS!
BAD SLEEP
GOOD SLEEP
FIRED
CAREER CHANGE
HUGE ARGUMENT
NEW BUSINESS
MOVE CITIES
HURRICANE

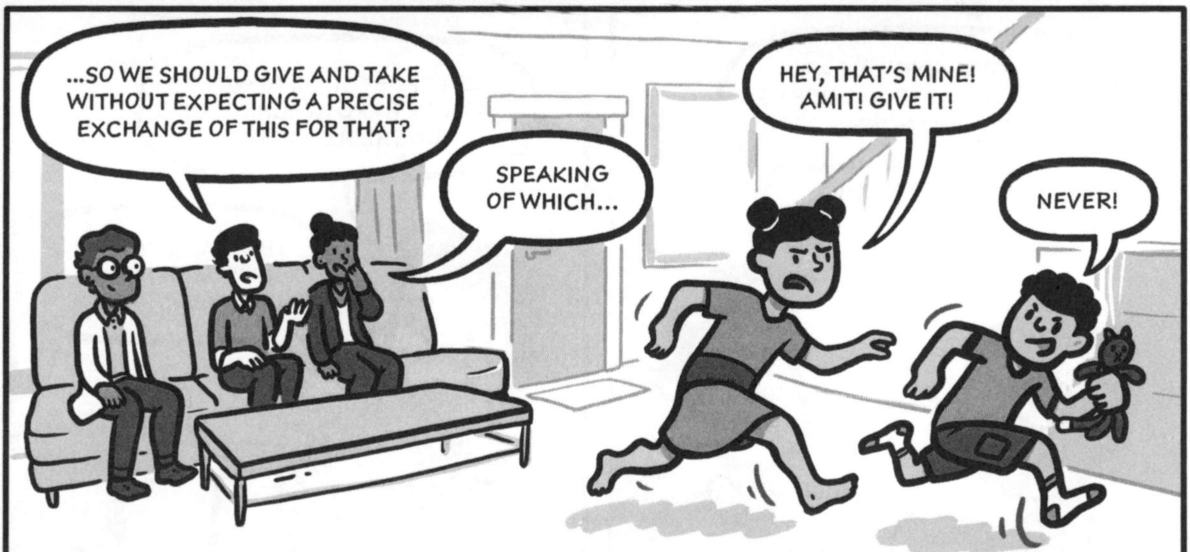
...SO WE SHOULD GIVE AND TAKE WITHOUT EXPECTING A PRECISE EXCHANGE OF THIS FOR THAT?
SPEAKING OF WHICH...
HEY, THAT'S MINE! AMIT! GIVE IT!
NEVER!

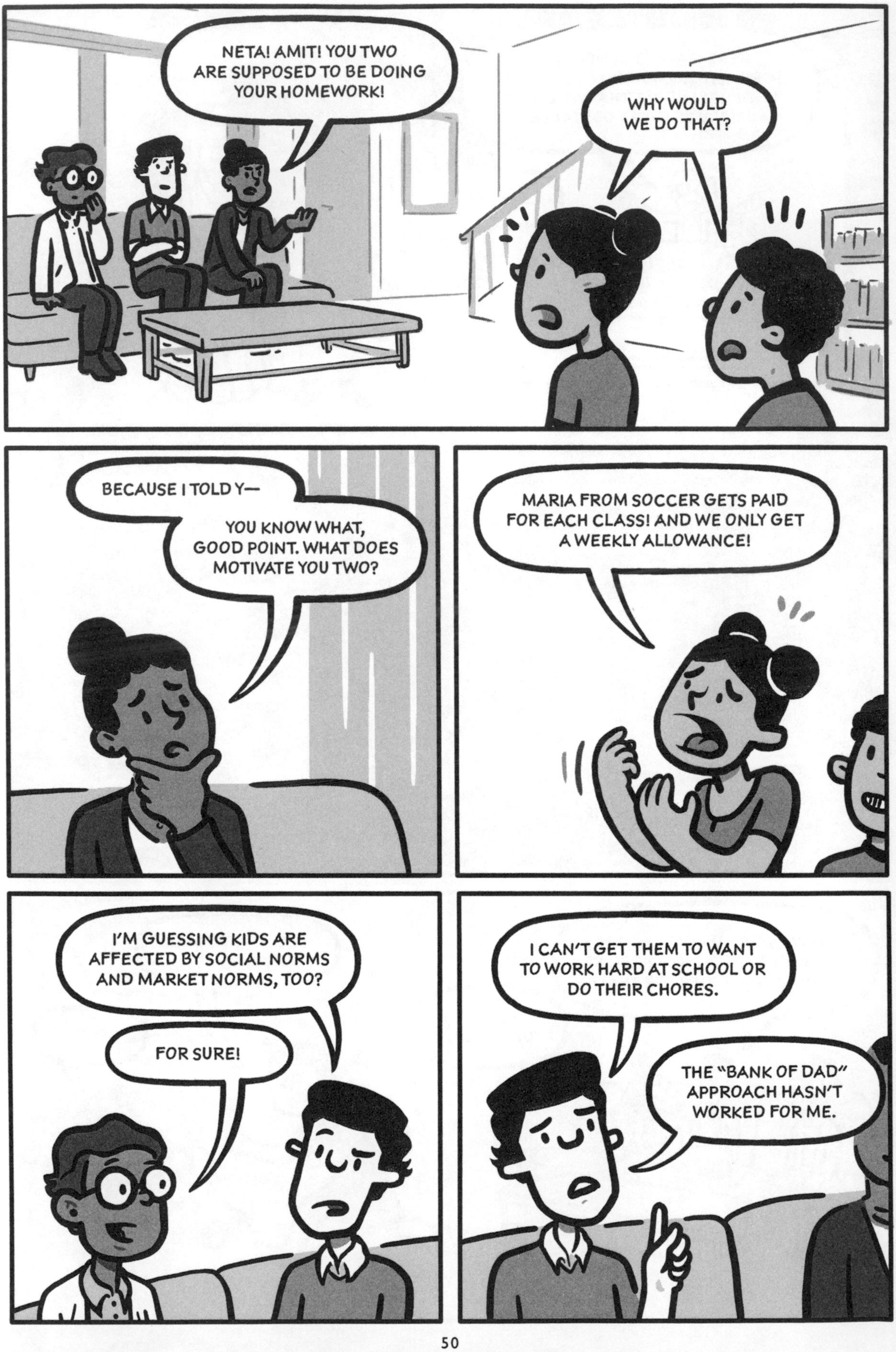
NETA! AMIT! YOU TWO ARE SUPPOSED TO BE DOING YOUR HOMEWORK!
WHY WOULD WE DO THAT?
BECAUSE I TOLD Y—
YOU KNOW WHAT, GOOD POINT. WHAT DOES MOTIVATE YOU TWO?
MARIA FROM SOCCER GETS PAID FOR EACH CLASS! AND WE ONLY GET A WEEKLY ALLOWANCE!
I'M GUESSING KIDS ARE AFFECTED BY SOCIAL NORMS AND MARKET NORMS, TOO?
FOR SURE!
I CAN'T GET THEM TO WANT TO WORK HARD AT SCHOOL OR DO THEIR CHORES.
THE "BANK OF DAD" APPROACH HASN'T WORKED FOR ME.

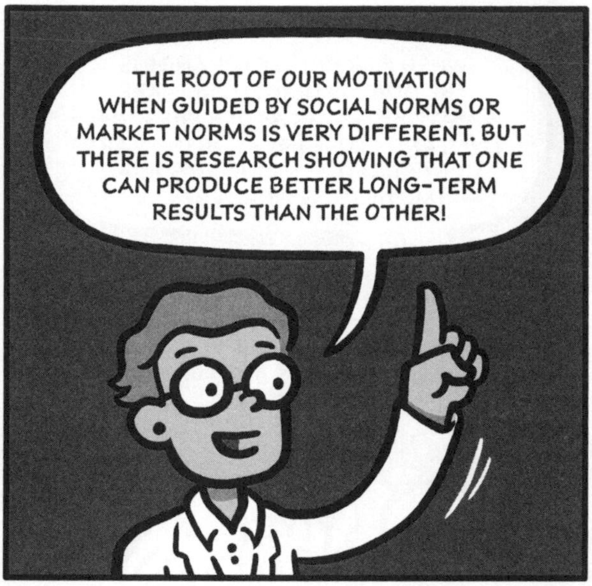
THE ROOT OF OUR MOTIVATION WHEN GUIDED BY SOCIAL NORMS OR MARKET NORMS IS VERY DIFFERENT. BUT THERE IS RESEARCH SHOWING THAT ONE CAN PRODUCE BETTER LONG-TERM RESULTS THAN THE OTHER!

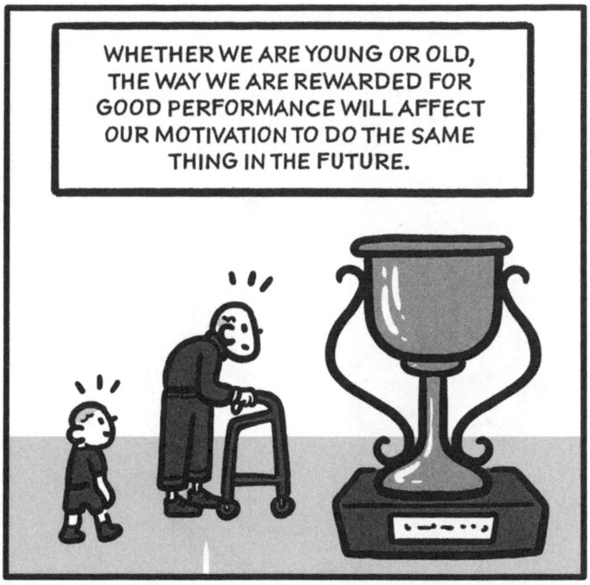
WHETHER WE ARE YOUNG OR OLD, THE WAY WE ARE REWARDED FOR GOOD PERFORMANCE WILL AFFECT OUR MOTIVATION TO DO THE SAME THING IN THE FUTURE.

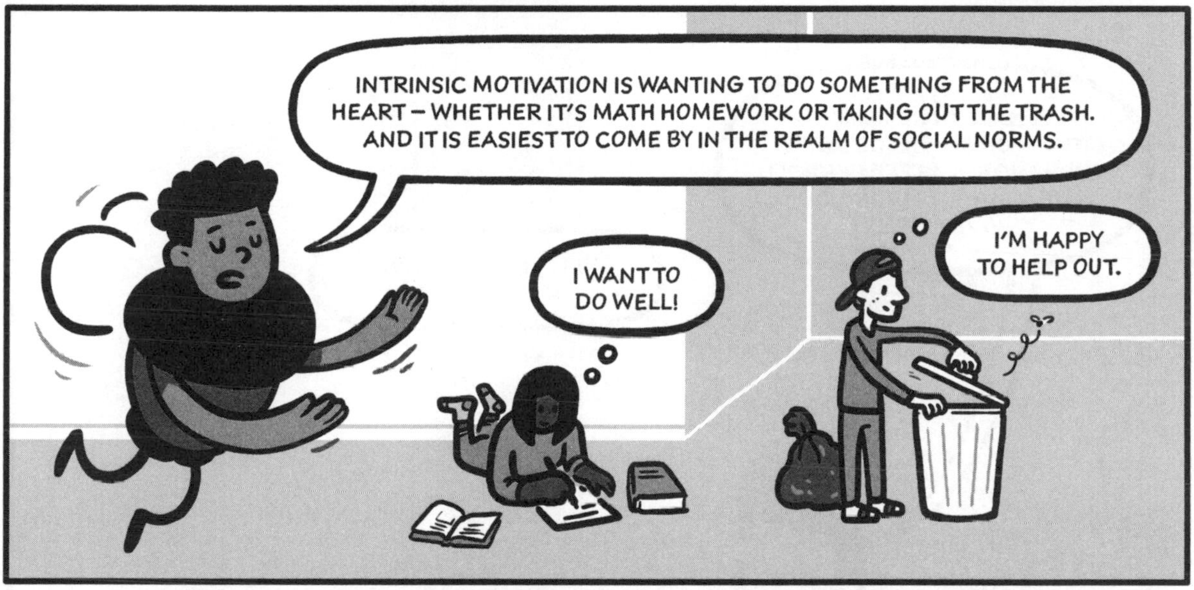
INTRINSIC MOTIVATION IS WANTING TO DO SOMETHING FROM THE HEART – WHETHER IT'S MATH HOMEWORK OR TAKING OUT THE TRASH. AND IT IS EASIEST TO COME BY IN THE REALM OF SOCIAL NORMS.
I WANT TO DO WELL!
I'M HAPPY TO HELP OUT.

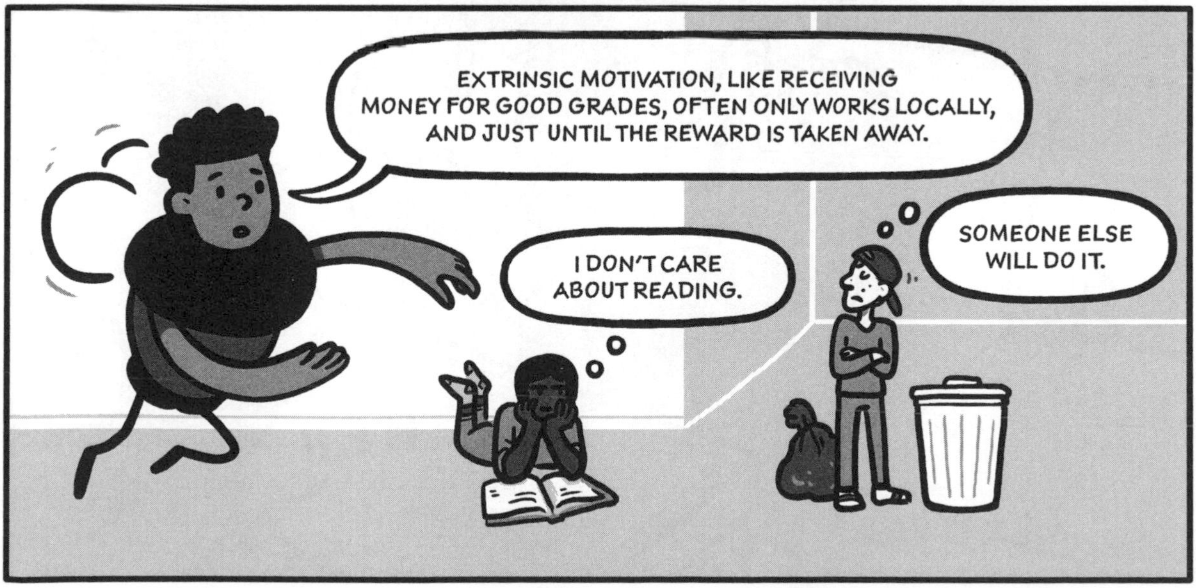
EXTRINSIC MOTIVATION, LIKE RECEIVING MONEY FOR GOOD GRADES, OFTEN ONLY WORKS LOCALLY, AND JUST UNTIL THE REWARD IS TAKEN AWAY.
I DON'T CARE ABOUT READING.
SOMEONE ELSE WILL DO IT.

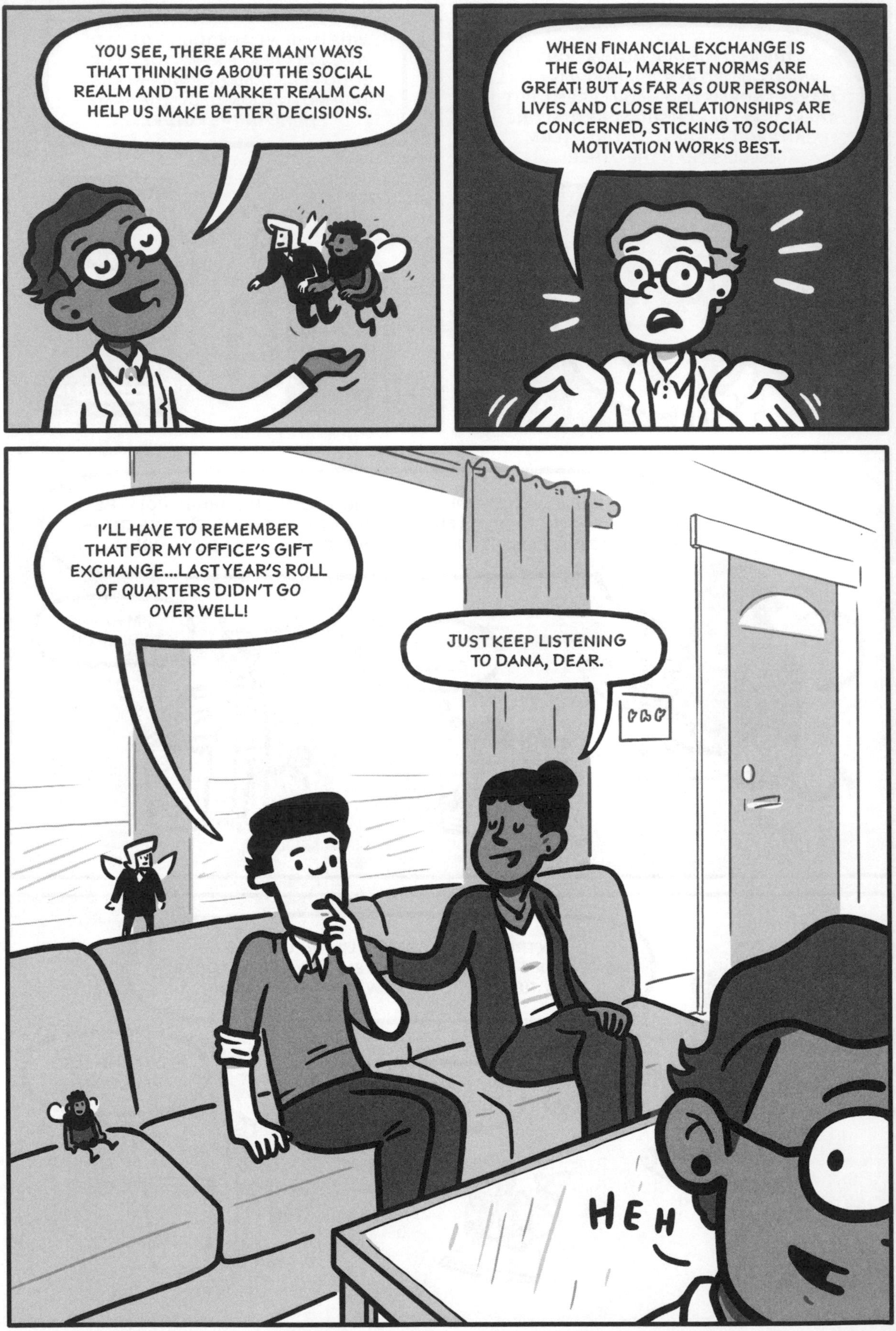
YOU SEE, THERE ARE MANY WAYS THAT THINKING ABOUT THE SOCIAL REALM AND THE MARKET REALM CAN HELP US MAKE BETTER DECISIONS.
WHEN FINANCIAL EXCHANGE IS THE GOAL, MARKET NORMS ARE GREAT! BUT AS FAR AS OUR PERSONAL LIVES AND CLOSE RELATIONSHIPS ARE CONCERNED, STICKING TO SOCIAL MOTIVATION WORKS BEST.
I'LL HAVE TO REMEMBER THAT FOR MY OFFICE'S GIFT EXCHANGE...LAST YEAR'S ROLL OF QUARTERS DIDN'T GO OVER WELL!
JUST KEEP LISTENING TO DANA, DEAR.
HEH

CHAPTER THREE

THE GIFT THAT GIVES

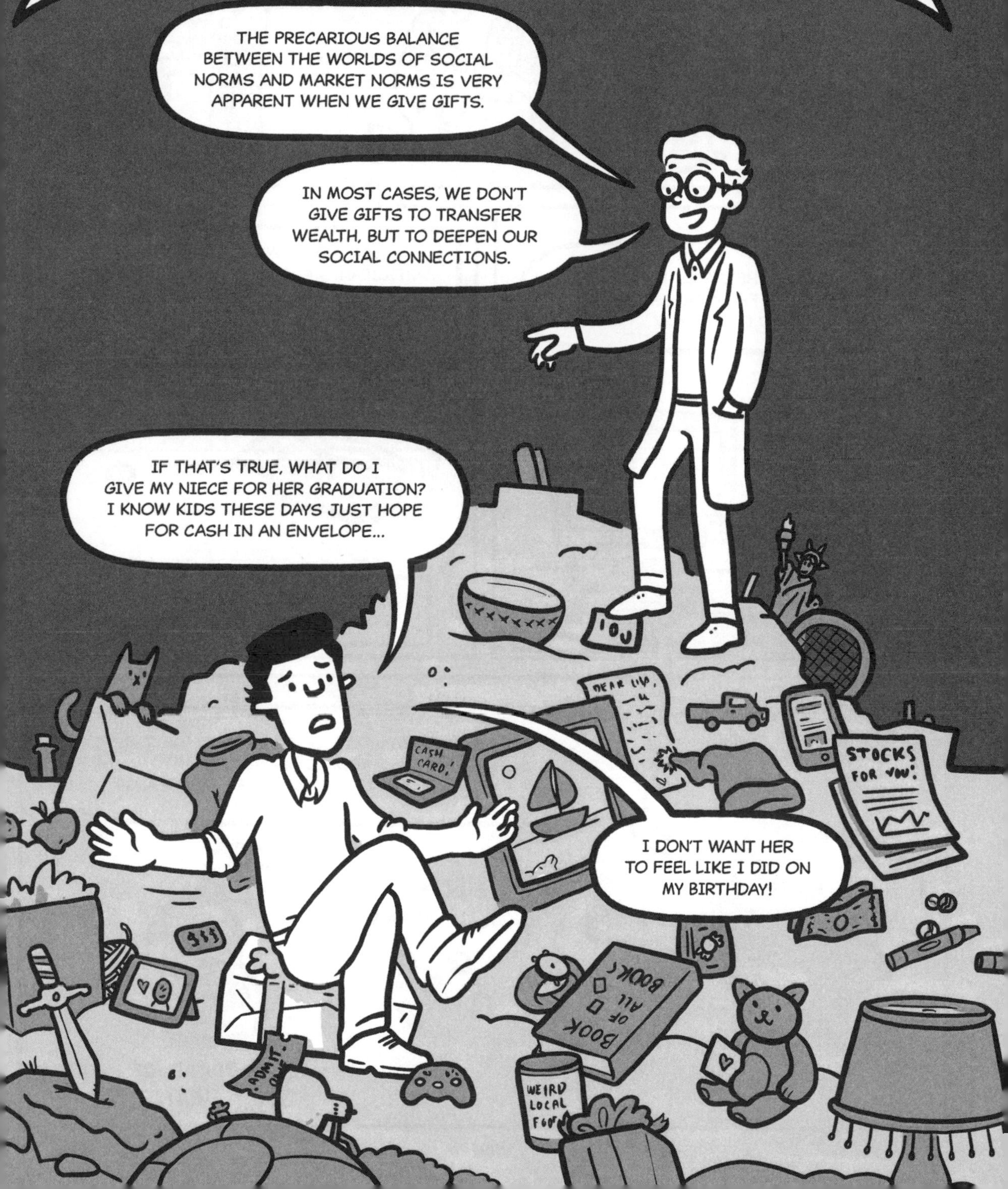
THE PRECARIOUS BALANCE BETWEEN THE WORLDS OF SOCIAL NORMS AND MARKET NORMS IS VERY APPARENT WHEN WE GIVE GIFTS.
IN MOST CASES, WE DON'T GIVE GIFTS TO TRANSFER WEALTH, BUT TO DEEPEN OUR SOCIAL CONNECTIONS.
IF THAT'S TRUE, WHAT DO I GIVE MY NIECE FOR HER GRADUATION? I KNOW KIDS THESE DAYS JUST HOPE FOR CASH IN AN ENVELOPE...
I DON'T WANT HER TO FEEL LIKE I DID ON MY BIRTHDAY!
IOU
CASH CARD!
STOCKS FOR YOU!
WEIRD LOCAL

WHILE GIFT GIVING IS A TYPE OF EXCHANGE, GIFTS OBSCURE THE TRANSACTION TAKING PLACE...

...ALLOWING EVERYONE TO FOCUS ON ITS SOCIAL VALUE INSTEAD.

REMEMBER THE CIRCLE-DRAGGING EXPERIMENT FROM JAMES HEYMAN AND DAN ARIELY?

RECALL THAT WHEN GIVEN CASH, PARTICIPANTS ADJUSTED TO PUT IN MORE EFFORT FOR $4 THAN FOR 10¢, BUT THEY WORKED HARDEST OF ALL FOR NO REWARD, THANKS TO SOCIAL NORMS.*

*10¢ → 101 CIRCLES, $4 → 159 CIRCLES, NO REWARD → 168 CIRCLES.

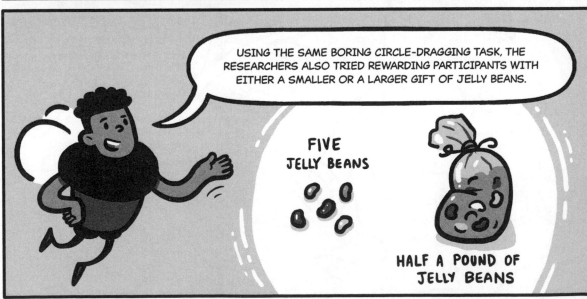

USING THE SAME BORING CIRCLE-DRAGGING TASK, THE RESEARCHERS ALSO TRIED REWARDING PARTICIPANTS WITH EITHER A SMALLER OR A LARGER GIFT OF JELLY BEANS.

FIVE JELLY BEANS

HALF A POUND OF JELLY BEANS

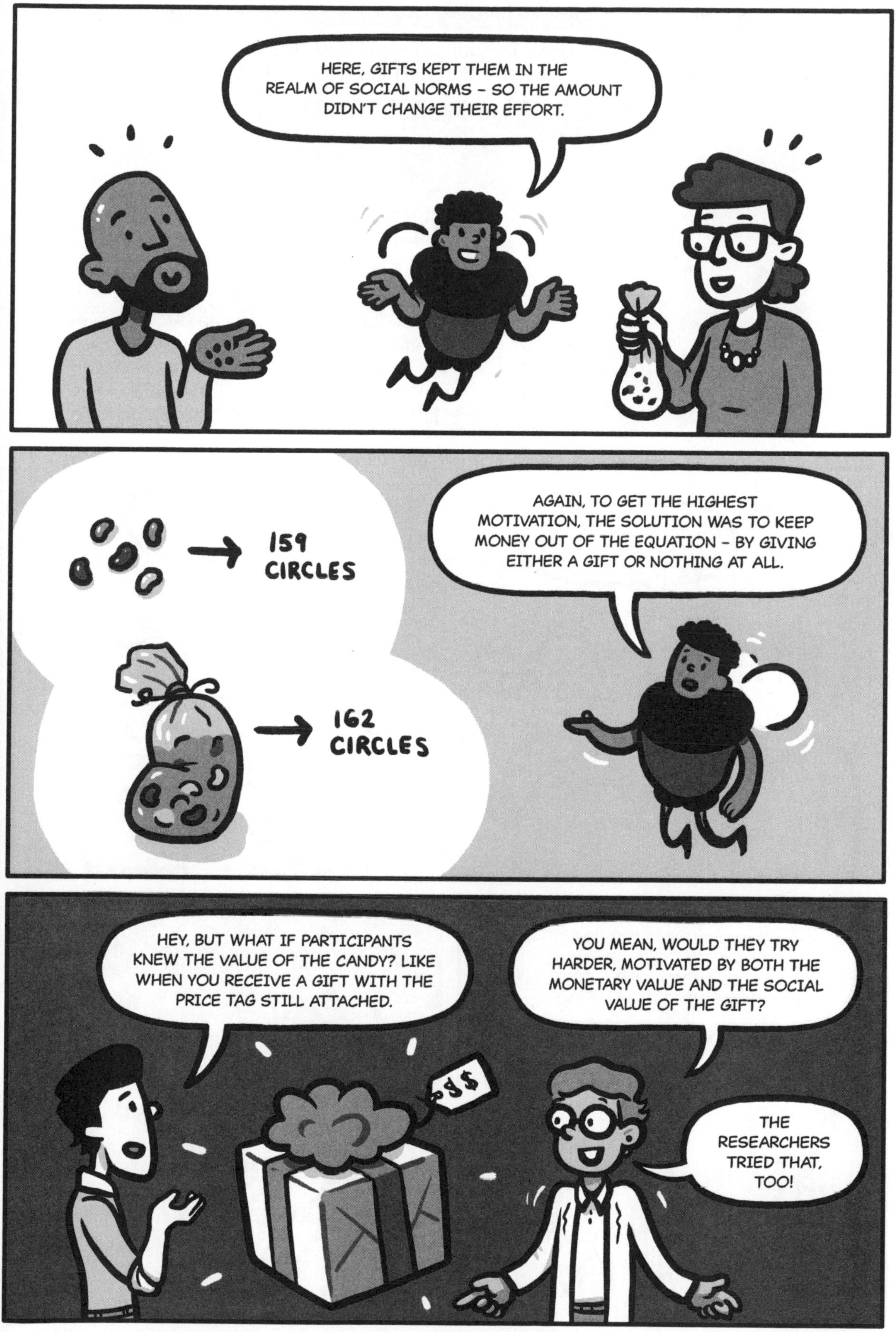
HERE, GIFTS KEPT THEM IN THE REALM OF SOCIAL NORMS – SO THE AMOUNT DIDN'T CHANGE THEIR EFFORT.
159 CIRCLES
162 CIRCLES
AGAIN, TO GET THE HIGHEST MOTIVATION, THE SOLUTION WAS TO KEEP MONEY OUT OF THE EQUATION – BY GIVING EITHER A GIFT OR NOTHING AT ALL.
HEY, BUT WHAT IF PARTICIPANTS KNEW THE VALUE OF THE CANDY? LIKE WHEN YOU RECEIVE A GIFT WITH THE PRICE TAG STILL ATTACHED.
$$
YOU MEAN, WOULD THEY TRY HARDER, MOTIVATED BY BOTH THE MONETARY VALUE AND THE SOCIAL VALUE OF THE GIFT?
THE RESEARCHERS TRIED THAT, TOO!

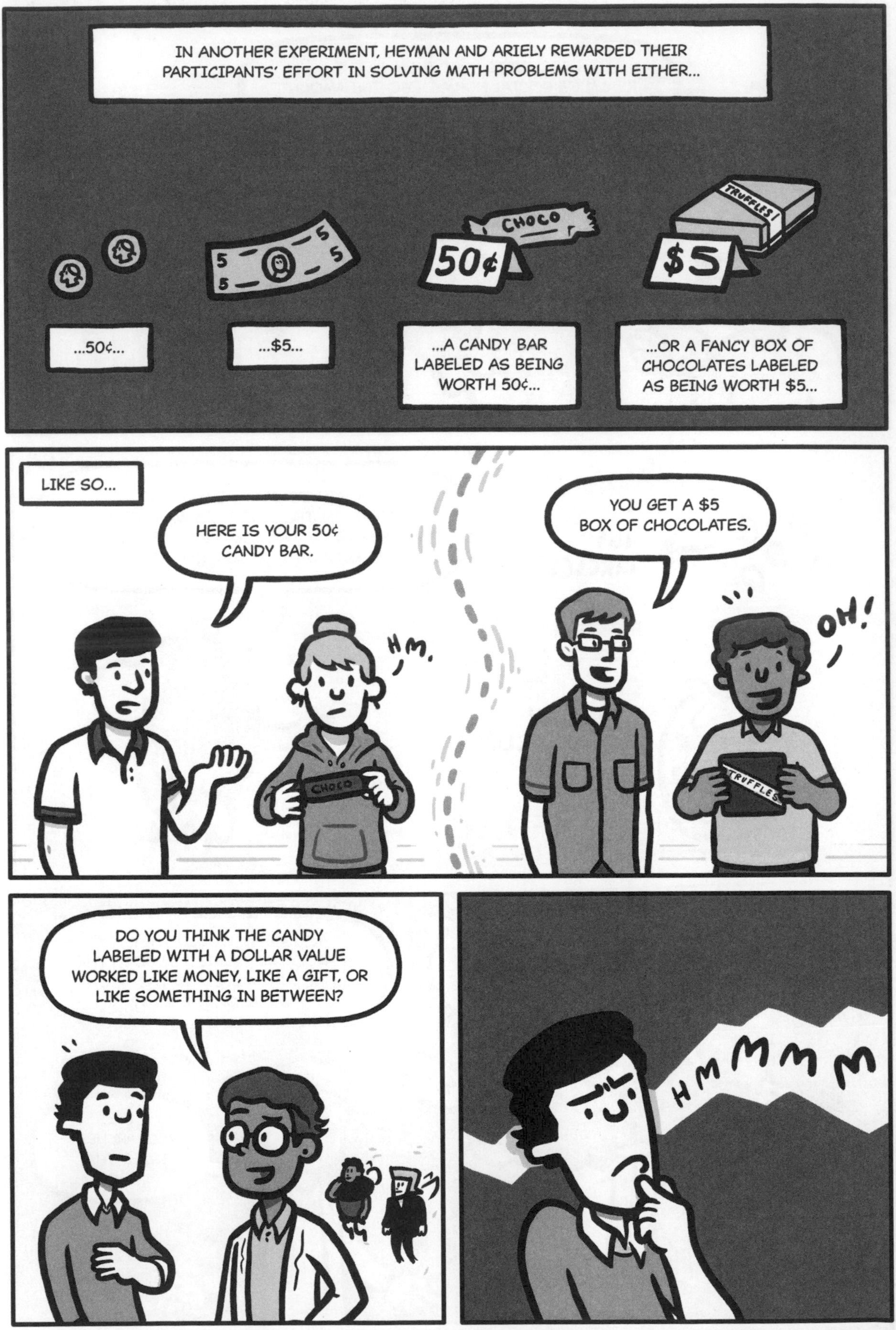
IN ANOTHER EXPERIMENT, HEYMAN AND ARIELY REWARDED THEIR PARTICIPANTS' EFFORT IN SOLVING MATH PROBLEMS WITH EITHER...
CHOCO
50¢
TRUFFLES!
$5
...50¢...
...$5...
...A CANDY BAR LABELED AS BEING WORTH 50¢...
...OR A FANCY BOX OF CHOCOLATES LABELED AS BEING WORTH $5...
LIKE SO...
HERE IS YOUR 50¢ CANDY BAR.
CHOCO
HM.
YOU GET A $5 BOX OF CHOCOLATES.
OH!
TRUFFLES
DO YOU THINK THE CANDY LABELED WITH A DOLLAR VALUE WORKED LIKE MONEY, LIKE A GIFT, OR LIKE SOMETHING IN BETWEEN?
HMMMMM

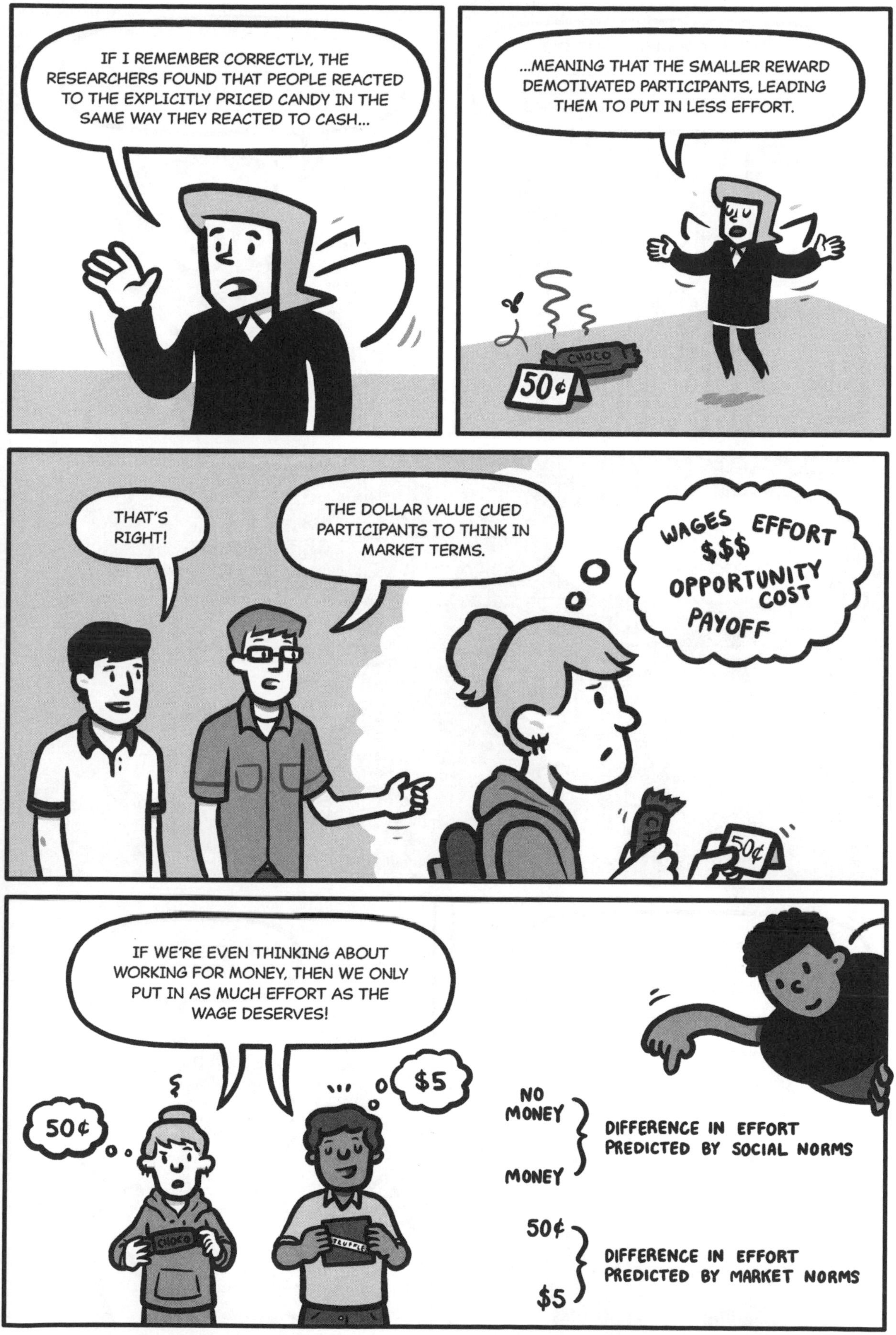
IF I REMEMBER CORRECTLY, THE RESEARCHERS FOUND THAT PEOPLE REACTED TO THE EXPLICITLY PRICED CANDY IN THE SAME WAY THEY REACTED TO CASH...
...MEANING THAT THE SMALLER REWARD DEMOTIVATED PARTICIPANTS, LEADING THEM TO PUT IN LESS EFFORT.
CHOCO
50¢
THAT'S RIGHT!
THE DOLLAR VALUE CUED PARTICIPANTS TO THINK IN MARKET TERMS.
WAGES EFFORT
$$$
OPPORTUNITY COST
PAYOFF
50¢
IF WE'RE EVEN THINKING ABOUT WORKING FOR MONEY, THEN WE ONLY PUT IN AS MUCH EFFORT AS THE WAGE DESERVES!
50¢
$5
CHOCO
NO MONEY
MONEY
DIFFERENCE IN EFFORT PREDICTED BY SOCIAL NORMS
50¢
$5
DIFFERENCE IN EFFORT PREDICTED BY MARKET NORMS

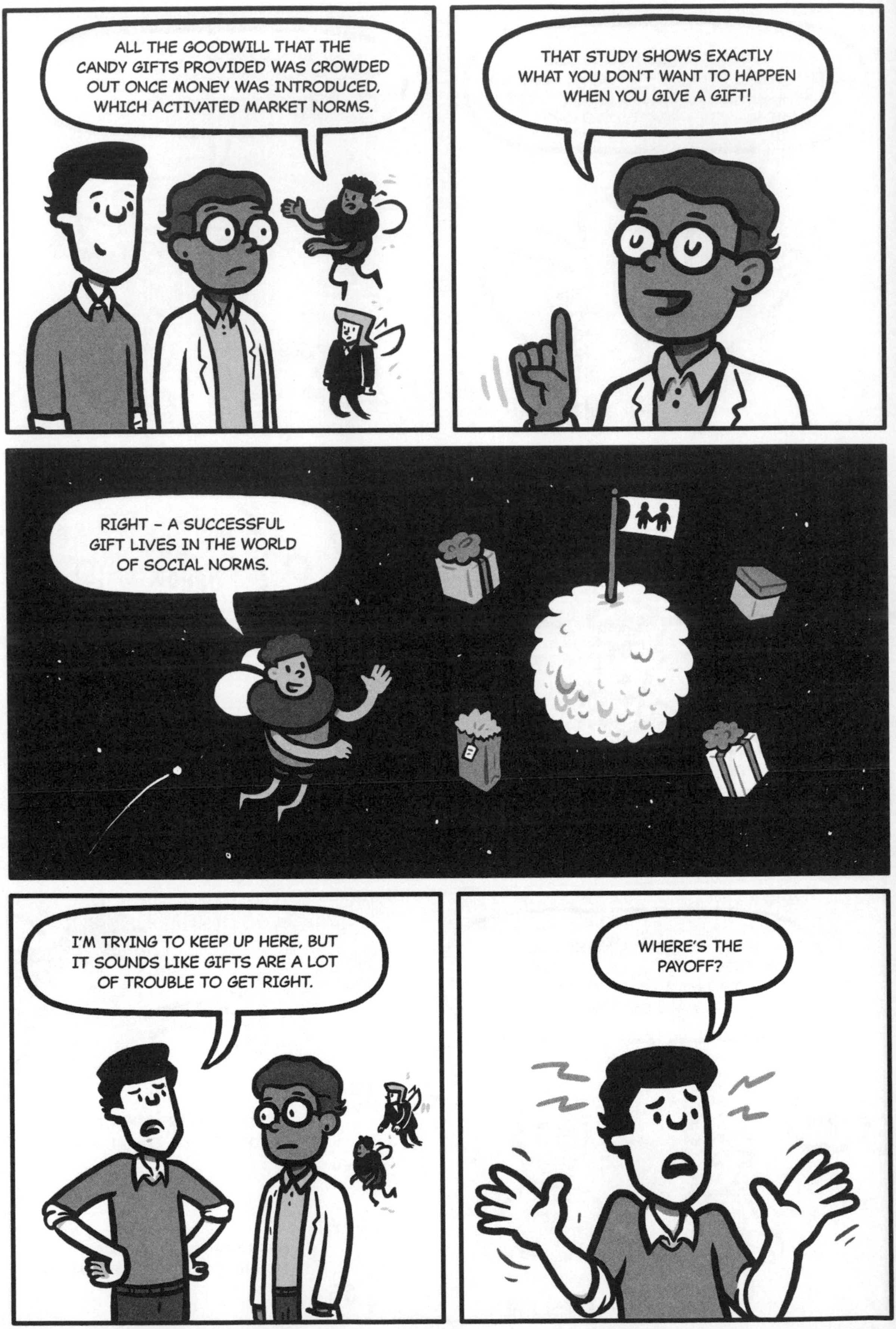
ALL THE GOODWILL THAT THE CANDY GIFTS PROVIDED WAS CROWDED OUT ONCE MONEY WAS INTRODUCED, WHICH ACTIVATED MARKET NORMS.
THAT STUDY SHOWS EXACTLY WHAT YOU DON'T WANT TO HAPPEN WHEN YOU GIVE A GIFT!
RIGHT – A SUCCESSFUL GIFT LIVES IN THE WORLD OF SOCIAL NORMS.
I'M TRYING TO KEEP UP HERE, BUT IT SOUNDS LIKE GIFTS ARE A LOT OF TROUBLE TO GET RIGHT.
WHERE'S THE PAYOFF?

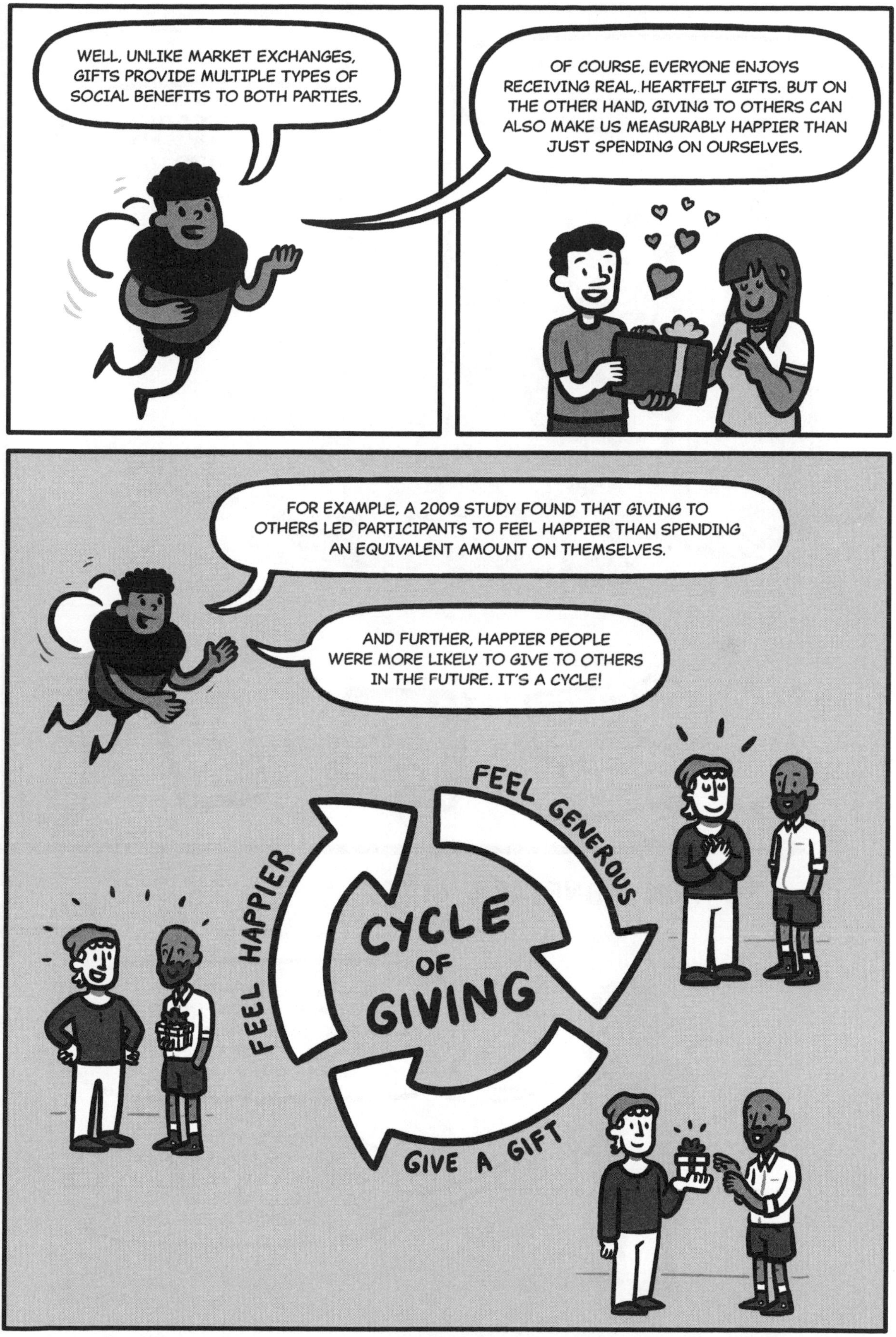
WELL, UNLIKE MARKET EXCHANGES, GIFTS PROVIDE MULTIPLE TYPES OF SOCIAL BENEFITS TO BOTH PARTIES.
OF COURSE, EVERYONE ENJOYS RECEIVING REAL, HEARTFELT GIFTS. BUT ON THE OTHER HAND, GIVING TO OTHERS CAN ALSO MAKE US MEASURABLY HAPPIER THAN JUST SPENDING ON OURSELVES.
FOR EXAMPLE, A 2009 STUDY FOUND THAT GIVING TO OTHERS LED PARTICIPANTS TO FEEL HAPPIER THAN SPENDING AN EQUIVALENT AMOUNT ON THEMSELVES.
AND FURTHER, HAPPIER PEOPLE WERE MORE LIKELY TO GIVE TO OTHERS IN THE FUTURE. IT'S A CYCLE!
CYCLE OF GIVING
FEEL GENEROUS
GIVE A GIFT
FEEL HAPPIER

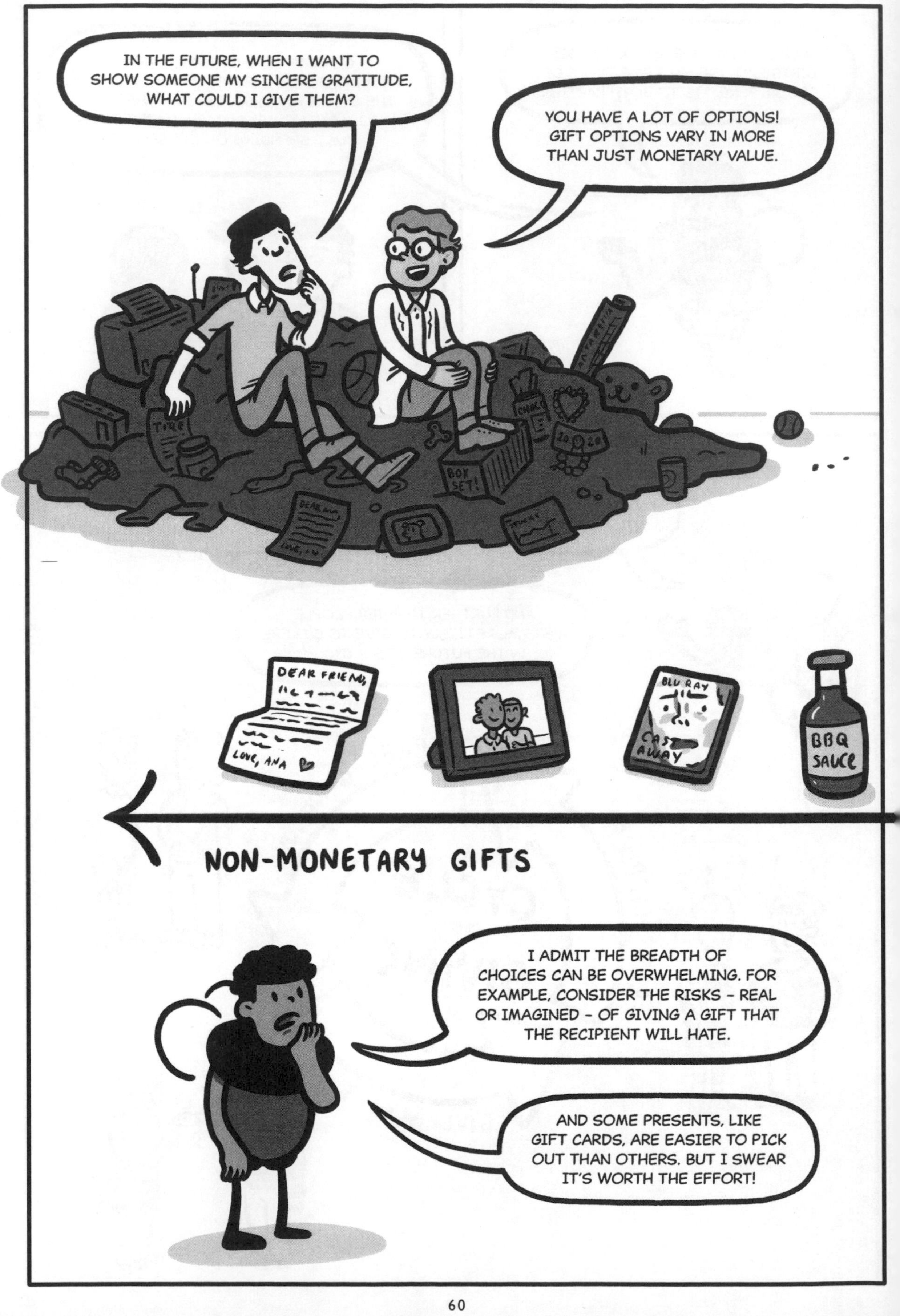
IN THE FUTURE, WHEN I WANT TO SHOW SOMEONE MY SINCERE GRATITUDE, WHAT COULD I GIVE THEM?
YOU HAVE A LOT OF OPTIONS! GIFT OPTIONS VARY IN MORE THAN JUST MONETARY VALUE.
BOX SET!
DEAR FRIENDS
LOVE, ANA
BLU RAY
CAST AWAY
BBQ SAUCE
NON-MONETARY GIFTS
I ADMIT THE BREADTH OF CHOICES CAN BE OVERWHELMING. FOR EXAMPLE, CONSIDER THE RISKS – REAL OR IMAGINED – OF GIVING A GIFT THAT THE RECIPIENT WILL HATE.
AND SOME PRESENTS, LIKE GIFT CARDS, ARE EASIER TO PICK OUT THAN OTHERS. BUT I SWEAR IT'S WORTH THE EFFORT!

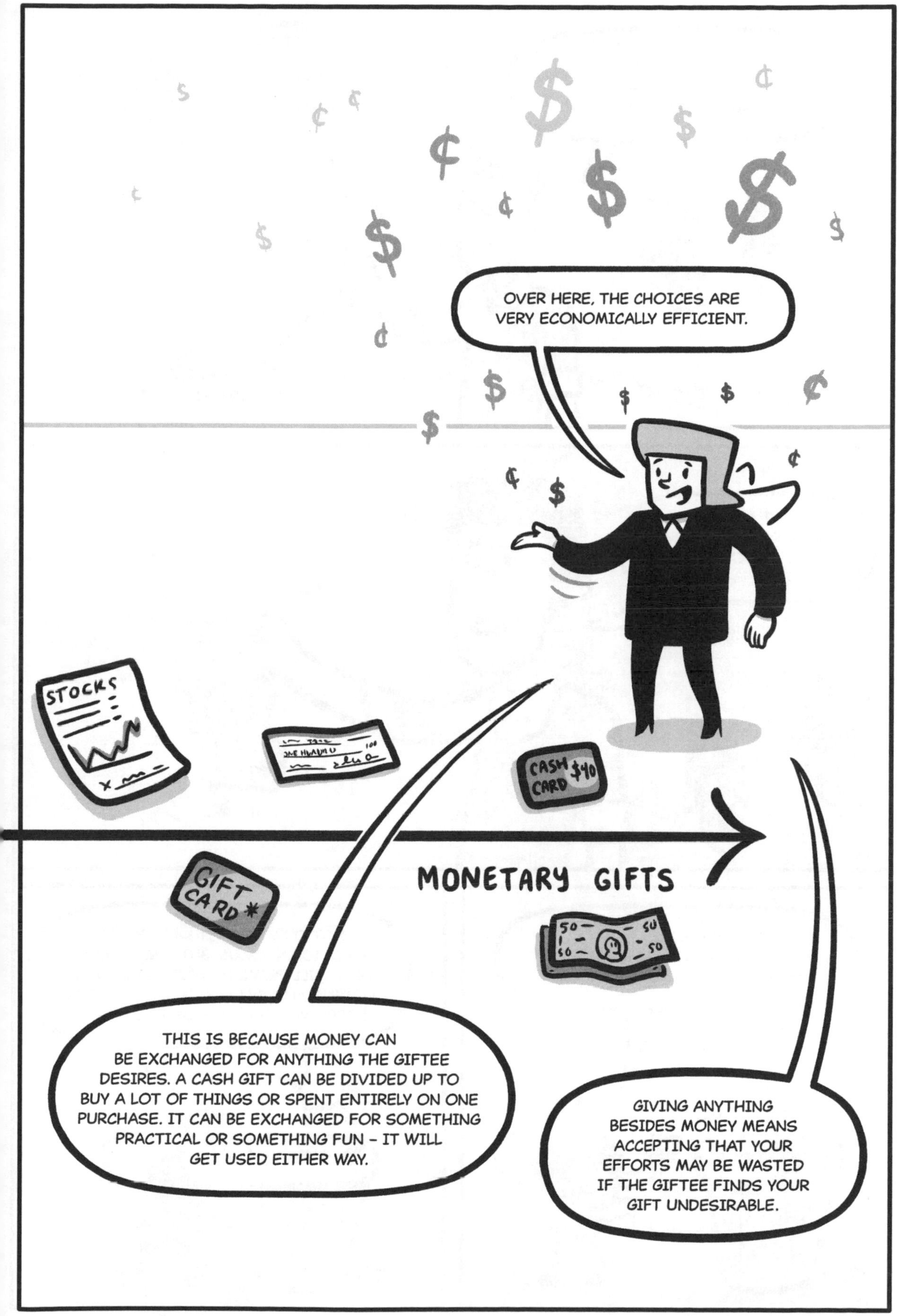
OVER HERE, THE CHOICES ARE VERY ECONOMICALLY EFFICIENT.
STOCKS
CASH CARD $40
GIFT CARD
MONETARY GIFTS
THIS IS BECAUSE MONEY CAN BE EXCHANGED FOR ANYTHING THE GIFTEE DESIRES. A CASH GIFT CAN BE DIVIDED UP TO BUY A LOT OF THINGS OR SPENT ENTIRELY ON ONE PURCHASE. IT CAN BE EXCHANGED FOR SOMETHING PRACTICAL OR SOMETHING FUN – IT WILL GET USED EITHER WAY.
GIVING ANYTHING BESIDES MONEY MEANS ACCEPTING THAT YOUR EFFORTS MAY BE WASTED IF THE GIFTEE FINDS YOUR GIFT UNDESIRABLE.

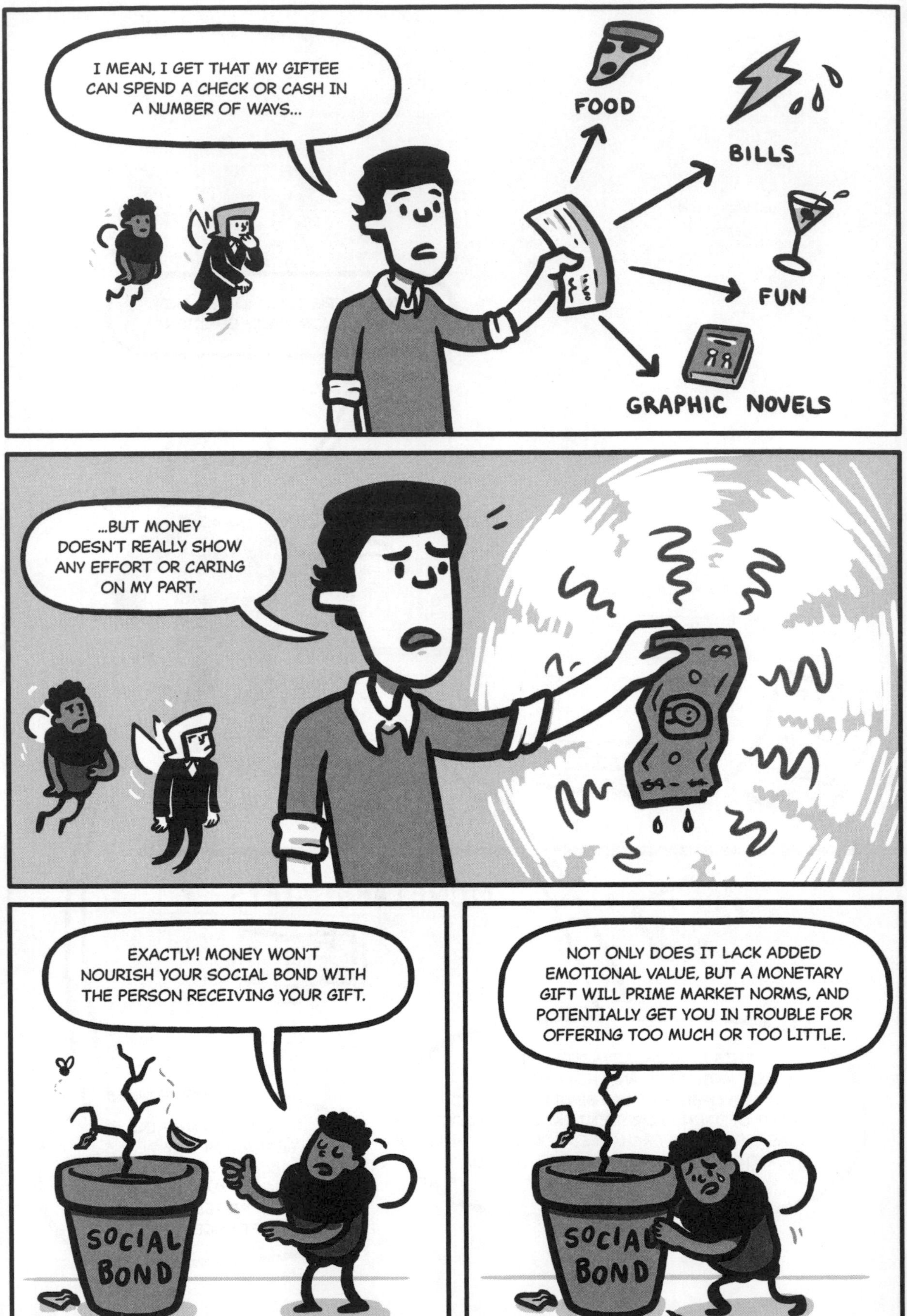
I MEAN, I GET THAT MY GIFTEE CAN SPEND A CHECK OR CASH IN A NUMBER OF WAYS...
FOOD
BILLS
FUN
GRAPHIC NOVELS
...BUT MONEY DOESN'T REALLY SHOW ANY EFFORT OR CARING ON MY PART.
EXACTLY! MONEY WON'T NOURISH YOUR SOCIAL BOND WITH THE PERSON RECEIVING YOUR GIFT.
SOCIAL BOND
NOT ONLY DOES IT LACK ADDED EMOTIONAL VALUE, BUT A MONETARY GIFT WILL PRIME MARKET NORMS, AND POTENTIALLY GET YOU IN TROUBLE FOR OFFERING TOO MUCH OR TOO LITTLE.
SOCIAL BOND

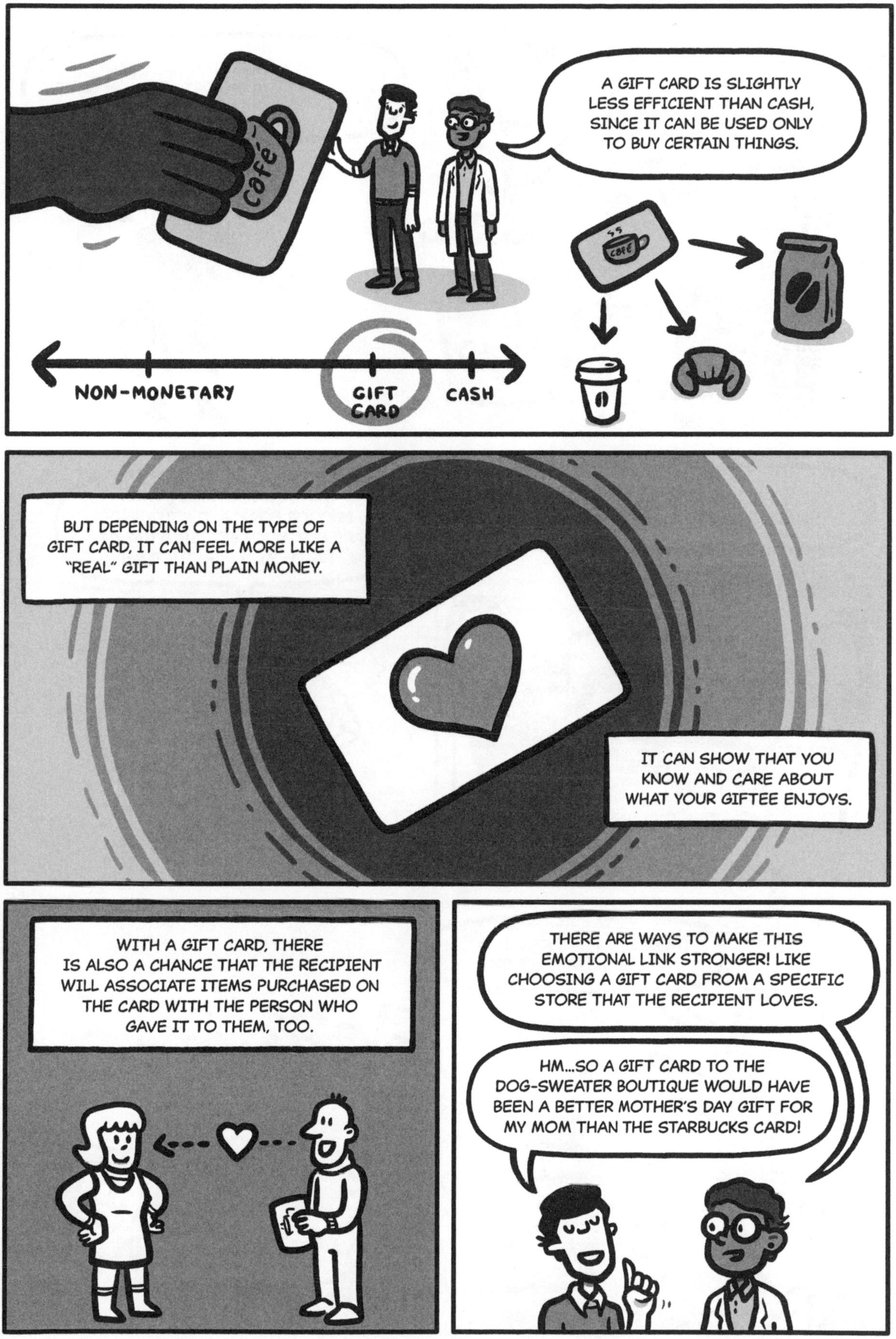
A GIFT CARD IS SLIGHTLY LESS EFFICIENT THAN CASH, SINCE IT CAN BE USED ONLY TO BUY CERTAIN THINGS.
CAFÉ
NON-MONETARY
GIFT CARD
CASH
BUT DEPENDING ON THE TYPE OF GIFT CARD, IT CAN FEEL MORE LIKE A "REAL" GIFT THAN PLAIN MONEY.
IT CAN SHOW THAT YOU KNOW AND CARE ABOUT WHAT YOUR GIFTEE ENJOYS.
WITH A GIFT CARD, THERE IS ALSO A CHANCE THAT THE RECIPIENT WILL ASSOCIATE ITEMS PURCHASED ON THE CARD WITH THE PERSON WHO GAVE IT TO THEM, TOO.
THERE ARE WAYS TO MAKE THIS EMOTIONAL LINK STRONGER! LIKE CHOOSING A GIFT CARD FROM A SPECIFIC STORE THAT THE RECIPIENT LOVES.
HM...SO A GIFT CARD TO THE DOG-SWEATER BOUTIQUE WOULD HAVE BEEN A BETTER MOTHER'S DAY GIFT FOR MY MOM THAN THE STARBUCKS CARD!

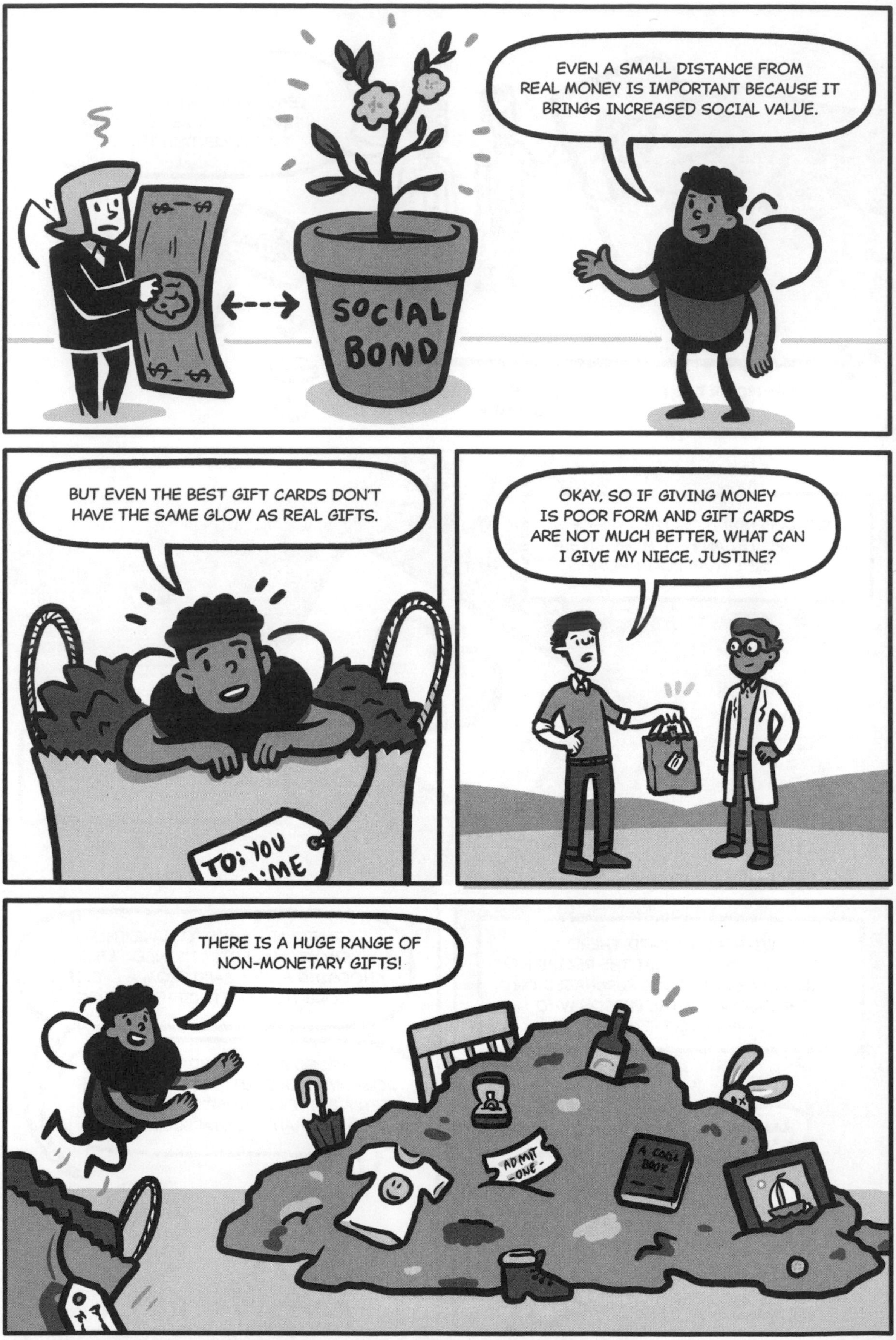
SOCIAL BOND
EVEN A SMALL DISTANCE FROM REAL MONEY IS IMPORTANT BECAUSE IT BRINGS INCREASED SOCIAL VALUE.
BUT EVEN THE BEST GIFT CARDS DON'T HAVE THE SAME GLOW AS REAL GIFTS.
TO: YOU
OKAY, SO IF GIVING MONEY IS POOR FORM AND GIFT CARDS ARE NOT MUCH BETTER, WHAT CAN I GIVE MY NIECE, JUSTINE?
THERE IS A HUGE RANGE OF NON-MONETARY GIFTS!
ADMIT ONE
A COOL BOOK

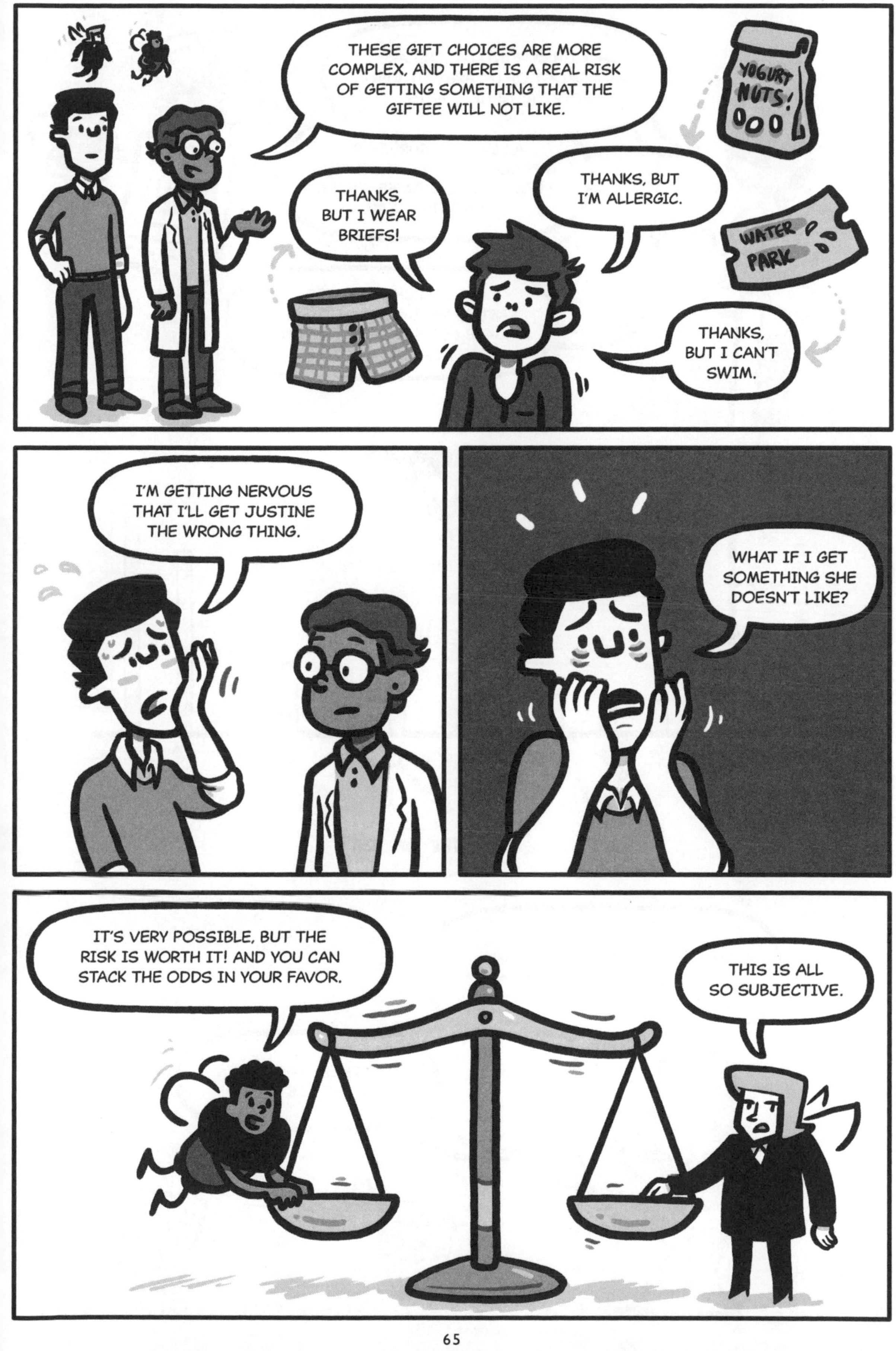

THESE GIFT CHOICES ARE MORE COMPLEX, AND THERE IS A REAL RISK OF GETTING SOMETHING THAT THE GIFTEE WILL NOT LIKE.
YOGURT NUTS!
THANKS, BUT I WEAR BRIEFS!
THANKS, BUT I'M ALLERGIC.
WATER PARK
THANKS, BUT I CAN'T SWIM.
I'M GETTING NERVOUS THAT I'LL GET JUSTINE THE WRONG THING.
WHAT IF I GET SOMETHING SHE DOESN'T LIKE?
IT'S VERY POSSIBLE, BUT THE RISK IS WORTH IT! AND YOU CAN STACK THE ODDS IN YOUR FAVOR.
THIS IS ALL SO SUBJECTIVE.

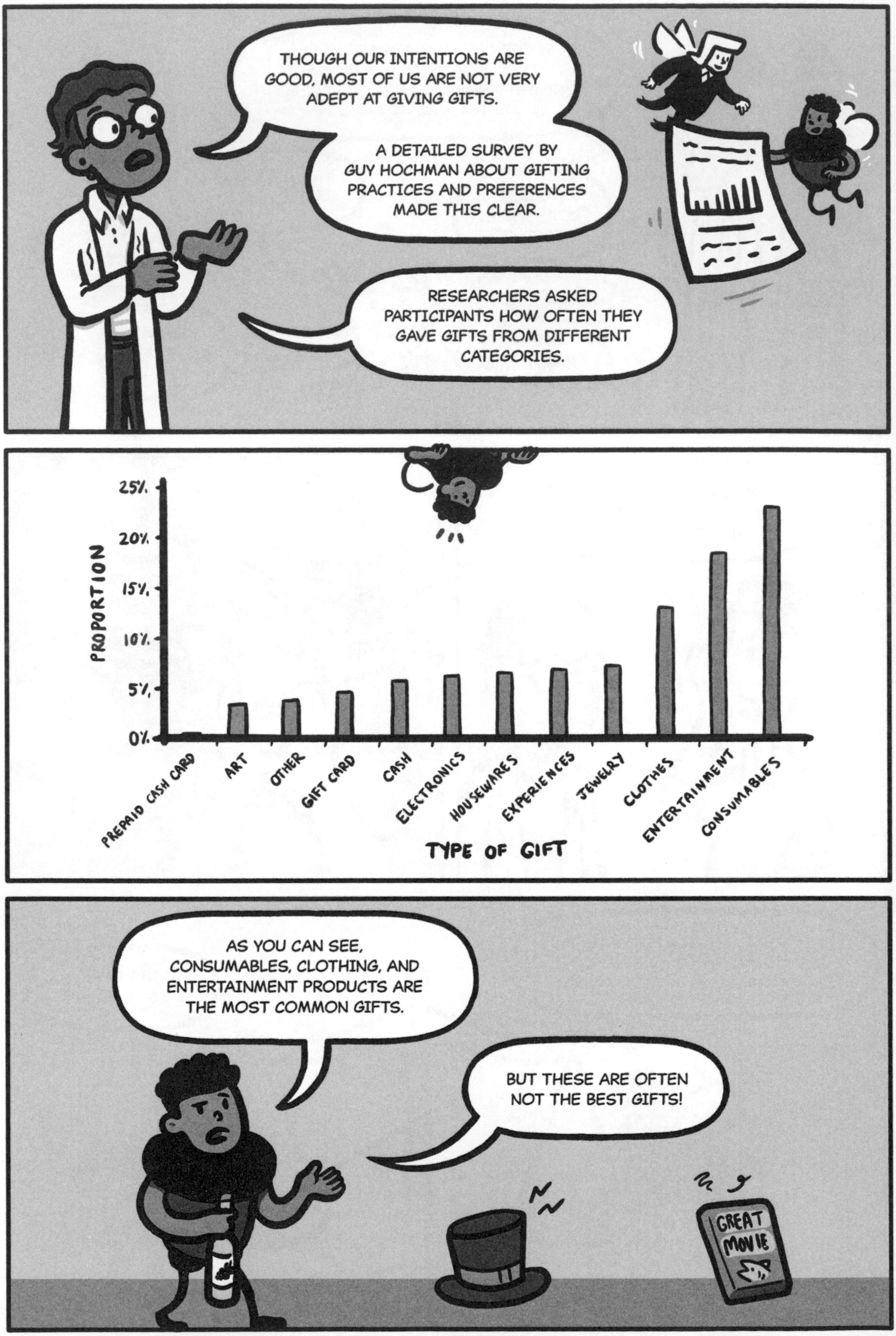
THOUGH OUR INTENTIONS ARE GOOD, MOST OF US ARE NOT VERY ADEPT AT GIVING GIFTS.
A DETAILED SURVEY BY GUY HOCHMAN ABOUT GIFTING PRACTICES AND PREFERENCES MADE THIS CLEAR.
RESEARCHERS ASKED PARTICIPANTS HOW OFTEN THEY GAVE GIFTS FROM DIFFERENT CATEGORIES.
25%
20%
15%
10%
5%
0%
PROPORTION
PREPAID CASH CARD
ART
OTHER
GIFT CARD
CASH
ELECTRONICS
HOUSEWARES
EXPERIENCES
JEWELRY
CLOTHES
ENTERTAINMENT
CONSUMABLES
TYPE OF GIFT
AS YOU CAN SEE, CONSUMABLES, CLOTHING, AND ENTERTAINMENT PRODUCTS ARE THE MOST COMMON GIFTS.
BUT THESE ARE OFTEN NOT THE BEST GIFTS!
GREAT MOVIE

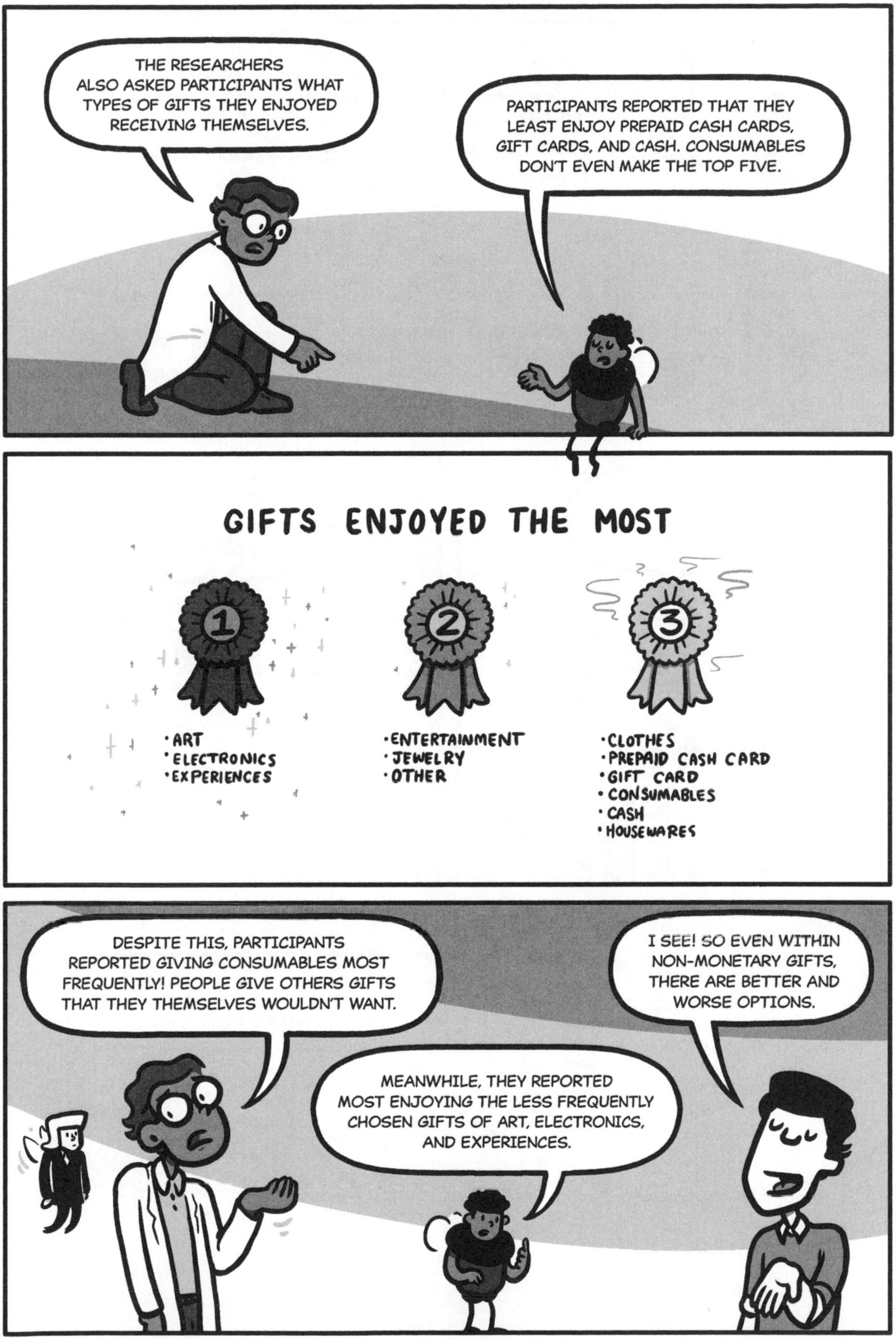
THE RESEARCHERS ALSO ASKED PARTICIPANTS WHAT TYPES OF GIFTS THEY ENJOYED RECEIVING THEMSELVES.
PARTICIPANTS REPORTED THAT THEY LEAST ENJOY PREPAID CASH CARDS, GIFT CARDS, AND CASH. CONSUMABLES DON'T EVEN MAKE THE TOP FIVE.
GIFTS ENJOYED THE MOST
1
•ART
•ELECTRONICS
•EXPERIENCES
2
•ENTERTAINMENT
•JEWELRY
•OTHER
3
•CLOTHES
•PREPAID CASH CARD
•GIFT CARD
•CONSUMABLES
•CASH
•HOUSEWARES
DESPITE THIS, PARTICIPANTS REPORTED GIVING CONSUMABLES MOST FREQUENTLY! PEOPLE GIVE OTHERS GIFTS THAT THEY THEMSELVES WOULDN'T WANT.
MEANWHILE, THEY REPORTED MOST ENJOYING THE LESS FREQUENTLY CHOSEN GIFTS OF ART, ELECTRONICS, AND EXPERIENCES.
I SEE! SO EVEN WITHIN NON-MONETARY GIFTS, THERE ARE BETTER AND WORSE OPTIONS.

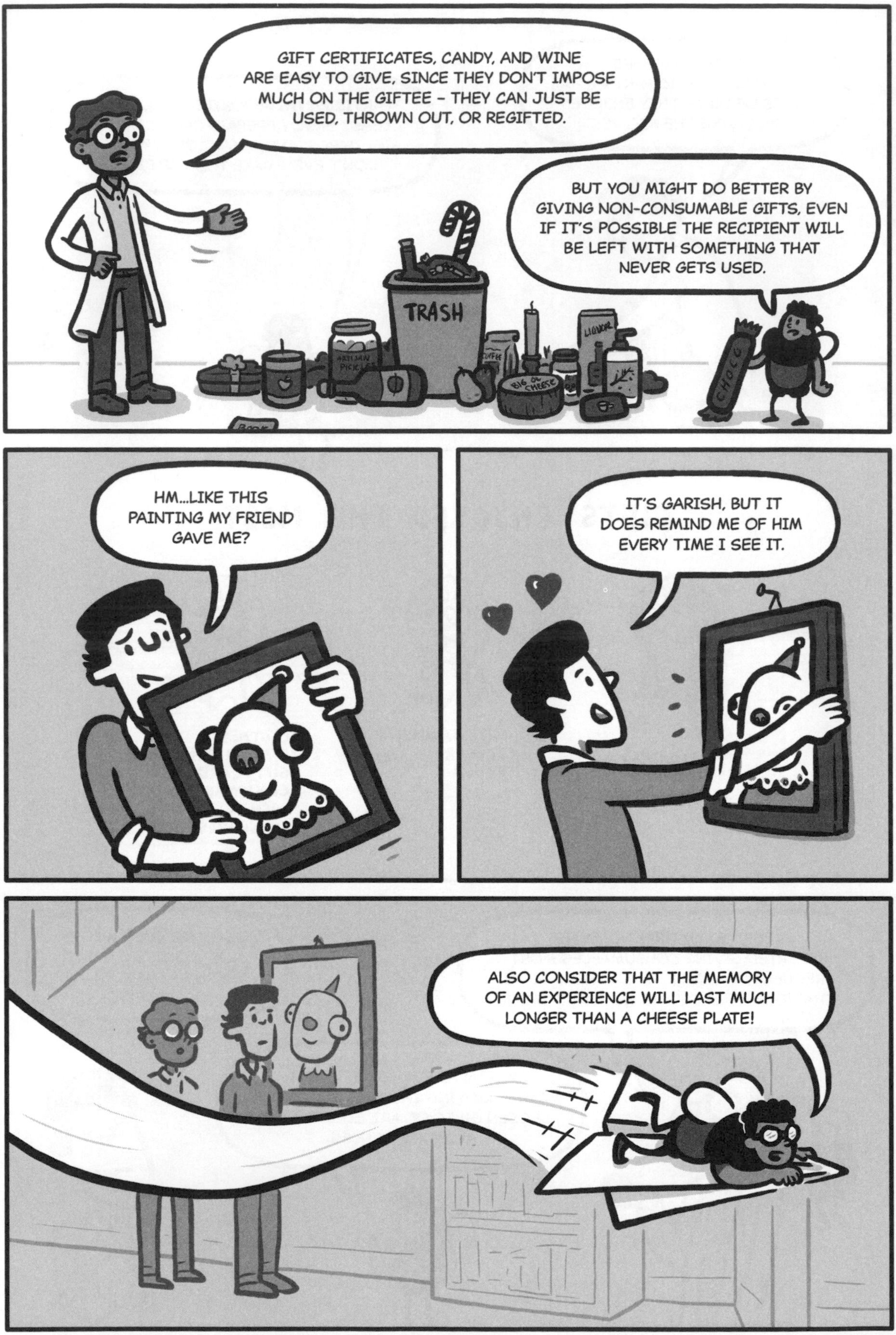
GIFT CERTIFICATES, CANDY, AND WINE ARE EASY TO GIVE, SINCE THEY DON'T IMPOSE MUCH ON THE GIFTEE – THEY CAN JUST BE USED, THROWN OUT, OR REGIFTED.
TRASH
BUT YOU MIGHT DO BETTER BY GIVING NON-CONSUMABLE GIFTS, EVEN IF IT'S POSSIBLE THE RECIPIENT WILL BE LEFT WITH SOMETHING THAT NEVER GETS USED.
HM...LIKE THIS PAINTING MY FRIEND GAVE ME?
IT'S GARISH, BUT IT DOES REMIND ME OF HIM EVERY TIME I SEE IT.
ALSO CONSIDER THAT THE MEMORY OF AN EXPERIENCE WILL LAST MUCH LONGER THAN A CHEESE PLATE!

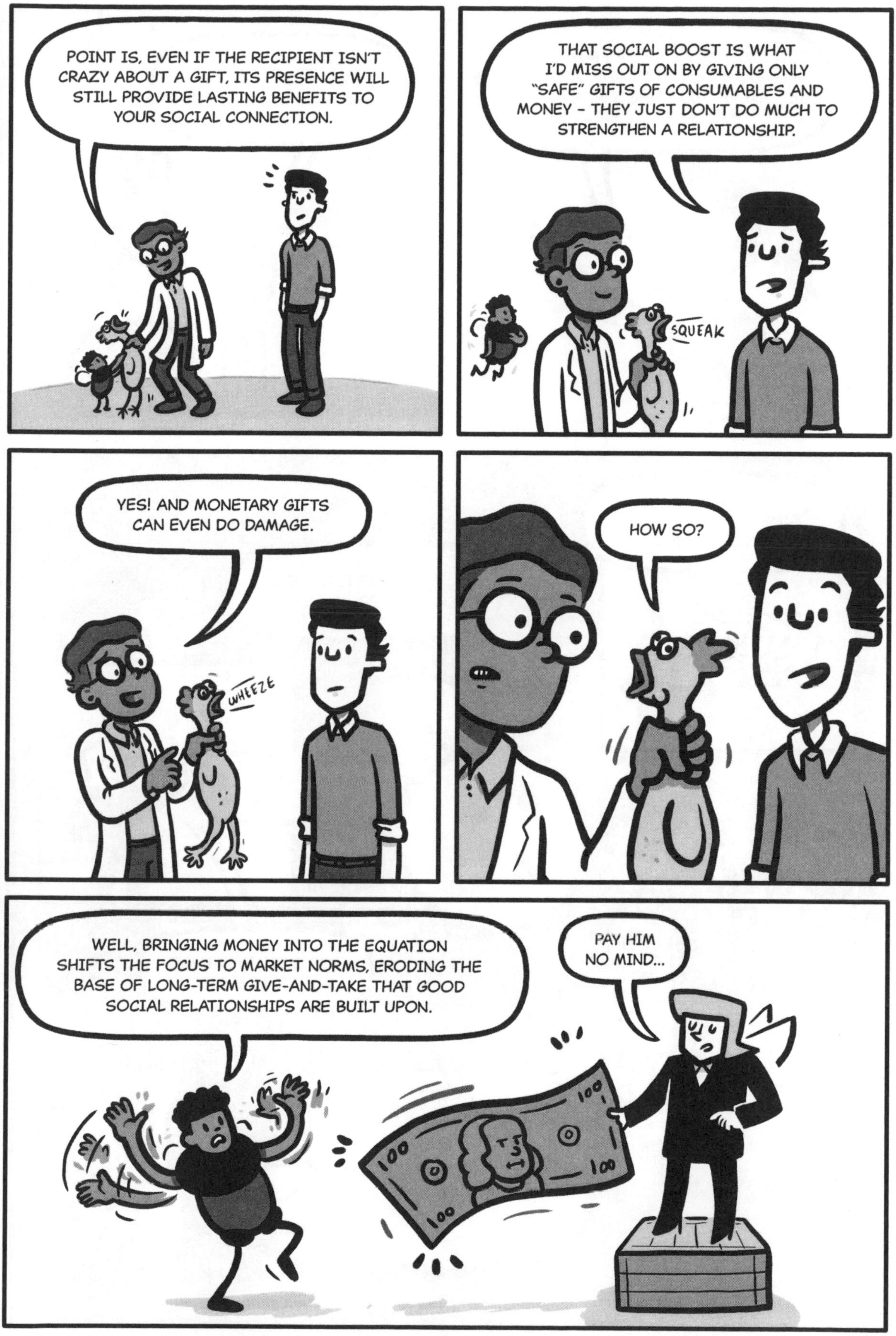
POINT IS, EVEN IF THE RECIPIENT ISN'T CRAZY ABOUT A GIFT, ITS PRESENCE WILL STILL PROVIDE LASTING BENEFITS TO YOUR SOCIAL CONNECTION.
THAT SOCIAL BOOST IS WHAT I'D MISS OUT ON BY GIVING ONLY "SAFE" GIFTS OF CONSUMABLES AND MONEY - THEY JUST DON'T DO MUCH TO STRENGTHEN A RELATIONSHIP.
SQUEAK
YES! AND MONETARY GIFTS CAN EVEN DO DAMAGE.
WHEEZE
HOW SO?
WELL, BRINGING MONEY INTO THE EQUATION SHIFTS THE FOCUS TO MARKET NORMS, ERODING THE BASE OF LONG-TERM GIVE-AND-TAKE THAT GOOD SOCIAL RELATIONSHIPS ARE BUILT UPON.
PAY HIM NO MIND...
100
100
100
100

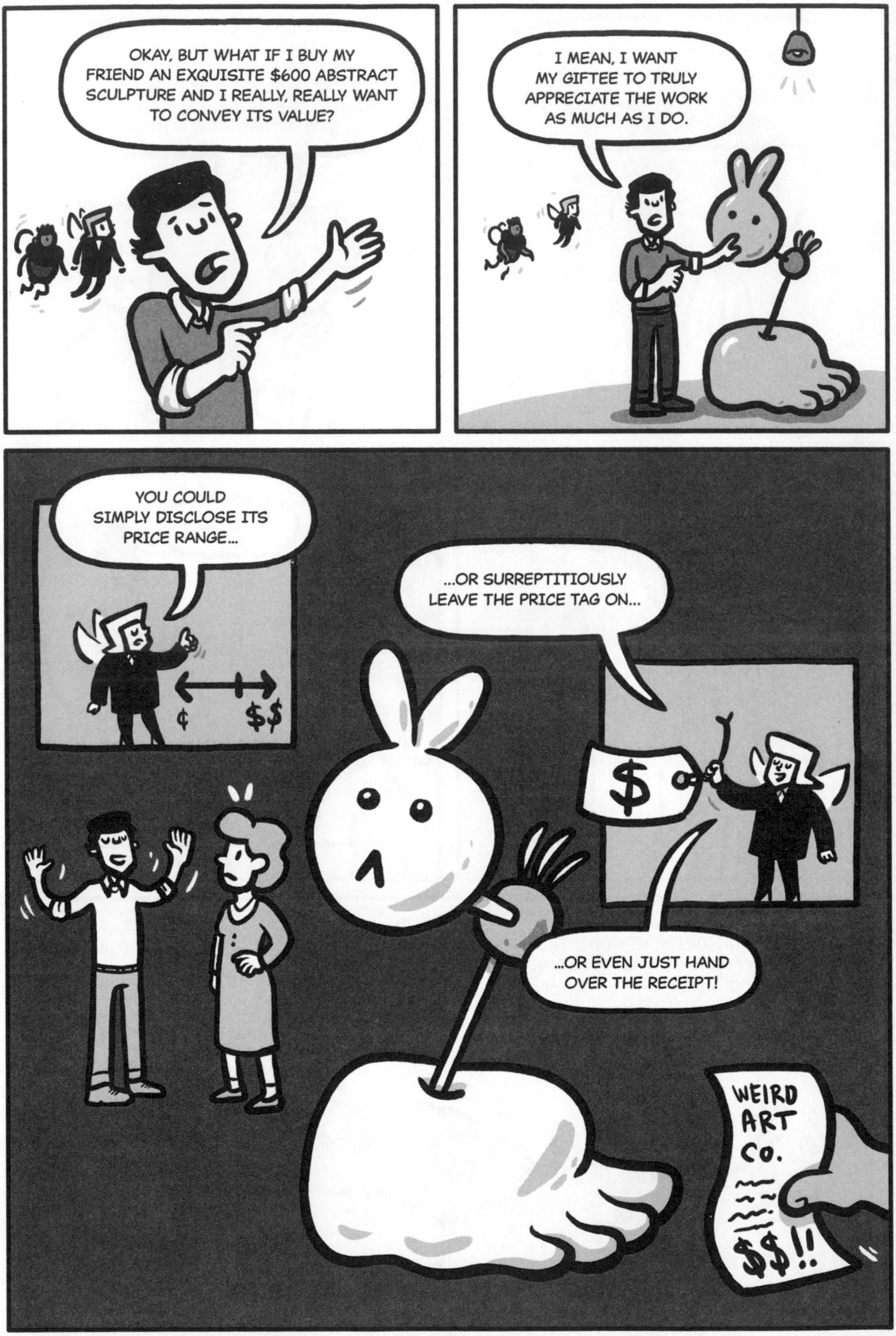
OKAY, BUT WHAT IF I BUY MY FRIEND AN EXQUISITE $600 ABSTRACT SCULPTURE AND I REALLY, REALLY WANT TO CONVEY ITS VALUE?
I MEAN, I WANT MY GIFTEE TO TRULY APPRECIATE THE WORK AS MUCH AS I DO.
YOU COULD SIMPLY DISCLOSE ITS PRICE RANGE...
¢
$$
...OR SURREPTITIOUSLY LEAVE THE PRICE TAG ON...
$
...OR EVEN JUST HAND OVER THE RECEIPT!
WEIRD ART CO.
$$!!

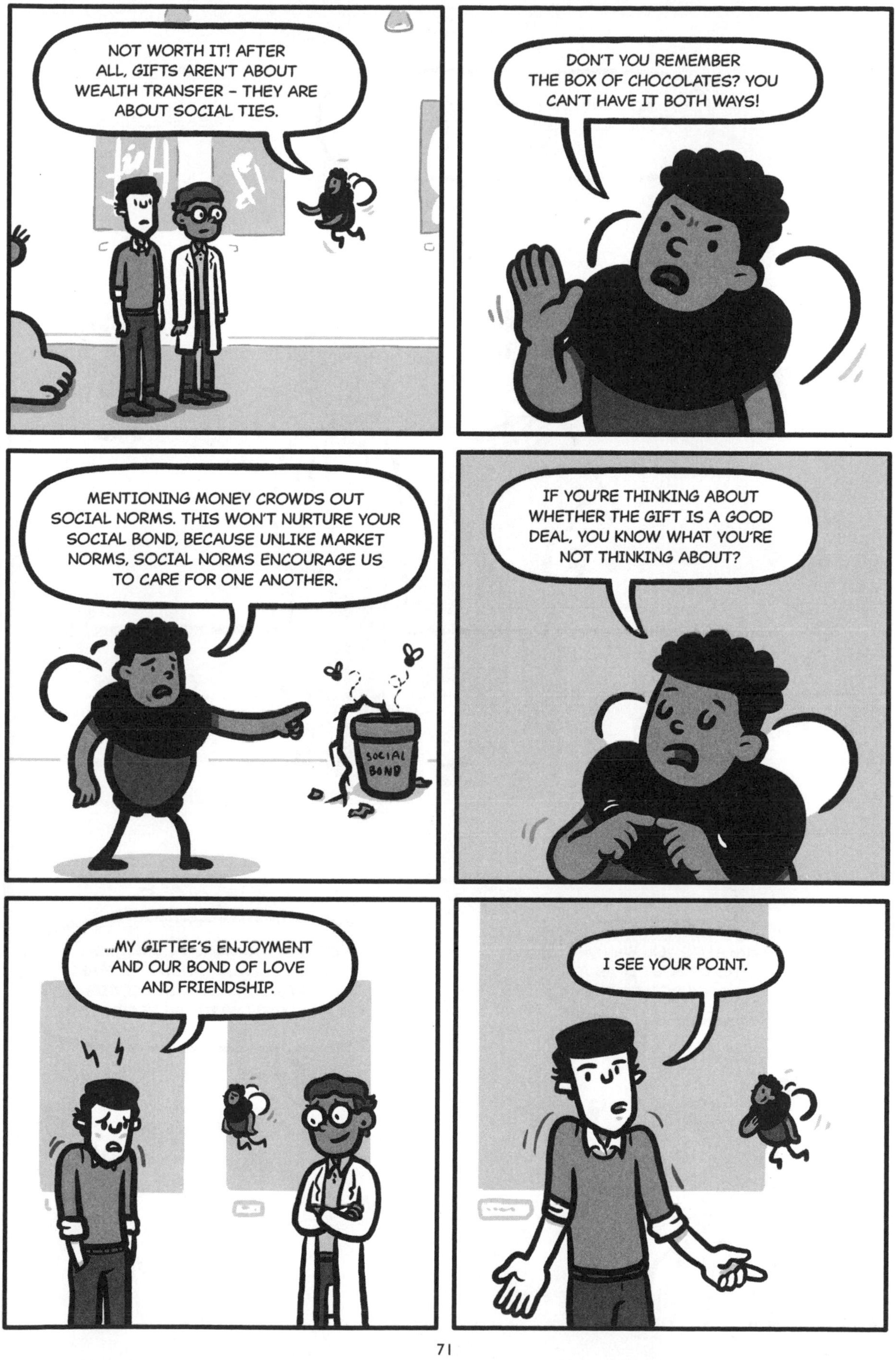
NOT WORTH IT! AFTER ALL, GIFTS AREN'T ABOUT WEALTH TRANSFER – THEY ARE ABOUT SOCIAL TIES.
DON'T YOU REMEMBER THE BOX OF CHOCOLATES? YOU CAN'T HAVE IT BOTH WAYS!
MENTIONING MONEY CROWDS OUT SOCIAL NORMS. THIS WON'T NURTURE YOUR SOCIAL BOND, BECAUSE UNLIKE MARKET NORMS, SOCIAL NORMS ENCOURAGE US TO CARE FOR ONE ANOTHER.
SOCIAL BOND
IF YOU'RE THINKING ABOUT WHETHER THE GIFT IS A GOOD DEAL, YOU KNOW WHAT YOU'RE NOT THINKING ABOUT?
...MY GIFTEE'S ENJOYMENT AND OUR BOND OF LOVE AND FRIENDSHIP.
I SEE YOUR POINT.

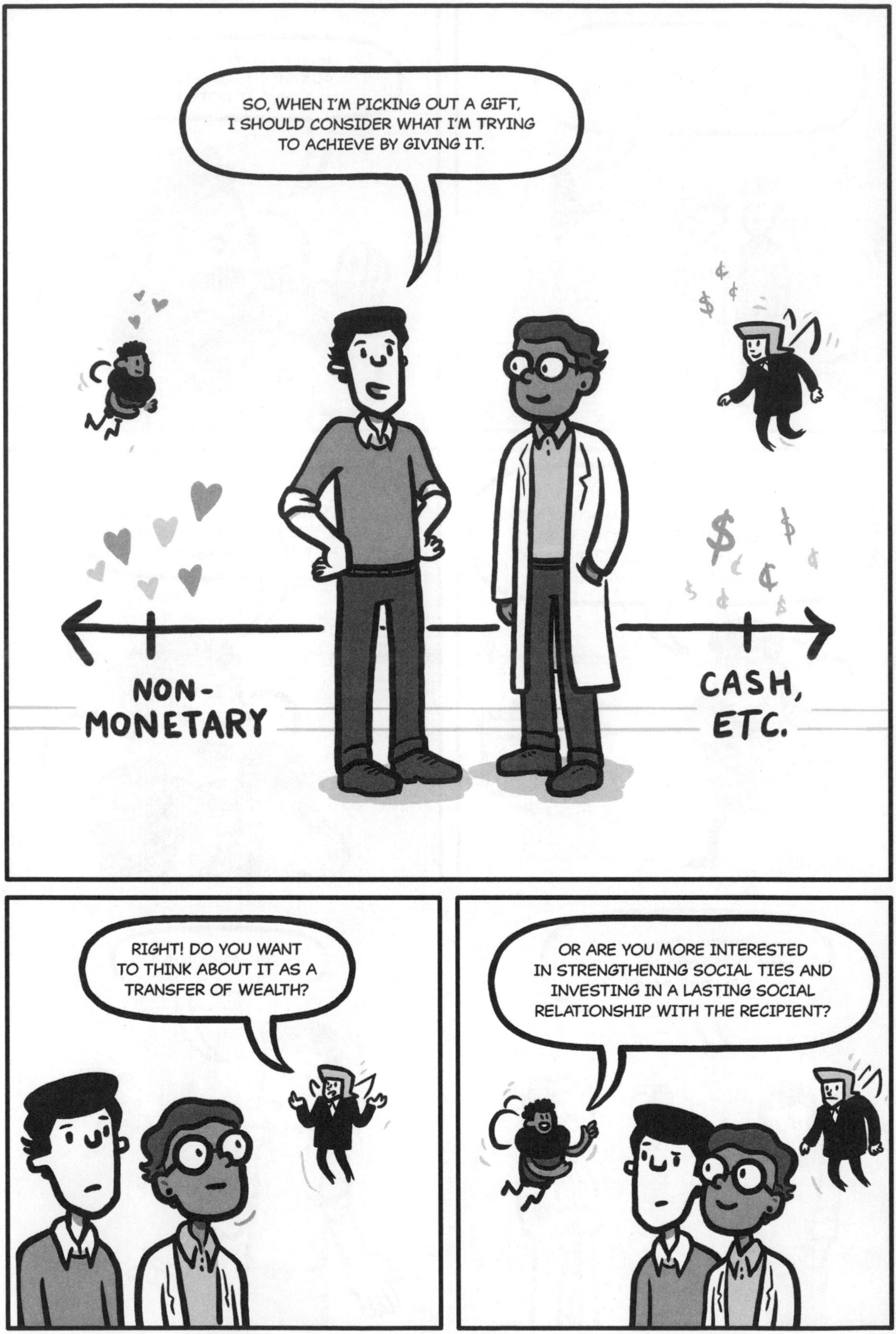
SO, WHEN I'M PICKING OUT A GIFT, I SHOULD CONSIDER WHAT I'M TRYING TO ACHIEVE BY GIVING IT.
NON-MONETARY
CASH, ETC.
RIGHT! DO YOU WANT TO THINK ABOUT IT AS A TRANSFER OF WEALTH?
OR ARE YOU MORE INTERESTED IN STRENGTHENING SOCIAL TIES AND INVESTING IN A LASTING SOCIAL RELATIONSHIP WITH THE RECIPIENT?

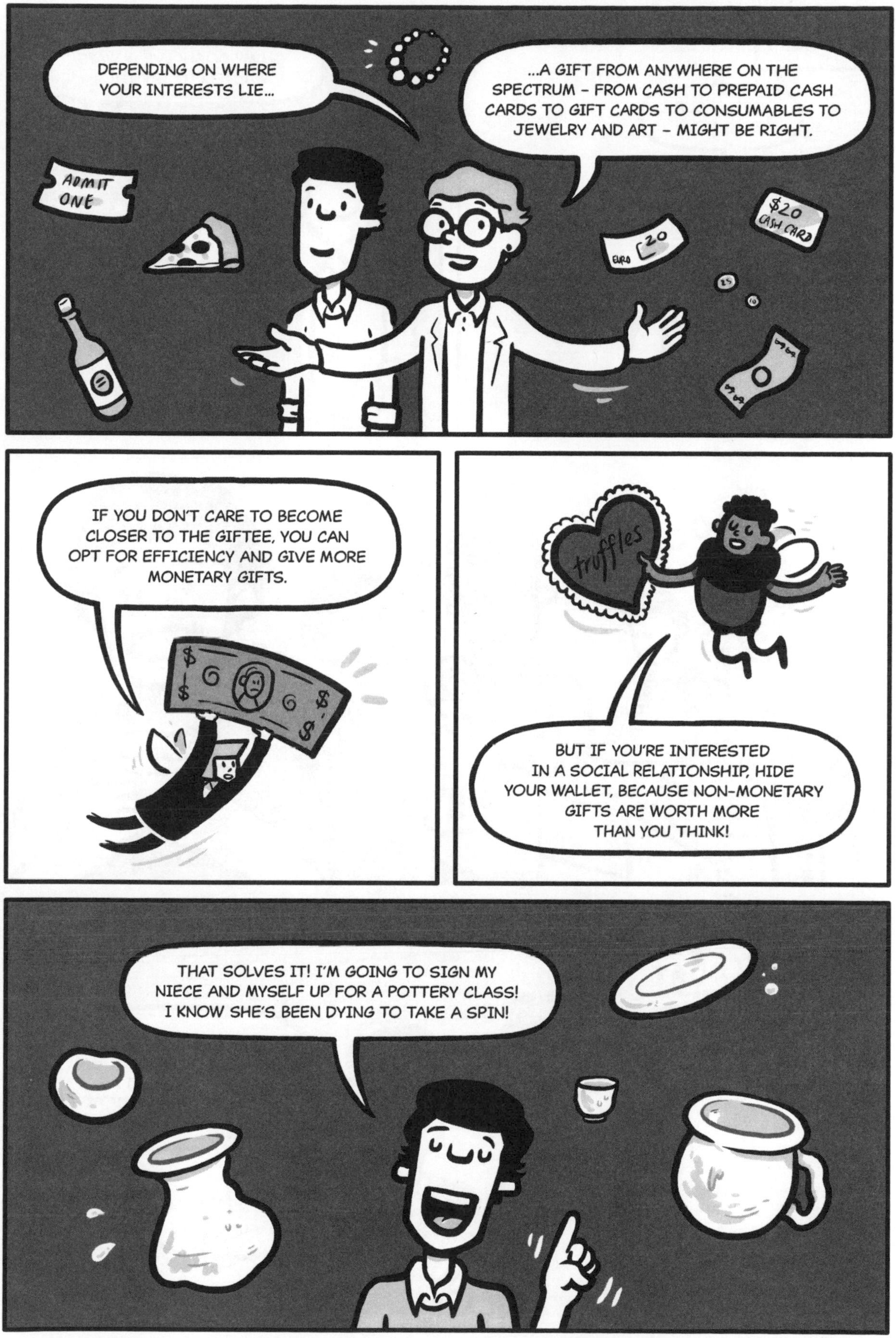
DEPENDING ON WHERE YOUR INTERESTS LIE...
...A GIFT FROM ANYWHERE ON THE SPECTRUM – FROM CASH TO PREPAID CASH CARDS TO GIFT CARDS TO CONSUMABLES TO JEWELRY AND ART – MIGHT BE RIGHT.
ADMIT ONE
EURO 20
$20 CASH CARD
IF YOU DON'T CARE TO BECOME CLOSER TO THE GIFTEE, YOU CAN OPT FOR EFFICIENCY AND GIVE MORE MONETARY GIFTS.
truffles
BUT IF YOU'RE INTERESTED IN A SOCIAL RELATIONSHIP, HIDE YOUR WALLET, BECAUSE NON-MONETARY GIFTS ARE WORTH MORE THAN YOU THINK!
THAT SOLVES IT! I'M GOING TO SIGN MY NIECE AND MYSELF UP FOR A POTTERY CLASS! I KNOW SHE'S BEEN DYING TO TAKE A SPIN!

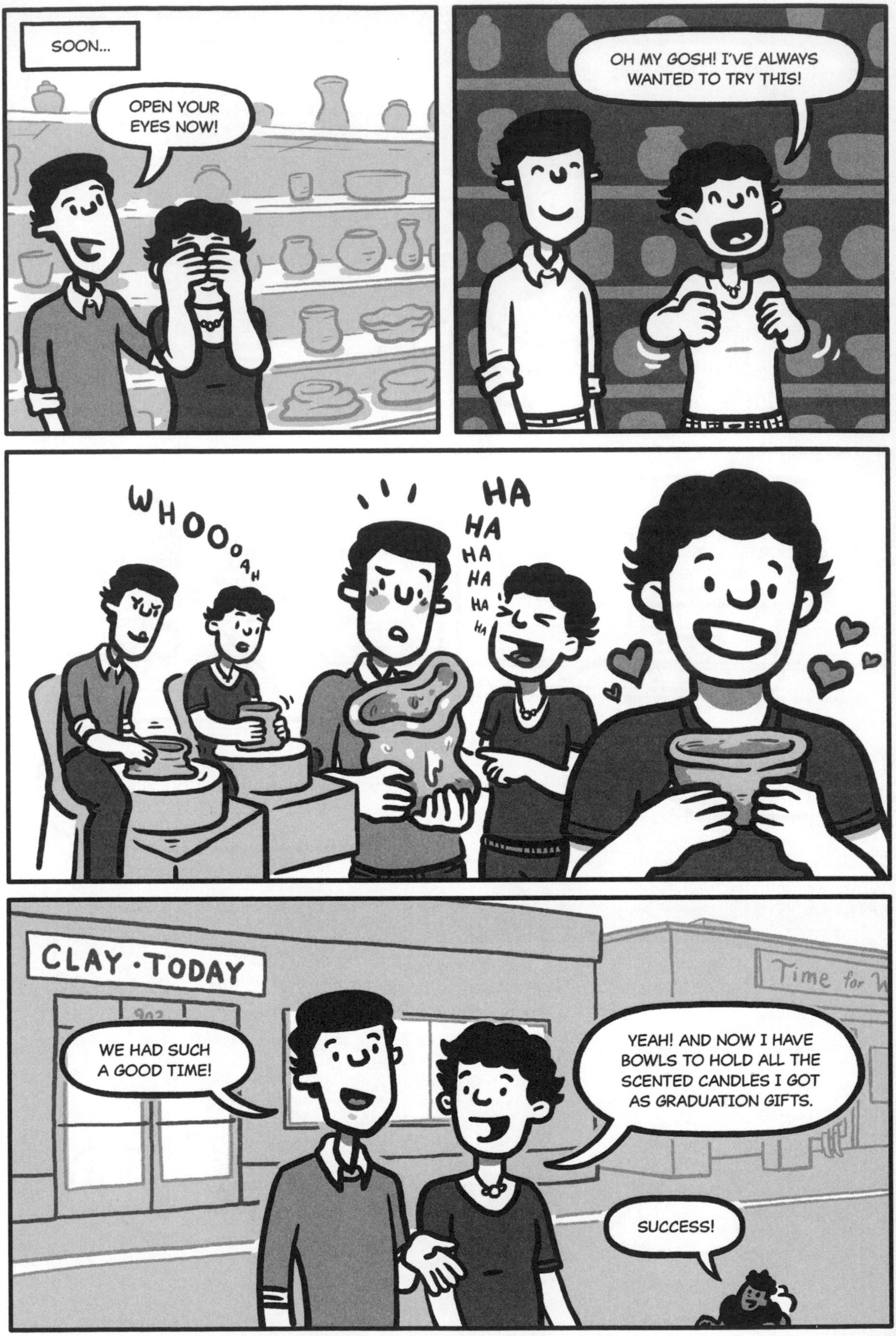
SOON...
OPEN YOUR EYES NOW!
OH MY GOSH! I'VE ALWAYS WANTED TO TRY THIS!
WHOOOOAH
HA HA HA HA HA HA
CLAY · TODAY
WE HAD SUCH A GOOD TIME!
YEAH! AND NOW I HAVE BOWLS TO HOLD ALL THE SCENTED CANDLES I GOT AS GRADUATION GIFTS.
SUCCESS!

CHAPTER FOUR

PUTTING IDEAS TO WORK

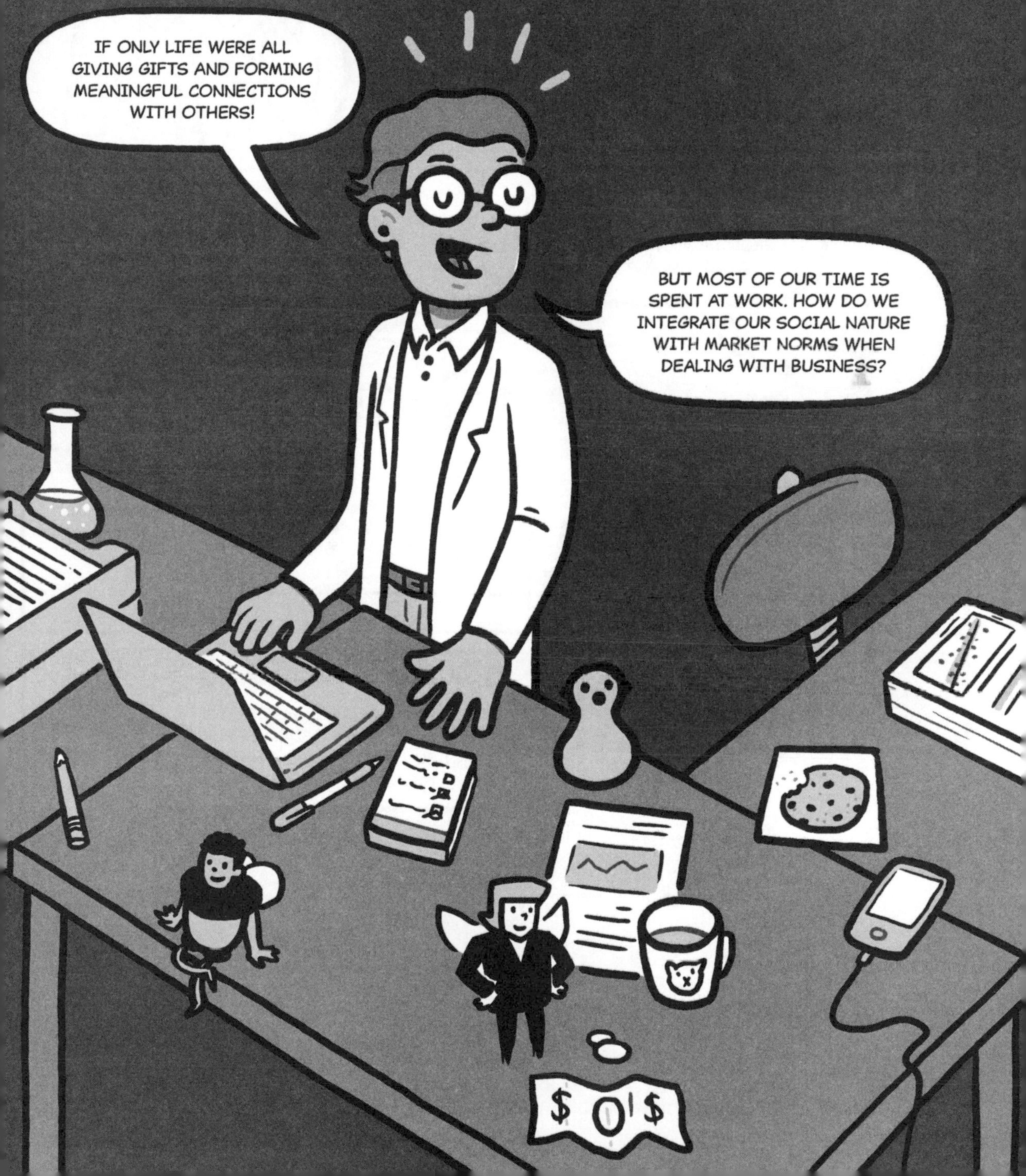

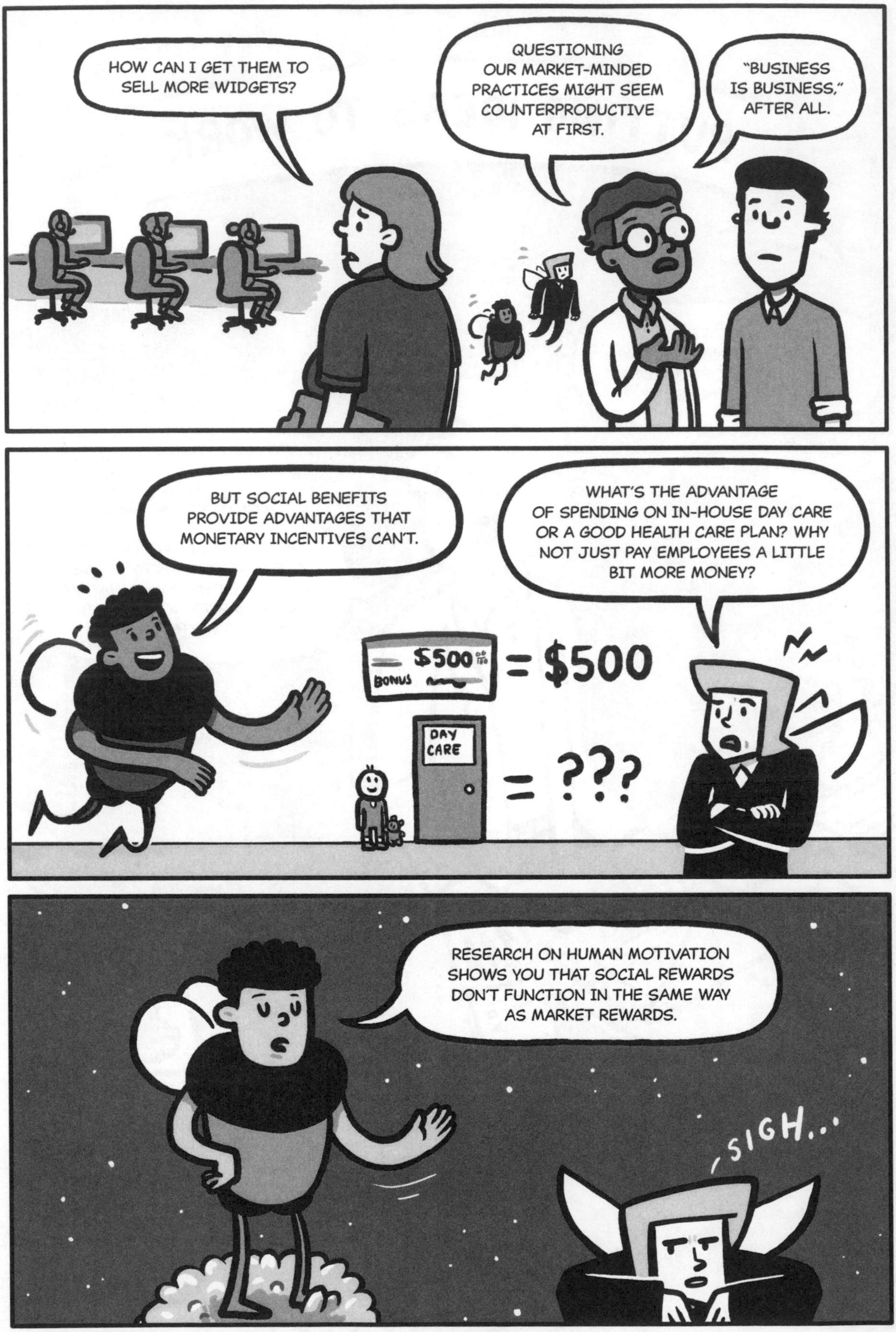
HOW CAN I GET THEM TO SELL MORE WIDGETS?
QUESTIONING OUR MARKET-MINDED PRACTICES MIGHT SEEM COUNTERPRODUCTIVE AT FIRST.
"BUSINESS IS BUSINESS," AFTER ALL.
BUT SOCIAL BENEFITS PROVIDE ADVANTAGES THAT MONETARY INCENTIVES CAN'T.
WHAT'S THE ADVANTAGE OF SPENDING ON IN-HOUSE DAY CARE OR A GOOD HEALTH CARE PLAN? WHY NOT JUST PAY EMPLOYEES A LITTLE BIT MORE MONEY?
$500
BONUS
= $500
DAY CARE
= ???
RESEARCH ON HUMAN MOTIVATION SHOWS YOU THAT SOCIAL REWARDS DON'T FUNCTION IN THE SAME WAY AS MARKET REWARDS.
SIGH...

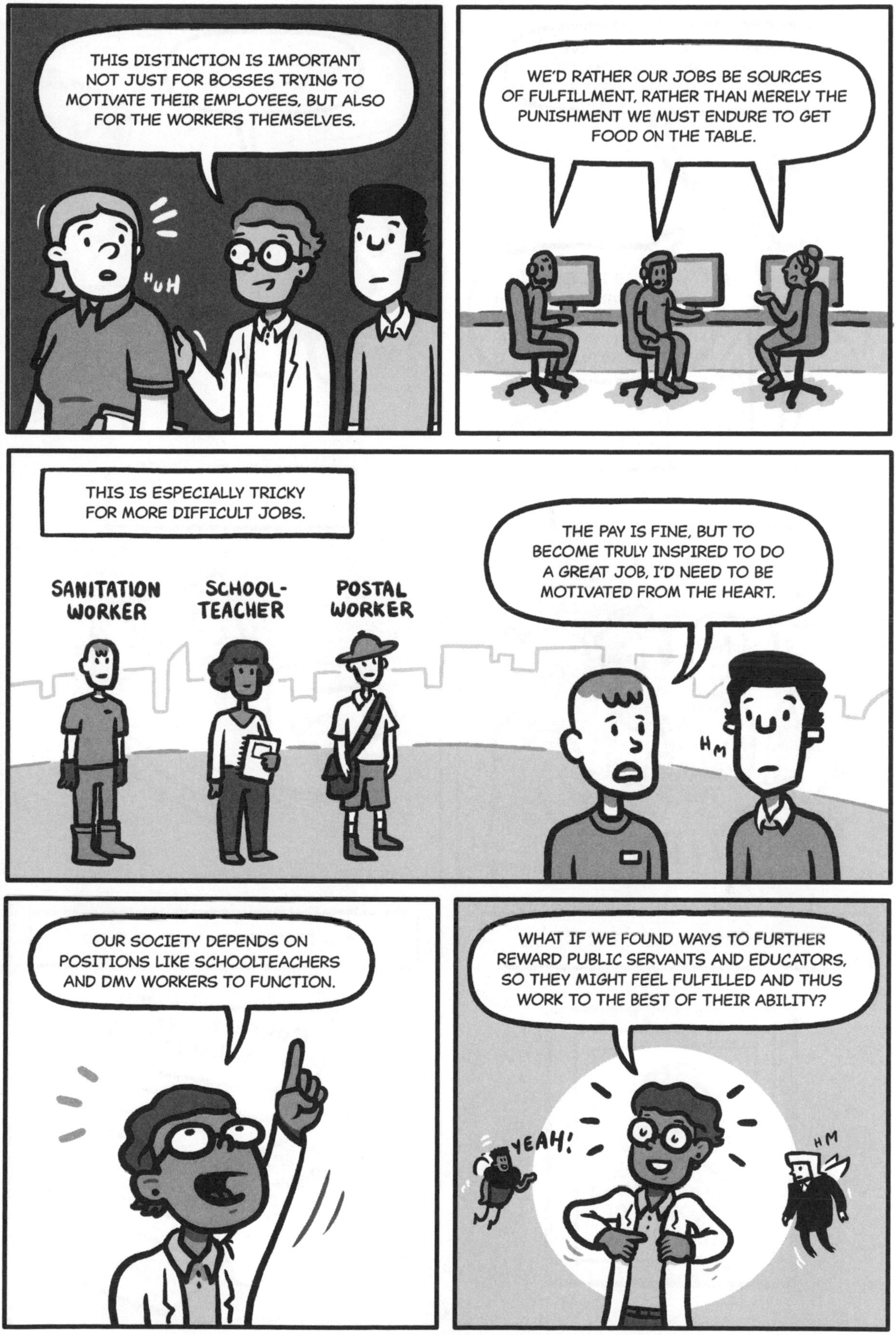
THIS DISTINCTION IS IMPORTANT NOT JUST FOR BOSSES TRYING TO MOTIVATE THEIR EMPLOYEES, BUT ALSO FOR THE WORKERS THEMSELVES.
HUH
WE'D RATHER OUR JOBS BE SOURCES OF FULFILLMENT, RATHER THAN MERELY THE PUNISHMENT WE MUST ENDURE TO GET FOOD ON THE TABLE.
THIS IS ESPECIALLY TRICKY FOR MORE DIFFICULT JOBS.
SANITATION WORKER
SCHOOL-TEACHER
POSTAL WORKER
THE PAY IS FINE, BUT TO BECOME TRULY INSPIRED TO DO A GREAT JOB, I'D NEED TO BE MOTIVATED FROM THE HEART.
HM
OUR SOCIETY DEPENDS ON POSITIONS LIKE SCHOOLTEACHERS AND DMV WORKERS TO FUNCTION.
WHAT IF WE FOUND WAYS TO FURTHER REWARD PUBLIC SERVANTS AND EDUCATORS, SO THEY MIGHT FEEL FULFILLED AND THUS WORK TO THE BEST OF THEIR ABILITY?
YEAH!
HM

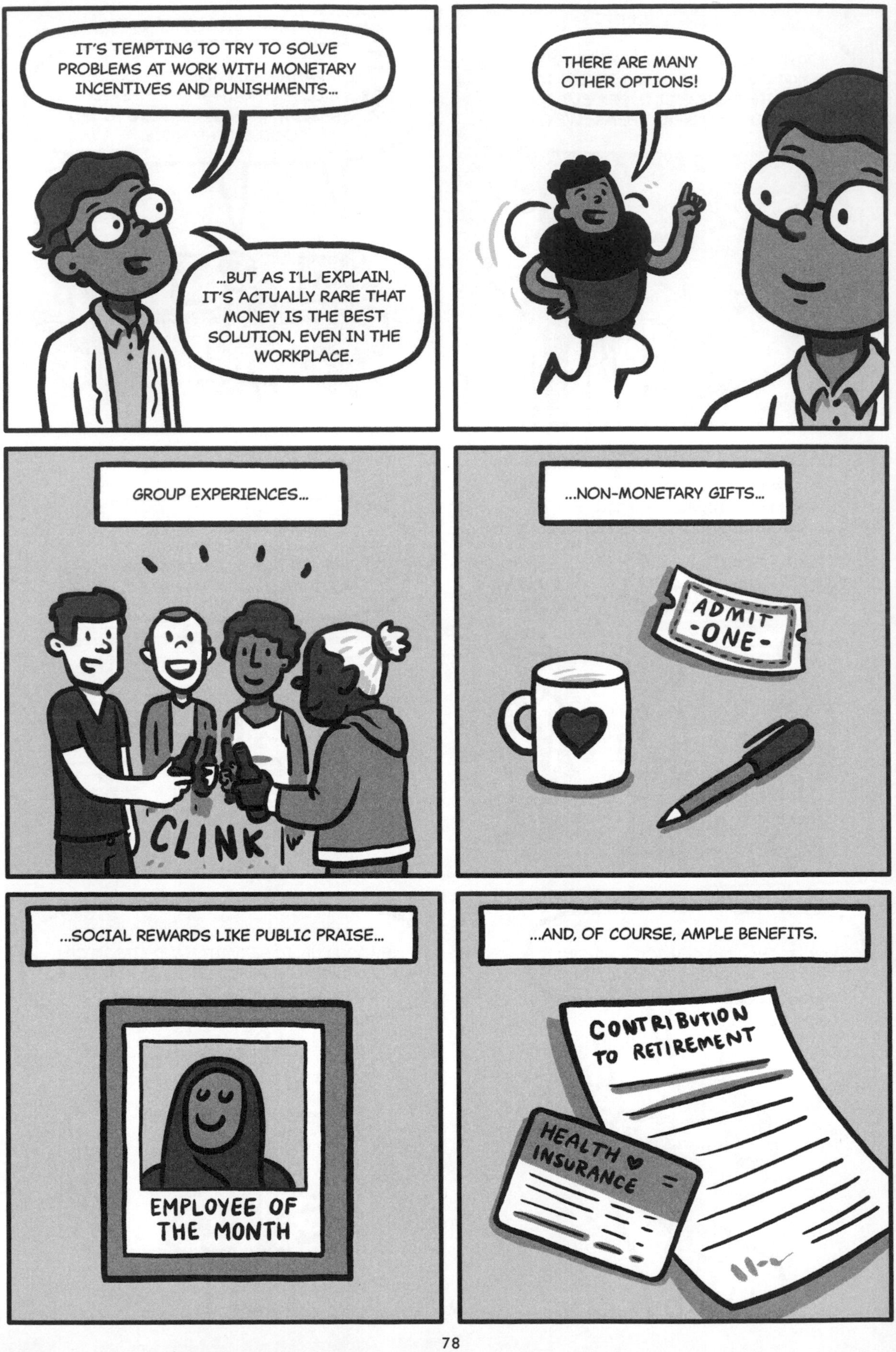
IT'S TEMPTING TO TRY TO SOLVE PROBLEMS AT WORK WITH MONETARY INCENTIVES AND PUNISHMENTS...
...BUT AS I'LL EXPLAIN, IT'S ACTUALLY RARE THAT MONEY IS THE BEST SOLUTION, EVEN IN THE WORKPLACE.
THERE ARE MANY OTHER OPTIONS!
GROUP EXPERIENCES...
CLINK
...NON-MONETARY GIFTS...
ADMIT ONE
...SOCIAL REWARDS LIKE PUBLIC PRAISE...
EMPLOYEE OF THE MONTH
...AND, OF COURSE, AMPLE BENEFITS.
CONTRIBUTION TO RETIREMENT
HEALTH INSURANCE

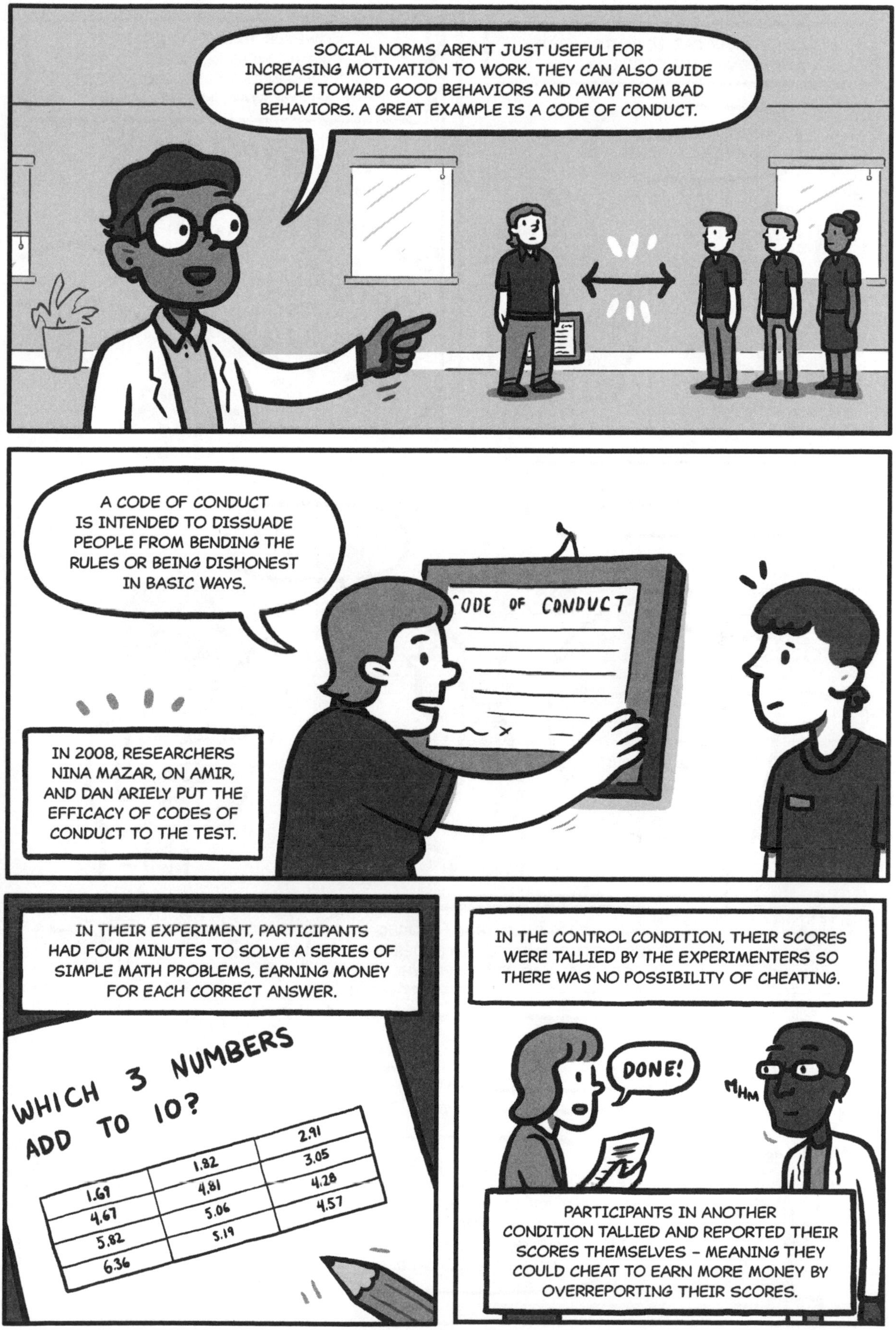
SOCIAL NORMS AREN'T JUST USEFUL FOR INCREASING MOTIVATION TO WORK. THEY CAN ALSO GUIDE PEOPLE TOWARD GOOD BEHAVIORS AND AWAY FROM BAD BEHAVIORS. A GREAT EXAMPLE IS A CODE OF CONDUCT.
A CODE OF CONDUCT IS INTENDED TO DISSUADE PEOPLE FROM BENDING THE RULES OR BEING DISHONEST IN BASIC WAYS.
CODE OF CONDUCT
IN 2008, RESEARCHERS NINA MAZAR, ON AMIR, AND DAN ARIELY PUT THE EFFICACY OF CODES OF CONDUCT TO THE TEST.
IN THEIR EXPERIMENT, PARTICIPANTS HAD FOUR MINUTES TO SOLVE A SERIES OF SIMPLE MATH PROBLEMS, EARNING MONEY FOR EACH CORRECT ANSWER.
WHICH 3 NUMBERS ADD TO 10?
1.69
4.67
5.82
6.36
1.82
4.81
5.06
5.19
2.91
3.05
4.28
4.57
IN THE CONTROL CONDITION, THEIR SCORES WERE TALLIED BY THE EXPERIMENTERS SO THERE WAS NO POSSIBILITY OF CHEATING.
DONE!
MHM
PARTICIPANTS IN ANOTHER CONDITION TALLIED AND REPORTED THEIR SCORES THEMSELVES – MEANING THEY COULD CHEAT TO EARN MORE MONEY BY OVERREPORTING THEIR SCORES.

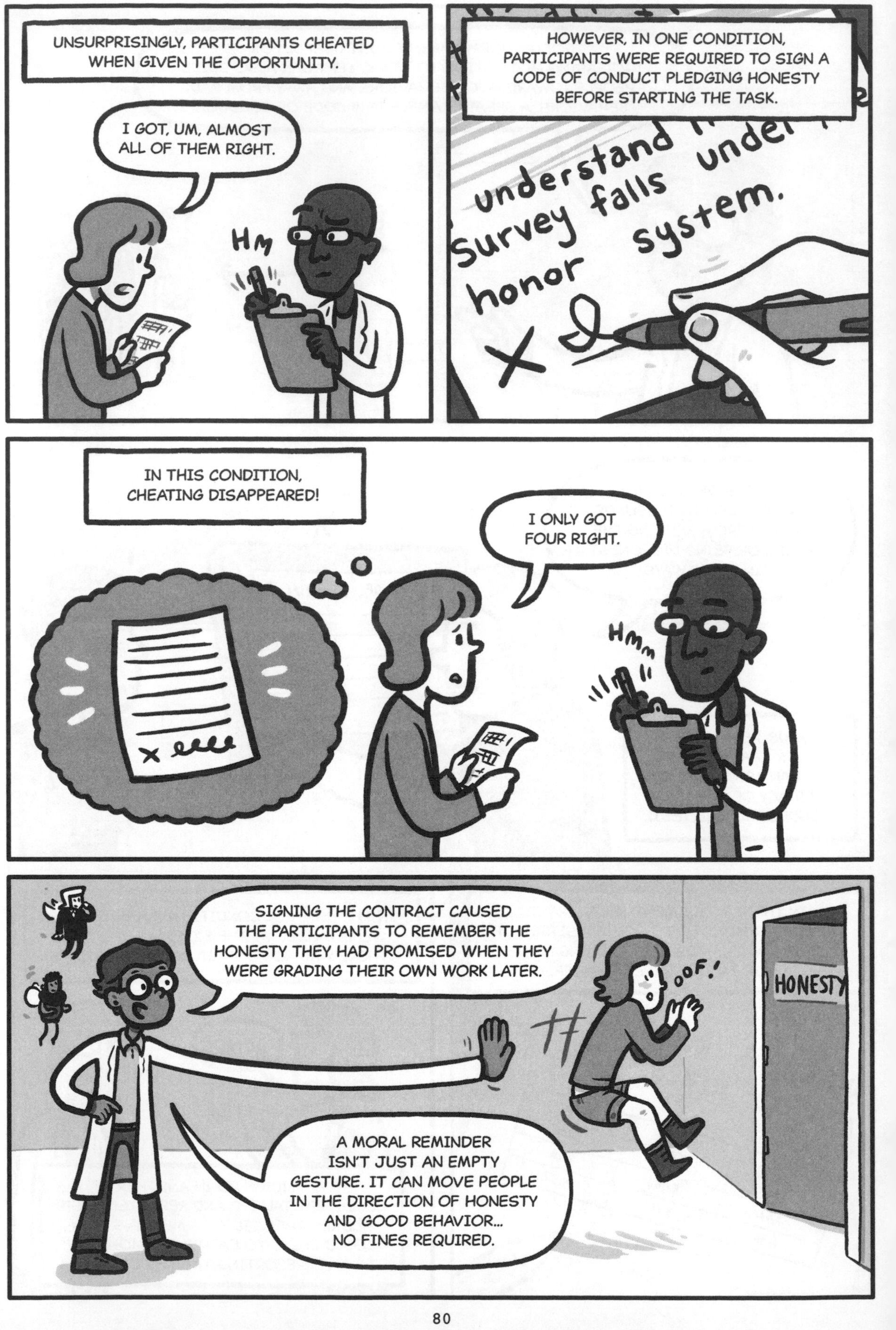
UNSURPRISINGLY, PARTICIPANTS CHEATED WHEN GIVEN THE OPPORTUNITY.
I GOT, UM, ALMOST ALL OF THEM RIGHT.
Hm
HOWEVER, IN ONE CONDITION, PARTICIPANTS WERE REQUIRED TO SIGN A CODE OF CONDUCT PLEDGING HONESTY BEFORE STARTING THE TASK.
understand
Survey falls
honor system.
IN THIS CONDITION, CHEATING DISAPPEARED!
I ONLY GOT FOUR RIGHT.
Hmm
SIGNING THE CONTRACT CAUSED THE PARTICIPANTS TO REMEMBER THE HONESTY THEY HAD PROMISED WHEN THEY WERE GRADING THEIR OWN WORK LATER.
OOF!
HONESTY
A MORAL REMINDER ISN'T JUST AN EMPTY GESTURE. IT CAN MOVE PEOPLE IN THE DIRECTION OF HONESTY AND GOOD BEHAVIOR... NO FINES REQUIRED.

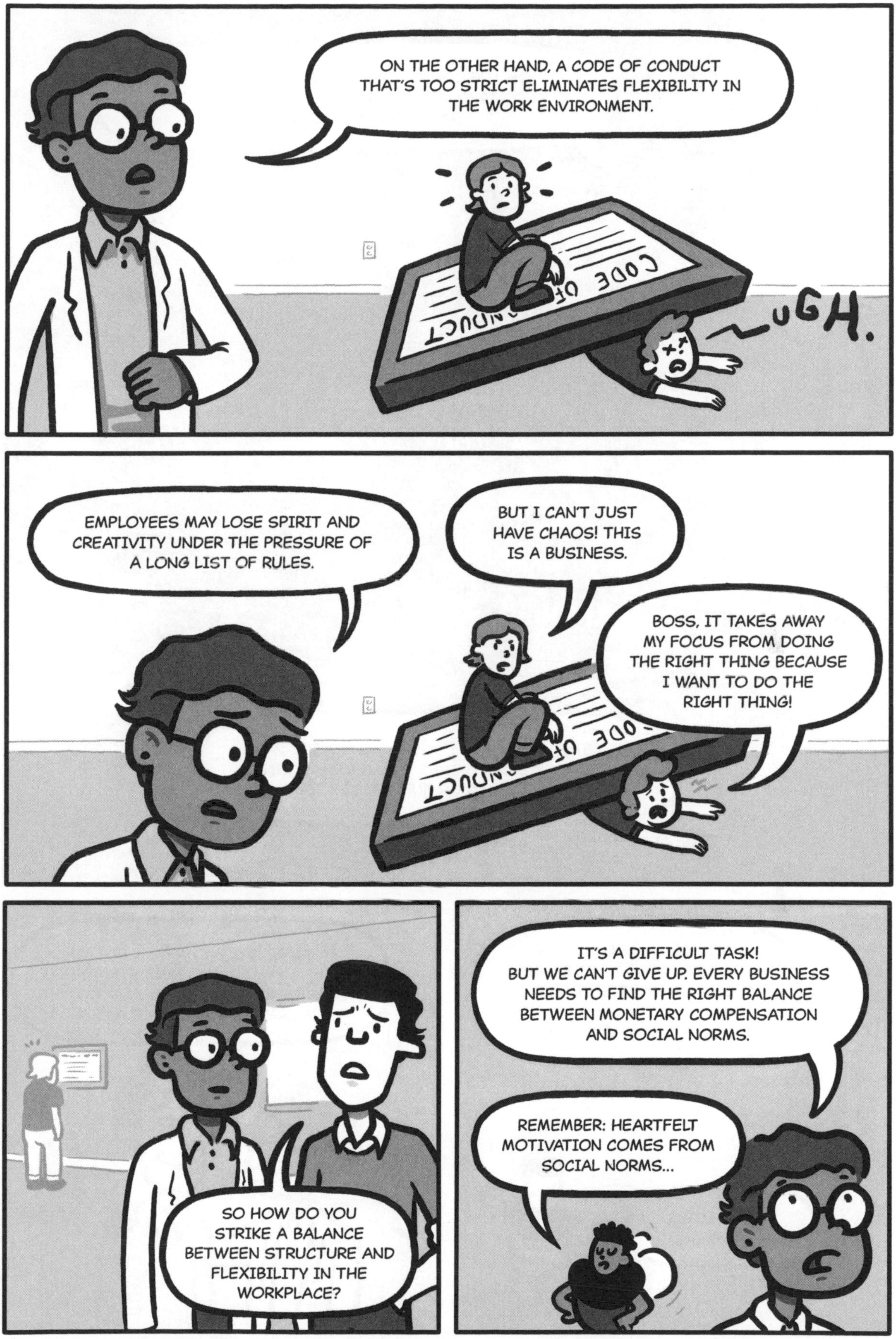

ON THE OTHER HAND, A CODE OF CONDUCT THAT'S TOO STRICT ELIMINATES FLEXIBILITY IN THE WORK ENVIRONMENT.
CODE OF CONDUCT
UGH.
EMPLOYEES MAY LOSE SPIRIT AND CREATIVITY UNDER THE PRESSURE OF A LONG LIST OF RULES.
BUT I CAN'T JUST HAVE CHAOS! THIS IS A BUSINESS.
BOSS, IT TAKES AWAY MY FOCUS FROM DOING THE RIGHT THING BECAUSE I WANT TO DO THE RIGHT THING!
SO HOW DO YOU STRIKE A BALANCE BETWEEN STRUCTURE AND FLEXIBILITY IN THE WORKPLACE?
IT'S A DIFFICULT TASK! BUT WE CAN'T GIVE UP. EVERY BUSINESS NEEDS TO FIND THE RIGHT BALANCE BETWEEN MONETARY COMPENSATION AND SOCIAL NORMS.
REMEMBER: HEARTFELT MOTIVATION COMES FROM SOCIAL NORMS...

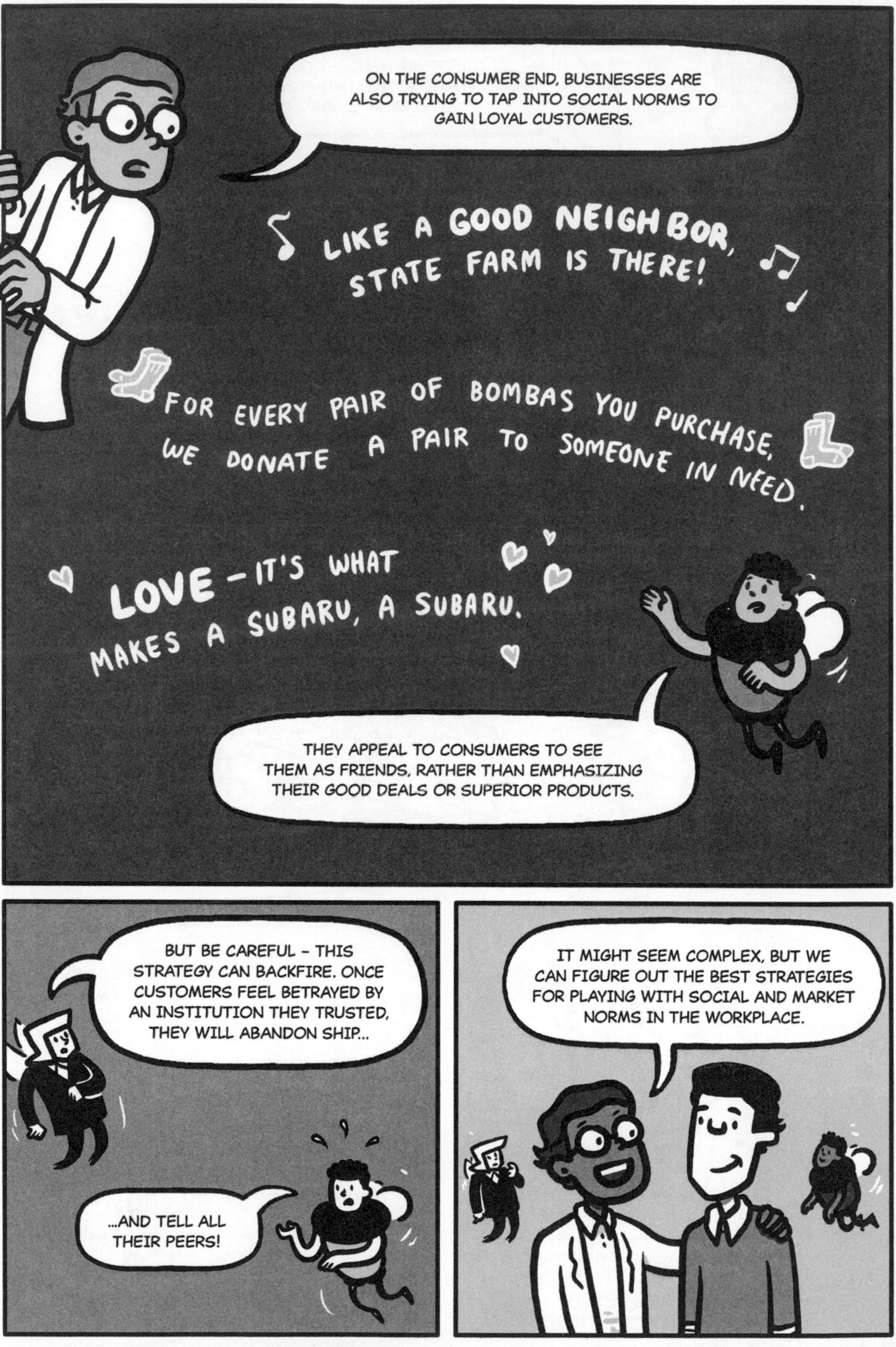

ON THE CONSUMER END, BUSINESSES ARE ALSO TRYING TO TAP INTO SOCIAL NORMS TO GAIN LOYAL CUSTOMERS.
LIKE A GOOD NEIGHBOR, STATE FARM IS THERE!
FOR EVERY PAIR OF BOMBAS YOU PURCHASE, WE DONATE A PAIR TO SOMEONE IN NEED.
LOVE - IT'S WHAT MAKES A SUBARU, A SUBARU.
THEY APPEAL TO CONSUMERS TO SEE THEM AS FRIENDS, RATHER THAN EMPHASIZING THEIR GOOD DEALS OR SUPERIOR PRODUCTS.
BUT BE CAREFUL – THIS STRATEGY CAN BACKFIRE. ONCE CUSTOMERS FEEL BETRAYED BY AN INSTITUTION THEY TRUSTED, THEY WILL ABANDON SHIP...
...AND TELL ALL THEIR PEERS!
IT MIGHT SEEM COMPLEX, BUT WE CAN FIGURE OUT THE BEST STRATEGIES FOR PLAYING WITH SOCIAL AND MARKET NORMS IN THE WORKPLACE.

CHAPTER FIVE

WILLINGNESS TO WORK AND MARKETPLACE MOTIVATION

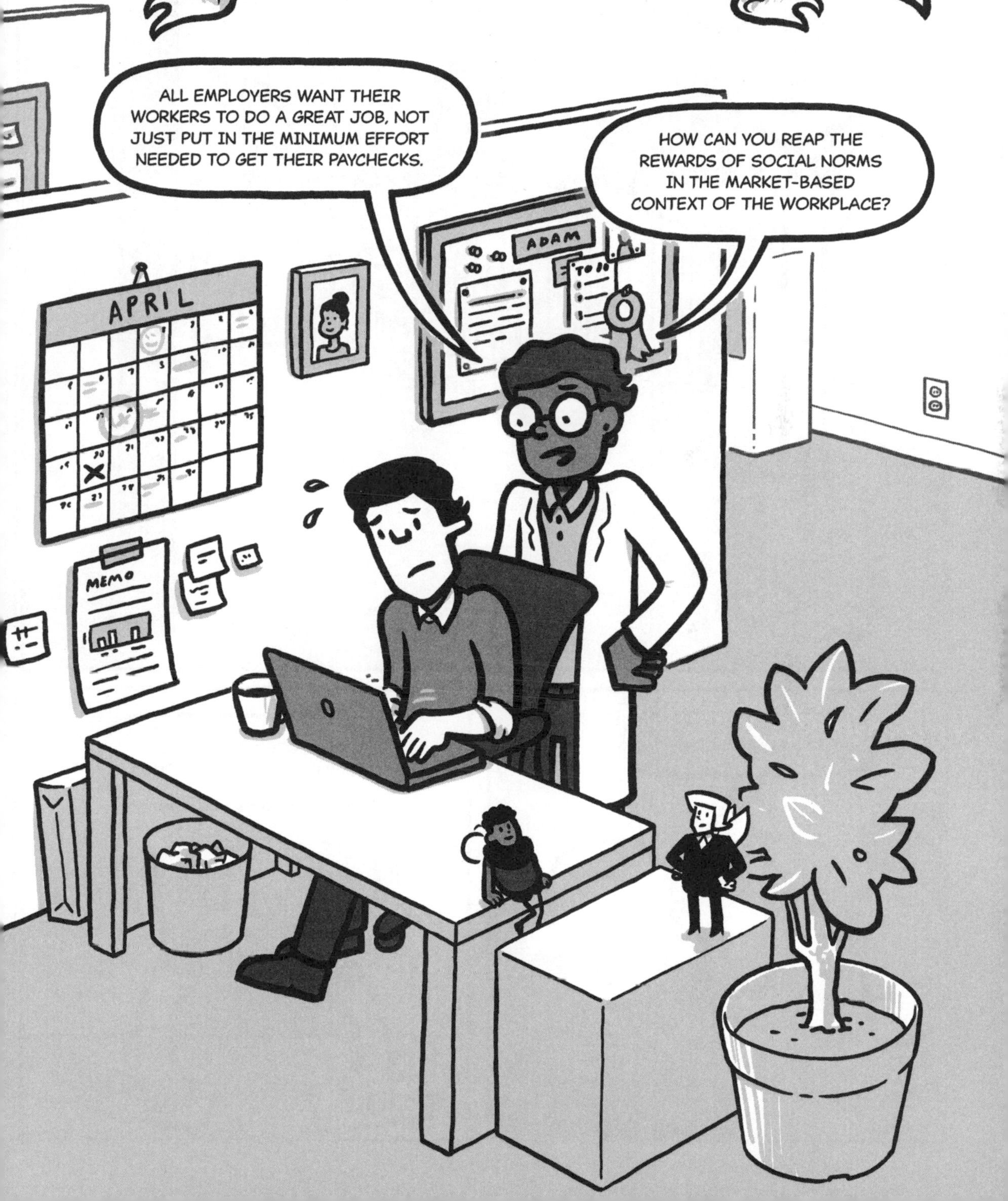
ALL EMPLOYERS WANT THEIR WORKERS TO DO A GREAT JOB, NOT JUST PUT IN THE MINIMUM EFFORT NEEDED TO GET THEIR PAYCHECKS.
HOW CAN YOU REAP THE REWARDS OF SOCIAL NORMS IN THE MARKET-BASED CONTEXT OF THE WORKPLACE?
ADAM
APRIL
MEMO

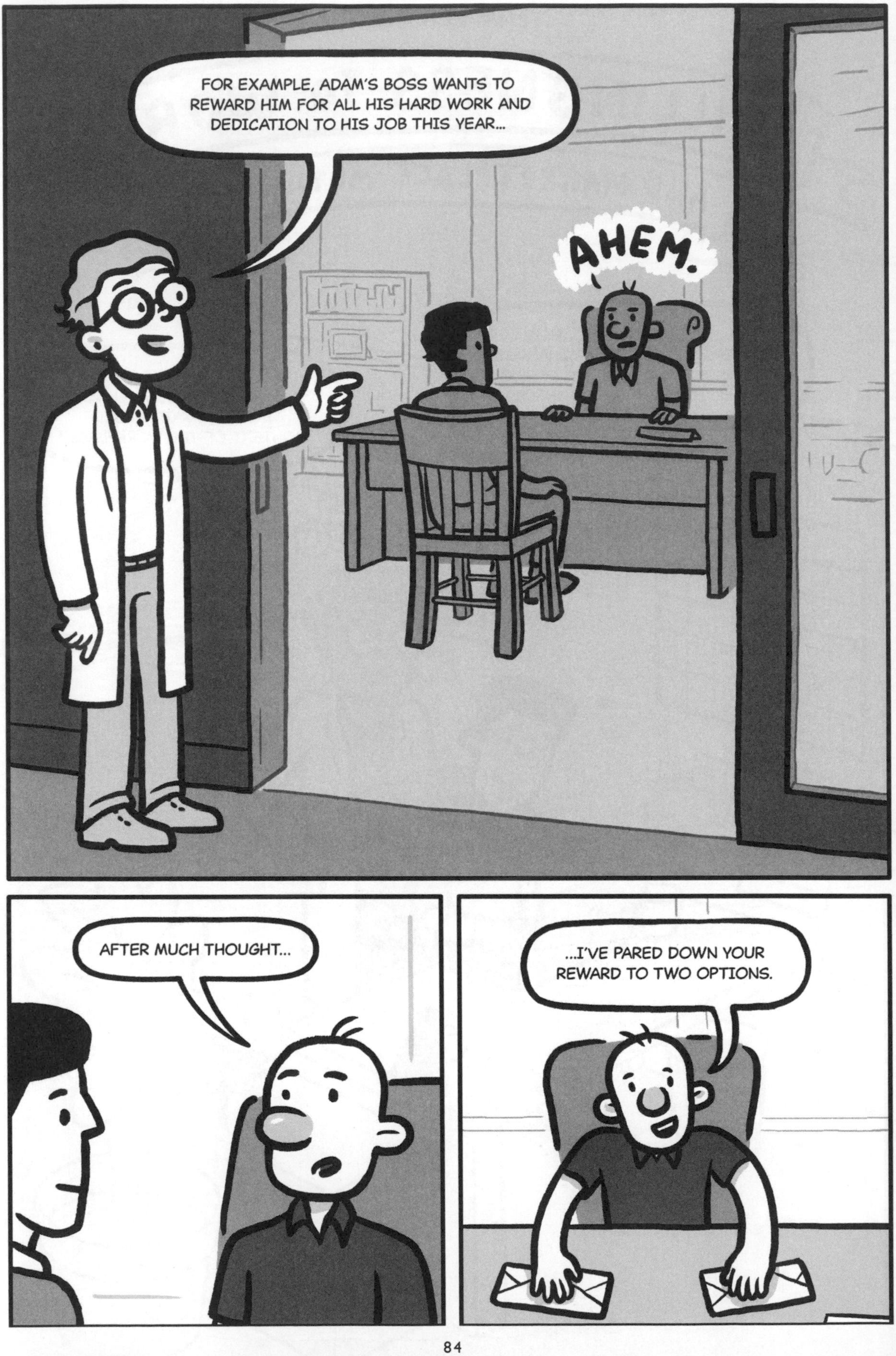
FOR EXAMPLE, ADAM'S BOSS WANTS TO REWARD HIM FOR ALL HIS HARD WORK AND DEDICATION TO HIS JOB THIS YEAR...
AHEM.
AFTER MUCH THOUGHT...
...I'VE PARED DOWN YOUR REWARD TO TWO OPTIONS.

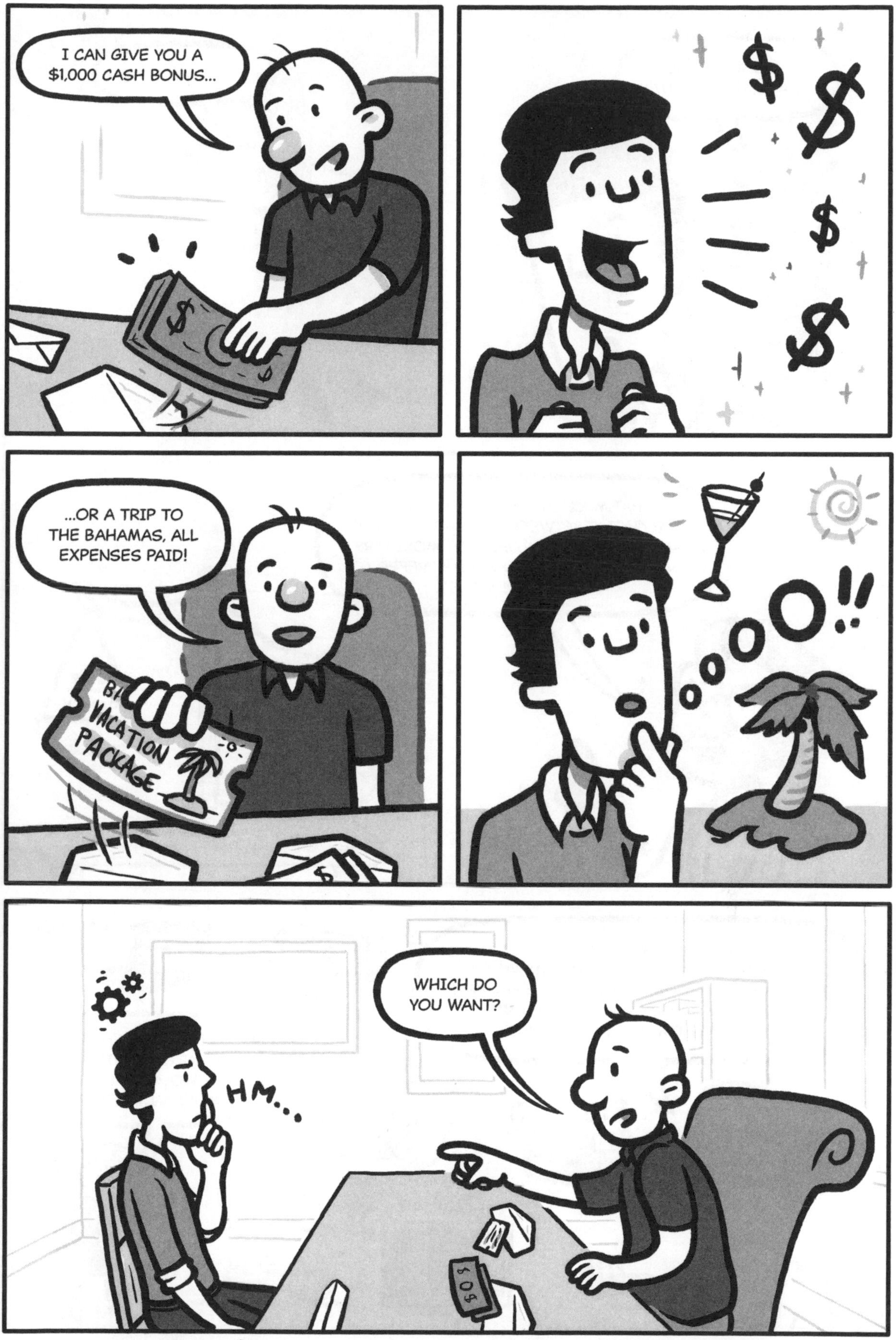
I CAN GIVE YOU A $1,000 CASH BONUS...
...OR A TRIP TO THE BAHAMAS, ALL EXPENSES PAID!
VACATION PACKAGE
oooOO!!
WHICH DO YOU WANT?
HM...

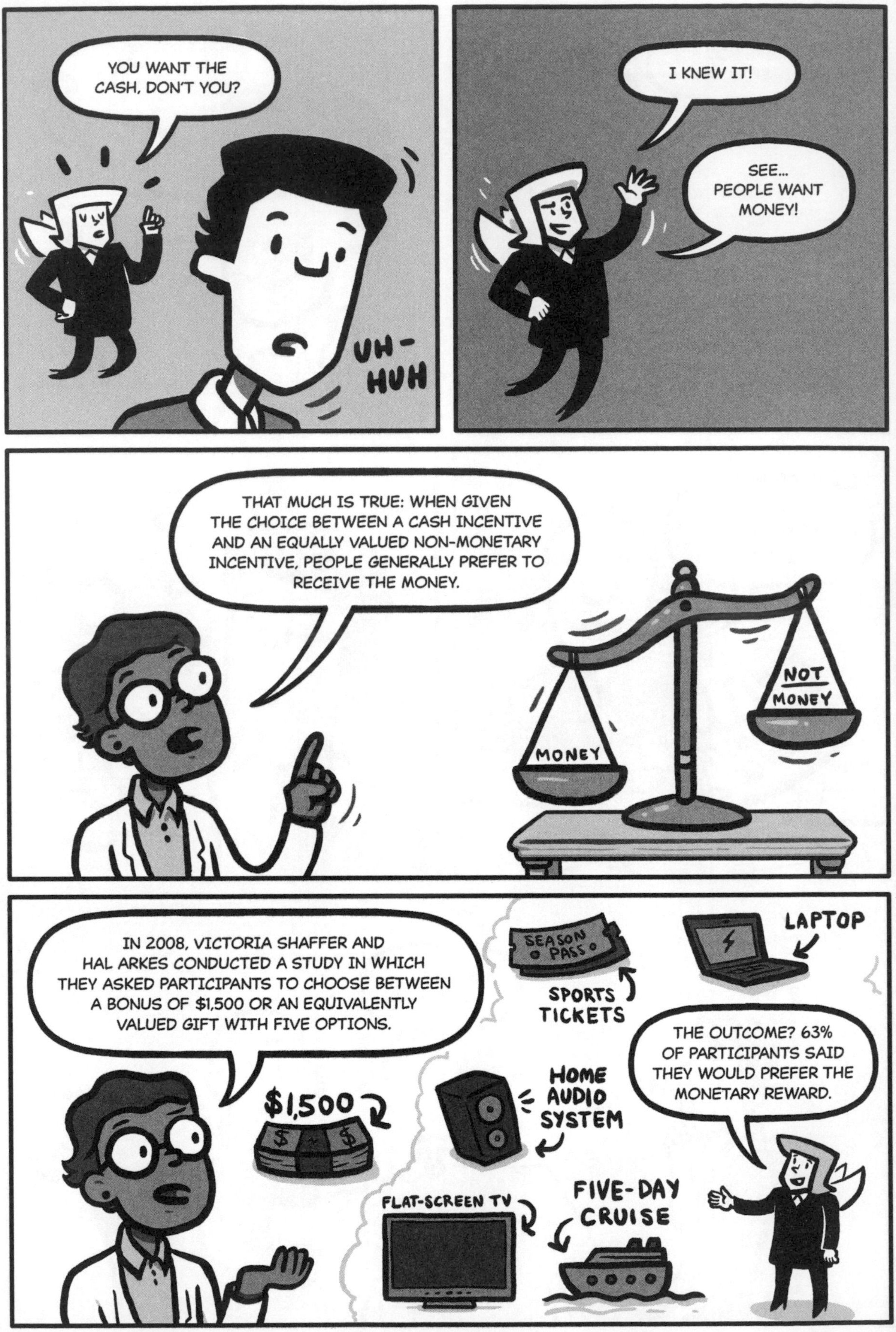
YOU WANT THE CASH, DON'T YOU?
UH-HUH
I KNEW IT!
SEE... PEOPLE WANT MONEY!
THAT MUCH IS TRUE: WHEN GIVEN THE CHOICE BETWEEN A CASH INCENTIVE AND AN EQUALLY VALUED NON-MONETARY INCENTIVE, PEOPLE GENERALLY PREFER TO RECEIVE THE MONEY.
MONEY
NOT MONEY
IN 2008, VICTORIA SHAFFER AND HAL ARKES CONDUCTED A STUDY IN WHICH THEY ASKED PARTICIPANTS TO CHOOSE BETWEEN A BONUS OF $1,500 OR AN EQUIVALENTLY VALUED GIFT WITH FIVE OPTIONS.
SEASON PASS
SPORTS TICKETS
LAPTOP
$1,500
HOME AUDIO SYSTEM
FLAT-SCREEN TV
FIVE-DAY CRUISE
THE OUTCOME? 63% OF PARTICIPANTS SAID THEY WOULD PREFER THE MONETARY REWARD.

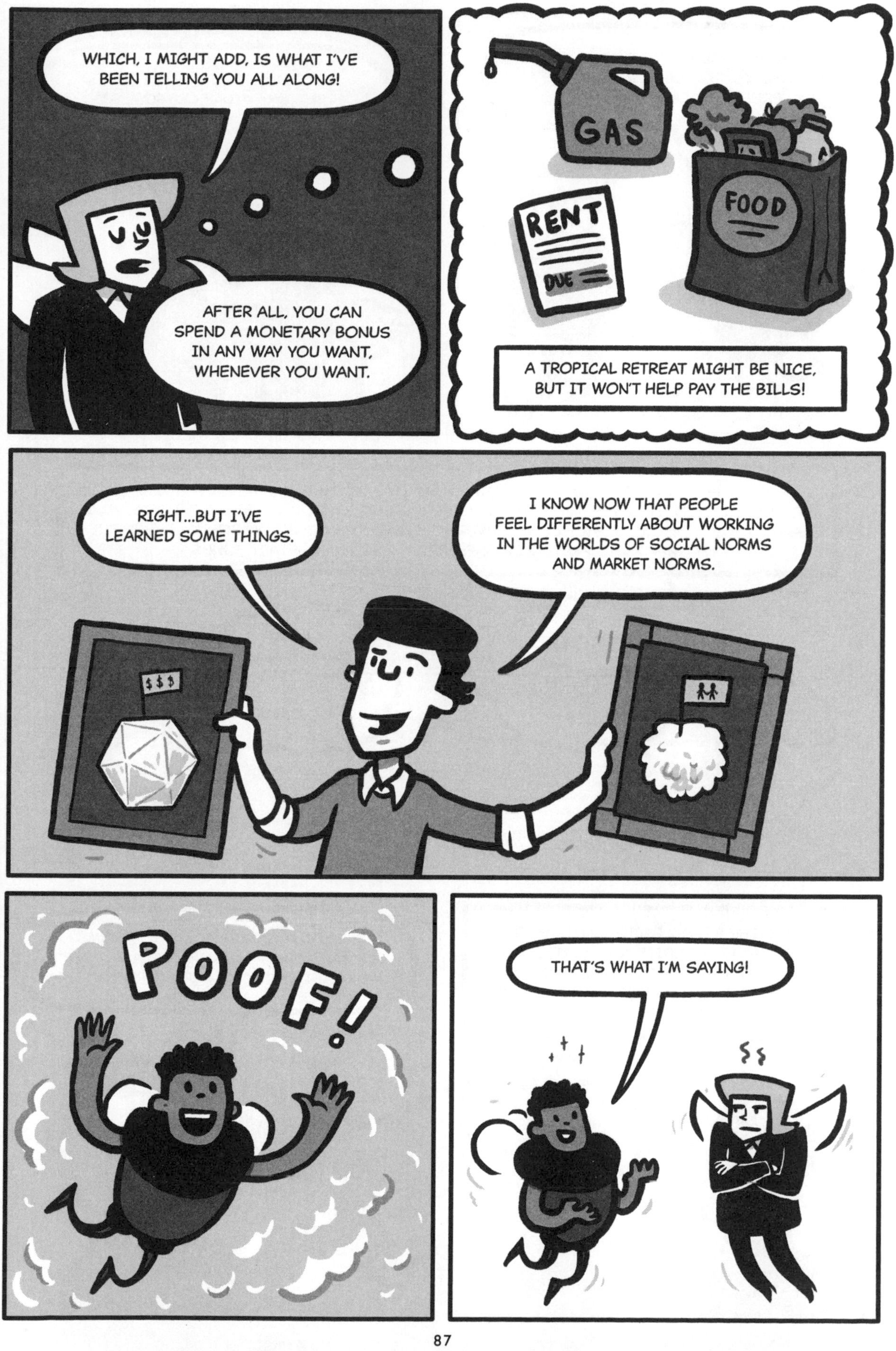
WHICH, I MIGHT ADD, IS WHAT I'VE BEEN TELLING YOU ALL ALONG!
AFTER ALL, YOU CAN SPEND A MONETARY BONUS IN ANY WAY YOU WANT, WHENEVER YOU WANT.
GAS
RENT
DUE
FOOD
A TROPICAL RETREAT MIGHT BE NICE, BUT IT WON'T HELP PAY THE BILLS!
RIGHT...BUT I'VE LEARNED SOME THINGS.
I KNOW NOW THAT PEOPLE FEEL DIFFERENTLY ABOUT WORKING IN THE WORLDS OF SOCIAL NORMS AND MARKET NORMS.
$$$
POOF!
THAT'S WHAT I'M SAYING!

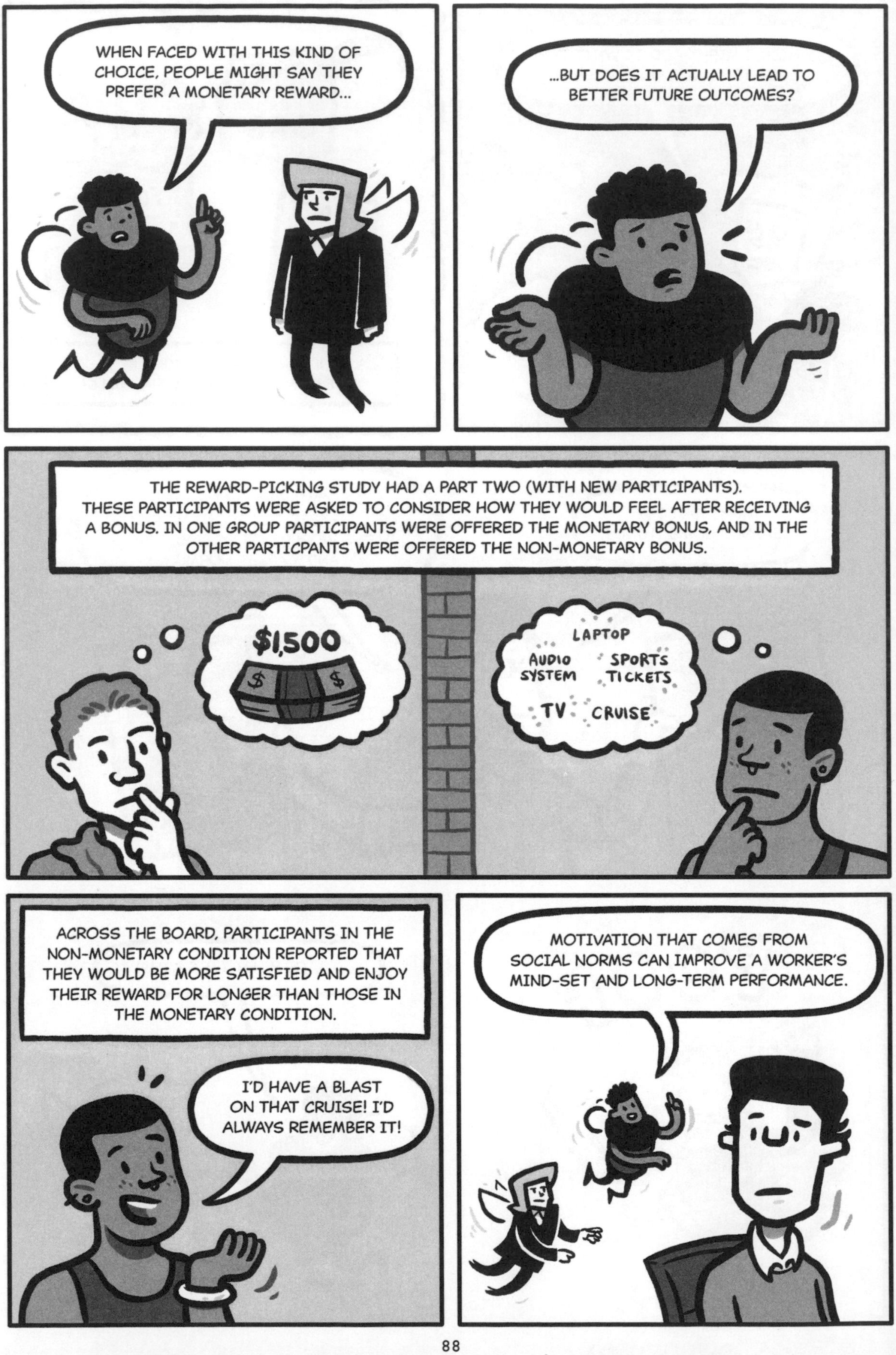

WHEN FACED WITH THIS KIND OF CHOICE, PEOPLE MIGHT SAY THEY PREFER A MONETARY REWARD...
...BUT DOES IT ACTUALLY LEAD TO BETTER FUTURE OUTCOMES?
THE REWARD-PICKING STUDY HAD A PART TWO (WITH NEW PARTICIPANTS). THESE PARTICIPANTS WERE ASKED TO CONSIDER HOW THEY WOULD FEEL AFTER RECEIVING A BONUS. IN ONE GROUP PARTICIPANTS WERE OFFERED THE MONETARY BONUS, AND IN THE OTHER PARTICPANTS WERE OFFERED THE NON-MONETARY BONUS.
$1,500
LAPTOP
AUDIO SYSTEM
SPORTS TICKETS
TV
CRUISE
ACROSS THE BOARD, PARTICIPANTS IN THE NON-MONETARY CONDITION REPORTED THAT THEY WOULD BE MORE SATISFIED AND ENJOY THEIR REWARD FOR LONGER THAN THOSE IN THE MONETARY CONDITION.
I'D HAVE A BLAST ON THAT CRUISE! I'D ALWAYS REMEMBER IT!
MOTIVATION THAT COMES FROM SOCIAL NORMS CAN IMPROVE A WORKER'S MIND-SET AND LONG-TERM PERFORMANCE.

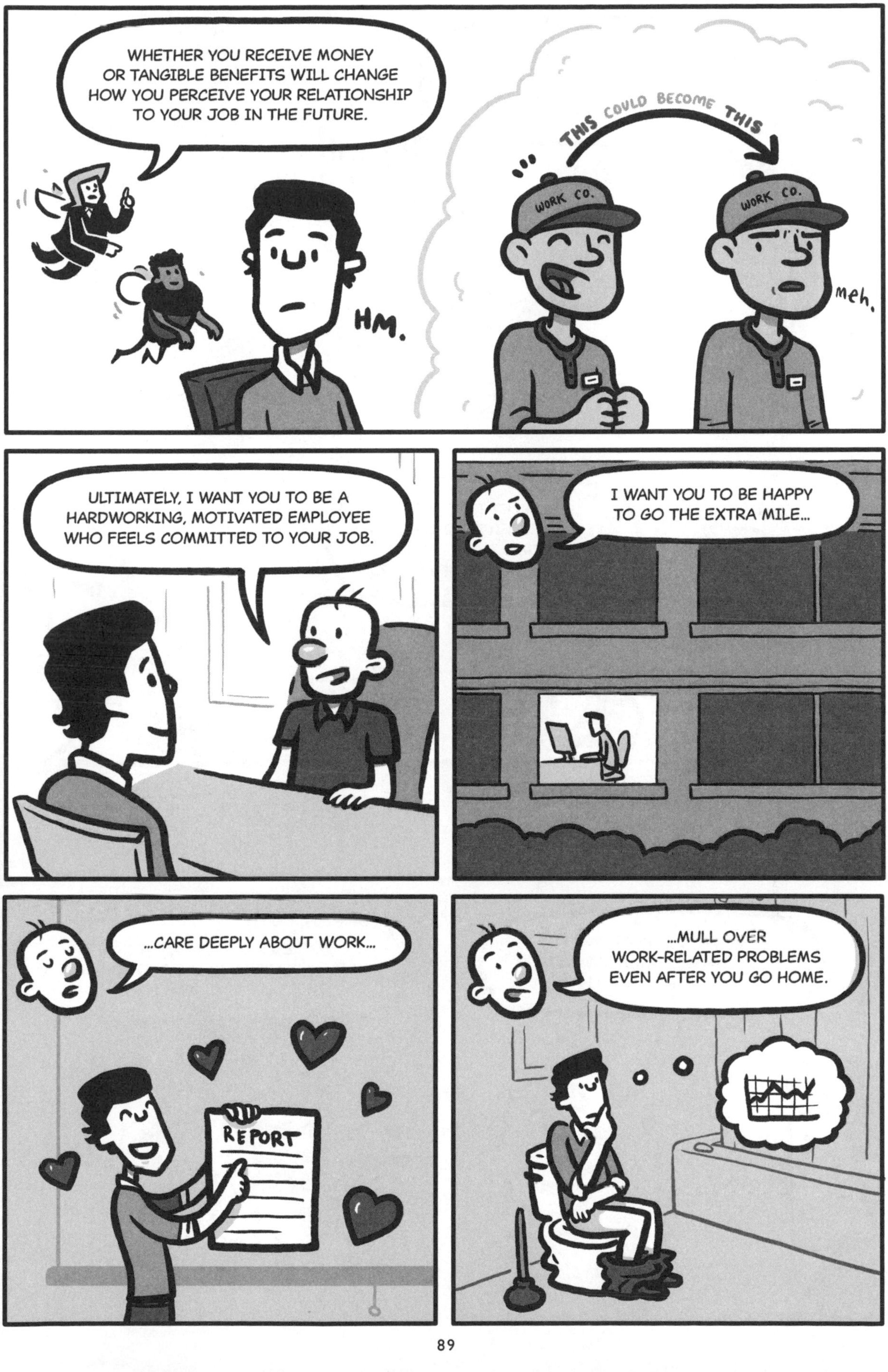
WHETHER YOU RECEIVE MONEY OR TANGIBLE BENEFITS WILL CHANGE HOW YOU PERCEIVE YOUR RELATIONSHIP TO YOUR JOB IN THE FUTURE.
HM.
THIS COULD BECOME THIS
WORK CO.
WORK CO.
meh.
ULTIMATELY, I WANT YOU TO BE A HARDWORKING, MOTIVATED EMPLOYEE WHO FEELS COMMITTED TO YOUR JOB.
I WANT YOU TO BE HAPPY TO GO THE EXTRA MILE...
...CARE DEEPLY ABOUT WORK...
REPORT
...MULL OVER WORK-RELATED PROBLEMS EVEN AFTER YOU GO HOME.

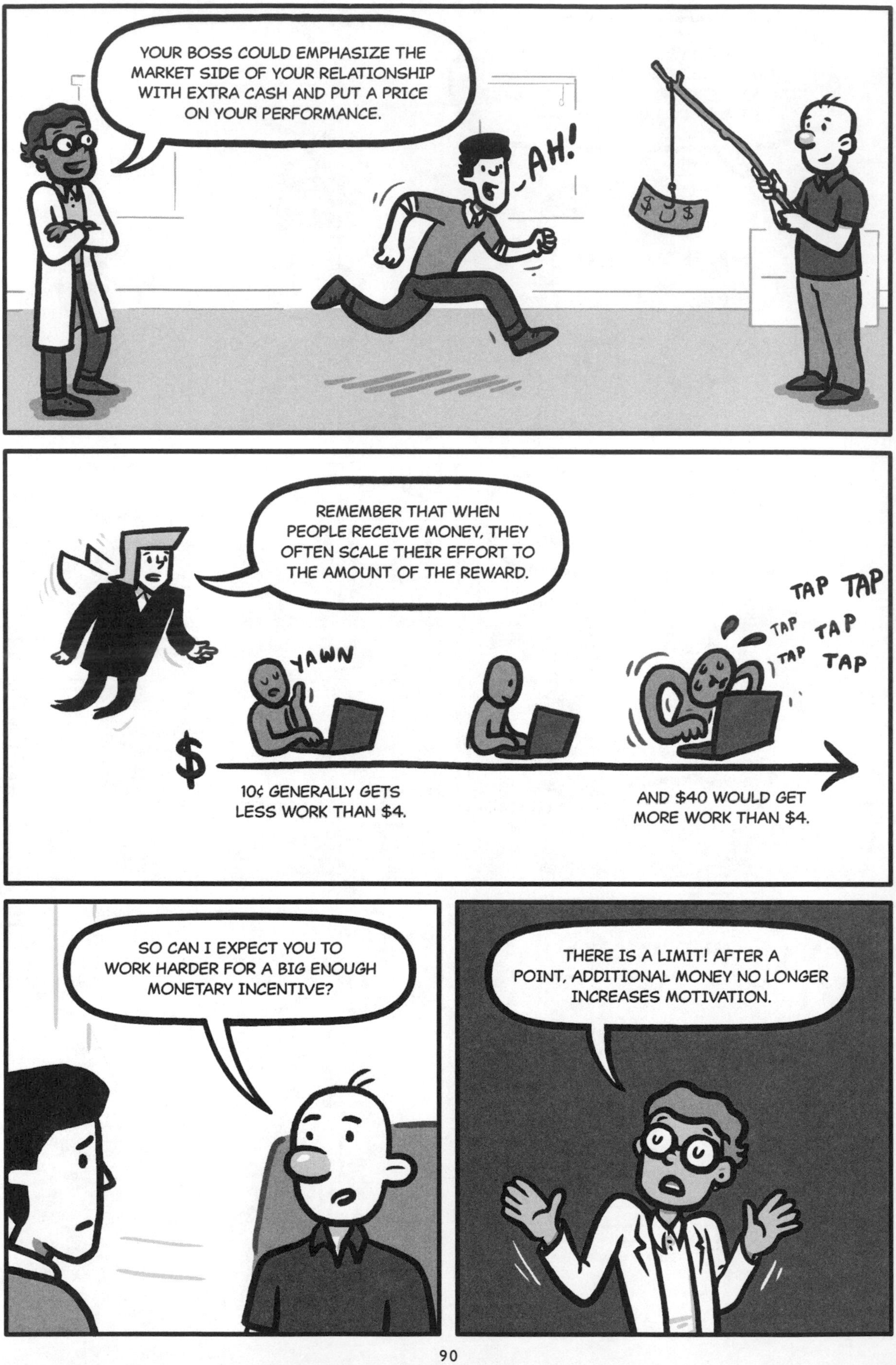
YOUR BOSS COULD EMPHASIZE THE MARKET SIDE OF YOUR RELATIONSHIP WITH EXTRA CASH AND PUT A PRICE ON YOUR PERFORMANCE.
AH!
REMEMBER THAT WHEN PEOPLE RECEIVE MONEY, THEY OFTEN SCALE THEIR EFFORT TO THE AMOUNT OF THE REWARD.
YAWN
TAP TAP
TAP
TAP
TAP
TAP
$
10¢ GENERALLY GETS LESS WORK THAN $4.
AND $40 WOULD GET MORE WORK THAN $4.
SO CAN I EXPECT YOU TO WORK HARDER FOR A BIG ENOUGH MONETARY INCENTIVE?
THERE IS A LIMIT! AFTER A POINT, ADDITIONAL MONEY NO LONGER INCREASES MOTIVATION.

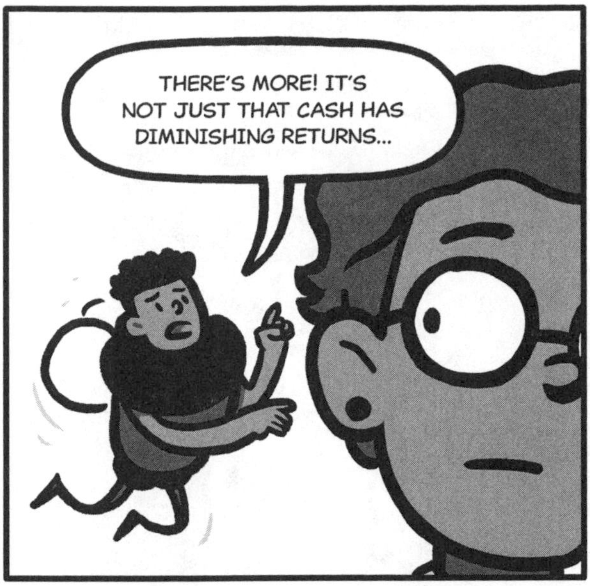
THERE'S MORE! IT'S NOT JUST THAT CASH HAS DIMINISHING RETURNS...

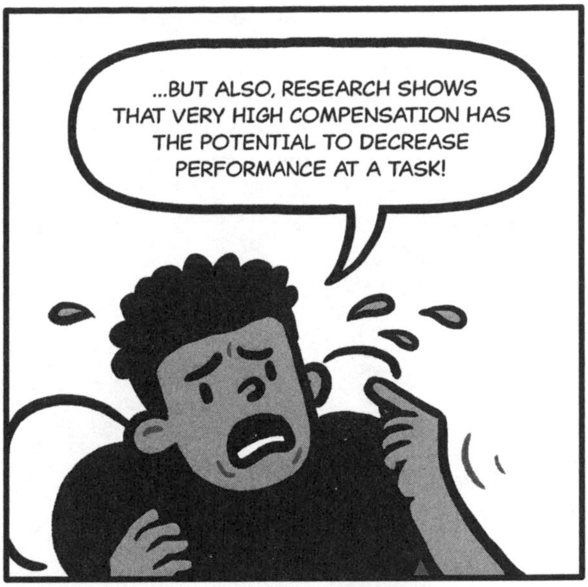
...BUT ALSO, RESEARCH SHOWS THAT VERY HIGH COMPENSATION HAS THE POTENTIAL TO DECREASE PERFORMANCE AT A TASK!

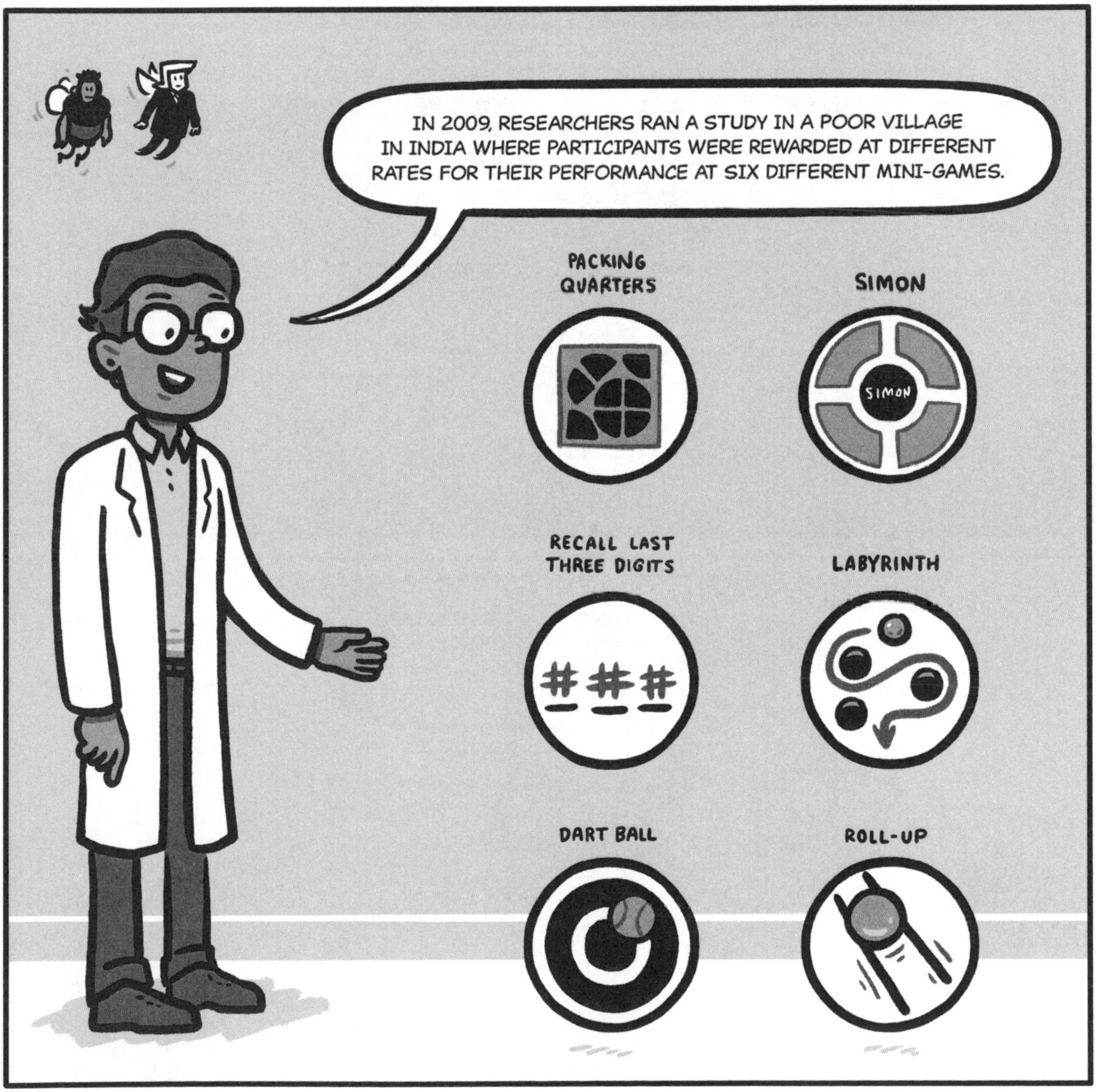
IN 2009, RESEARCHERS RAN A STUDY IN A POOR VILLAGE IN INDIA WHERE PARTICIPANTS WERE REWARDED AT DIFFERENT RATES FOR THEIR PERFORMANCE AT SIX DIFFERENT MINI-GAMES.
PACKING QUARTERS
SIMON
SIMON
RECALL LAST THREE DIGITS
LABYRINTH
DART BALL
ROLL-UP

IN EACH GAME, REACHING A GOOD OR VERY GOOD LEVEL OF PERFORMANCE BROUGHT A REWARD.

BUT POOR PERFORMANCE MEANT NO REWARD AT ALL.

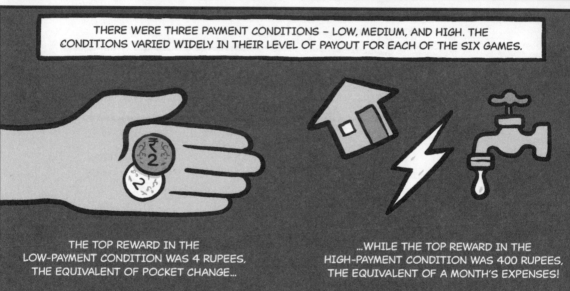

THERE WERE THREE PAYMENT CONDITIONS – LOW, MEDIUM, AND HIGH. THE CONDITIONS VARIED WIDELY IN THEIR LEVEL OF PAYOUT FOR EACH OF THE SIX GAMES.

THE TOP REWARD IN THE LOW-PAYMENT CONDITION WAS 4 RUPEES, THE EQUIVALENT OF POCKET CHANGE...

...WHILE THE TOP REWARD IN THE HIGH-PAYMENT CONDITION WAS 400 RUPEES, THE EQUIVALENT OF A MONTH'S EXPENSES!

AT FIRST GLANCE, YOU MIGHT GUESS THAT PEOPLE WOULD DO THE BEST WITH THE HIGHEST MONETARY MOTIVATION. BUT WHAT DID HAPPEN?

400 RUPEES?!

MHM

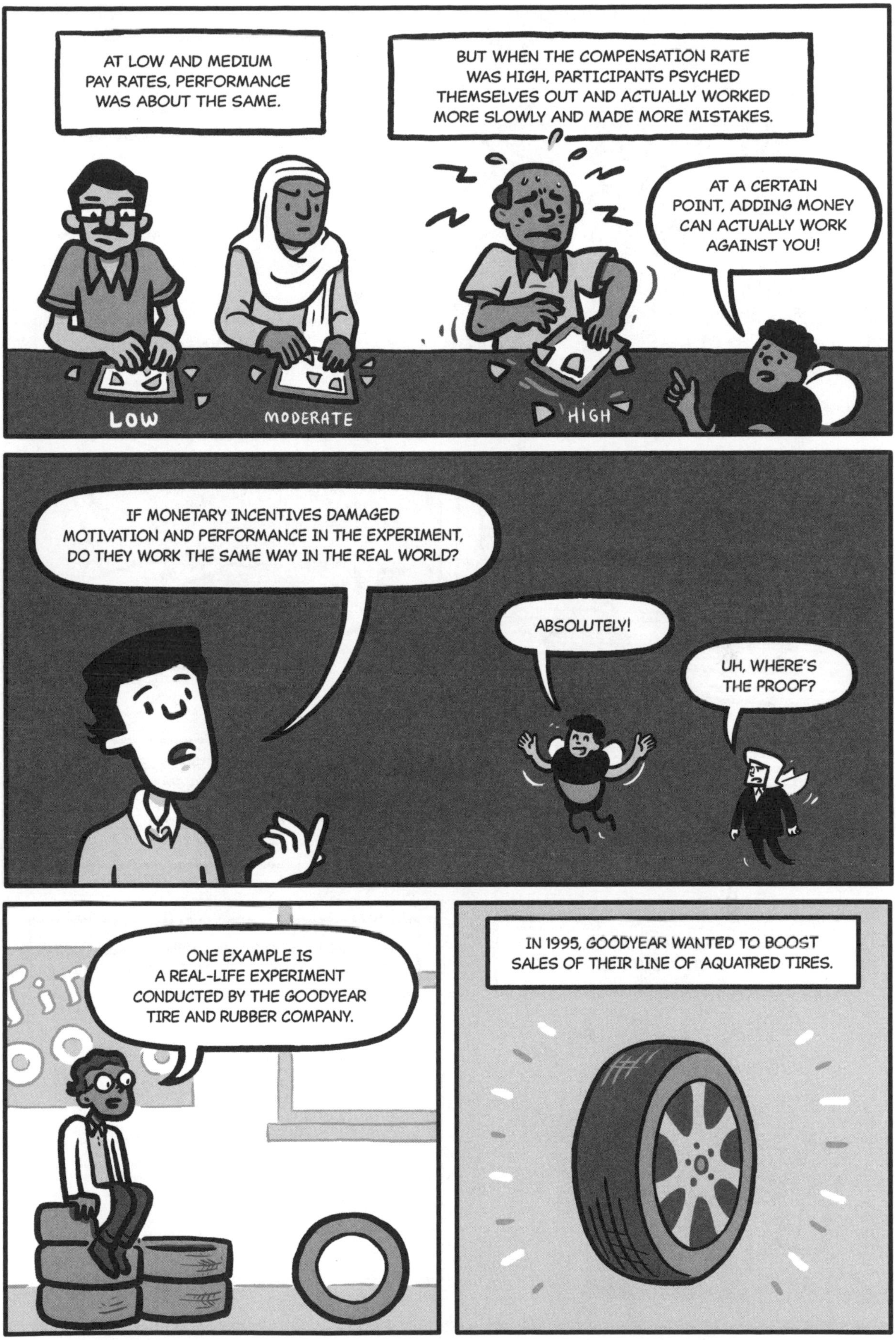
AT LOW AND MEDIUM PAY RATES, PERFORMANCE WAS ABOUT THE SAME.
BUT WHEN THE COMPENSATION RATE WAS HIGH, PARTICIPANTS PSYCHED THEMSELVES OUT AND ACTUALLY WORKED MORE SLOWLY AND MADE MORE MISTAKES.
LOW
MODERATE
HIGH
AT A CERTAIN POINT, ADDING MONEY CAN ACTUALLY WORK AGAINST YOU!
IF MONETARY INCENTIVES DAMAGED MOTIVATION AND PERFORMANCE IN THE EXPERIMENT, DO THEY WORK THE SAME WAY IN THE REAL WORLD?
ABSOLUTELY!
UH, WHERE'S THE PROOF?
ONE EXAMPLE IS A REAL-LIFE EXPERIMENT CONDUCTED BY THE GOODYEAR TIRE AND RUBBER COMPANY.
IN 1995, GOODYEAR WANTED TO BOOST SALES OF THEIR LINE OF AQUATRED TIRES.

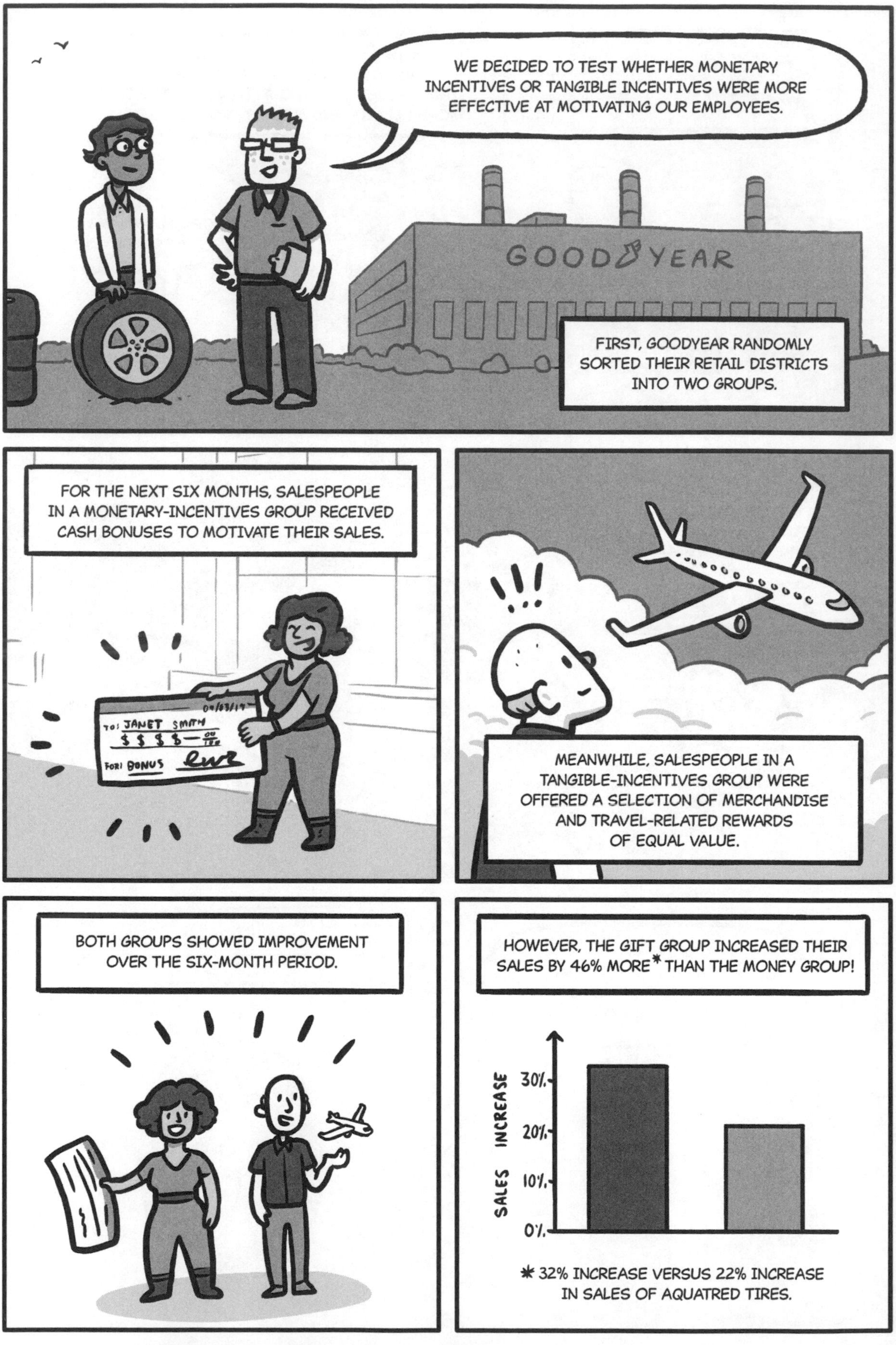
WE DECIDED TO TEST WHETHER MONETARY INCENTIVES OR TANGIBLE INCENTIVES WERE MORE EFFECTIVE AT MOTIVATING OUR EMPLOYEES.
GOODYEAR
FIRST, GOODYEAR RANDOMLY SORTED THEIR RETAIL DISTRICTS INTO TWO GROUPS.
FOR THE NEXT SIX MONTHS, SALESPEOPLE IN A MONETARY-INCENTIVES GROUP RECEIVED CASH BONUSES TO MOTIVATE THEIR SALES.
TO: JANET SMITH
FOR: BONUS
MEANWHILE, SALESPEOPLE IN A TANGIBLE-INCENTIVES GROUP WERE OFFERED A SELECTION OF MERCHANDISE AND TRAVEL-RELATED REWARDS OF EQUAL VALUE.
BOTH GROUPS SHOWED IMPROVEMENT OVER THE SIX-MONTH PERIOD.
HOWEVER, THE GIFT GROUP INCREASED THEIR SALES BY 46% MORE* THAN THE MONEY GROUP!
SALES INCREASE
30%
20%
10%
0%
* 32% INCREASE VERSUS 22% INCREASE IN SALES OF AQUATRED TIRES.

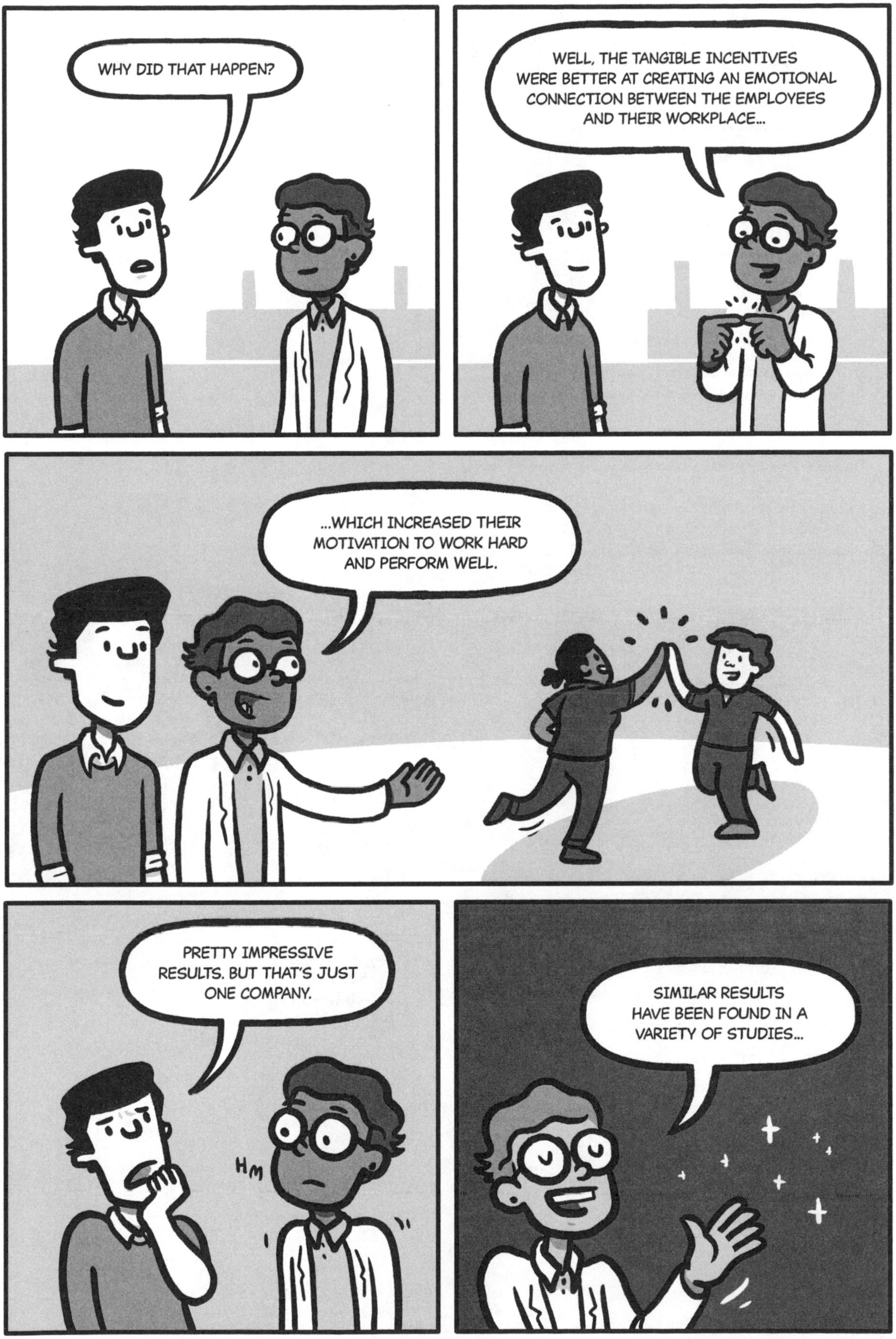
WHY DID THAT HAPPEN?
WELL, THE TANGIBLE INCENTIVES WERE BETTER AT CREATING AN EMOTIONAL CONNECTION BETWEEN THE EMPLOYEES AND THEIR WORKPLACE...
...WHICH INCREASED THEIR MOTIVATION TO WORK HARD AND PERFORM WELL.
PRETTY IMPRESSIVE RESULTS. BUT THAT'S JUST ONE COMPANY.
HM
SIMILAR RESULTS HAVE BEEN FOUND IN A VARIETY OF STUDIES...

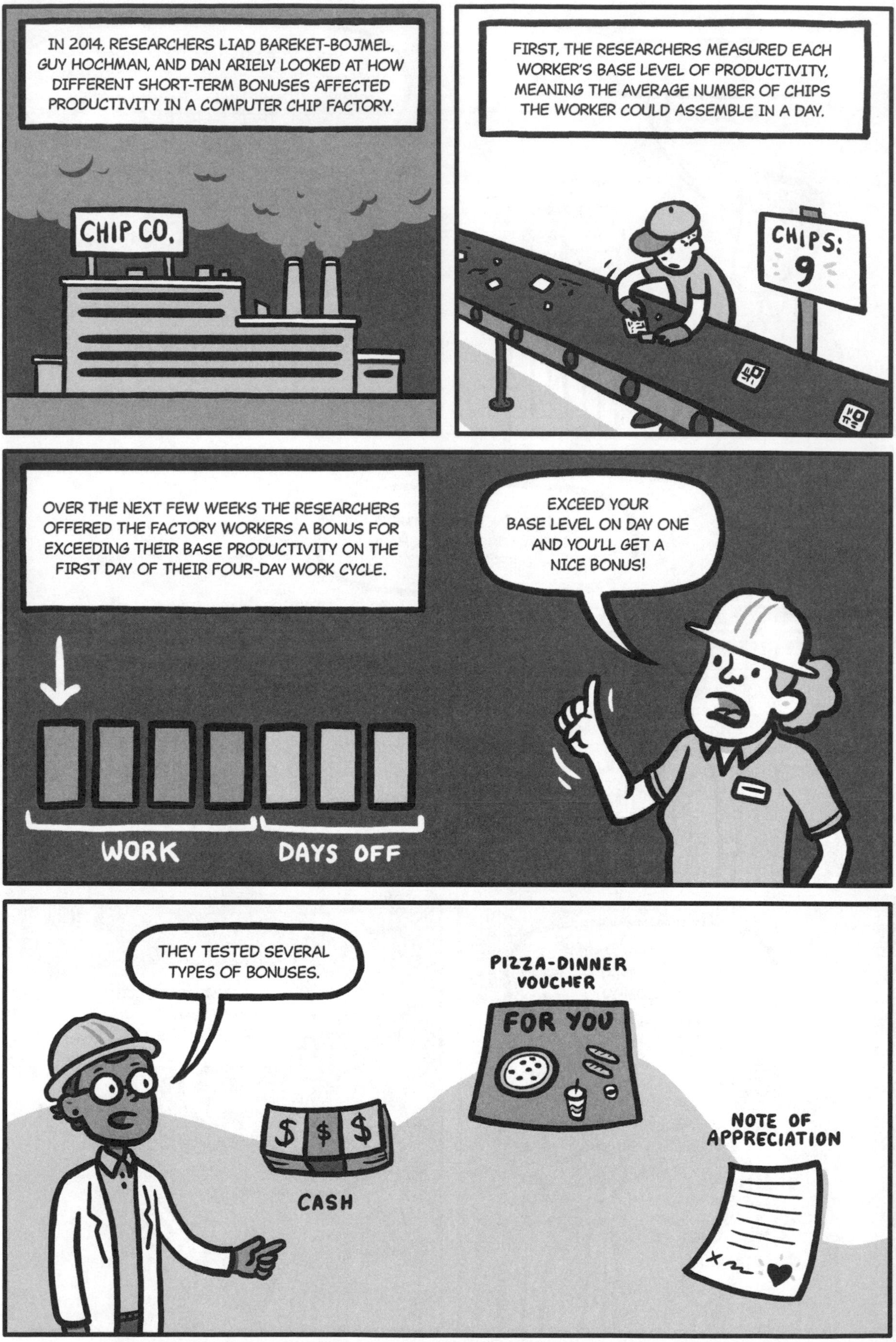
IN 2014, RESEARCHERS LIAD BAREKET-BOJMEL, GUY HOCHMAN, AND DAN ARIELY LOOKED AT HOW DIFFERENT SHORT-TERM BONUSES AFFECTED PRODUCTIVITY IN A COMPUTER CHIP FACTORY.
CHIP CO.
FIRST, THE RESEARCHERS MEASURED EACH WORKER'S BASE LEVEL OF PRODUCTIVITY, MEANING THE AVERAGE NUMBER OF CHIPS THE WORKER COULD ASSEMBLE IN A DAY.
CHIPS: 9
OVER THE NEXT FEW WEEKS THE RESEARCHERS OFFERED THE FACTORY WORKERS A BONUS FOR EXCEEDING THEIR BASE PRODUCTIVITY ON THE FIRST DAY OF THEIR FOUR-DAY WORK CYCLE.
EXCEED YOUR BASE LEVEL ON DAY ONE AND YOU'LL GET A NICE BONUS!
WORK
DAYS OFF
THEY TESTED SEVERAL TYPES OF BONUSES.
PIZZA-DINNER VOUCHER
FOR YOU
CASH
NOTE OF APPRECIATION

WHAT WORKED BEST?

UNSURPRISINGLY, ALL THE REWARDS LED TO INCREASED PERFORMANCE ON THE DAY OF THE BONUS – ABOUT 5% ABOVE WORKERS' BASE PRODUCTIVITY.

5%

BASELINE

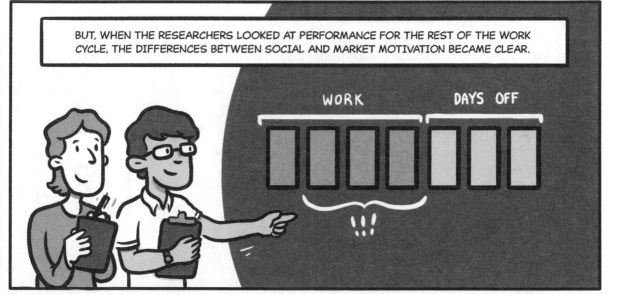

BUT, WHEN THE RESEARCHERS LOOKED AT PERFORMANCE FOR THE REST OF THE WORK CYCLE, THE DIFFERENCES BETWEEN SOCIAL AND MARKET MOTIVATION BECAME CLEAR.

WORK

DAYS OFF

WHEN WORKERS RECEIVED THE PIZZA VOUCHER OR NOTE OF APPRECIATION, THEIR PRODUCTIVITY RETURNED TO ITS BASE LEVEL ON THE WORK DAYS FOLLOWING THE BONUS.

FOR YOU

SHRUG   SHRUG

BUT WHEN THEY'D BEEN MOTIVATED BY THE CASH BONUS, WORKERS WERE ACTUALLY 6.5% LESS PRODUCTIVE THAN THEIR BASE LEVEL OVER THE REMAINDER OF THEIR WORK CYCLE!

$ $ $

BLIP BLOOP

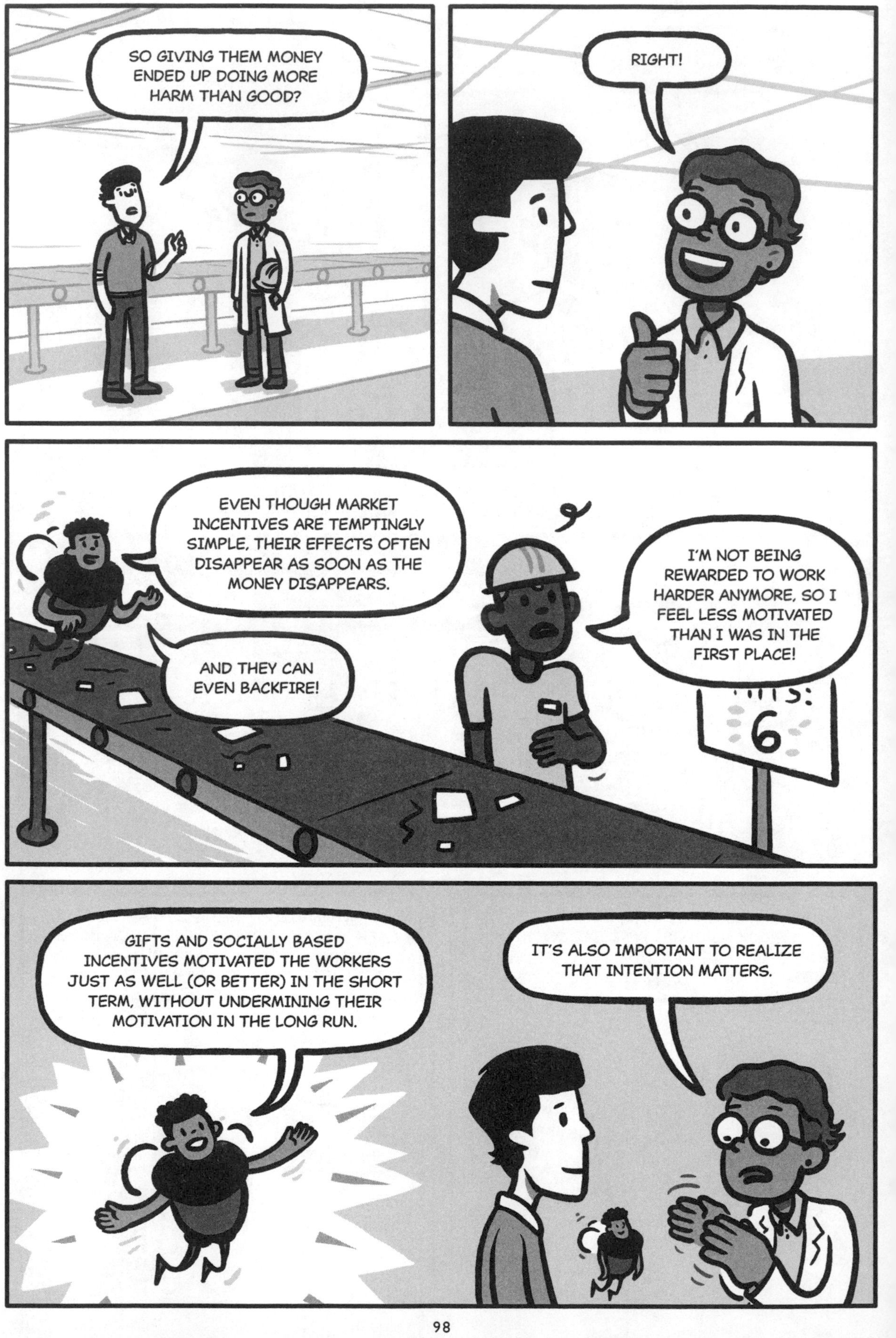
SO GIVING THEM MONEY ENDED UP DOING MORE HARM THAN GOOD?
RIGHT!
EVEN THOUGH MARKET INCENTIVES ARE TEMPTINGLY SIMPLE, THEIR EFFECTS OFTEN DISAPPEAR AS SOON AS THE MONEY DISAPPEARS.
AND THEY CAN EVEN BACKFIRE!
I'M NOT BEING REWARDED TO WORK HARDER ANYMORE, SO I FEEL LESS MOTIVATED THAN I WAS IN THE FIRST PLACE!
6
GIFTS AND SOCIALLY BASED INCENTIVES MOTIVATED THE WORKERS JUST AS WELL (OR BETTER) IN THE SHORT TERM, WITHOUT UNDERMINING THEIR MOTIVATION IN THE LONG RUN.
IT'S ALSO IMPORTANT TO REALIZE THAT INTENTION MATTERS.

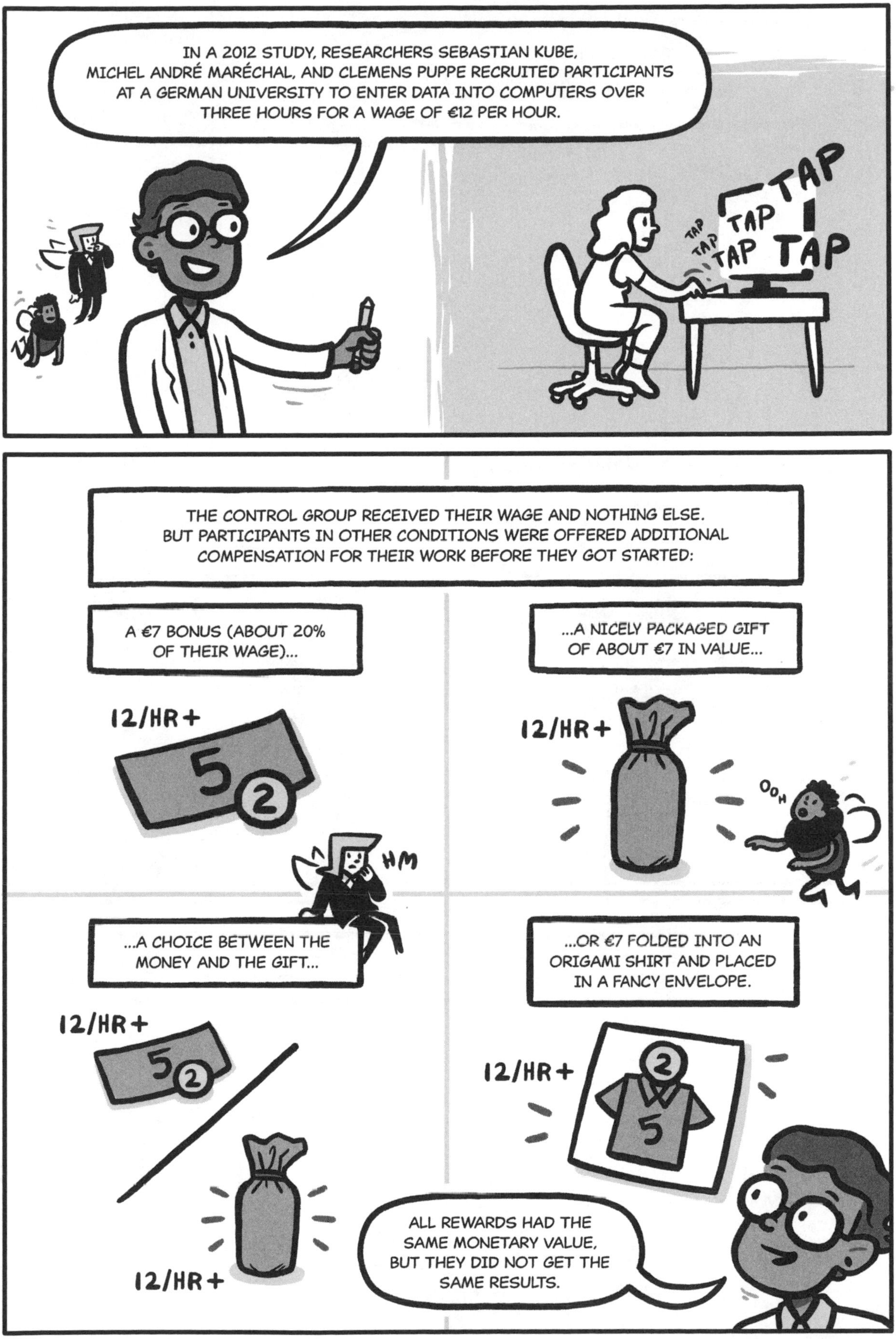
IN A 2012 STUDY, RESEARCHERS SEBASTIAN KUBE, MICHEL ANDRÉ MARÉCHAL, AND CLEMENS PUPPE RECRUITED PARTICIPANTS AT A GERMAN UNIVERSITY TO ENTER DATA INTO COMPUTERS OVER THREE HOURS FOR A WAGE OF €12 PER HOUR.
TAP TAP TAP TAP TAP TAP TAP
THE CONTROL GROUP RECEIVED THEIR WAGE AND NOTHING ELSE. BUT PARTICIPANTS IN OTHER CONDITIONS WERE OFFERED ADDITIONAL COMPENSATION FOR THEIR WORK BEFORE THEY GOT STARTED:
A €7 BONUS (ABOUT 20% OF THEIR WAGE)...
12/HR +
5
2
HM
...A NICELY PACKAGED GIFT OF ABOUT €7 IN VALUE...
12/HR +
OOH
...A CHOICE BETWEEN THE MONEY AND THE GIFT...
12/HR +
5
2
12/HR +
...OR €7 FOLDED INTO AN ORIGAMI SHIRT AND PLACED IN A FANCY ENVELOPE.
12/HR +
2
5
ALL REWARDS HAD THE SAME MONETARY VALUE, BUT THEY DID NOT GET THE SAME RESULTS.

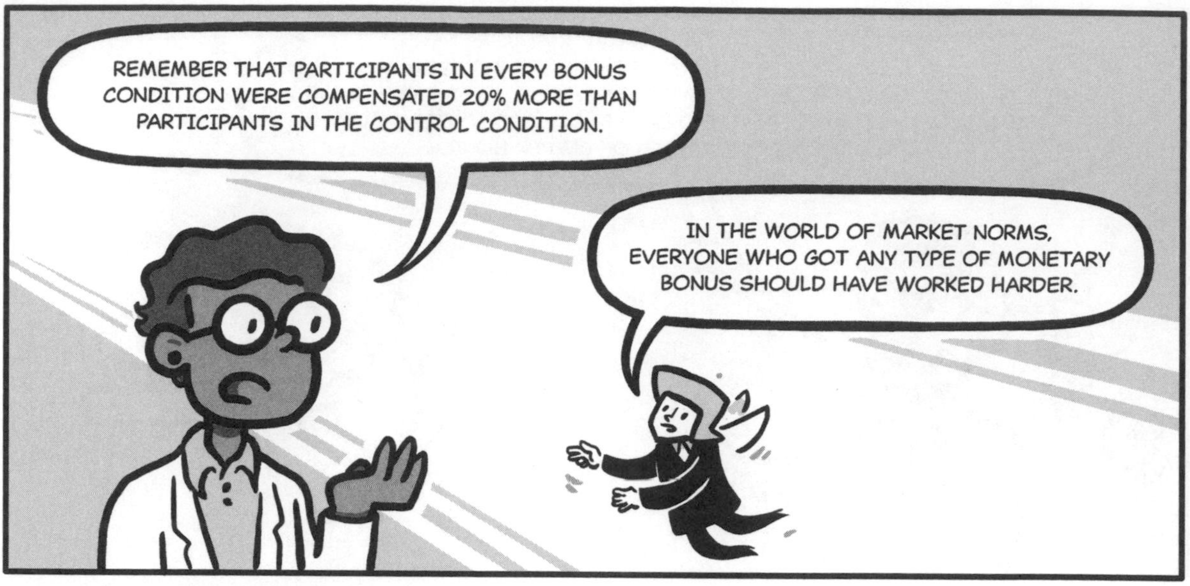
REMEMBER THAT PARTICIPANTS IN EVERY BONUS CONDITION WERE COMPENSATED 20% MORE THAN PARTICIPANTS IN THE CONTROL CONDITION.
IN THE WORLD OF MARKET NORMS, EVERYONE WHO GOT ANY TYPE OF MONETARY BONUS SHOULD HAVE WORKED HARDER.

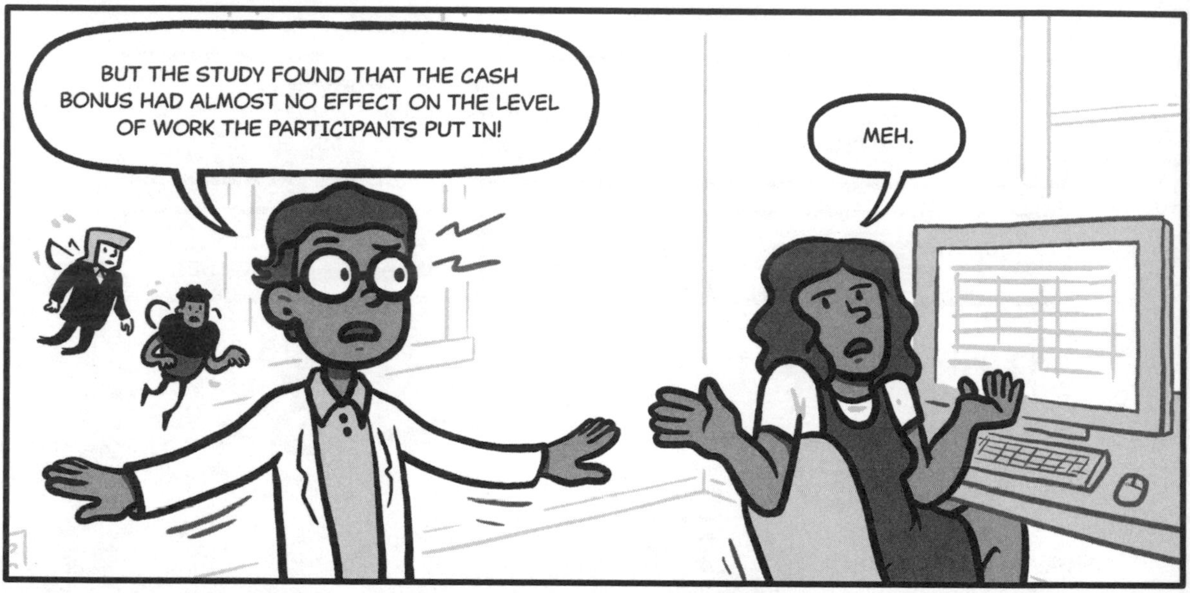
BUT THE STUDY FOUND THAT THE CASH BONUS HAD ALMOST NO EFFECT ON THE LEVEL OF WORK THE PARTICIPANTS PUT IN!
MEH.

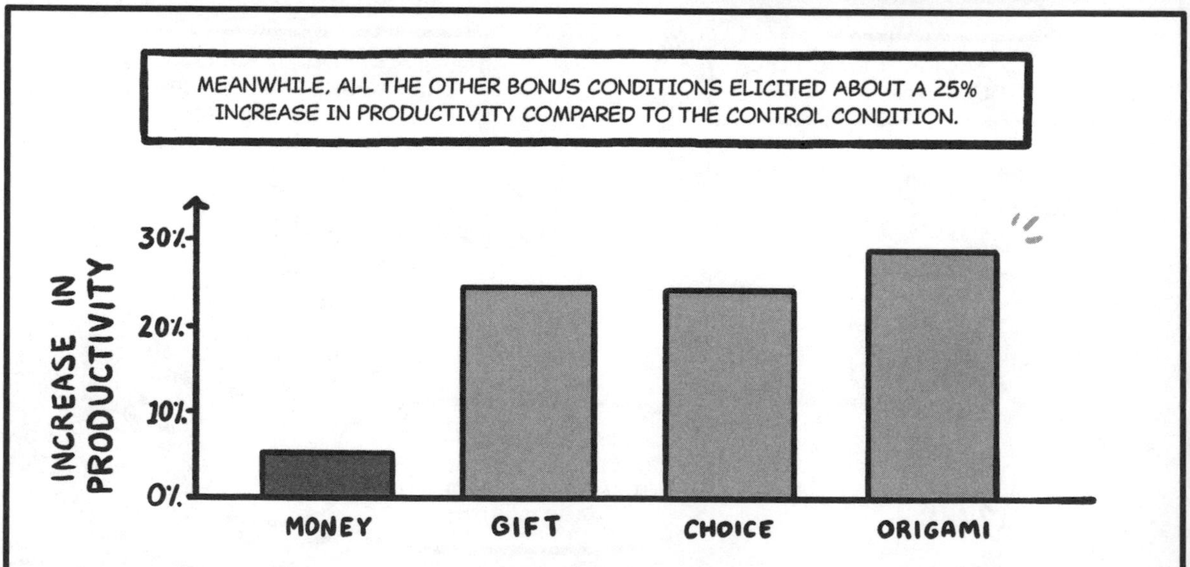
MEANWHILE, ALL THE OTHER BONUS CONDITIONS ELICITED ABOUT A 25% INCREASE IN PRODUCTIVITY COMPARED TO THE CONTROL CONDITION.
INCREASE IN PRODUCTIVITY
30%
20%
10%
0%
MONEY
GIFT
CHOICE
ORIGAMI

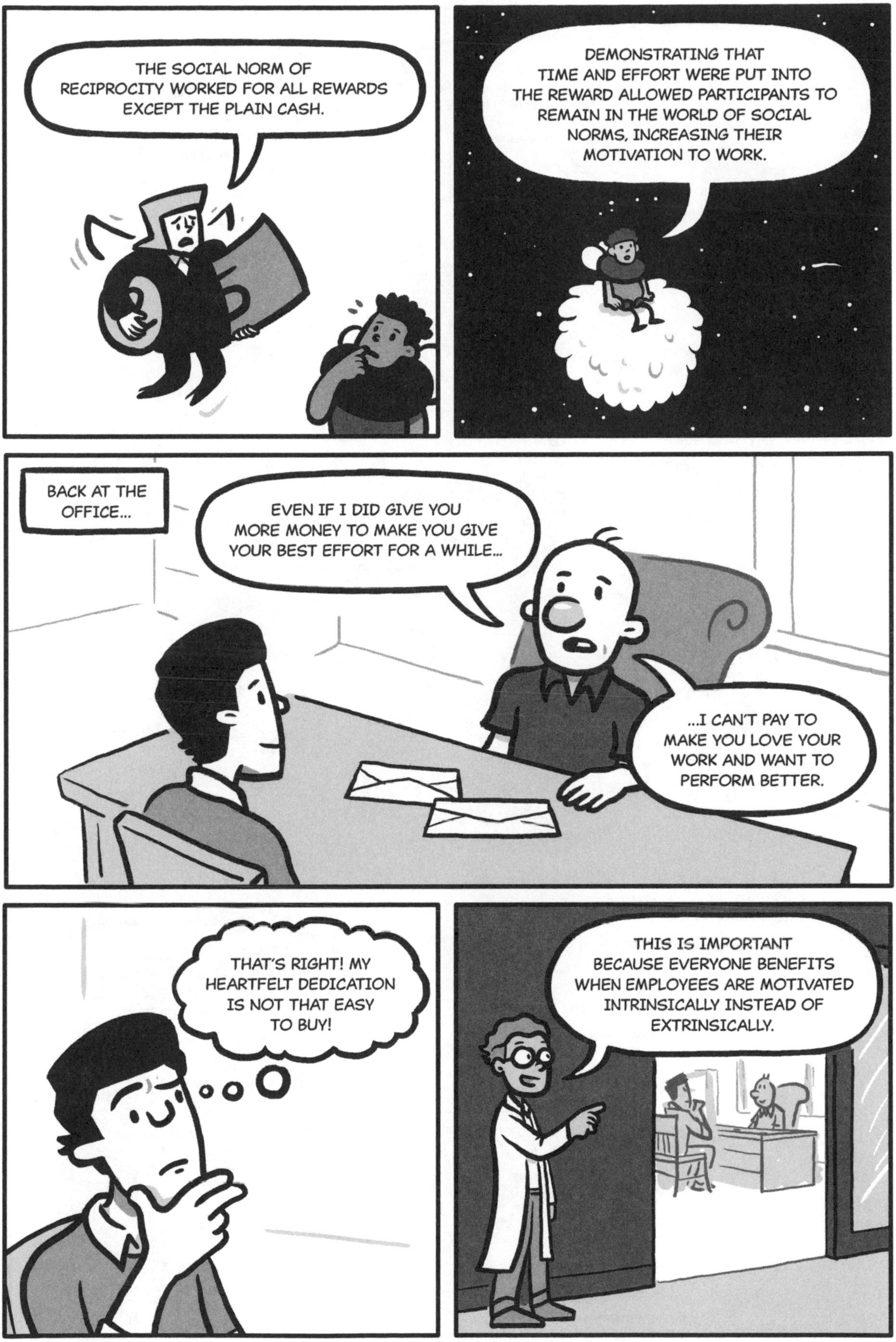
THE SOCIAL NORM OF RECIPROCITY WORKED FOR ALL REWARDS EXCEPT THE PLAIN CASH.
DEMONSTRATING THAT TIME AND EFFORT WERE PUT INTO THE REWARD ALLOWED PARTICIPANTS TO REMAIN IN THE WORLD OF SOCIAL NORMS, INCREASING THEIR MOTIVATION TO WORK.
BACK AT THE OFFICE...
EVEN IF I DID GIVE YOU MORE MONEY TO MAKE YOU GIVE YOUR BEST EFFORT FOR A WHILE...
...I CAN'T PAY TO MAKE YOU LOVE YOUR WORK AND WANT TO PERFORM BETTER.
THAT'S RIGHT! MY HEARTFELT DEDICATION IS NOT THAT EASY TO BUY!
THIS IS IMPORTANT BECAUSE EVERYONE BENEFITS WHEN EMPLOYEES ARE MOTIVATED INTRINSICALLY INSTEAD OF EXTRINSICALLY.

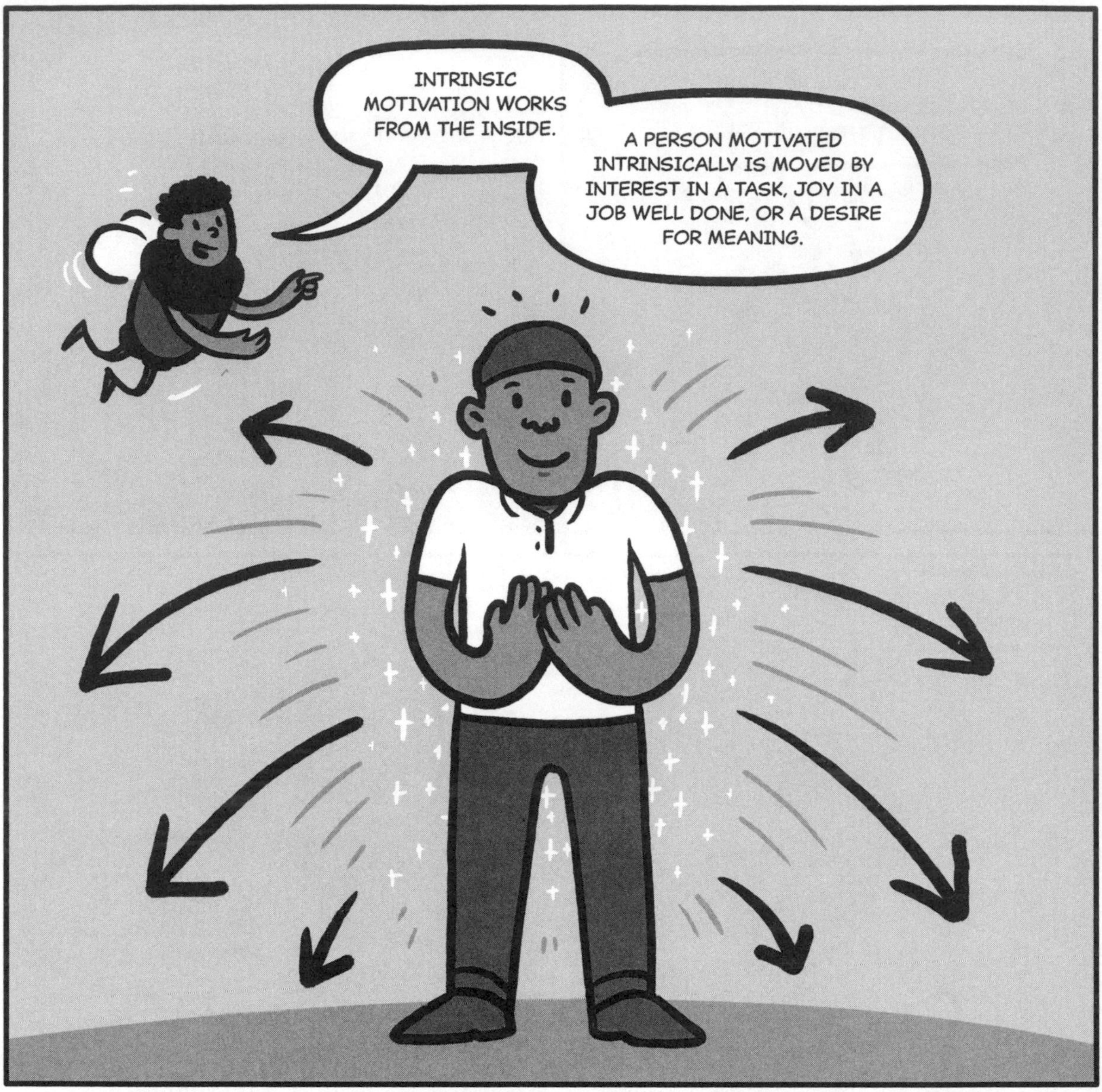
INTRINSIC MOTIVATION WORKS FROM THE INSIDE.
A PERSON MOTIVATED INTRINSICALLY IS MOVED BY INTEREST IN A TASK, JOY IN A JOB WELL DONE, OR A DESIRE FOR MEANING.

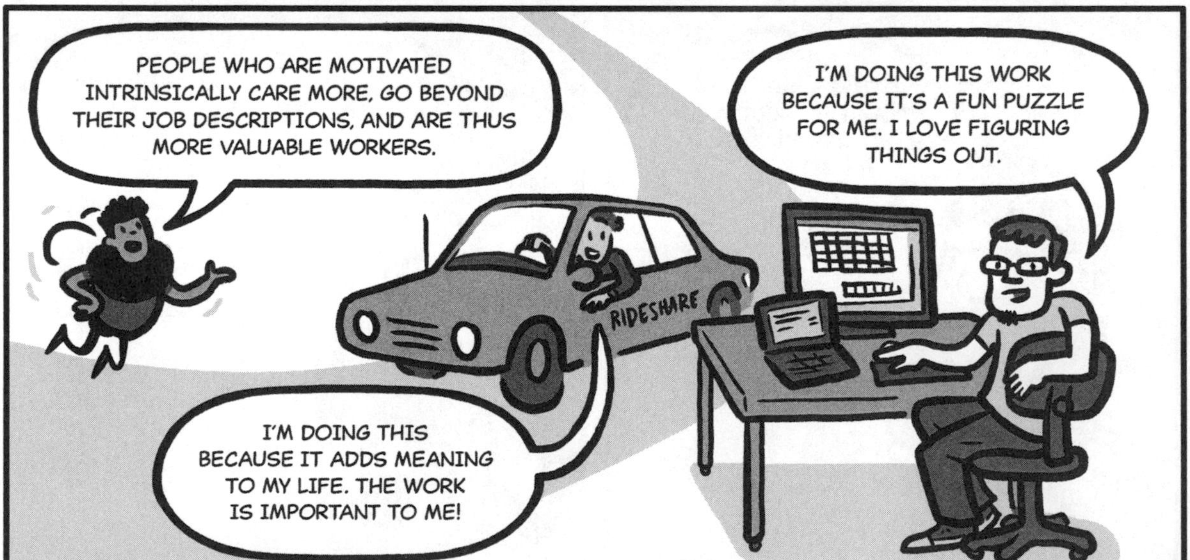
PEOPLE WHO ARE MOTIVATED INTRINSICALLY CARE MORE, GO BEYOND THEIR JOB DESCRIPTIONS, AND ARE THUS MORE VALUABLE WORKERS.
I'M DOING THIS WORK BECAUSE IT'S A FUN PUZZLE FOR ME. I LOVE FIGURING THINGS OUT.
RIDESHARE
I'M DOING THIS BECAUSE IT ADDS MEANING TO MY LIFE. THE WORK IS IMPORTANT TO ME!

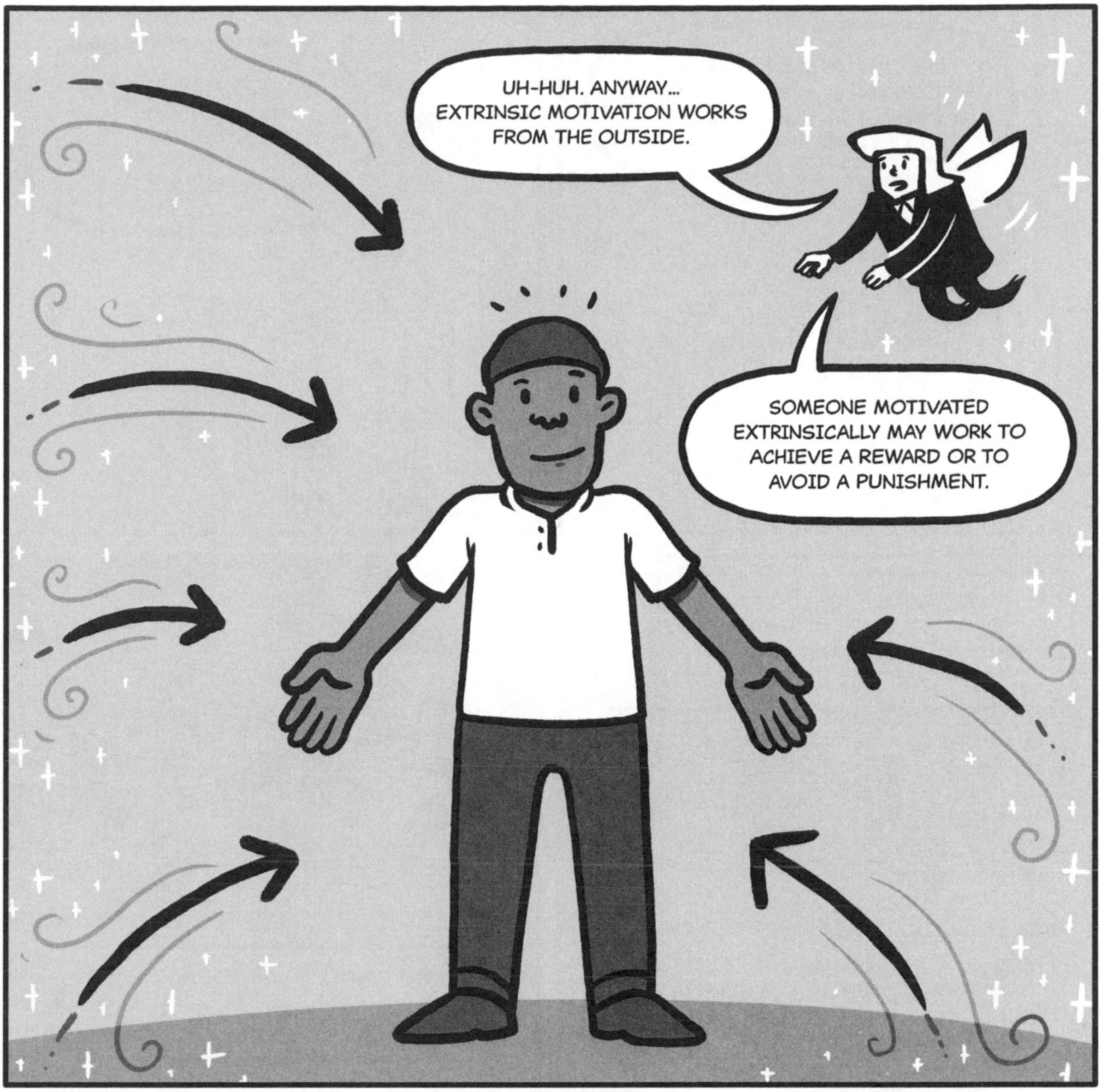
UH-HUH. ANYWAY... EXTRINSIC MOTIVATION WORKS FROM THE OUTSIDE.
SOMEONE MOTIVATED EXTRINSICALLY MAY WORK TO ACHIEVE A REWARD OR TO AVOID A PUNISHMENT.

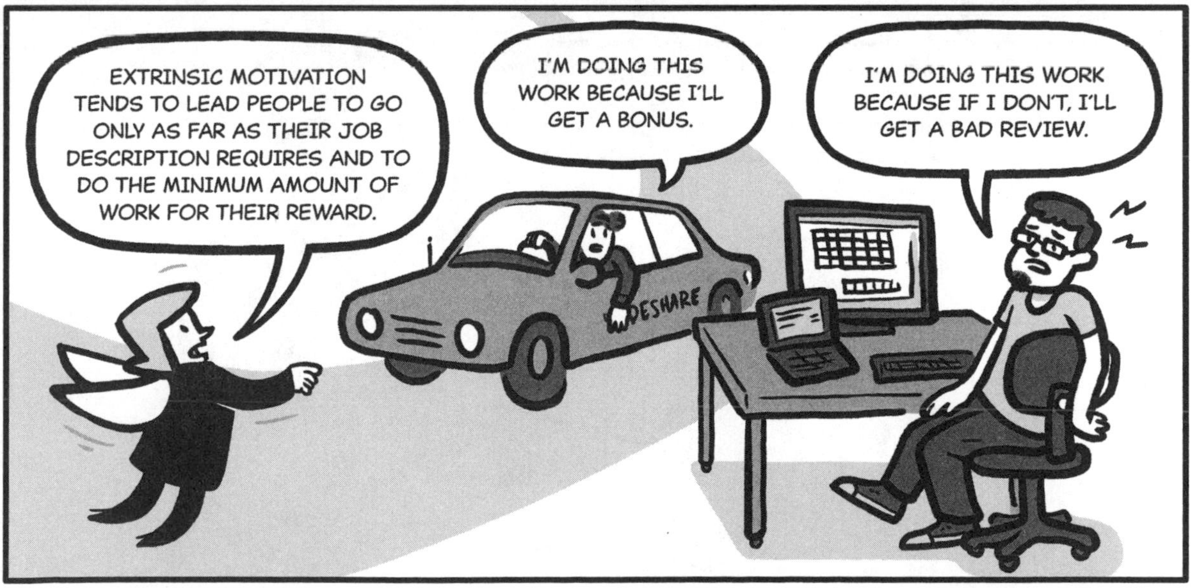
EXTRINSIC MOTIVATION TENDS TO LEAD PEOPLE TO GO ONLY AS FAR AS THEIR JOB DESCRIPTION REQUIRES AND TO DO THE MINIMUM AMOUNT OF WORK FOR THEIR REWARD.
I'M DOING THIS WORK BECAUSE I'LL GET A BONUS.
I'M DOING THIS WORK BECAUSE IF I DON'T, I'LL GET A BAD REVIEW.

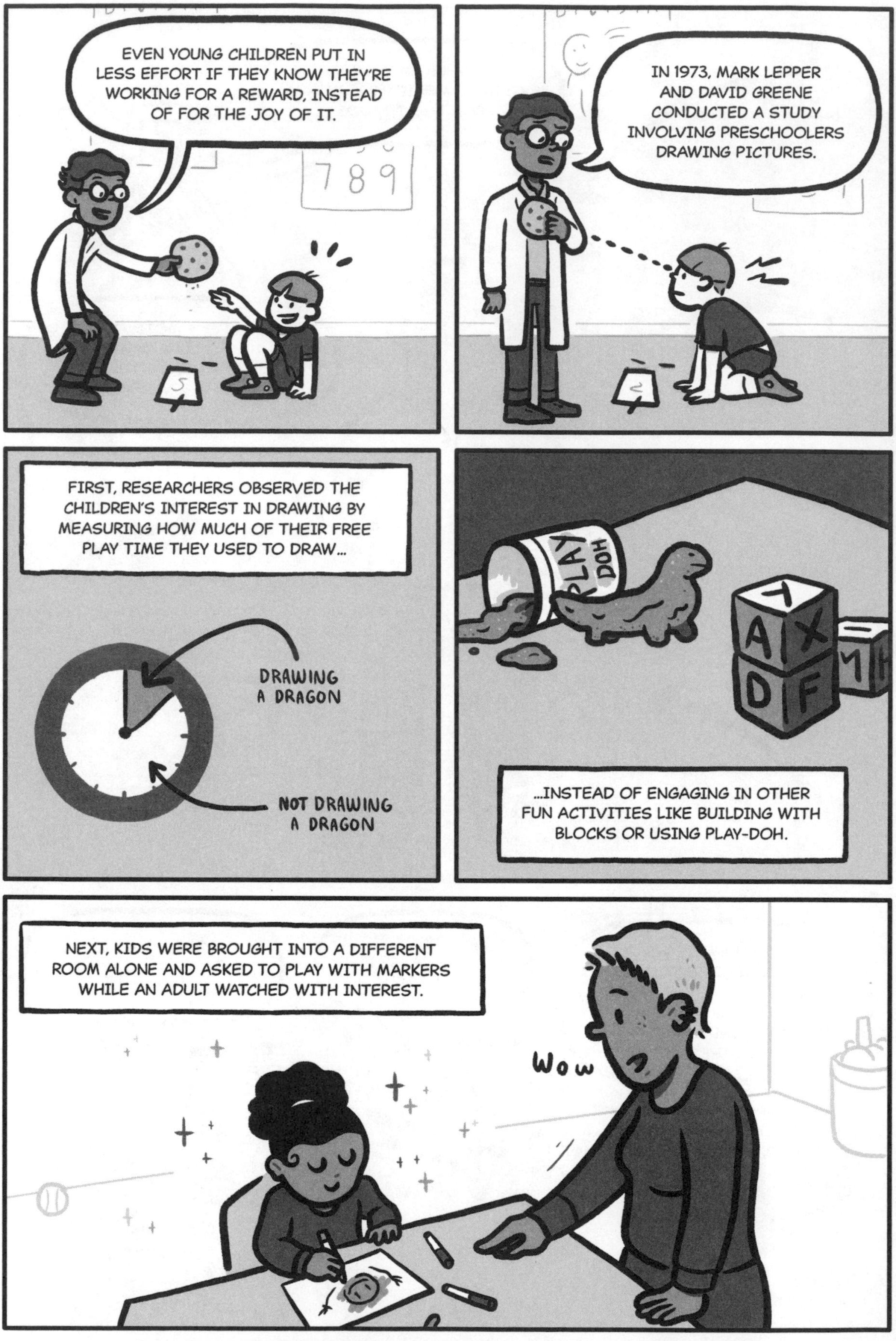

EVEN YOUNG CHILDREN PUT IN LESS EFFORT IF THEY KNOW THEY'RE WORKING FOR A REWARD, INSTEAD OF FOR THE JOY OF IT.
IN 1973, MARK LEPPER AND DAVID GREENE CONDUCTED A STUDY INVOLVING PRESCHOOLERS DRAWING PICTURES.
FIRST, RESEARCHERS OBSERVED THE CHILDREN'S INTEREST IN DRAWING BY MEASURING HOW MUCH OF THEIR FREE PLAY TIME THEY USED TO DRAW...
DRAWING A DRAGON
NOT DRAWING A DRAGON
PLAY DOH
...INSTEAD OF ENGAGING IN OTHER FUN ACTIVITIES LIKE BUILDING WITH BLOCKS OR USING PLAY-DOH.
NEXT, KIDS WERE BROUGHT INTO A DIFFERENT ROOM ALONE AND ASKED TO PLAY WITH MARKERS WHILE AN ADULT WATCHED WITH INTEREST.
Wow

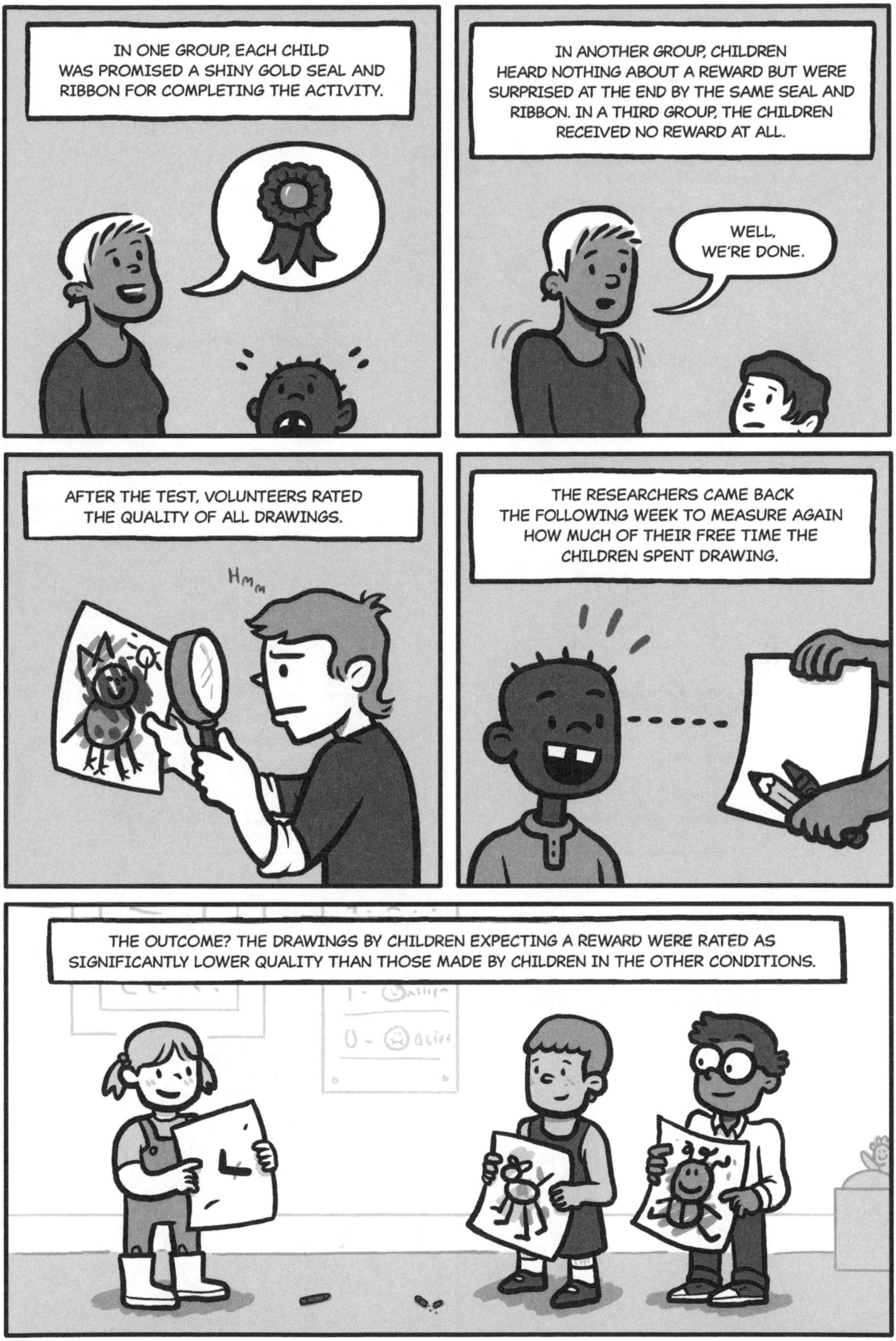
IN ONE GROUP, EACH CHILD WAS PROMISED A SHINY GOLD SEAL AND RIBBON FOR COMPLETING THE ACTIVITY.
IN ANOTHER GROUP, CHILDREN HEARD NOTHING ABOUT A REWARD BUT WERE SURPRISED AT THE END BY THE SAME SEAL AND RIBBON. IN A THIRD GROUP, THE CHILDREN RECEIVED NO REWARD AT ALL.
WELL, WE'RE DONE.
AFTER THE TEST, VOLUNTEERS RATED THE QUALITY OF ALL DRAWINGS.
Hmm
THE RESEARCHERS CAME BACK THE FOLLOWING WEEK TO MEASURE AGAIN HOW MUCH OF THEIR FREE TIME THE CHILDREN SPENT DRAWING.
THE OUTCOME? THE DRAWINGS BY CHILDREN EXPECTING A REWARD WERE RATED AS SIGNIFICANTLY LOWER QUALITY THAN THOSE MADE BY CHILDREN IN THE OTHER CONDITIONS.

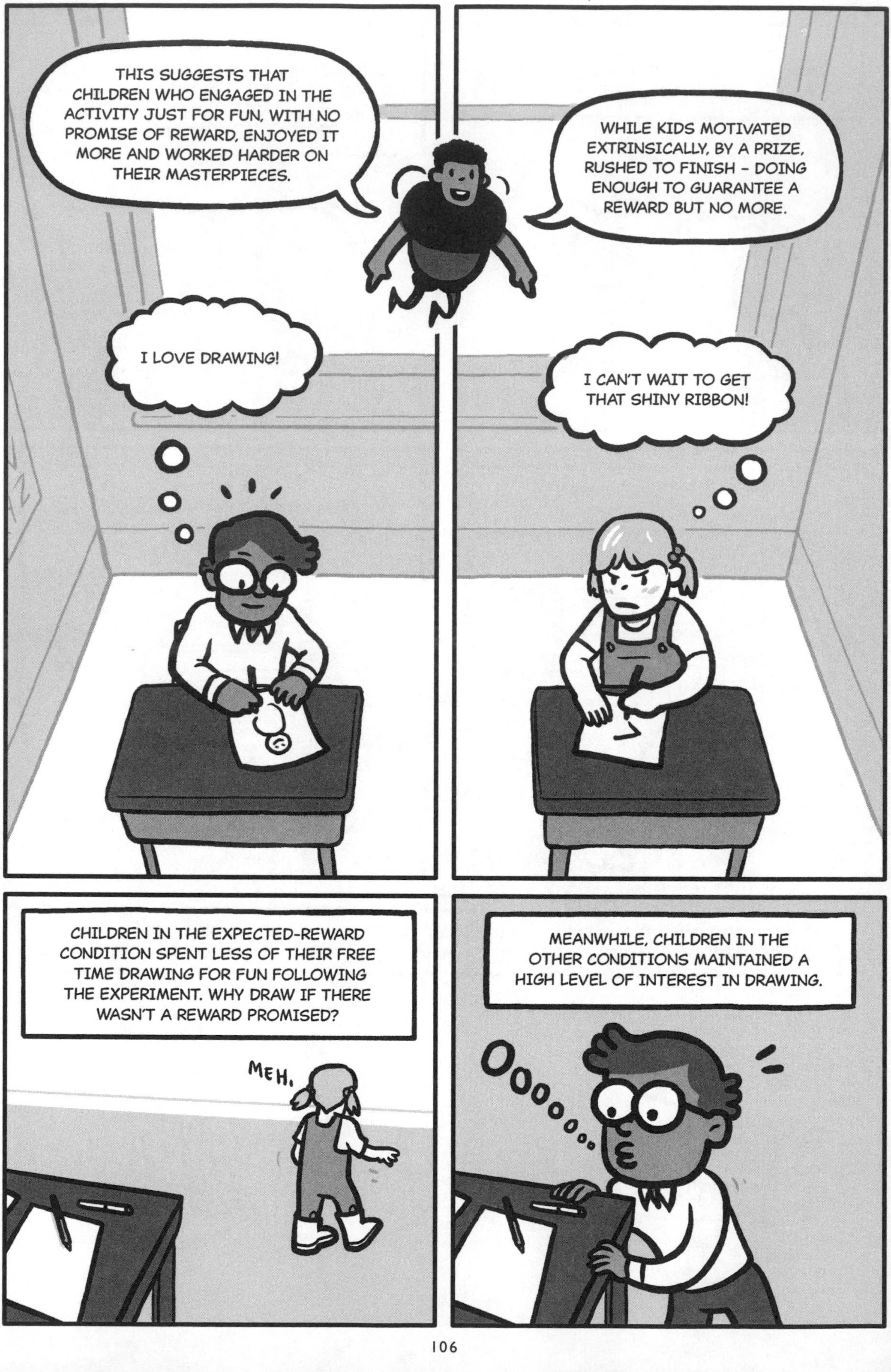
THIS SUGGESTS THAT CHILDREN WHO ENGAGED IN THE ACTIVITY JUST FOR FUN, WITH NO PROMISE OF REWARD, ENJOYED IT MORE AND WORKED HARDER ON THEIR MASTERPIECES.
WHILE KIDS MOTIVATED EXTRINSICALLY, BY A PRIZE, RUSHED TO FINISH – DOING ENOUGH TO GUARANTEE A REWARD BUT NO MORE.
I LOVE DRAWING!
I CAN'T WAIT TO GET THAT SHINY RIBBON!
CHILDREN IN THE EXPECTED-REWARD CONDITION SPENT LESS OF THEIR FREE TIME DRAWING FOR FUN FOLLOWING THE EXPERIMENT. WHY DRAW IF THERE WASN'T A REWARD PROMISED?
MEH.
MEANWHILE, CHILDREN IN THE OTHER CONDITIONS MAINTAINED A HIGH LEVEL OF INTEREST IN DRAWING.
OOOOooo

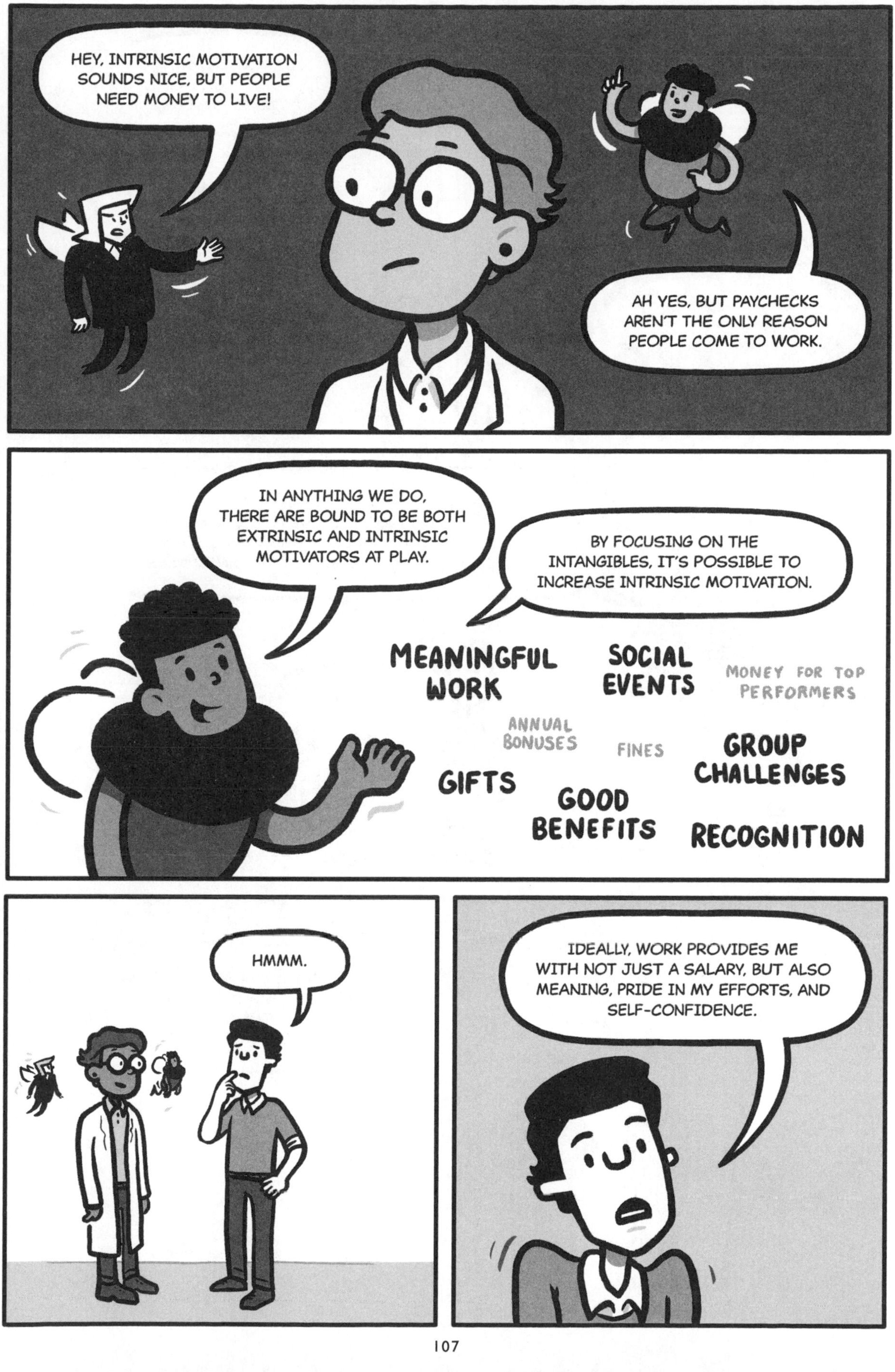
HEY, INTRINSIC MOTIVATION SOUNDS NICE, BUT PEOPLE NEED MONEY TO LIVE!
AH YES, BUT PAYCHECKS AREN'T THE ONLY REASON PEOPLE COME TO WORK.
IN ANYTHING WE DO, THERE ARE BOUND TO BE BOTH EXTRINSIC AND INTRINSIC MOTIVATORS AT PLAY.
BY FOCUSING ON THE INTANGIBLES, IT'S POSSIBLE TO INCREASE INTRINSIC MOTIVATION.
MEANINGFUL WORK
SOCIAL EVENTS
MONEY FOR TOP PERFORMERS
ANNUAL BONUSES
FINES
GROUP CHALLENGES
GIFTS
GOOD BENEFITS
RECOGNITION
HMMM.
IDEALLY, WORK PROVIDES ME WITH NOT JUST A SALARY, BUT ALSO MEANING, PRIDE IN MY EFFORTS, AND SELF-CONFIDENCE.

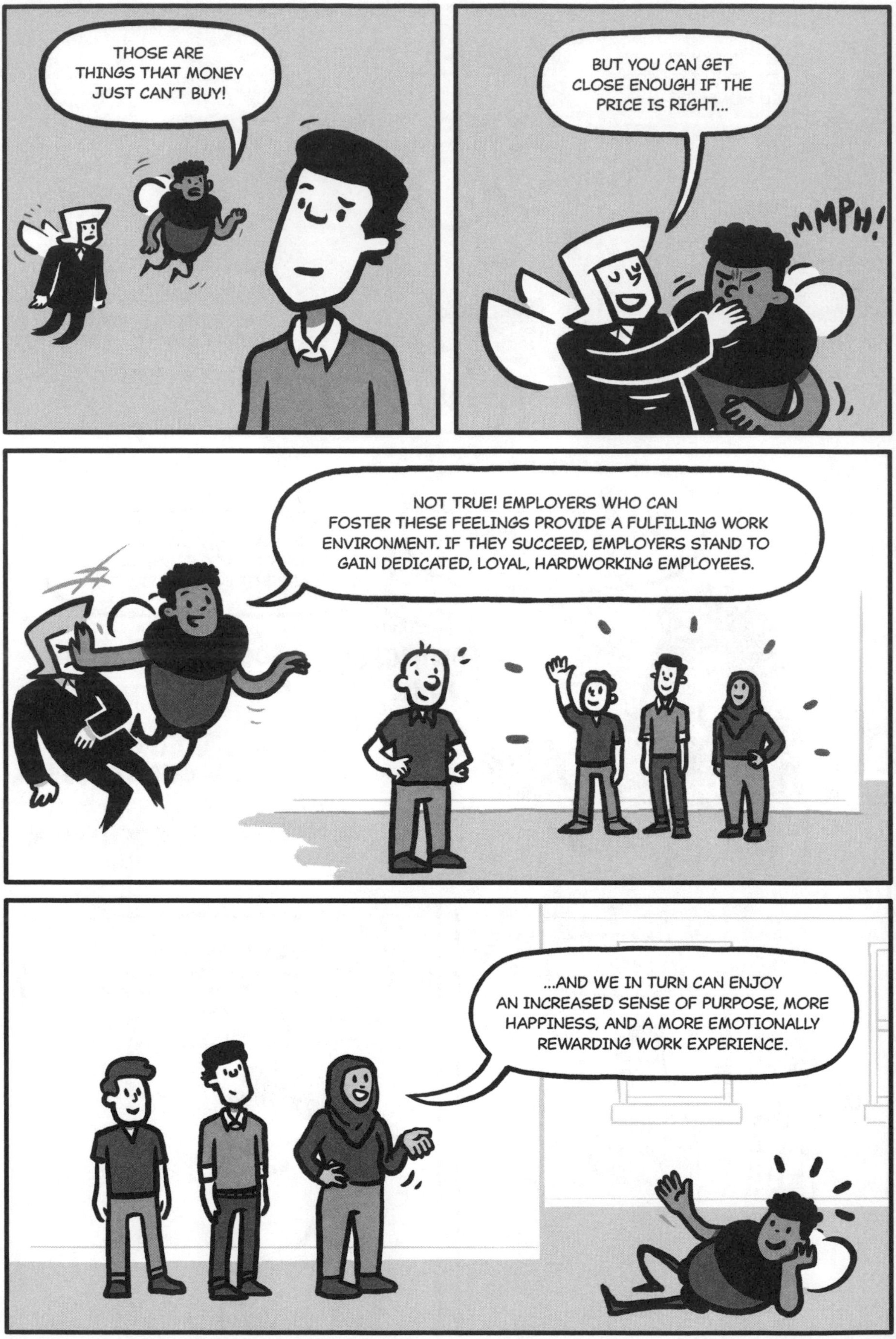
THOSE ARE THINGS THAT MONEY JUST CAN'T BUY!
BUT YOU CAN GET CLOSE ENOUGH IF THE PRICE IS RIGHT...
MMPH!
NOT TRUE! EMPLOYERS WHO CAN FOSTER THESE FEELINGS PROVIDE A FULFILLING WORK ENVIRONMENT. IF THEY SUCCEED, EMPLOYERS STAND TO GAIN DEDICATED, LOYAL, HARDWORKING EMPLOYEES.
...AND WE IN TURN CAN ENJOY AN INCREASED SENSE OF PURPOSE, MORE HAPPINESS, AND A MORE EMOTIONALLY REWARDING WORK EXPERIENCE.

IF THIS SOUNDS TOO WARM AND FUZZY FOR YOU, CONSIDER THIS NEXT STUDY, EXAMINING THE LONG-TERM PERFORMANCE OF CADETS AT WEST POINT, AN ELITE U.S. MILITARY ACADEMY.

RESEARCHERS EXAMINED WHY NEW CADETS WERE MOTIVATED TO ATTEND WEST POINT.

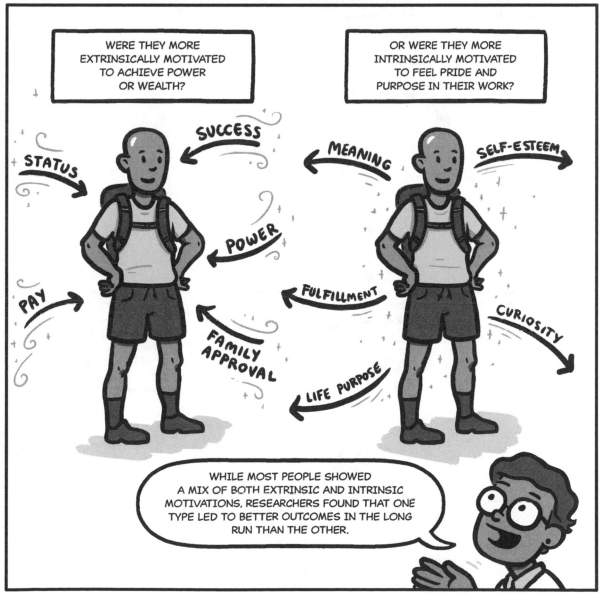

WERE THEY MORE EXTRINSICALLY MOTIVATED TO ACHIEVE POWER OR WEALTH?

OR WERE THEY MORE INTRINSICALLY MOTIVATED TO FEEL PRIDE AND PURPOSE IN THEIR WORK?

SUCCESS

STATUS

POWER

PAY

FAMILY APPROVAL

MEANING

SELF-ESTEEM

FULFILLMENT

CURIOSITY

LIFE PURPOSE

WHILE MOST PEOPLE SHOWED A MIX OF BOTH EXTRINSIC AND INTRINSIC MOTIVATIONS, RESEARCHERS FOUND THAT ONE TYPE LED TO BETTER OUTCOMES IN THE LONG RUN THAN THE OTHER.

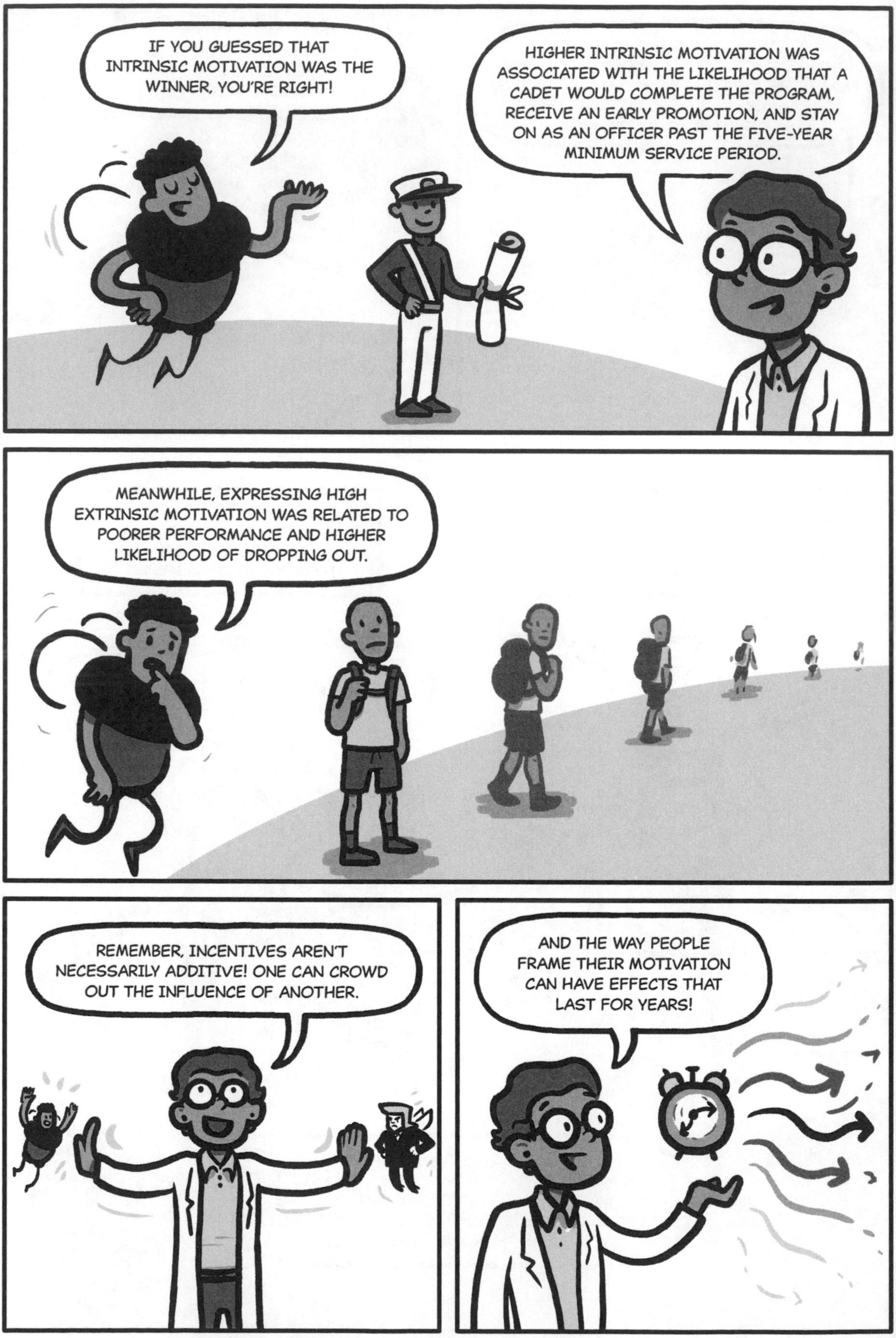
IF YOU GUESSED THAT INTRINSIC MOTIVATION WAS THE WINNER, YOU'RE RIGHT!
HIGHER INTRINSIC MOTIVATION WAS ASSOCIATED WITH THE LIKELIHOOD THAT A CADET WOULD COMPLETE THE PROGRAM, RECEIVE AN EARLY PROMOTION, AND STAY ON AS AN OFFICER PAST THE FIVE-YEAR MINIMUM SERVICE PERIOD.
MEANWHILE, EXPRESSING HIGH EXTRINSIC MOTIVATION WAS RELATED TO POORER PERFORMANCE AND HIGHER LIKELIHOOD OF DROPPING OUT.
REMEMBER, INCENTIVES AREN'T NECESSARILY ADDITIVE! ONE CAN CROWD OUT THE INFLUENCE OF ANOTHER.
AND THE WAY PEOPLE FRAME THEIR MOTIVATION CAN HAVE EFFECTS THAT LAST FOR YEARS!

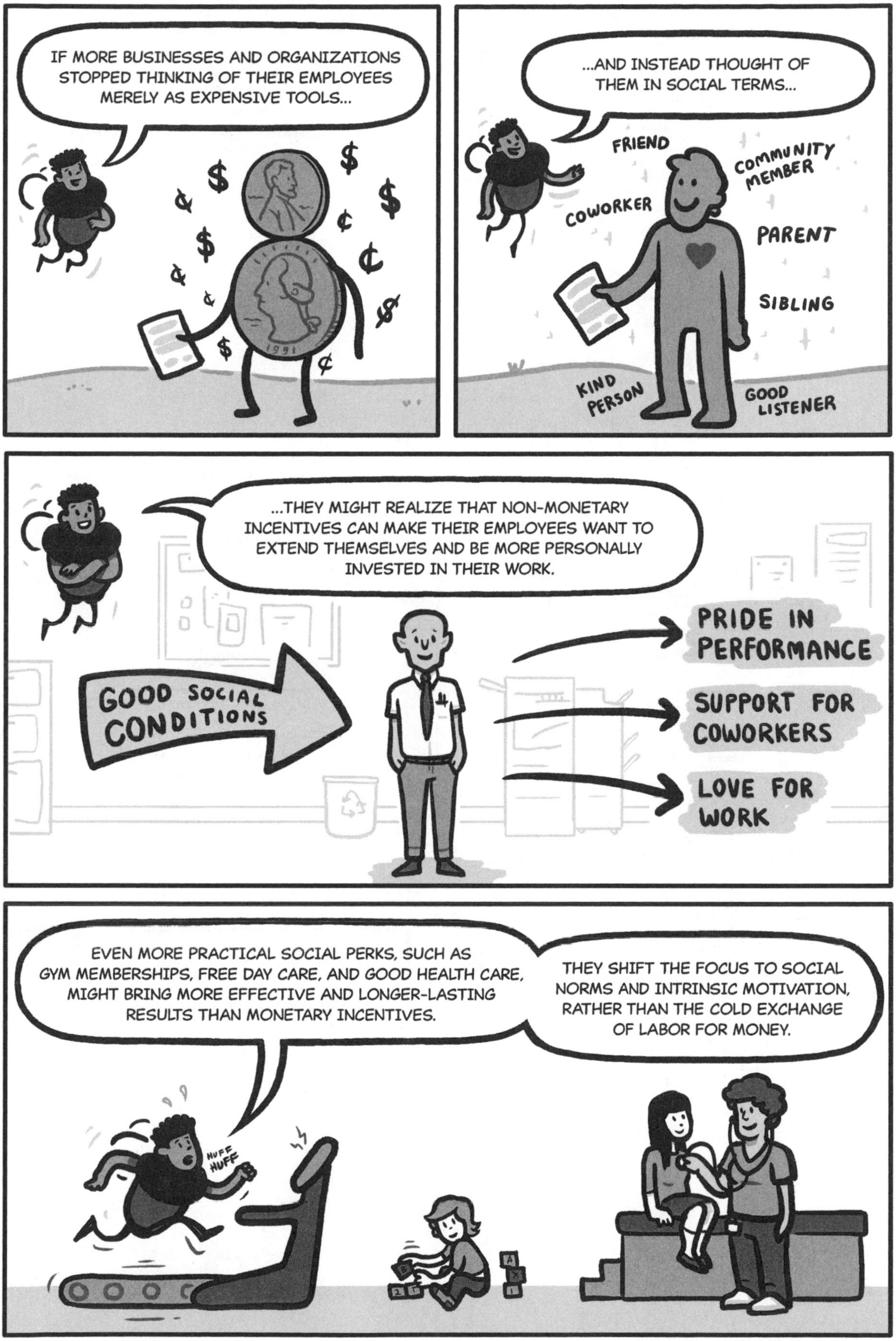
IF MORE BUSINESSES AND ORGANIZATIONS STOPPED THINKING OF THEIR EMPLOYEES MERELY AS EXPENSIVE TOOLS...
1991
...AND INSTEAD THOUGHT OF THEM IN SOCIAL TERMS...
FRIEND
COMMUNITY MEMBER
COWORKER
PARENT
SIBLING
KIND PERSON
GOOD LISTENER
...THEY MIGHT REALIZE THAT NON-MONETARY INCENTIVES CAN MAKE THEIR EMPLOYEES WANT TO EXTEND THEMSELVES AND BE MORE PERSONALLY INVESTED IN THEIR WORK.
GOOD SOCIAL CONDITIONS
PRIDE IN PERFORMANCE
SUPPORT FOR COWORKERS
LOVE FOR WORK
EVEN MORE PRACTICAL SOCIAL PERKS, SUCH AS GYM MEMBERSHIPS, FREE DAY CARE, AND GOOD HEALTH CARE, MIGHT BRING MORE EFFECTIVE AND LONGER-LASTING RESULTS THAN MONETARY INCENTIVES.
THEY SHIFT THE FOCUS TO SOCIAL NORMS AND INTRINSIC MOTIVATION, RATHER THAN THE COLD EXCHANGE OF LABOR FOR MONEY.
HUFF HUFF

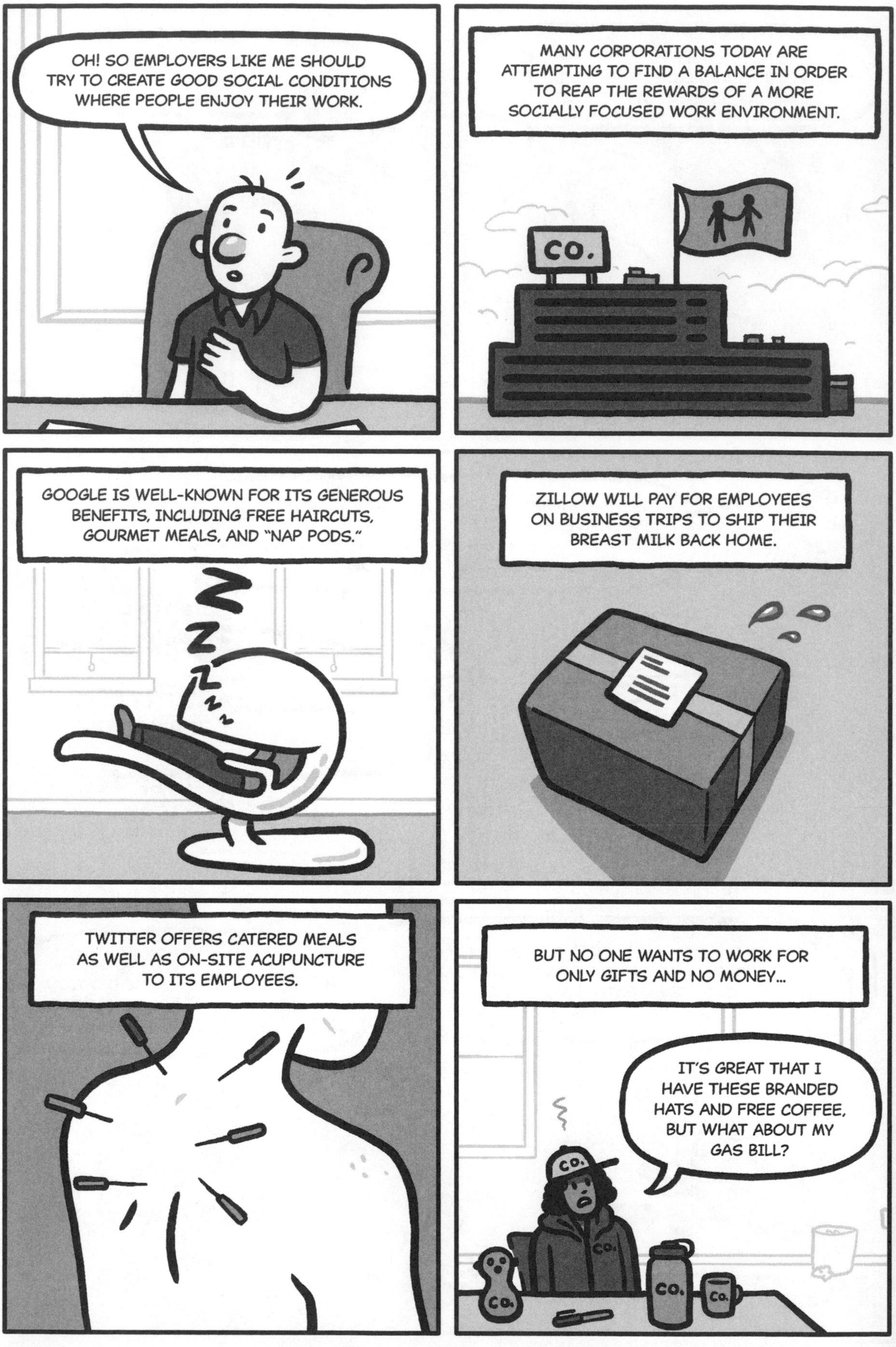
OH! SO EMPLOYERS LIKE ME SHOULD TRY TO CREATE GOOD SOCIAL CONDITIONS WHERE PEOPLE ENJOY THEIR WORK.
MANY CORPORATIONS TODAY ARE ATTEMPTING TO FIND A BALANCE IN ORDER TO REAP THE REWARDS OF A MORE SOCIALLY FOCUSED WORK ENVIRONMENT.
CO.
GOOGLE IS WELL-KNOWN FOR ITS GENEROUS BENEFITS, INCLUDING FREE HAIRCUTS, GOURMET MEALS, AND "NAP PODS."
Z
Z
ZILLOW WILL PAY FOR EMPLOYEES ON BUSINESS TRIPS TO SHIP THEIR BREAST MILK BACK HOME.
TWITTER OFFERS CATERED MEALS AS WELL AS ON-SITE ACUPUNCTURE TO ITS EMPLOYEES.
BUT NO ONE WANTS TO WORK FOR ONLY GIFTS AND NO MONEY...
IT'S GREAT THAT I HAVE THESE BRANDED HATS AND FREE COFFEE, BUT WHAT ABOUT MY GAS BILL?
CO.
CO.
CO.
CO.
CO.

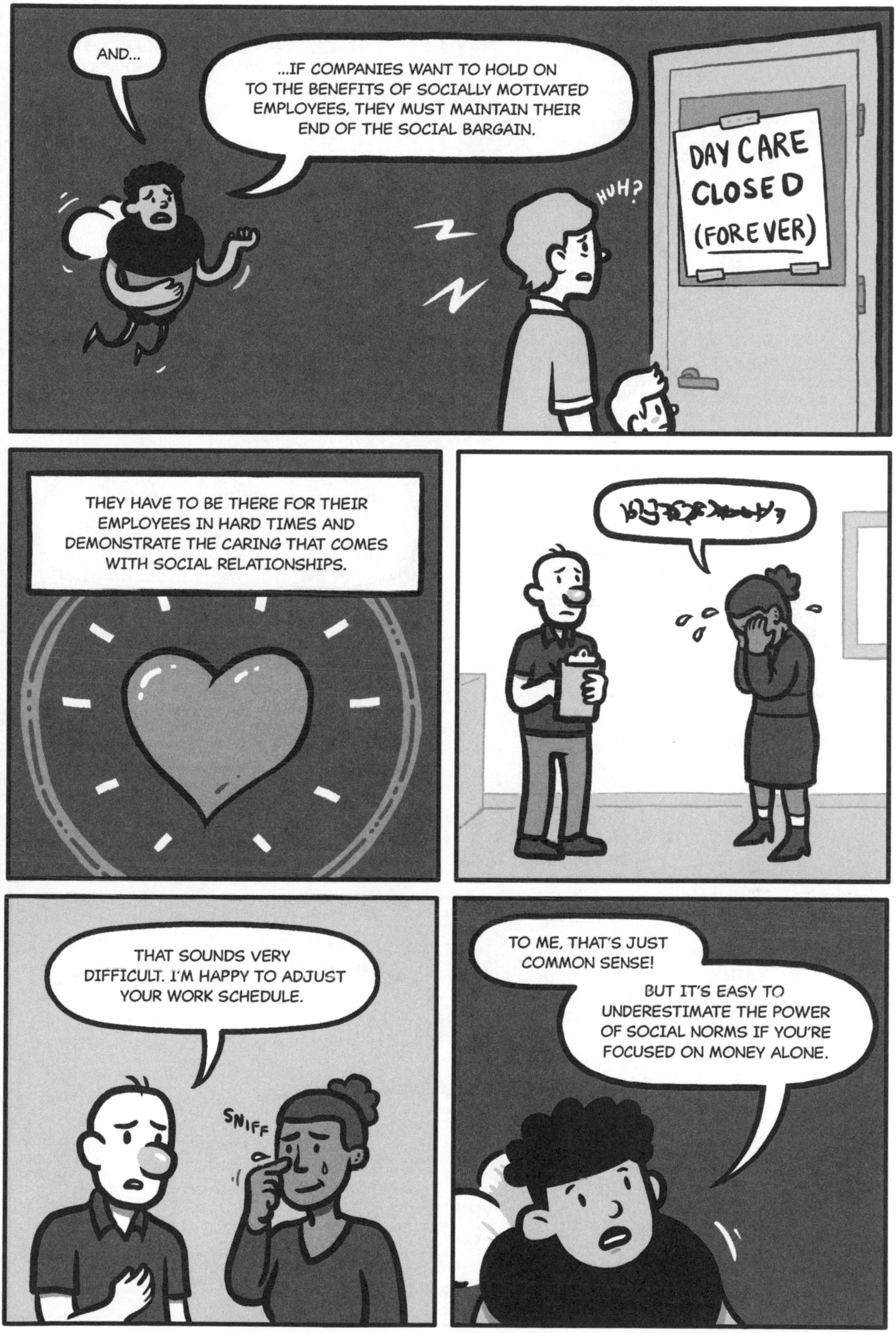
AND...
...IF COMPANIES WANT TO HOLD ON TO THE BENEFITS OF SOCIALLY MOTIVATED EMPLOYEES, THEY MUST MAINTAIN THEIR END OF THE SOCIAL BARGAIN.
HUH?
DAY CARE CLOSED (FOREVER)
THEY HAVE TO BE THERE FOR THEIR EMPLOYEES IN HARD TIMES AND DEMONSTRATE THE CARING THAT COMES WITH SOCIAL RELATIONSHIPS.
THAT SOUNDS VERY DIFFICULT. I'M HAPPY TO ADJUST YOUR WORK SCHEDULE.
SNIFF
TO ME, THAT'S JUST COMMON SENSE!
BUT IT'S EASY TO UNDERESTIMATE THE POWER OF SOCIAL NORMS IF YOU'RE FOCUSED ON MONEY ALONE.

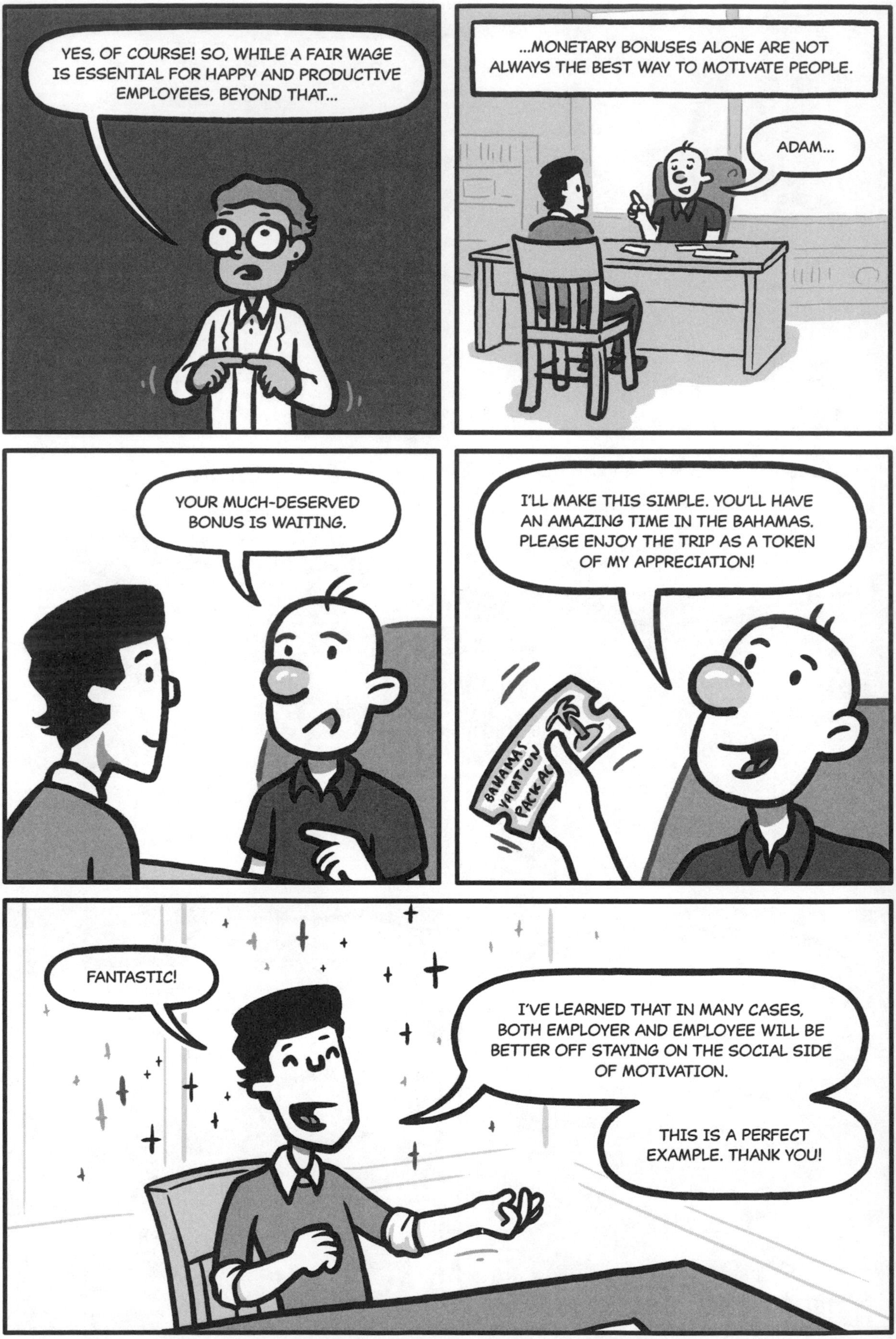
YES, OF COURSE! SO, WHILE A FAIR WAGE IS ESSENTIAL FOR HAPPY AND PRODUCTIVE EMPLOYEES, BEYOND THAT...
...MONETARY BONUSES ALONE ARE NOT ALWAYS THE BEST WAY TO MOTIVATE PEOPLE.
ADAM...
YOUR MUCH-DESERVED BONUS IS WAITING.
I'LL MAKE THIS SIMPLE. YOU'LL HAVE AN AMAZING TIME IN THE BAHAMAS. PLEASE ENJOY THE TRIP AS A TOKEN OF MY APPRECIATION!
BAHAMAS VACATION PACKAG
FANTASTIC!
I'VE LEARNED THAT IN MANY CASES, BOTH EMPLOYER AND EMPLOYEE WILL BE BETTER OFF STAYING ON THE SOCIAL SIDE OF MOTIVATION.
THIS IS A PERFECT EXAMPLE. THANK YOU!

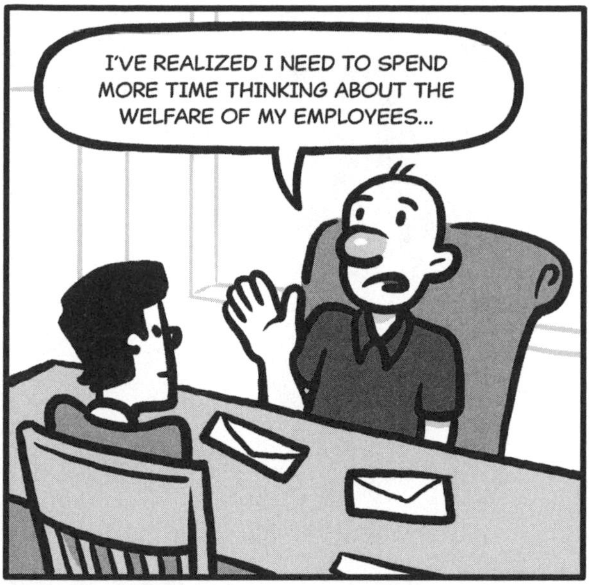
I'VE REALIZED I NEED TO SPEND MORE TIME THINKING ABOUT THE WELFARE OF MY EMPLOYEES...

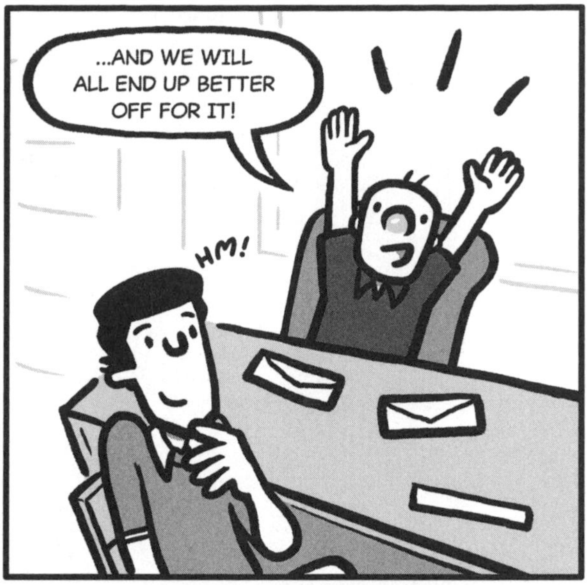
...AND WE WILL ALL END UP BETTER OFF FOR IT!
HM!

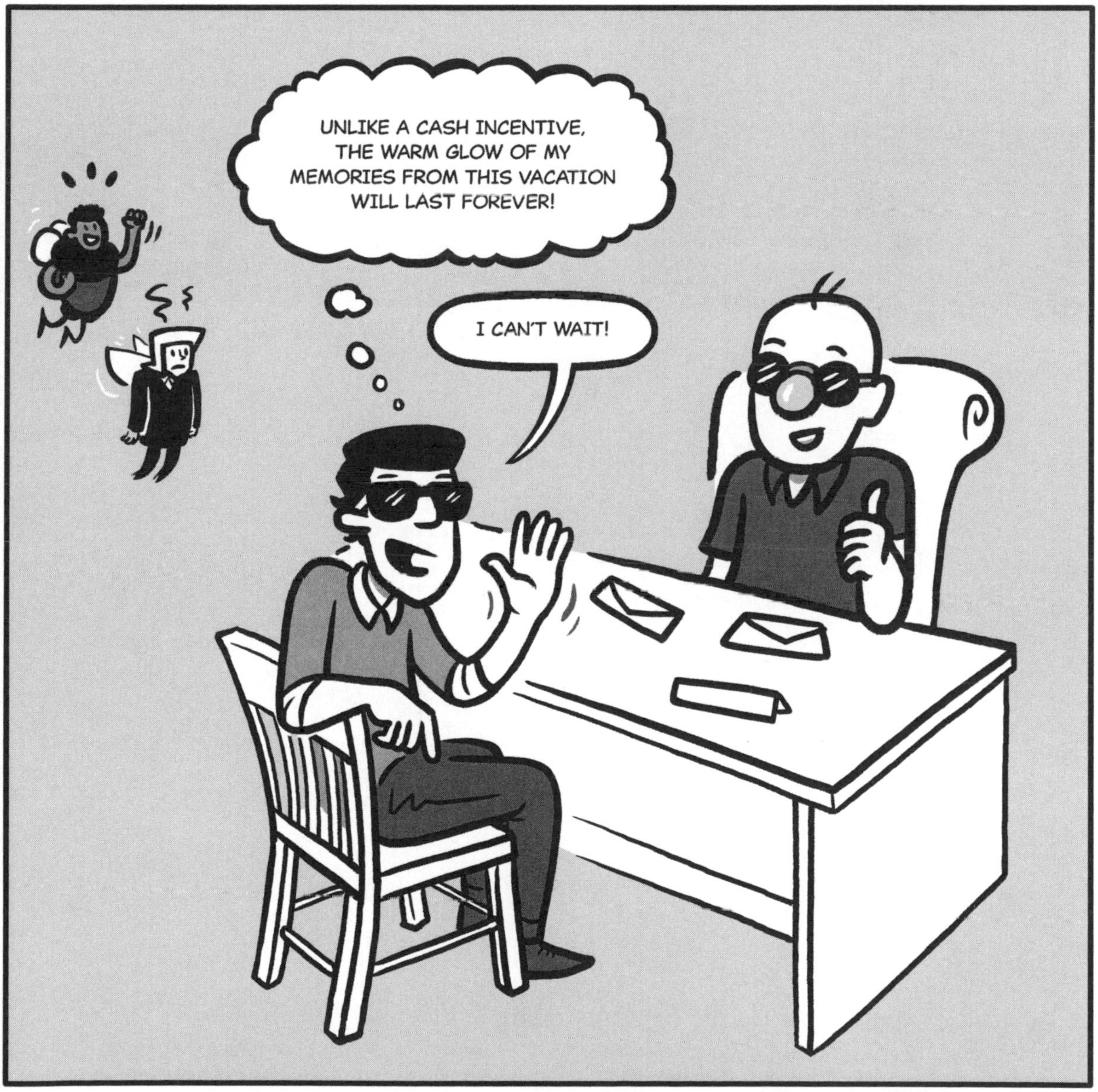
UNLIKE A CASH INCENTIVE, THE WARM GLOW OF MY MEMORIES FROM THIS VACATION WILL LAST FOREVER!
I CAN'T WAIT!

CHAPTER SIX

GOING TO THE MARKET AND BACK AGAIN

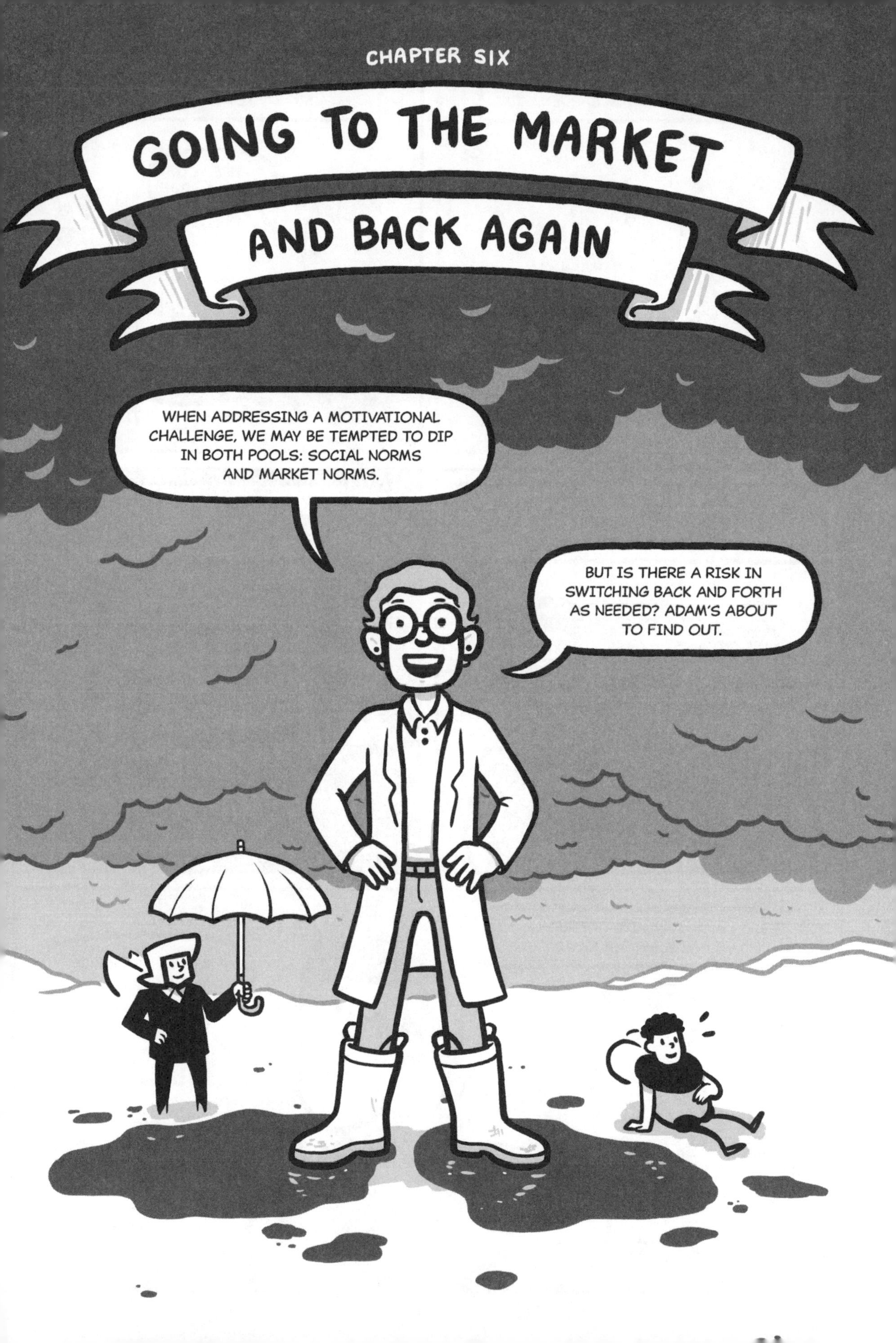
WHEN ADDRESSING A MOTIVATIONAL CHALLENGE, WE MAY BE TEMPTED TO DIP IN BOTH POOLS: SOCIAL NORMS AND MARKET NORMS.
BUT IS THERE A RISK IN SWITCHING BACK AND FORTH AS NEEDED? ADAM'S ABOUT TO FIND OUT.

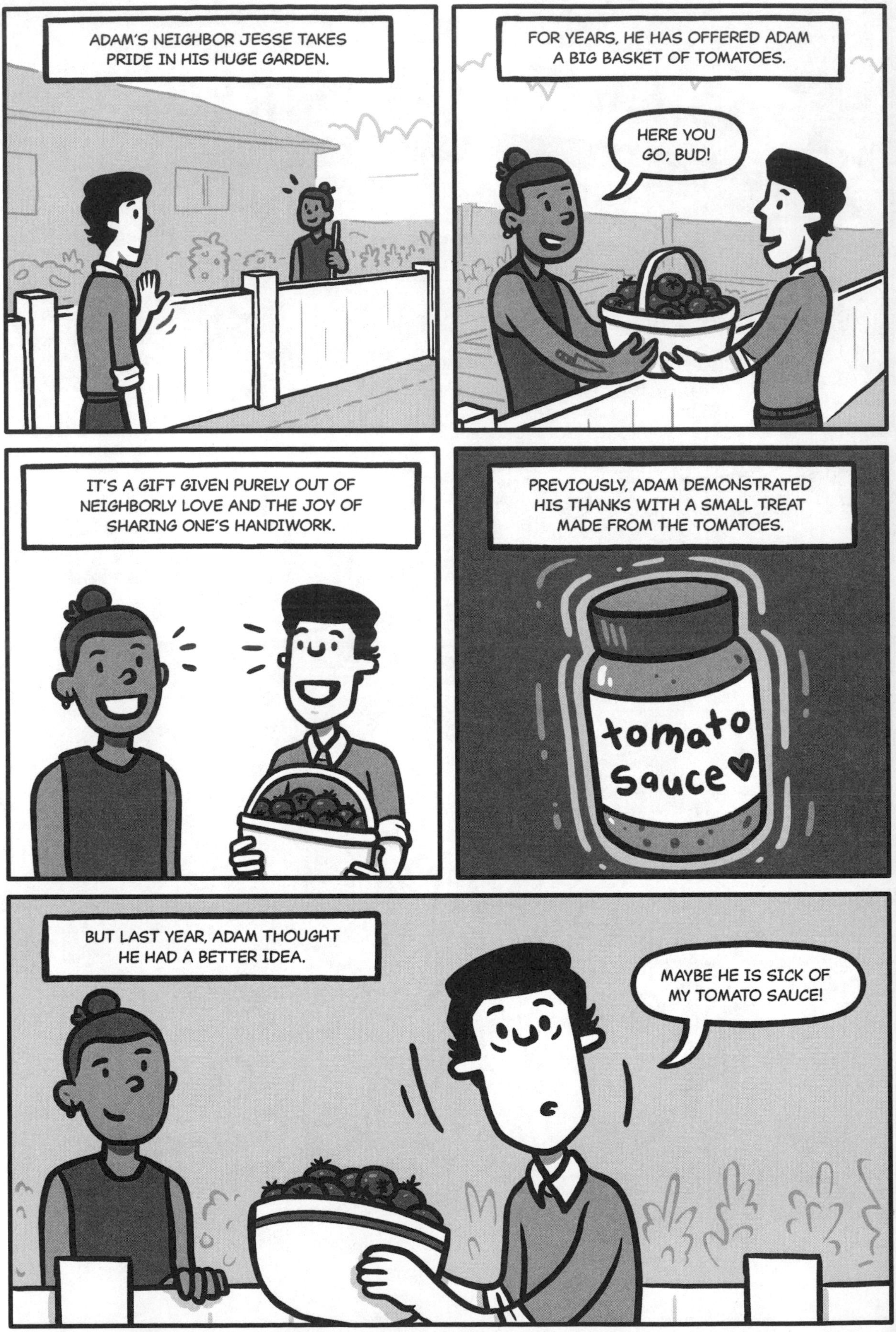
ADAM'S NEIGHBOR JESSE TAKES PRIDE IN HIS HUGE GARDEN.
FOR YEARS, HE HAS OFFERED ADAM A BIG BASKET OF TOMATOES.
HERE YOU GO, BUD!
IT'S A GIFT GIVEN PURELY OUT OF NEIGHBORLY LOVE AND THE JOY OF SHARING ONE'S HANDIWORK.
PREVIOUSLY, ADAM DEMONSTRATED HIS THANKS WITH A SMALL TREAT MADE FROM THE TOMATOES.
tomato Sauce
BUT LAST YEAR, ADAM THOUGHT HE HAD A BETTER IDEA.
MAYBE HE IS SICK OF MY TOMATO SAUCE!

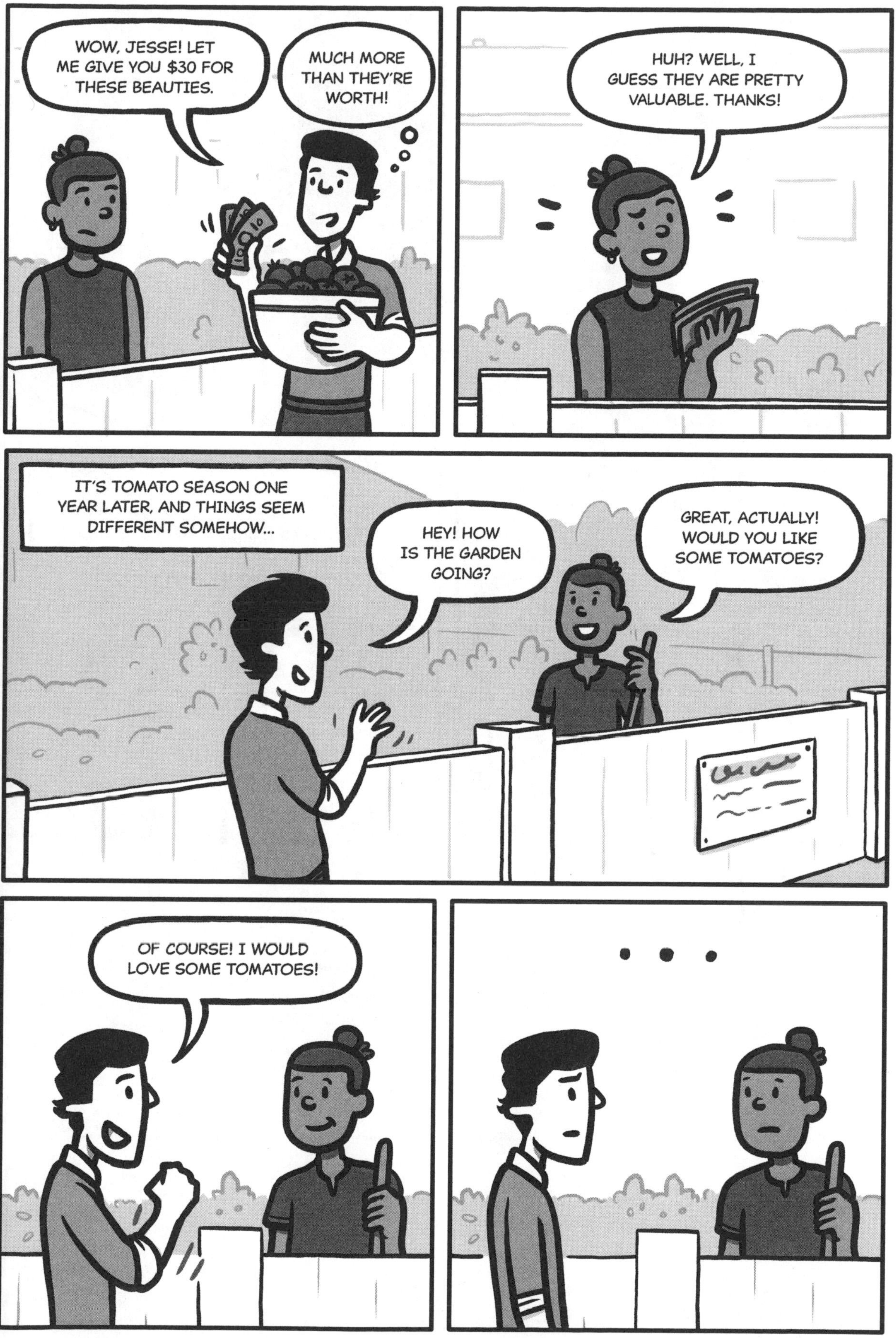
WOW, JESSE! LET ME GIVE YOU $30 FOR THESE BEAUTIES.
MUCH MORE THAN THEY'RE WORTH!
HUH? WELL, I GUESS THEY ARE PRETTY VALUABLE. THANKS!
IT'S TOMATO SEASON ONE YEAR LATER, AND THINGS SEEM DIFFERENT SOMEHOW...
HEY! HOW IS THE GARDEN GOING?
GREAT, ACTUALLY! WOULD YOU LIKE SOME TOMATOES?
OF COURSE! I WOULD LOVE SOME TOMATOES!
• • •

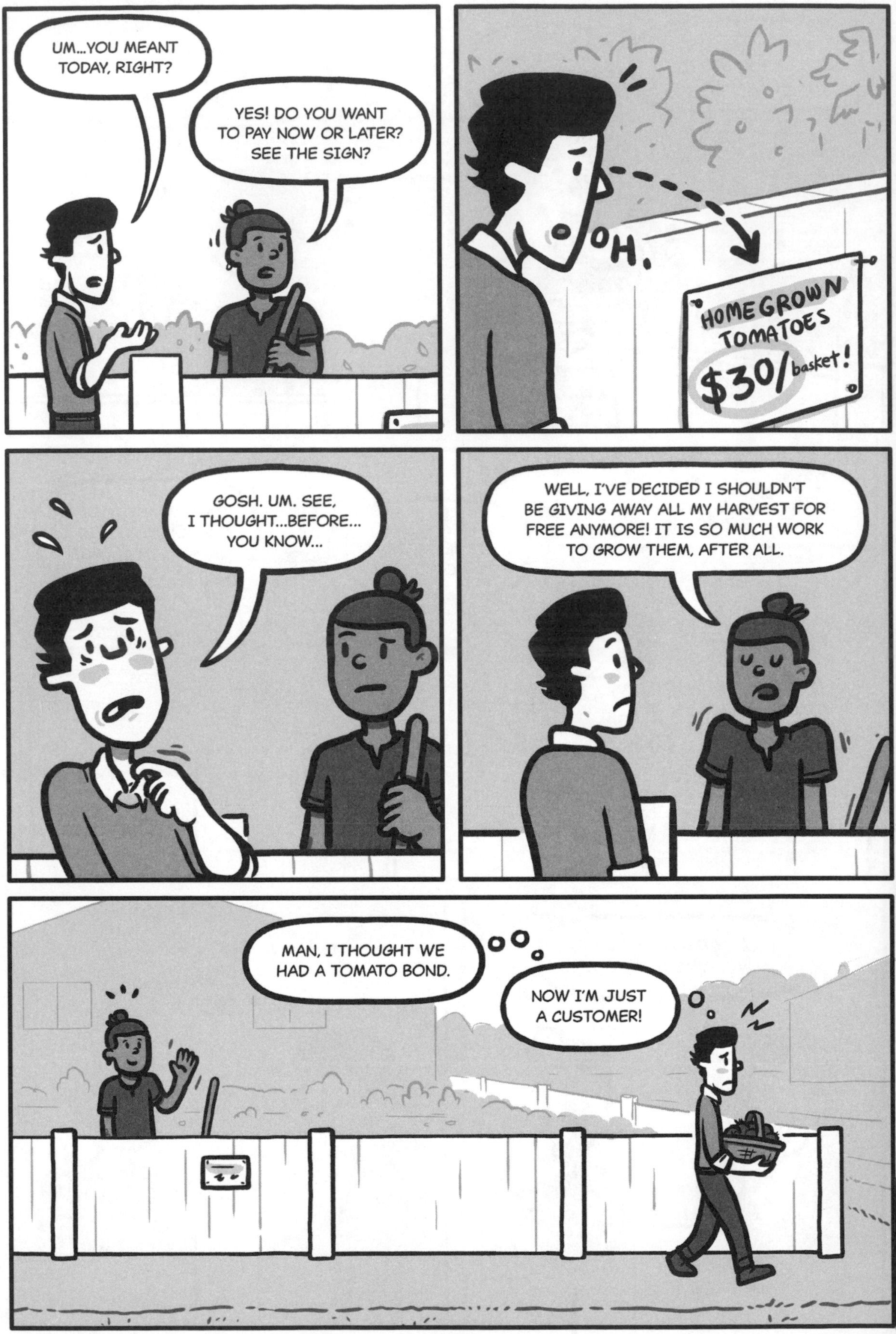
UM...YOU MEANT TODAY, RIGHT?
YES! DO YOU WANT TO PAY NOW OR LATER? SEE THE SIGN?
OH.
HOMEGROWN TOMATOES $30/basket!
GOSH. UM. SEE, I THOUGHT...BEFORE... YOU KNOW...
WELL, I'VE DECIDED I SHOULDN'T BE GIVING AWAY ALL MY HARVEST FOR FREE ANYMORE! IT IS SO MUCH WORK TO GROW THEM, AFTER ALL.
MAN, I THOUGHT WE HAD A TOMATO BOND.
NOW I'M JUST A CUSTOMER!

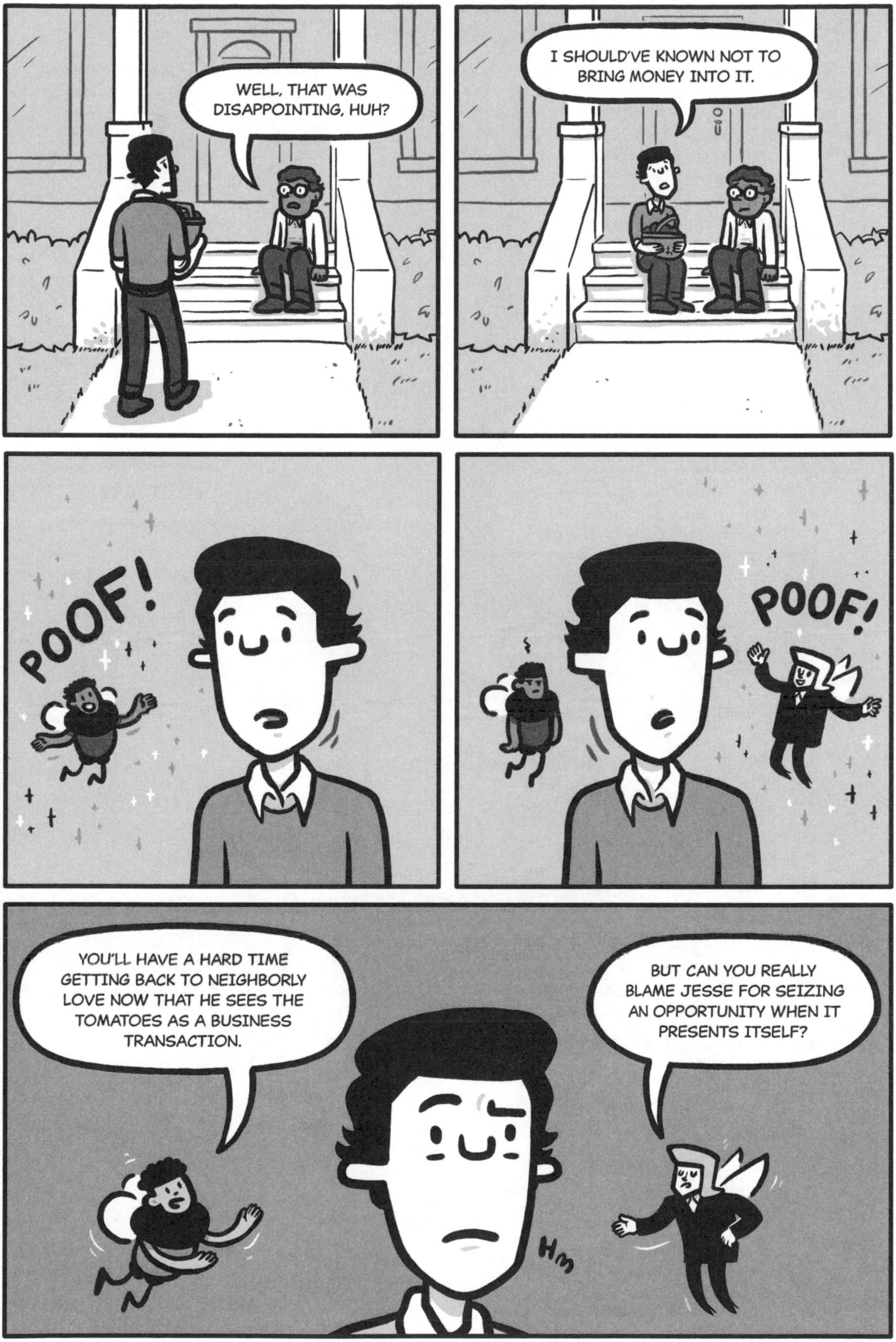
WELL, THAT WAS DISAPPOINTING, HUH?
I SHOULD'VE KNOWN NOT TO BRING MONEY INTO IT.
POOF!
POOF!
YOU'LL HAVE A HARD TIME GETTING BACK TO NEIGHBORLY LOVE NOW THAT HE SEES THE TOMATOES AS A BUSINESS TRANSACTION.
BUT CAN YOU REALLY BLAME JESSE FOR SEIZING AN OPPORTUNITY WHEN IT PRESENTS ITSELF?
Hm

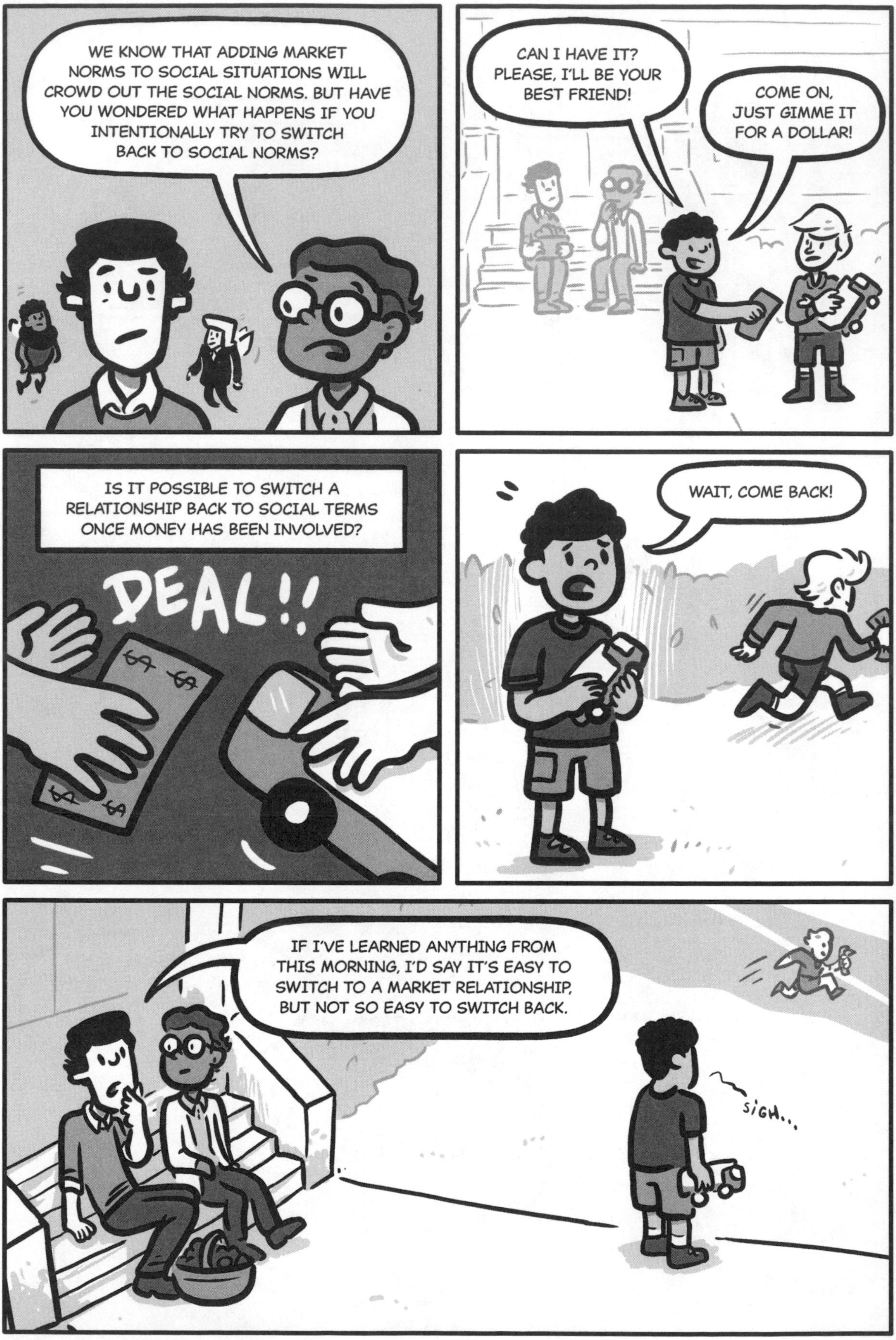
WE KNOW THAT ADDING MARKET NORMS TO SOCIAL SITUATIONS WILL CROWD OUT THE SOCIAL NORMS. BUT HAVE YOU WONDERED WHAT HAPPENS IF YOU INTENTIONALLY TRY TO SWITCH BACK TO SOCIAL NORMS?
CAN I HAVE IT? PLEASE, I'LL BE YOUR BEST FRIEND!
COME ON, JUST GIMME IT FOR A DOLLAR!
IS IT POSSIBLE TO SWITCH A RELATIONSHIP BACK TO SOCIAL TERMS ONCE MONEY HAS BEEN INVOLVED?
DEAL!!
WAIT, COME BACK!
IF I'VE LEARNED ANYTHING FROM THIS MORNING, I'D SAY IT'S EASY TO SWITCH TO A MARKET RELATIONSHIP, BUT NOT SO EASY TO SWITCH BACK.
SIGH...

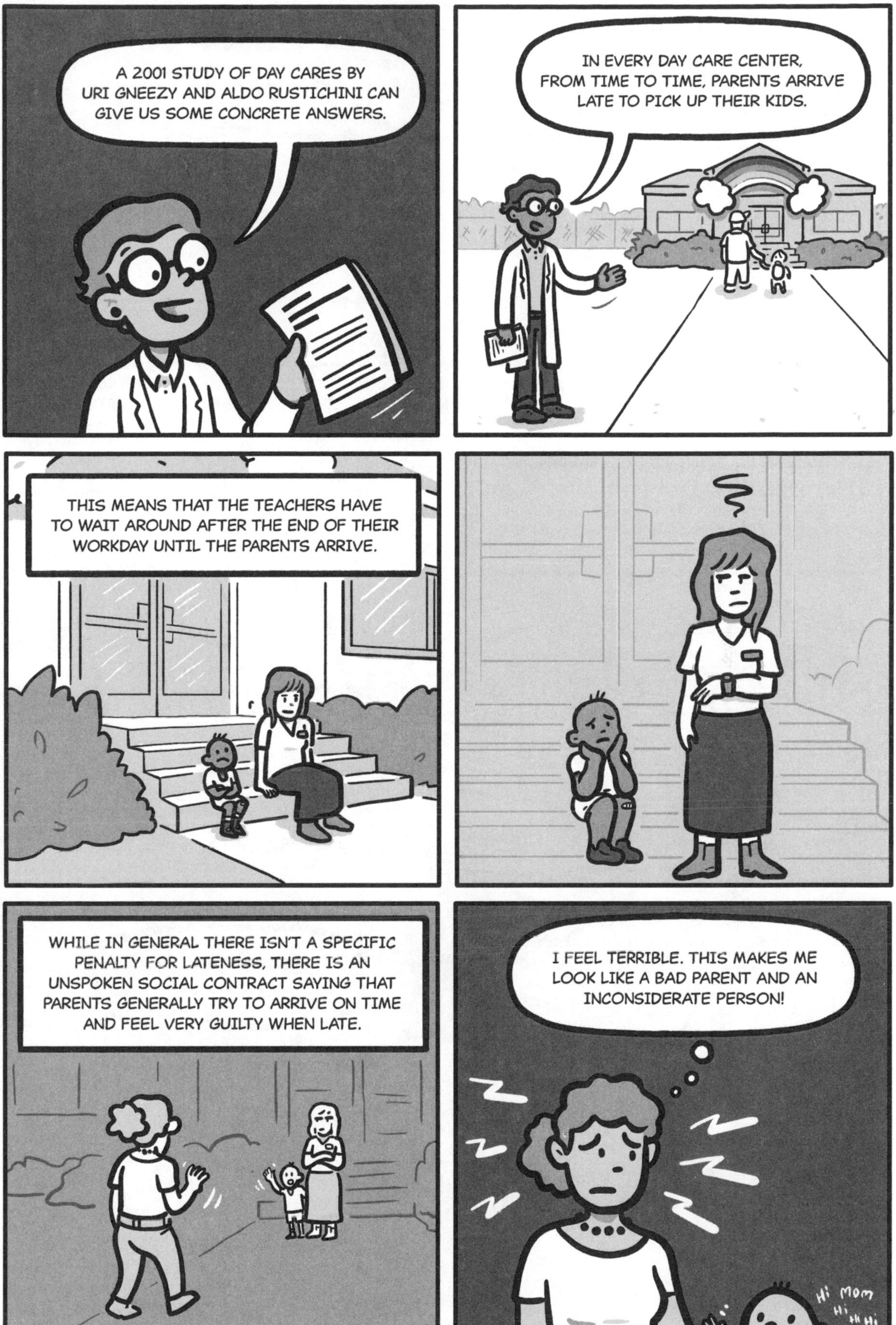
A 2001 STUDY OF DAY CARES BY URI GNEEZY AND ALDO RUSTICHINI CAN GIVE US SOME CONCRETE ANSWERS.
IN EVERY DAY CARE CENTER, FROM TIME TO TIME, PARENTS ARRIVE LATE TO PICK UP THEIR KIDS.
THIS MEANS THAT THE TEACHERS HAVE TO WAIT AROUND AFTER THE END OF THEIR WORKDAY UNTIL THE PARENTS ARRIVE.
WHILE IN GENERAL THERE ISN'T A SPECIFIC PENALTY FOR LATENESS, THERE IS AN UNSPOKEN SOCIAL CONTRACT SAYING THAT PARENTS GENERALLY TRY TO ARRIVE ON TIME AND FEEL VERY GUILTY WHEN LATE.
I FEEL TERRIBLE. THIS MAKES ME LOOK LIKE A BAD PARENT AND AN INCONSIDERATE PERSON!
Hi Mom
Hi
Hi Hi

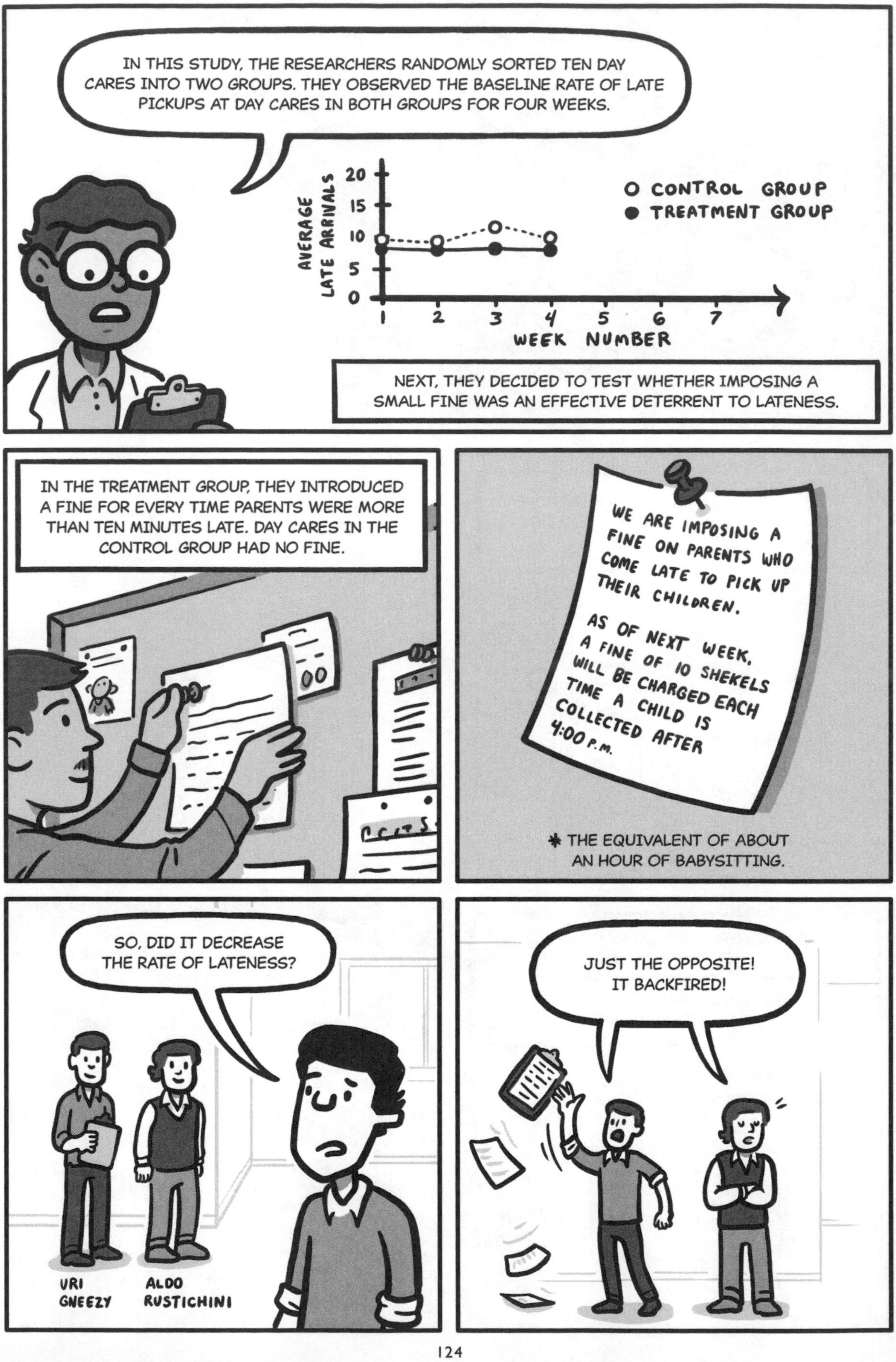

IN THIS STUDY, THE RESEARCHERS RANDOMLY SORTED TEN DAY CARES INTO TWO GROUPS. THEY OBSERVED THE BASELINE RATE OF LATE PICKUPS AT DAY CARES IN BOTH GROUPS FOR FOUR WEEKS.
AVERAGE LATE ARRIVALS
20
15
10
5
0
1 2 3 4 5 6 7
WEEK NUMBER
CONTROL GROUP
TREATMENT GROUP
NEXT, THEY DECIDED TO TEST WHETHER IMPOSING A SMALL FINE WAS AN EFFECTIVE DETERRENT TO LATENESS.
IN THE TREATMENT GROUP, THEY INTRODUCED A FINE FOR EVERY TIME PARENTS WERE MORE THAN TEN MINUTES LATE. DAY CARES IN THE CONTROL GROUP HAD NO FINE.
WE ARE IMPOSING A FINE ON PARENTS WHO COME LATE TO PICK UP THEIR CHILDREN.
AS OF NEXT WEEK, A FINE OF 10 SHEKELS WILL BE CHARGED EACH TIME A CHILD IS COLLECTED AFTER 4:00 P.M.
* THE EQUIVALENT OF ABOUT AN HOUR OF BABYSITTING.
SO, DID IT DECREASE THE RATE OF LATENESS?
URI GNEEZY
ALDO RUSTICHINI
JUST THE OPPOSITE! IT BACKFIRED!

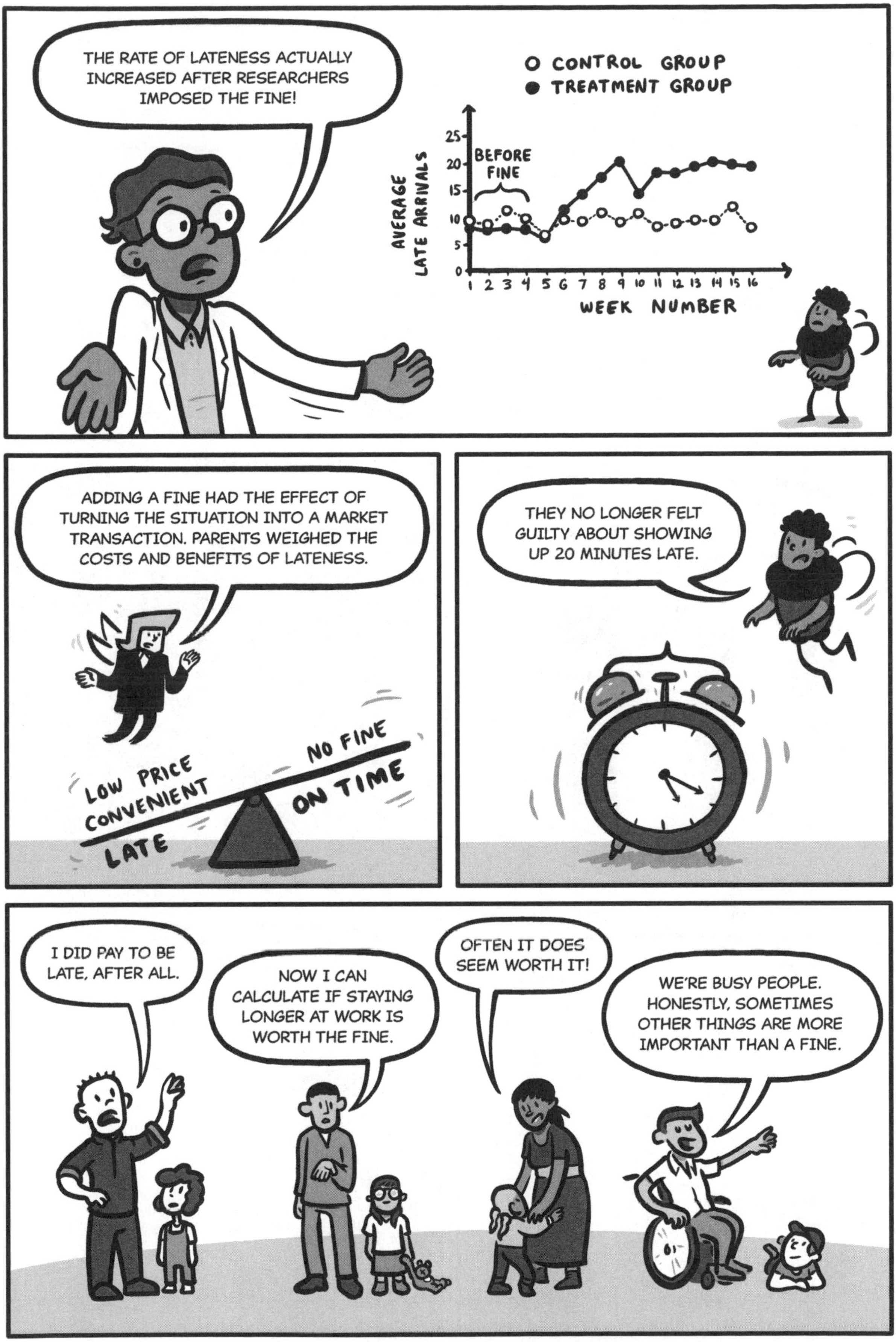
THE RATE OF LATENESS ACTUALLY INCREASED AFTER RESEARCHERS IMPOSED THE FINE!
CONTROL GROUP
TREATMENT GROUP
BEFORE FINE
AVERAGE LATE ARRIVALS
0 5 10 15 20 25
1 2 3 4 5 6 7 8 9 10 11 12 13 14 15 16
WEEK NUMBER
ADDING A FINE HAD THE EFFECT OF TURNING THE SITUATION INTO A MARKET TRANSACTION. PARENTS WEIGHED THE COSTS AND BENEFITS OF LATENESS.
LOW PRICE
CONVENIENT
LATE
NO FINE
ON TIME
THEY NO LONGER FELT GUILTY ABOUT SHOWING UP 20 MINUTES LATE.
I DID PAY TO BE LATE, AFTER ALL.
NOW I CAN CALCULATE IF STAYING LONGER AT WORK IS WORTH THE FINE.
OFTEN IT DOES SEEM WORTH IT!
WE'RE BUSY PEOPLE. HONESTLY, SOMETIMES OTHER THINGS ARE MORE IMPORTANT THAN A FINE.

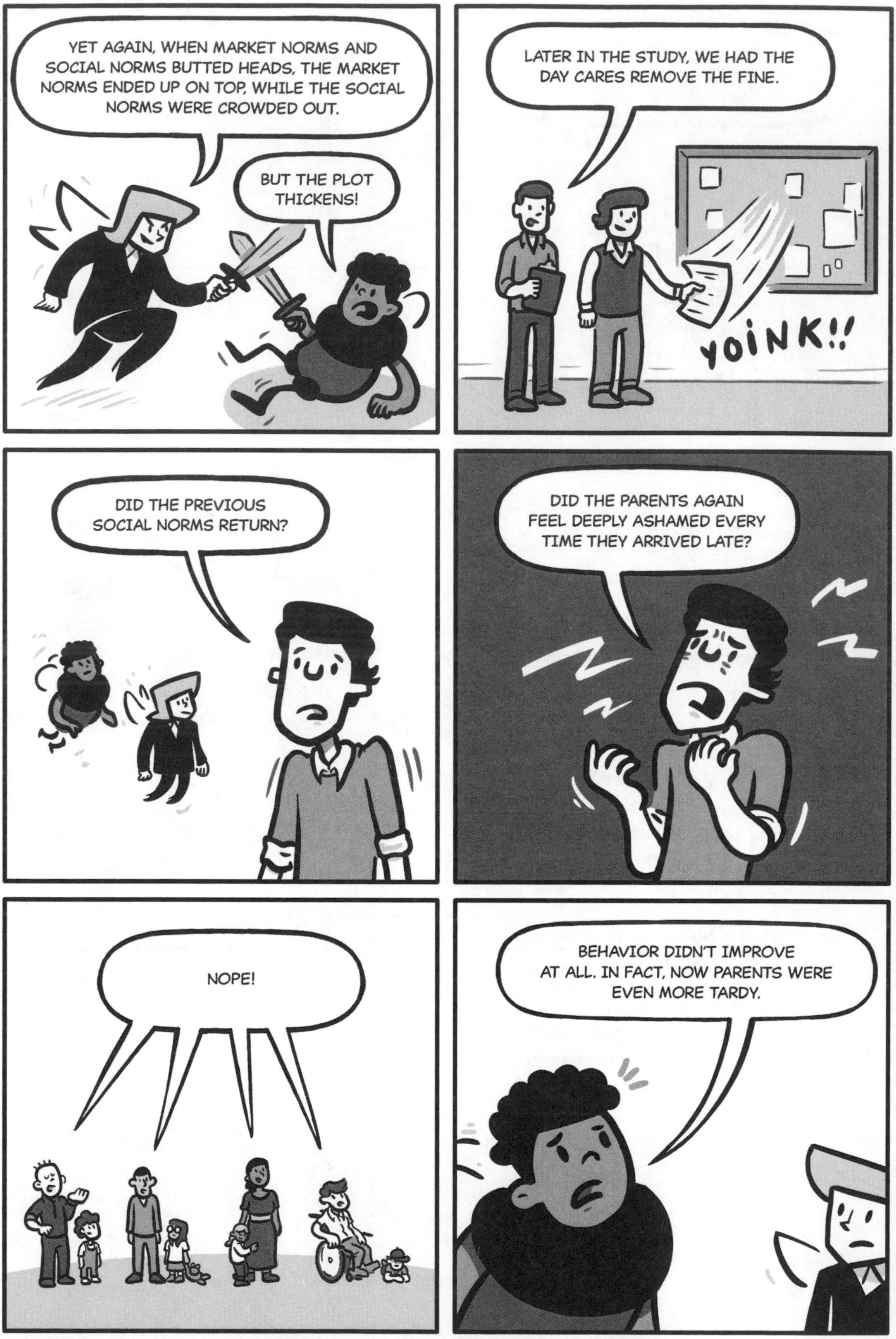
YET AGAIN, WHEN MARKET NORMS AND SOCIAL NORMS BUTTED HEADS, THE MARKET NORMS ENDED UP ON TOP, WHILE THE SOCIAL NORMS WERE CROWDED OUT.
BUT THE PLOT THICKENS!
LATER IN THE STUDY, WE HAD THE DAY CARES REMOVE THE FINE.
YOINK!!
DID THE PREVIOUS SOCIAL NORMS RETURN?
DID THE PARENTS AGAIN FEEL DEEPLY ASHAMED EVERY TIME THEY ARRIVED LATE?
NOPE!
BEHAVIOR DIDN'T IMPROVE AT ALL. IN FACT, NOW PARENTS WERE EVEN MORE TARDY.

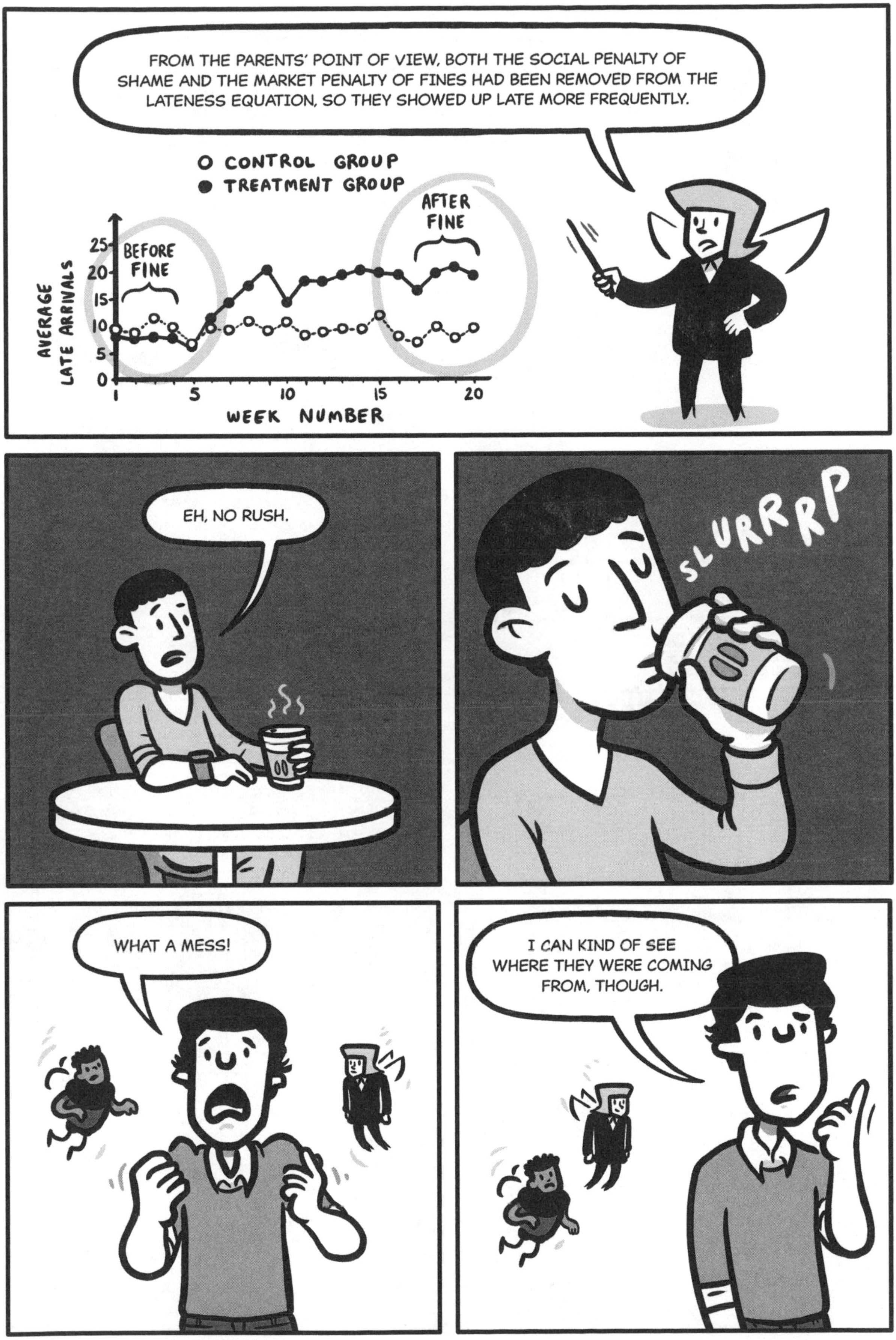
FROM THE PARENTS' POINT OF VIEW, BOTH THE SOCIAL PENALTY OF SHAME AND THE MARKET PENALTY OF FINES HAD BEEN REMOVED FROM THE LATENESS EQUATION, SO THEY SHOWED UP LATE MORE FREQUENTLY.
CONTROL GROUP
TREATMENT GROUP
BEFORE FINE
AFTER FINE
AVERAGE LATE ARRIVALS
0 5 10 15 20 25
WEEK NUMBER
1 5 10 15 20
EH, NO RUSH.
SLURRRP
WHAT A MESS!
I CAN KIND OF SEE WHERE THEY WERE COMING FROM, THOUGH.

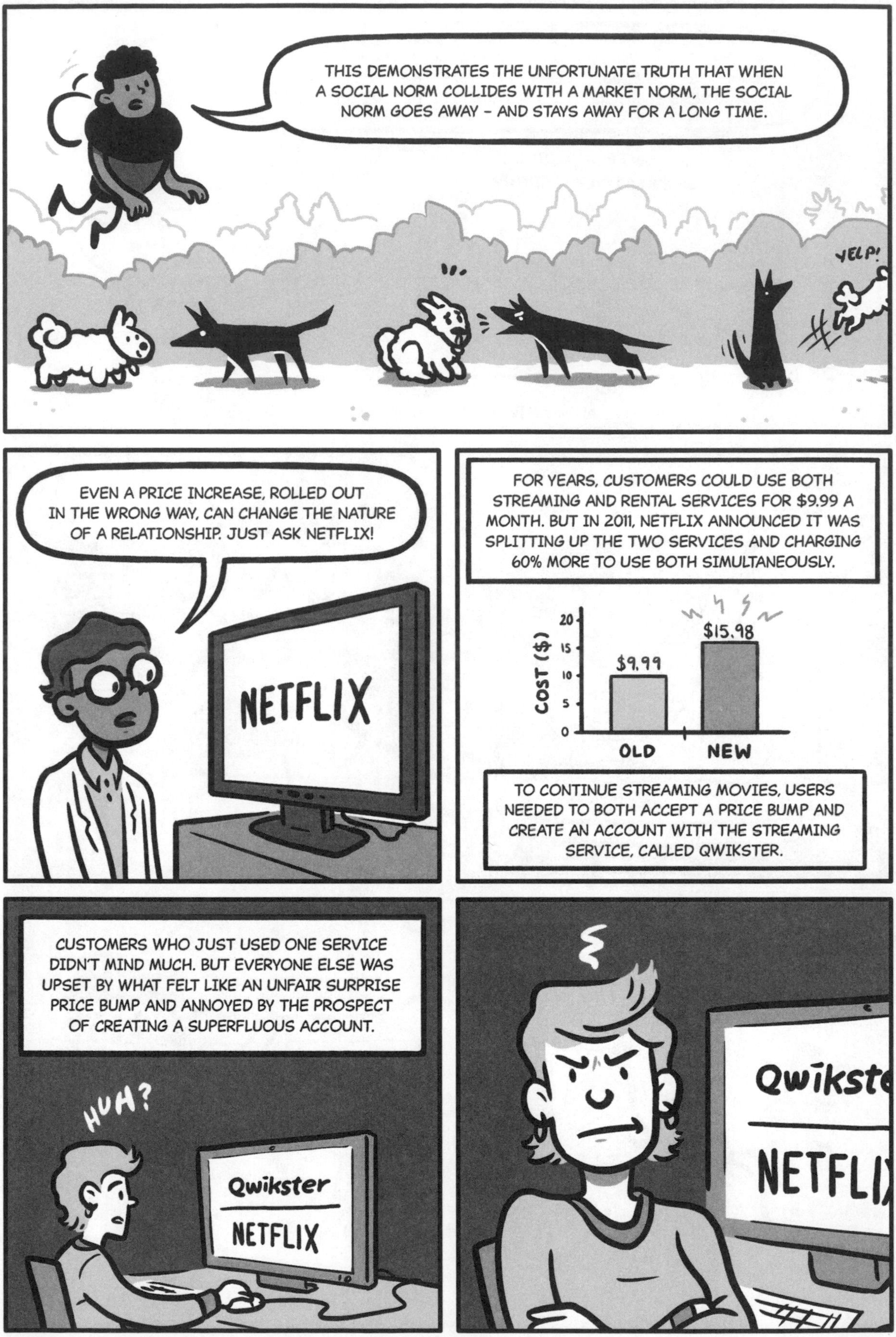
THIS DEMONSTRATES THE UNFORTUNATE TRUTH THAT WHEN A SOCIAL NORM COLLIDES WITH A MARKET NORM, THE SOCIAL NORM GOES AWAY – AND STAYS AWAY FOR A LONG TIME.
YELP!
EVEN A PRICE INCREASE, ROLLED OUT IN THE WRONG WAY, CAN CHANGE THE NATURE OF A RELATIONSHIP. JUST ASK NETFLIX!
NETFLIX
FOR YEARS, CUSTOMERS COULD USE BOTH STREAMING AND RENTAL SERVICES FOR $9.99 A MONTH. BUT IN 2011, NETFLIX ANNOUNCED IT WAS SPLITTING UP THE TWO SERVICES AND CHARGING 60% MORE TO USE BOTH SIMULTANEOUSLY.
COST ($)
20
15
10
5
0
$9.99
$15.98
OLD
NEW
TO CONTINUE STREAMING MOVIES, USERS NEEDED TO BOTH ACCEPT A PRICE BUMP AND CREATE AN ACCOUNT WITH THE STREAMING SERVICE, CALLED QWIKSTER.
CUSTOMERS WHO JUST USED ONE SERVICE DIDN'T MIND MUCH. BUT EVERYONE ELSE WAS UPSET BY WHAT FELT LIKE AN UNFAIR SURPRISE PRICE BUMP AND ANNOYED BY THE PROSPECT OF CREATING A SUPERFLUOUS ACCOUNT.
HUH?
Qwikster
NETFLIX

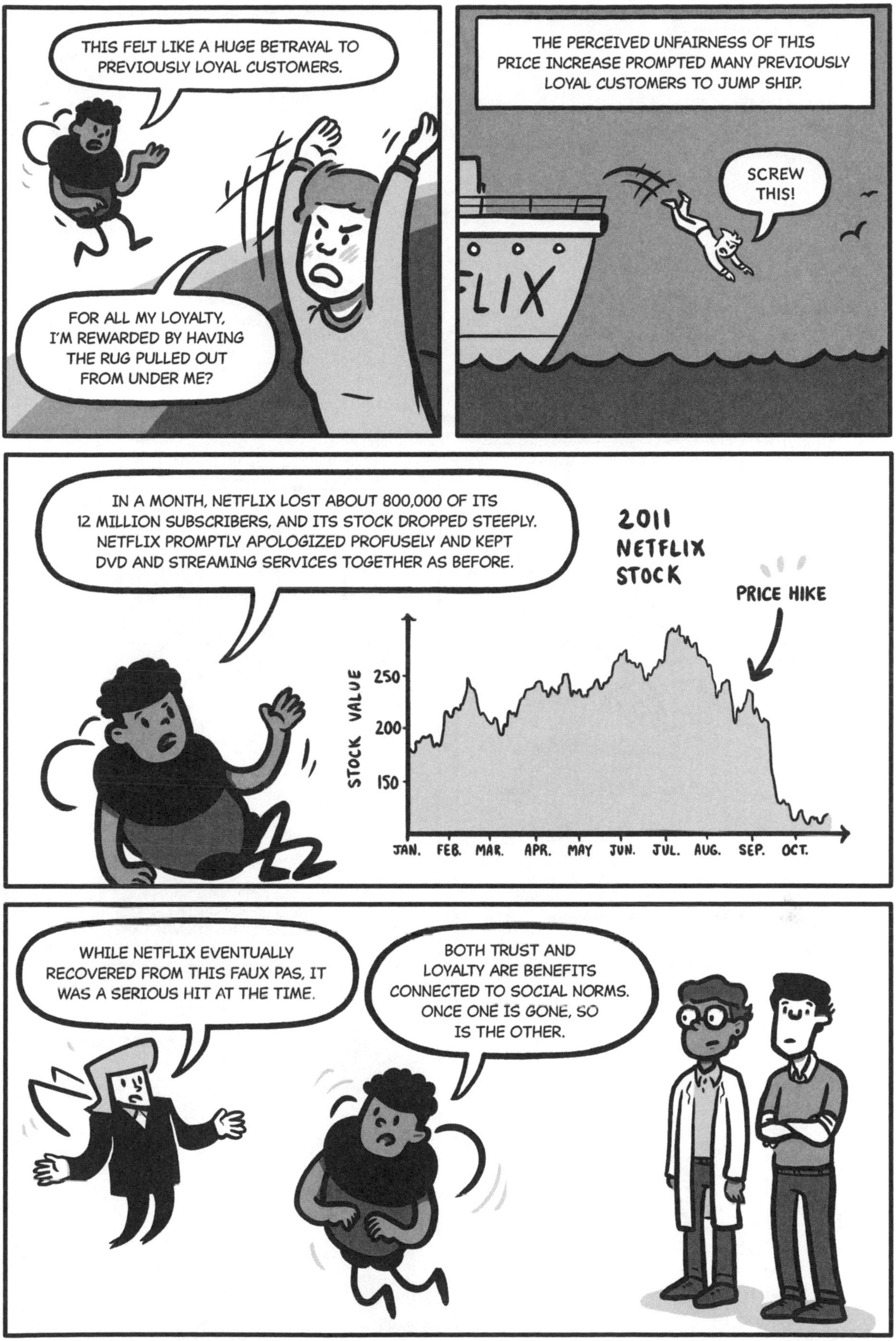
THIS FELT LIKE A HUGE BETRAYAL TO PREVIOUSLY LOYAL CUSTOMERS.
FOR ALL MY LOYALTY, I'M REWARDED BY HAVING THE RUG PULLED OUT FROM UNDER ME?
THE PERCEIVED UNFAIRNESS OF THIS PRICE INCREASE PROMPTED MANY PREVIOUSLY LOYAL CUSTOMERS TO JUMP SHIP.
FLIX
SCREW THIS!
IN A MONTH, NETFLIX LOST ABOUT 800,000 OF ITS 12 MILLION SUBSCRIBERS, AND ITS STOCK DROPPED STEEPLY. NETFLIX PROMPTLY APOLOGIZED PROFUSELY AND KEPT DVD AND STREAMING SERVICES TOGETHER AS BEFORE.
2011 NETFLIX STOCK
PRICE HIKE
STOCK VALUE
250
200
150
JAN. FEB. MAR. APR. MAY JUN. JUL. AUG. SEP. OCT.
WHILE NETFLIX EVENTUALLY RECOVERED FROM THIS FAUX PAS, IT WAS A SERIOUS HIT AT THE TIME.
BOTH TRUST AND LOYALTY ARE BENEFITS CONNECTED TO SOCIAL NORMS. ONCE ONE IS GONE, SO IS THE OTHER.

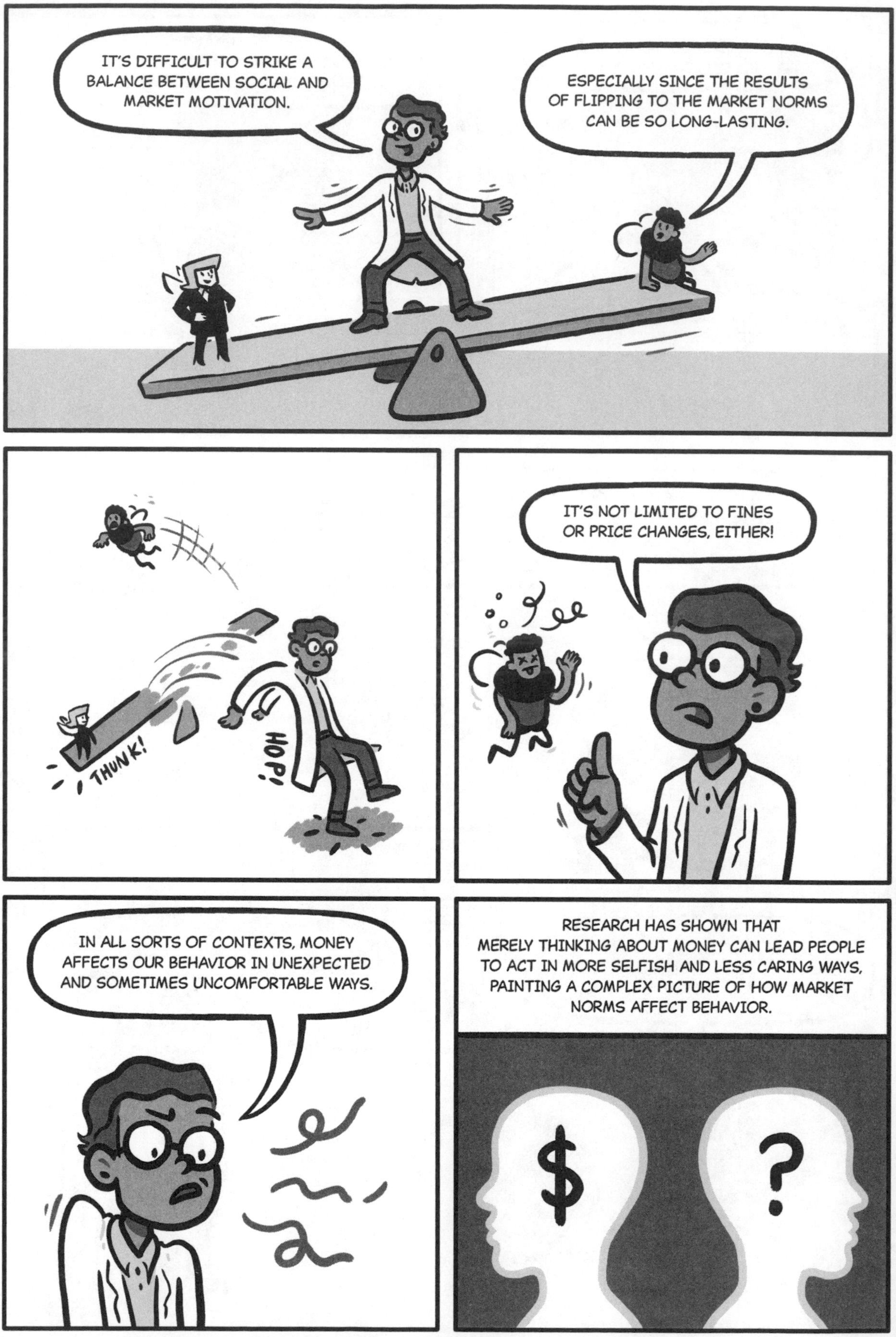
IT'S DIFFICULT TO STRIKE A BALANCE BETWEEN SOCIAL AND MARKET MOTIVATION.
ESPECIALLY SINCE THE RESULTS OF FLIPPING TO THE MARKET NORMS CAN BE SO LONG-LASTING.
THUNK!
HOP!
IT'S NOT LIMITED TO FINES OR PRICE CHANGES, EITHER!
IN ALL SORTS OF CONTEXTS, MONEY AFFECTS OUR BEHAVIOR IN UNEXPECTED AND SOMETIMES UNCOMFORTABLE WAYS.
RESEARCH HAS SHOWN THAT MERELY THINKING ABOUT MONEY CAN LEAD PEOPLE TO ACT IN MORE SELFISH AND LESS CARING WAYS, PAINTING A COMPLEX PICTURE OF HOW MARKET NORMS AFFECT BEHAVIOR.
$
?

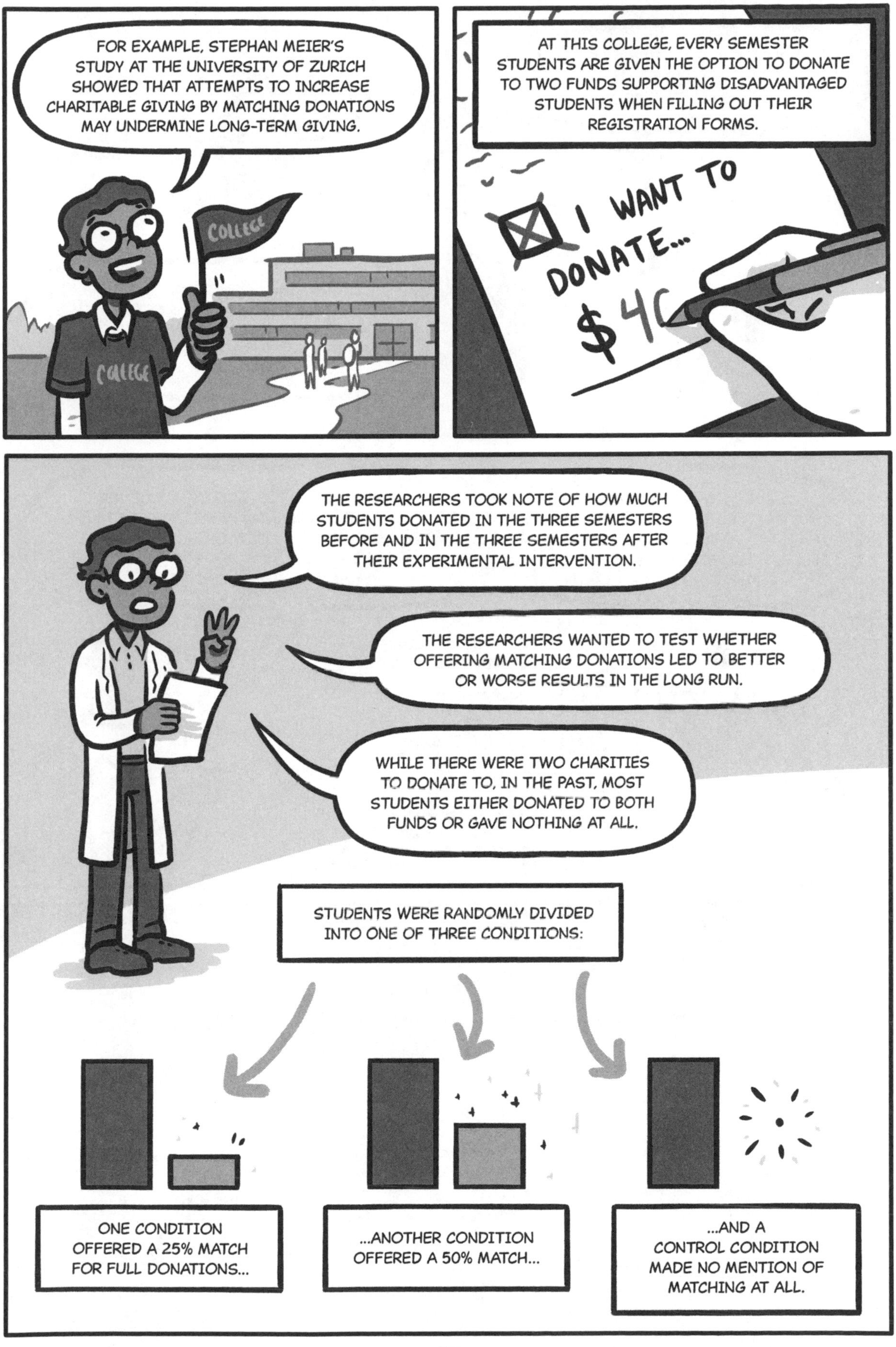
FOR EXAMPLE, STEPHAN MEIER'S STUDY AT THE UNIVERSITY OF ZURICH SHOWED THAT ATTEMPTS TO INCREASE CHARITABLE GIVING BY MATCHING DONATIONS MAY UNDERMINE LONG-TERM GIVING.
COLLEGE
COLLEGE
AT THIS COLLEGE, EVERY SEMESTER STUDENTS ARE GIVEN THE OPTION TO DONATE TO TWO FUNDS SUPPORTING DISADVANTAGED STUDENTS WHEN FILLING OUT THEIR REGISTRATION FORMS.
I WANT TO DONATE...
$ 40
THE RESEARCHERS TOOK NOTE OF HOW MUCH STUDENTS DONATED IN THE THREE SEMESTERS BEFORE AND IN THE THREE SEMESTERS AFTER THEIR EXPERIMENTAL INTERVENTION.
THE RESEARCHERS WANTED TO TEST WHETHER OFFERING MATCHING DONATIONS LED TO BETTER OR WORSE RESULTS IN THE LONG RUN.
WHILE THERE WERE TWO CHARITIES TO DONATE TO, IN THE PAST, MOST STUDENTS EITHER DONATED TO BOTH FUNDS OR GAVE NOTHING AT ALL.
STUDENTS WERE RANDOMLY DIVIDED INTO ONE OF THREE CONDITIONS:
ONE CONDITION OFFERED A 25% MATCH FOR FULL DONATIONS...
...ANOTHER CONDITION OFFERED A 50% MATCH...
...AND A CONTROL CONDITION MADE NO MENTION OF MATCHING AT ALL.

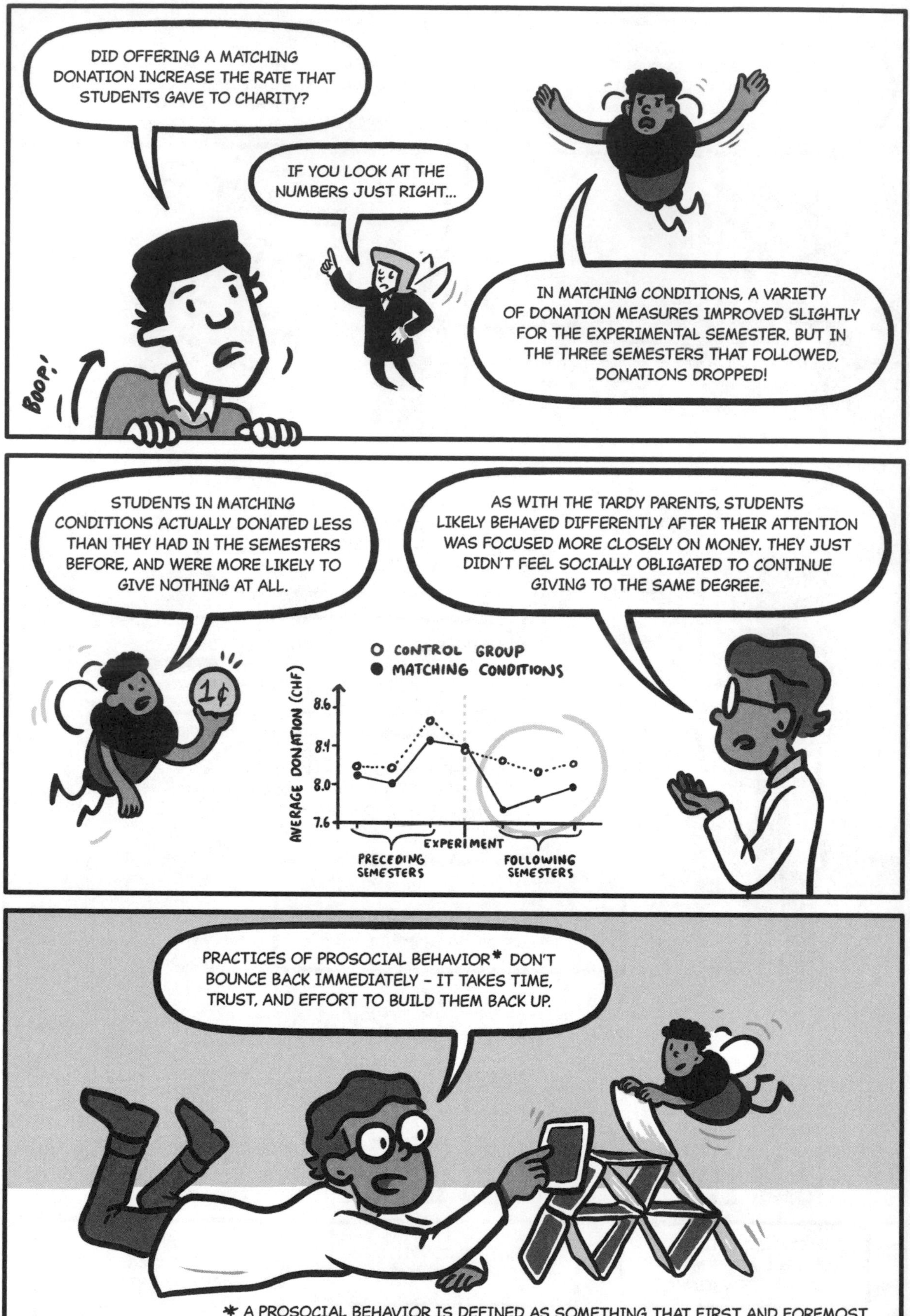
DID OFFERING A MATCHING DONATION INCREASE THE RATE THAT STUDENTS GAVE TO CHARITY?
IF YOU LOOK AT THE NUMBERS JUST RIGHT...
IN MATCHING CONDITIONS, A VARIETY OF DONATION MEASURES IMPROVED SLIGHTLY FOR THE EXPERIMENTAL SEMESTER. BUT IN THE THREE SEMESTERS THAT FOLLOWED, DONATIONS DROPPED!
BOOP!
STUDENTS IN MATCHING CONDITIONS ACTUALLY DONATED LESS THAN THEY HAD IN THE SEMESTERS BEFORE, AND WERE MORE LIKELY TO GIVE NOTHING AT ALL.
AS WITH THE TARDY PARENTS, STUDENTS LIKELY BEHAVED DIFFERENTLY AFTER THEIR ATTENTION WAS FOCUSED MORE CLOSELY ON MONEY. THEY JUST DIDN'T FEEL SOCIALLY OBLIGATED TO CONTINUE GIVING TO THE SAME DEGREE.
1¢
CONTROL GROUP
MATCHING CONDITIONS
AVERAGE DONATION (CHF)
8.6
8.4
8.0
7.6
EXPERIMENT
PRECEDING SEMESTERS
FOLLOWING SEMESTERS
PRACTICES OF PROSOCIAL BEHAVIOR* DON'T BOUNCE BACK IMMEDIATELY – IT TAKES TIME, TRUST, AND EFFORT TO BUILD THEM BACK UP.
* A PROSOCIAL BEHAVIOR IS DEFINED AS SOMETHING THAT FIRST AND FOREMOST BENEFITS OTHERS, SUCH AS SHARING, MAKING DONATIONS, OR OFFERING HELP.

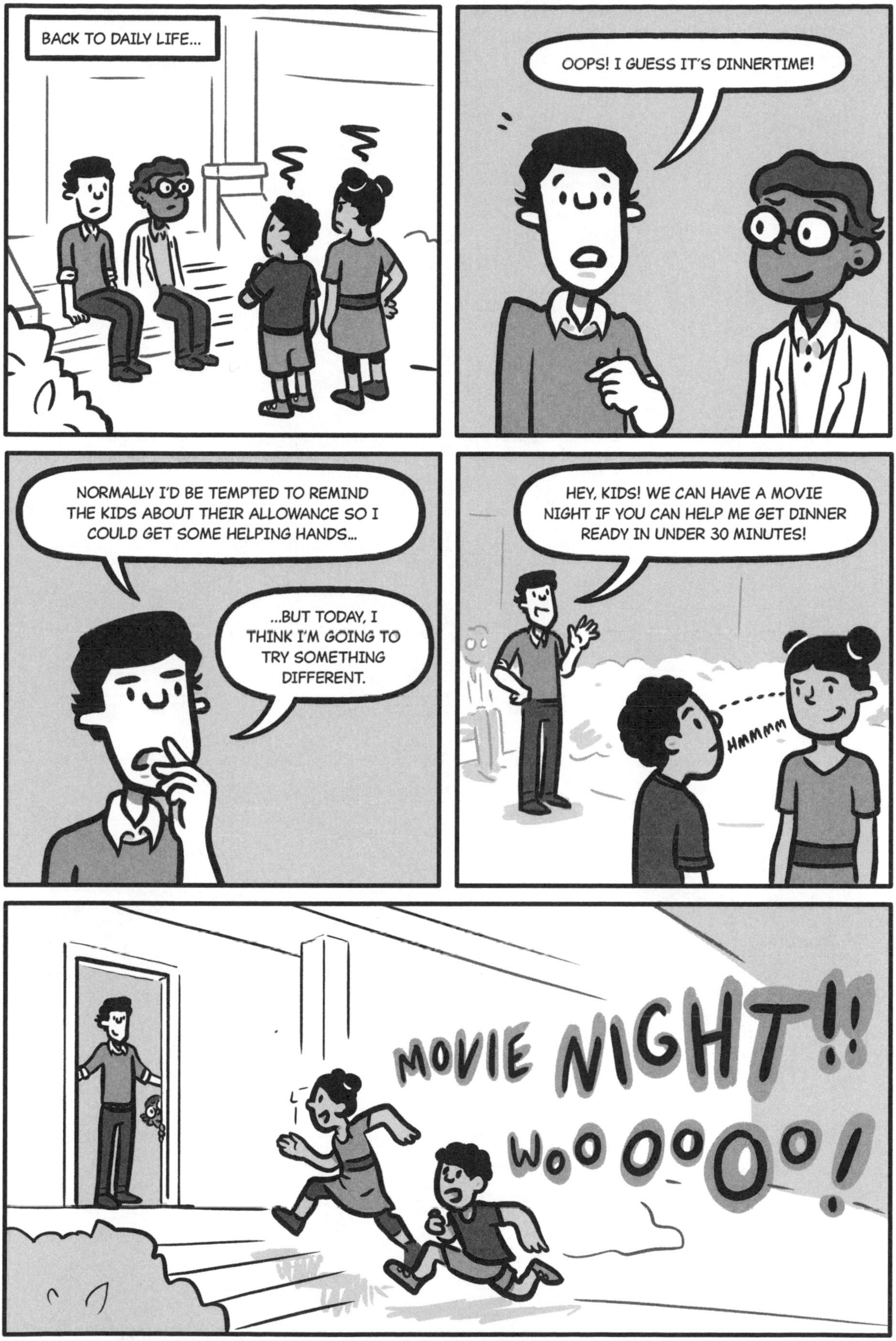
BACK TO DAILY LIFE...
OOPS! I GUESS IT'S DINNERTIME!
NORMALLY I'D BE TEMPTED TO REMIND THE KIDS ABOUT THEIR ALLOWANCE SO I COULD GET SOME HELPING HANDS...
...BUT TODAY, I THINK I'M GOING TO TRY SOMETHING DIFFERENT.
HEY, KIDS! WE CAN HAVE A MOVIE NIGHT IF YOU CAN HELP ME GET DINNER READY IN UNDER 30 MINUTES!
HMMMM
MOVIE NIGHT!!
WoOOOOO!

CHAPTER SEVEN

FEELING COMPLETE

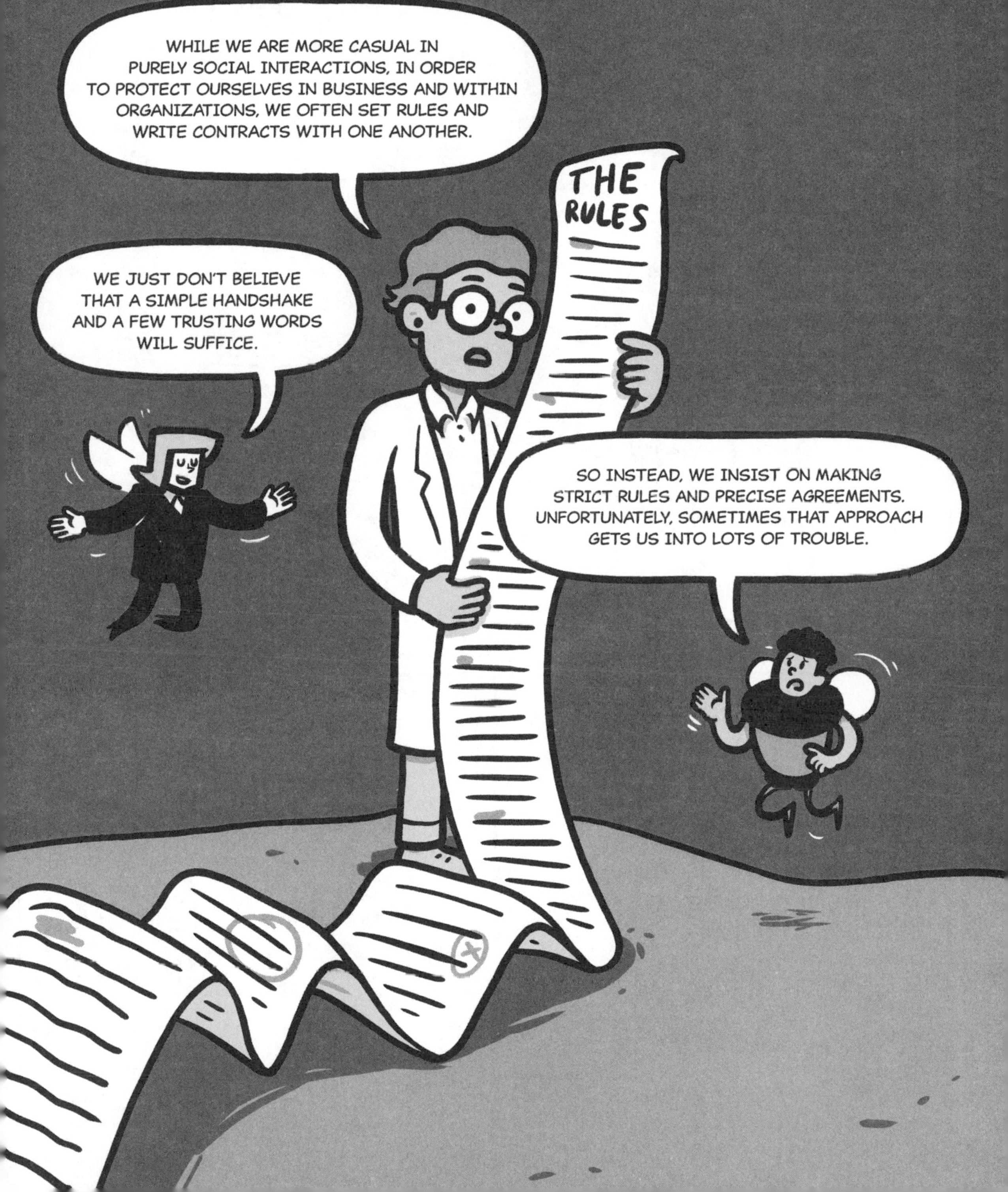

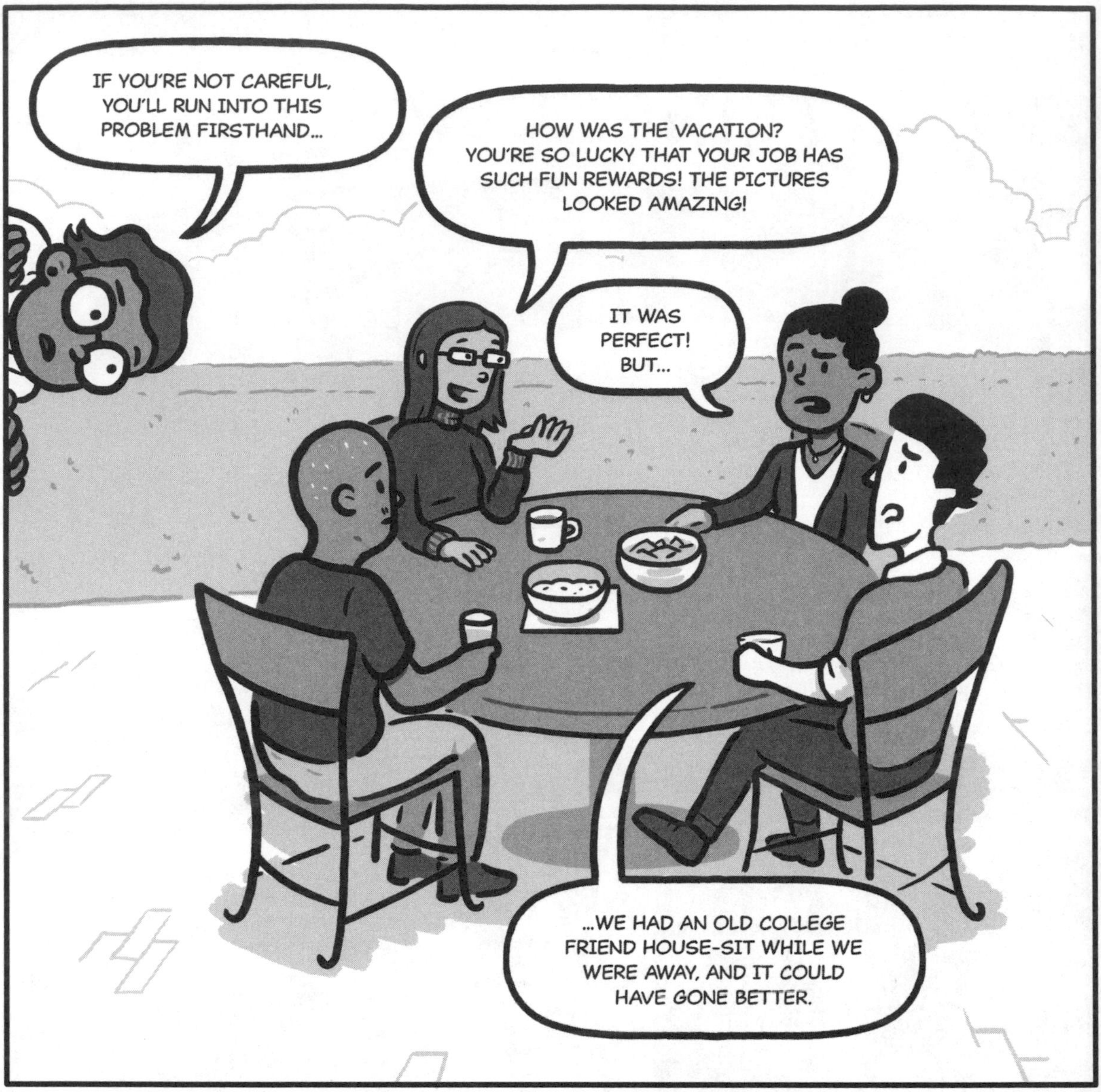
IF YOU'RE NOT CAREFUL, YOU'LL RUN INTO THIS PROBLEM FIRSTHAND...
HOW WAS THE VACATION? YOU'RE SO LUCKY THAT YOUR JOB HAS SUCH FUN REWARDS! THE PICTURES LOOKED AMAZING!
IT WAS PERFECT! BUT...
...WE HAD AN OLD COLLEGE FRIEND HOUSE-SIT WHILE WE WERE AWAY, AND IT COULD HAVE GONE BETTER.

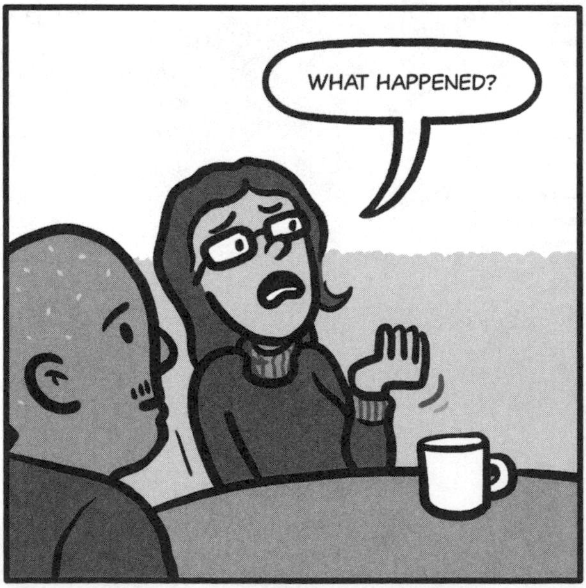
WHAT HAPPENED?

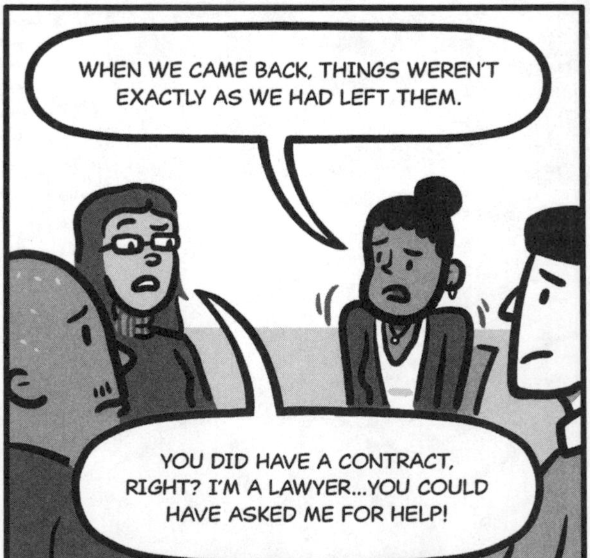
WHEN WE CAME BACK, THINGS WEREN'T EXACTLY AS WE HAD LEFT THEM.
YOU DID HAVE A CONTRACT, RIGHT? I'M A LAWYER...YOU COULD HAVE ASKED ME FOR HELP!

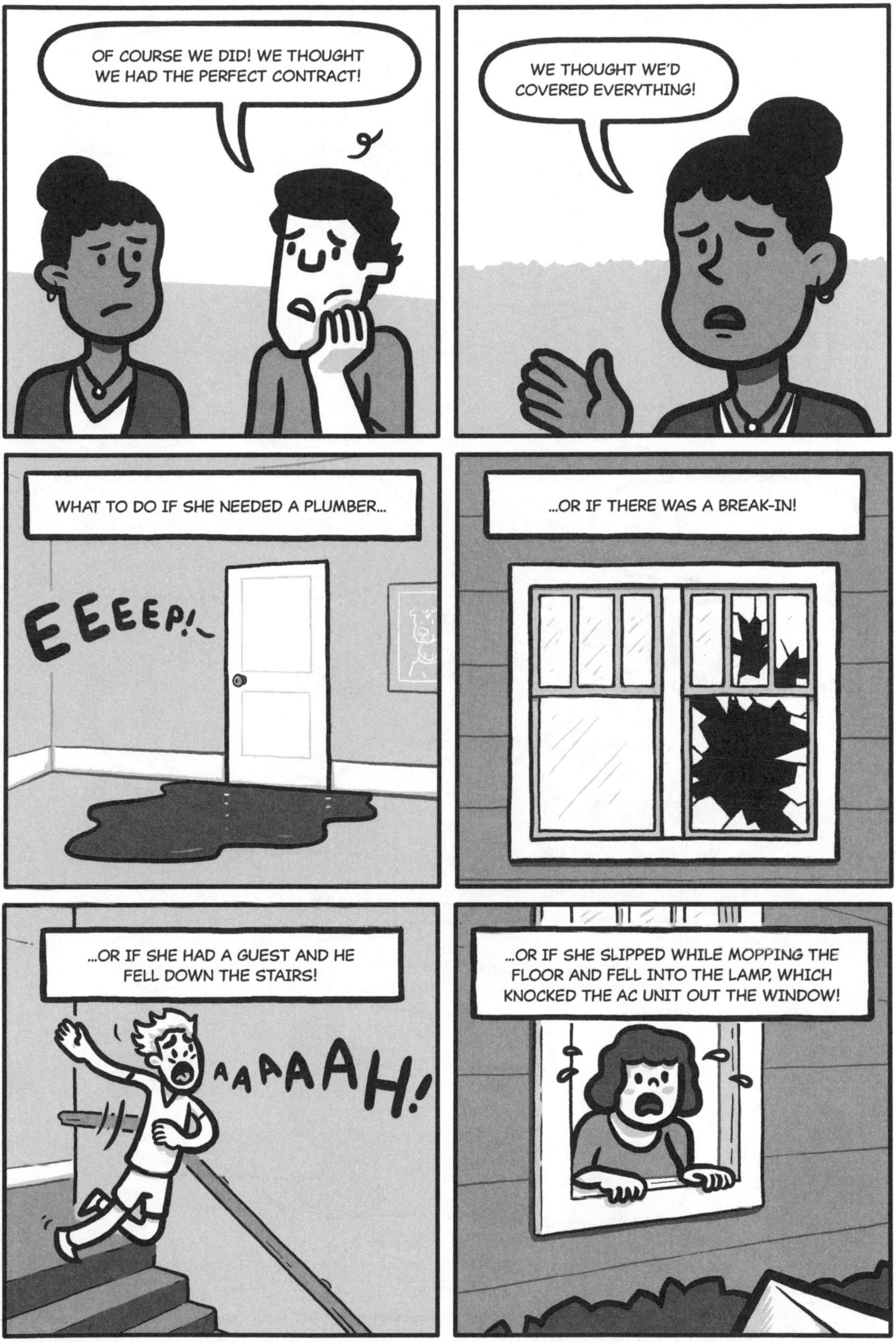
OF COURSE WE DID! WE THOUGHT WE HAD THE PERFECT CONTRACT!
WE THOUGHT WE'D COVERED EVERYTHING!
WHAT TO DO IF SHE NEEDED A PLUMBER...
EEEEP!
...OR IF THERE WAS A BREAK-IN!
...OR IF SHE HAD A GUEST AND HE FELL DOWN THE STAIRS!
AAAAAAH!
...OR IF SHE SLIPPED WHILE MOPPING THE FLOOR AND FELL INTO THE LAMP, WHICH KNOCKED THE AC UNIT OUT THE WINDOW!

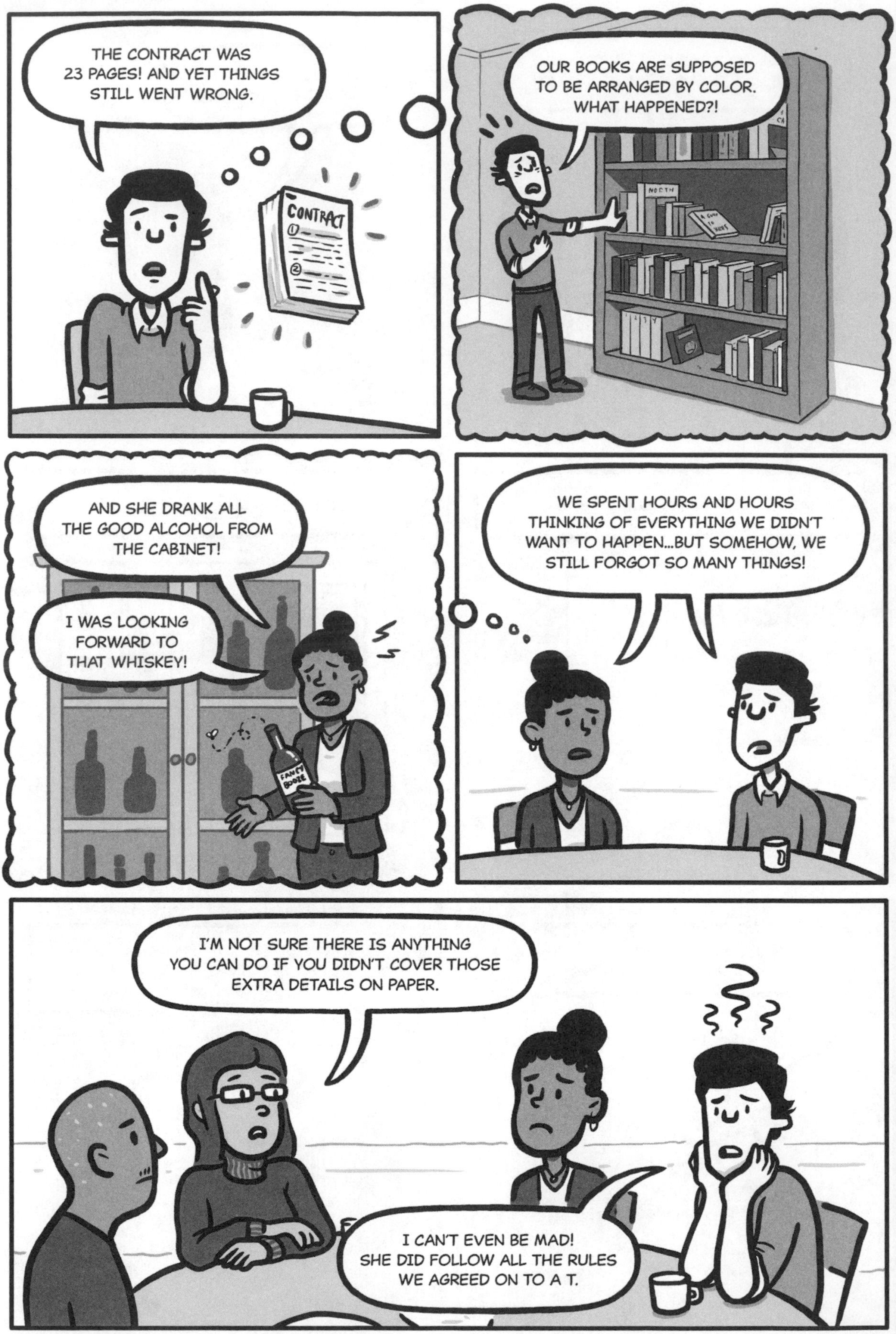
THE CONTRACT WAS 23 PAGES! AND YET THINGS STILL WENT WRONG.
CONTRACT
OUR BOOKS ARE SUPPOSED TO BE ARRANGED BY COLOR. WHAT HAPPENED?!
NORTH
AND SHE DRANK ALL THE GOOD ALCOHOL FROM THE CABINET!
I WAS LOOKING FORWARD TO THAT WHISKEY!
FANCY BOOZE
WE SPENT HOURS AND HOURS THINKING OF EVERYTHING WE DIDN'T WANT TO HAPPEN...BUT SOMEHOW, WE STILL FORGOT SO MANY THINGS!
I'M NOT SURE THERE IS ANYTHING YOU CAN DO IF YOU DIDN'T COVER THOSE EXTRA DETAILS ON PAPER.
I CAN'T EVEN BE MAD! SHE DID FOLLOW ALL THE RULES WE AGREED ON TO A T.

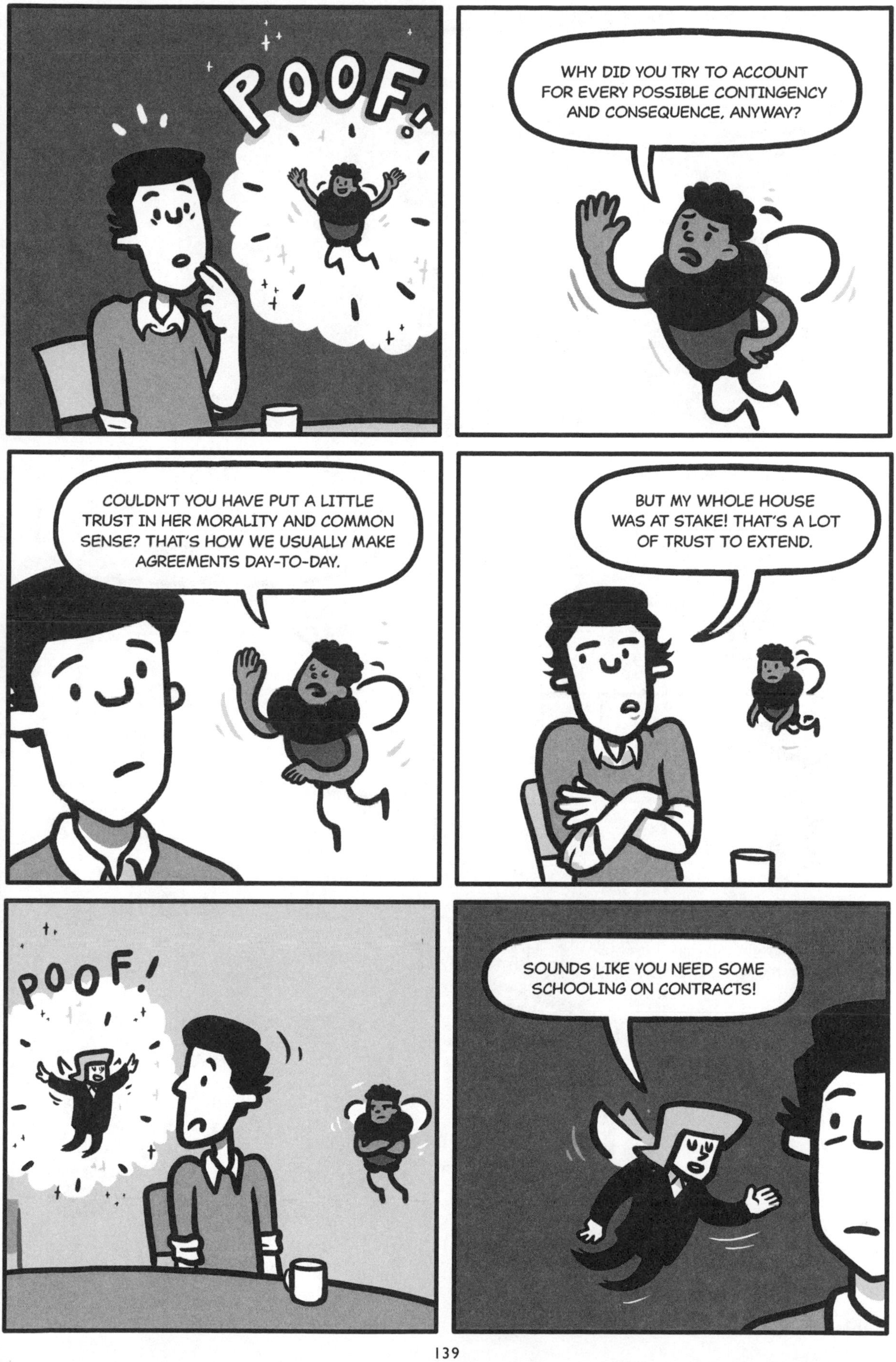
POOF!
WHY DID YOU TRY TO ACCOUNT FOR EVERY POSSIBLE CONTINGENCY AND CONSEQUENCE, ANYWAY?
COULDN'T YOU HAVE PUT A LITTLE TRUST IN HER MORALITY AND COMMON SENSE? THAT'S HOW WE USUALLY MAKE AGREEMENTS DAY-TO-DAY.
BUT MY WHOLE HOUSE WAS AT STAKE! THAT'S A LOT OF TRUST TO EXTEND.
POOF!
SOUNDS LIKE YOU NEED SOME SCHOOLING ON CONTRACTS!

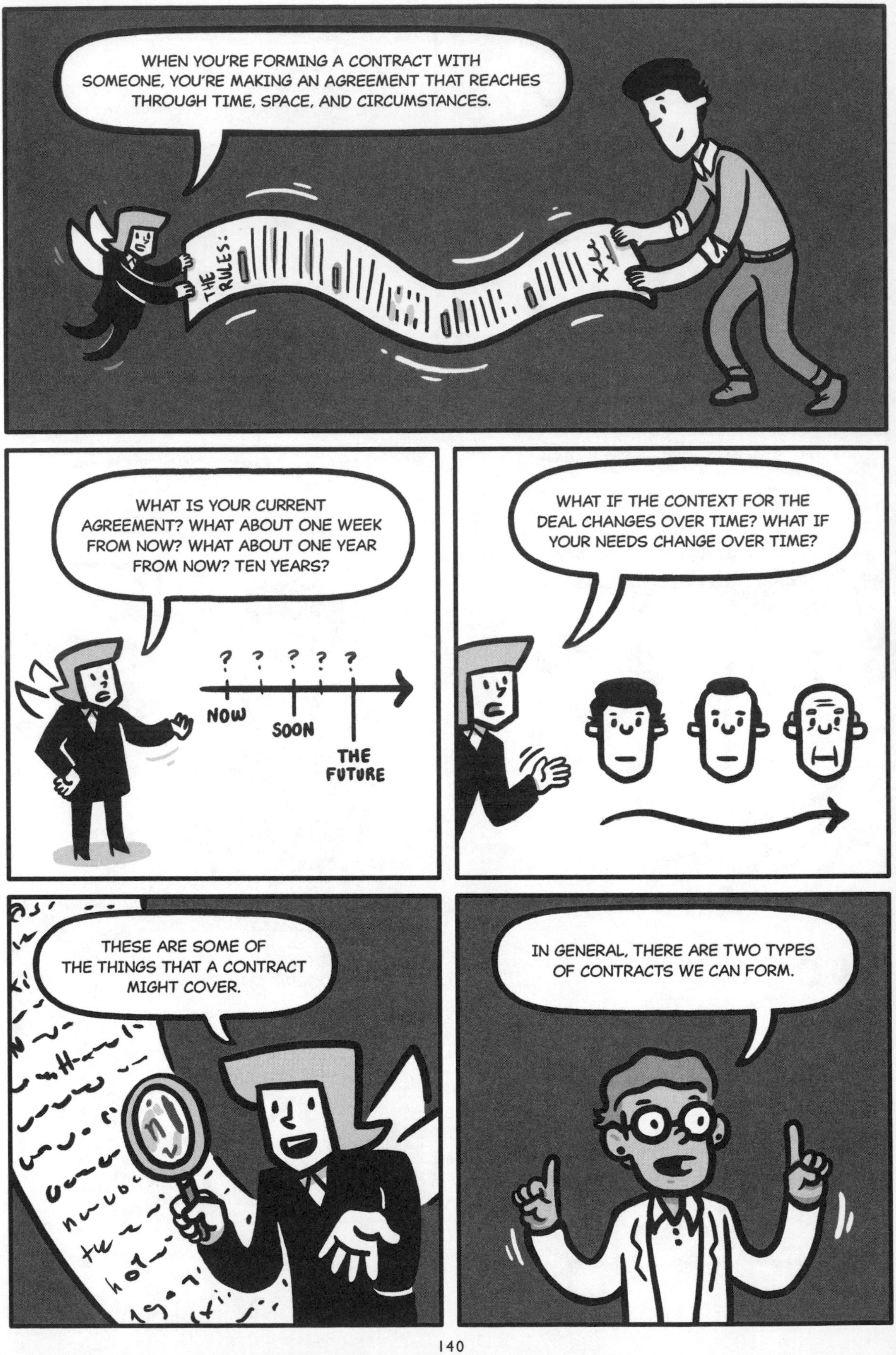
WHEN YOU'RE FORMING A CONTRACT WITH SOMEONE, YOU'RE MAKING AN AGREEMENT THAT REACHES THROUGH TIME, SPACE, AND CIRCUMSTANCES.
THE RULES:
WHAT IS YOUR CURRENT AGREEMENT? WHAT ABOUT ONE WEEK FROM NOW? WHAT ABOUT ONE YEAR FROM NOW? TEN YEARS?
NOW
SOON
THE FUTURE
WHAT IF THE CONTEXT FOR THE DEAL CHANGES OVER TIME? WHAT IF YOUR NEEDS CHANGE OVER TIME?
THESE ARE SOME OF THE THINGS THAT A CONTRACT MIGHT COVER.
IN GENERAL, THERE ARE TWO TYPES OF CONTRACTS WE CAN FORM.

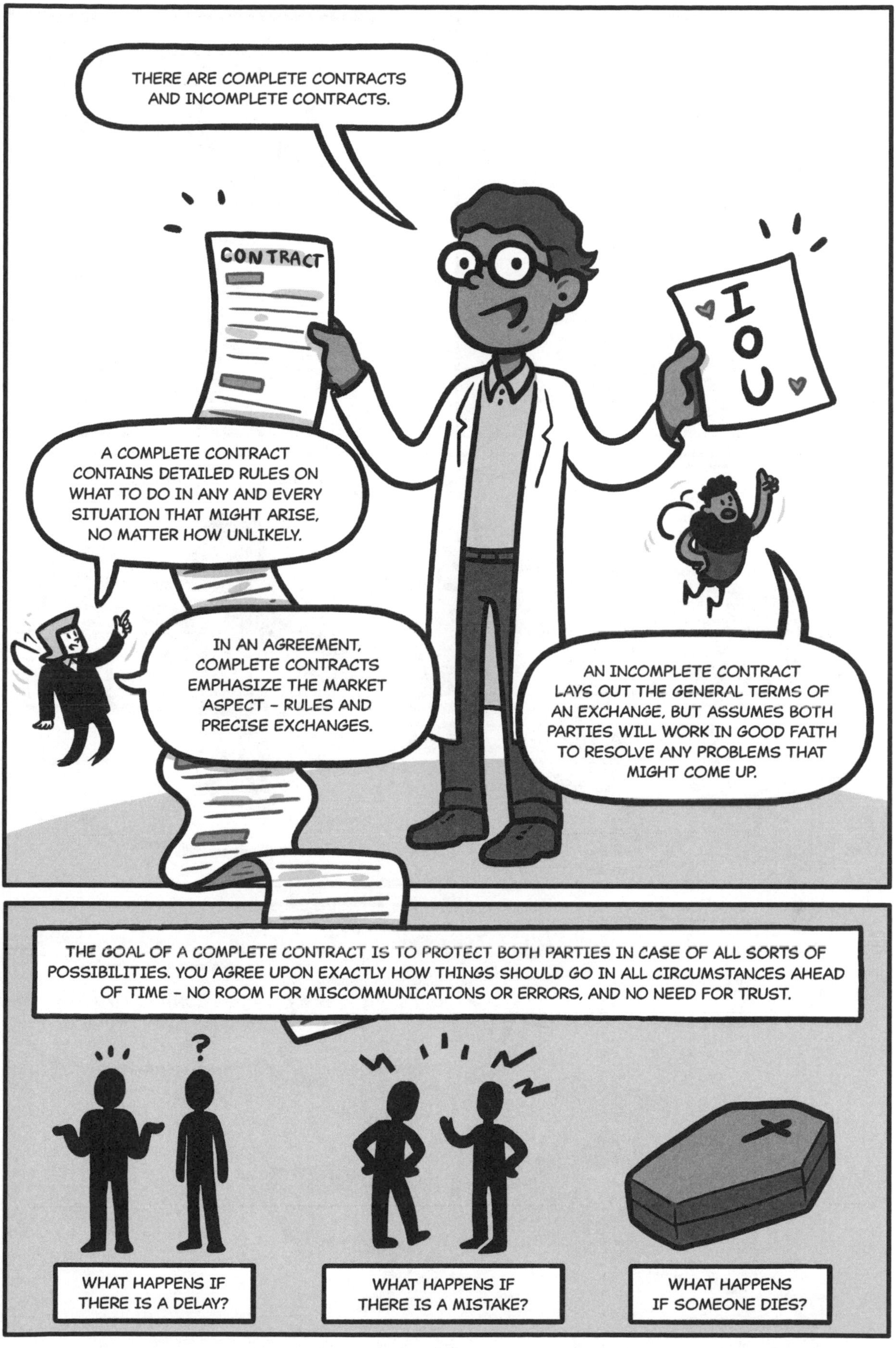
THERE ARE COMPLETE CONTRACTS AND INCOMPLETE CONTRACTS.
CONTRACT
IOU
A COMPLETE CONTRACT CONTAINS DETAILED RULES ON WHAT TO DO IN ANY AND EVERY SITUATION THAT MIGHT ARISE, NO MATTER HOW UNLIKELY.
IN AN AGREEMENT, COMPLETE CONTRACTS EMPHASIZE THE MARKET ASPECT – RULES AND PRECISE EXCHANGES.
AN INCOMPLETE CONTRACT LAYS OUT THE GENERAL TERMS OF AN EXCHANGE, BUT ASSUMES BOTH PARTIES WILL WORK IN GOOD FAITH TO RESOLVE ANY PROBLEMS THAT MIGHT COME UP.
THE GOAL OF A COMPLETE CONTRACT IS TO PROTECT BOTH PARTIES IN CASE OF ALL SORTS OF POSSIBILITIES. YOU AGREE UPON EXACTLY HOW THINGS SHOULD GO IN ALL CIRCUMSTANCES AHEAD OF TIME – NO ROOM FOR MISCOMMUNICATIONS OR ERRORS, AND NO NEED FOR TRUST.
WHAT HAPPENS IF THERE IS A DELAY?
WHAT HAPPENS IF THERE IS A MISTAKE?
WHAT HAPPENS IF SOMEONE DIES?

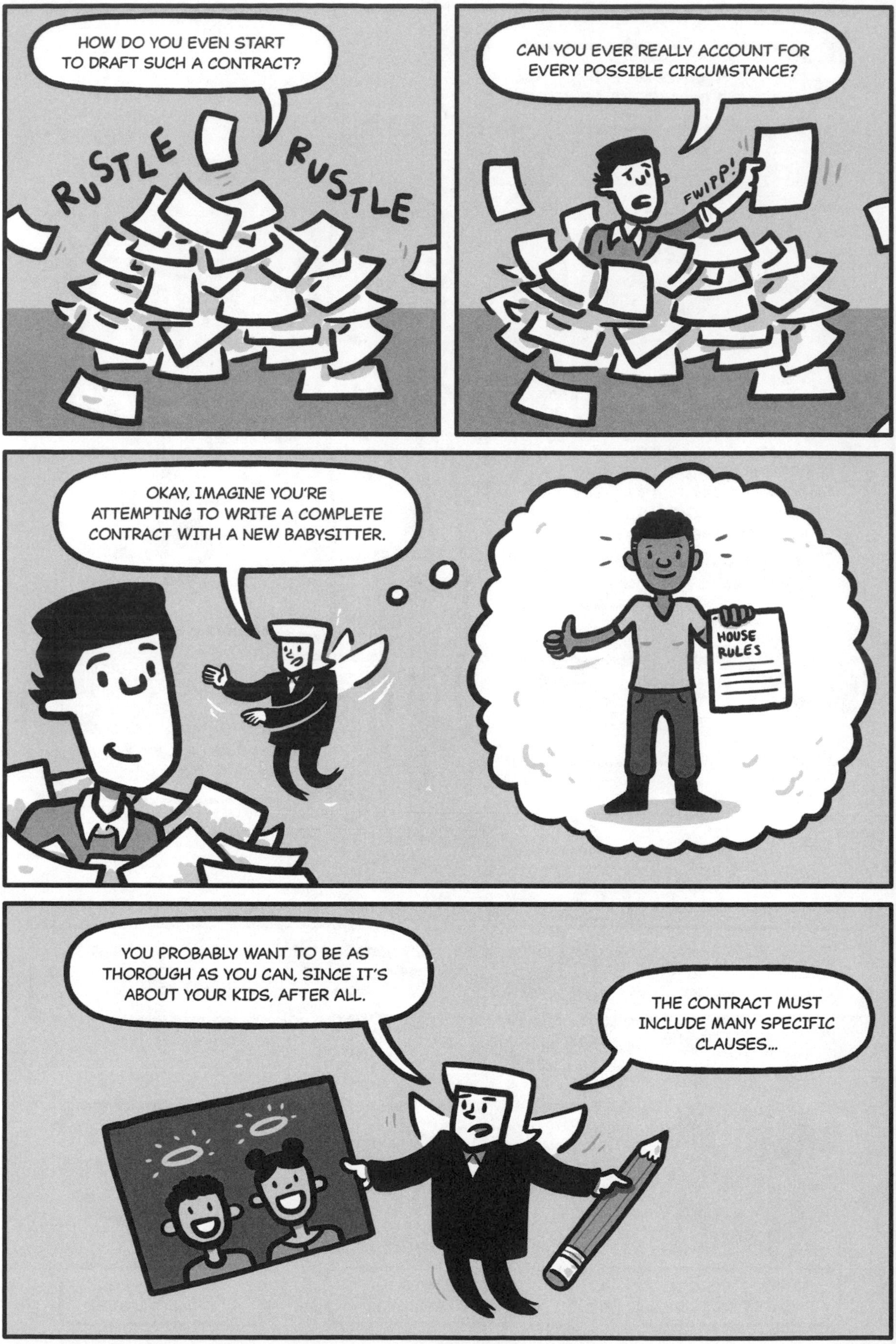
HOW DO YOU EVEN START TO DRAFT SUCH A CONTRACT?
RUSTLE RUSTLE
CAN YOU EVER REALLY ACCOUNT FOR EVERY POSSIBLE CIRCUMSTANCE?
FWIPP!
OKAY, IMAGINE YOU'RE ATTEMPTING TO WRITE A COMPLETE CONTRACT WITH A NEW BABYSITTER.
HOUSE RULES
YOU PROBABLY WANT TO BE AS THOROUGH AS YOU CAN, SINCE IT'S ABOUT YOUR KIDS, AFTER ALL.
THE CONTRACT MUST INCLUDE MANY SPECIFIC CLAUSES...

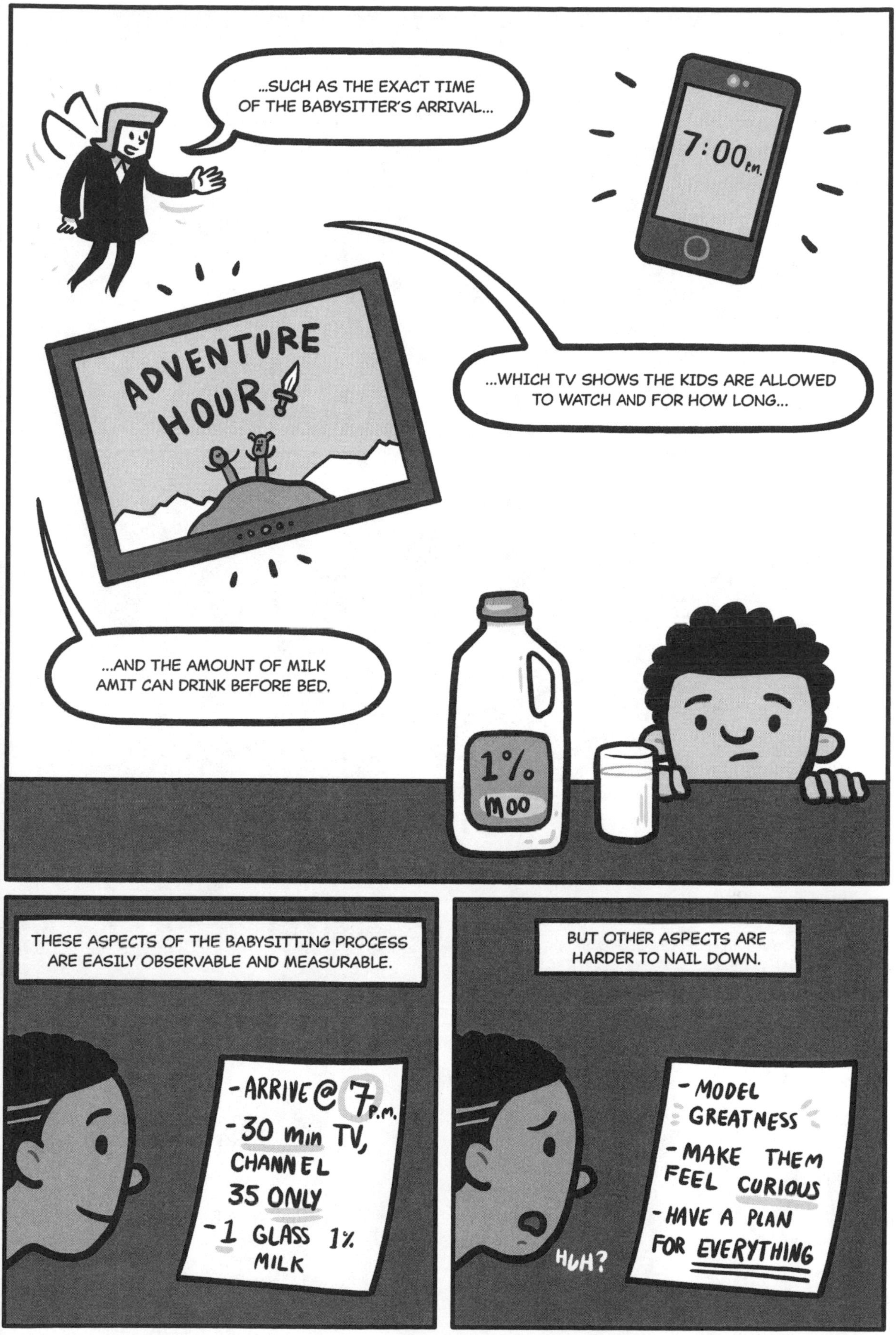
...SUCH AS THE EXACT TIME OF THE BABYSITTER'S ARRIVAL...
7:00 P.M.
...WHICH TV SHOWS THE KIDS ARE ALLOWED TO WATCH AND FOR HOW LONG...
ADVENTURE HOUR
...AND THE AMOUNT OF MILK AMIT CAN DRINK BEFORE BED.
1%
MOO
THESE ASPECTS OF THE BABYSITTING PROCESS ARE EASILY OBSERVABLE AND MEASURABLE.
-ARRIVE @ 7 P.M.
-30 min TV, CHANNEL 35 ONLY
-1 GLASS 1% MILK
BUT OTHER ASPECTS ARE HARDER TO NAIL DOWN.
-MODEL GREATNESS
-MAKE THEM FEEL CURIOUS
-HAVE A PLAN FOR EVERYTHING
HUH?

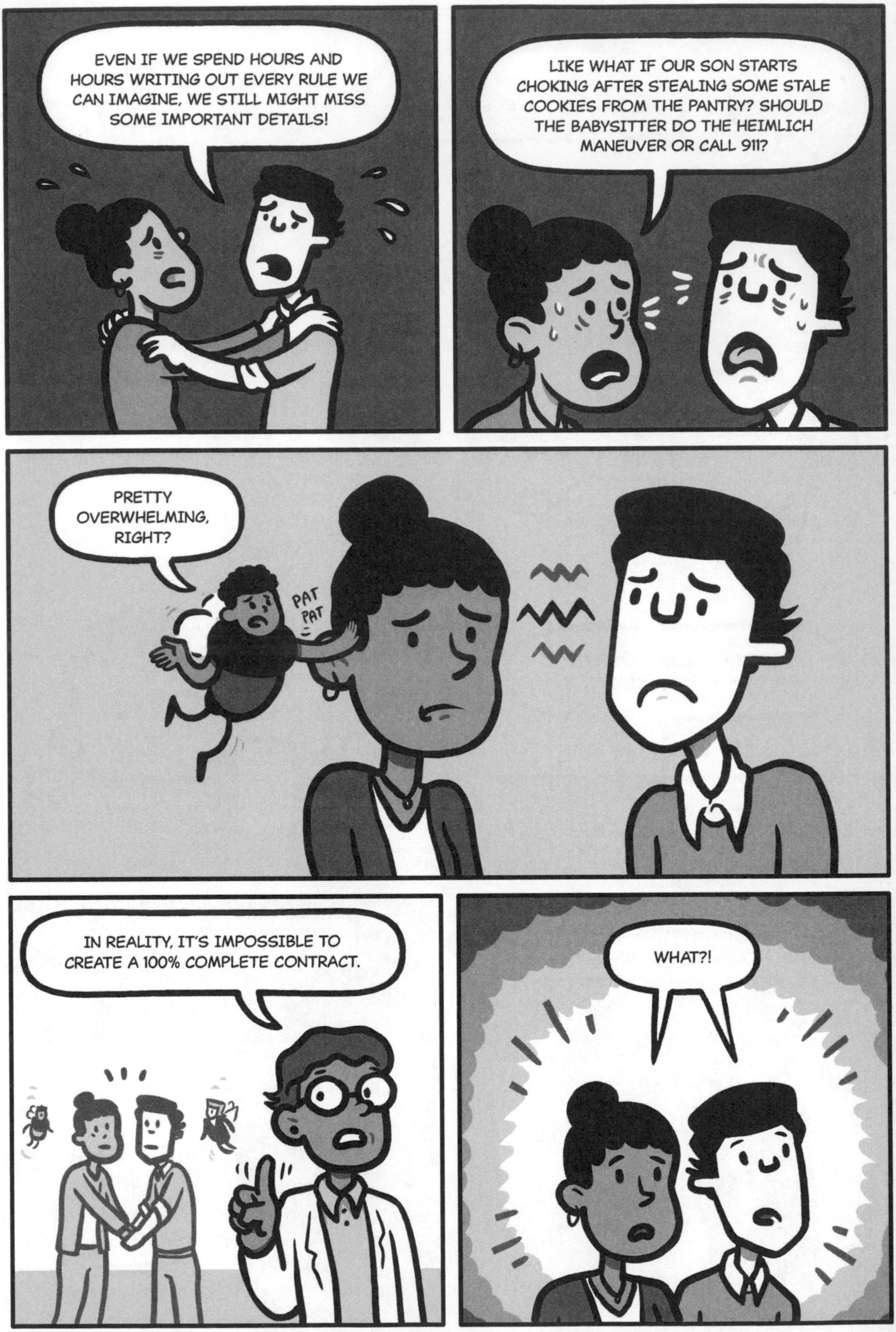
EVEN IF WE SPEND HOURS AND HOURS WRITING OUT EVERY RULE WE CAN IMAGINE, WE STILL MIGHT MISS SOME IMPORTANT DETAILS!
LIKE WHAT IF OUR SON STARTS CHOKING AFTER STEALING SOME STALE COOKIES FROM THE PANTRY? SHOULD THE BABYSITTER DO THE HEIMLICH MANEUVER OR CALL 911?
PRETTY OVERWHELMING, RIGHT?
PAT PAT
IN REALITY, IT'S IMPOSSIBLE TO CREATE A 100% COMPLETE CONTRACT.
WHAT?!

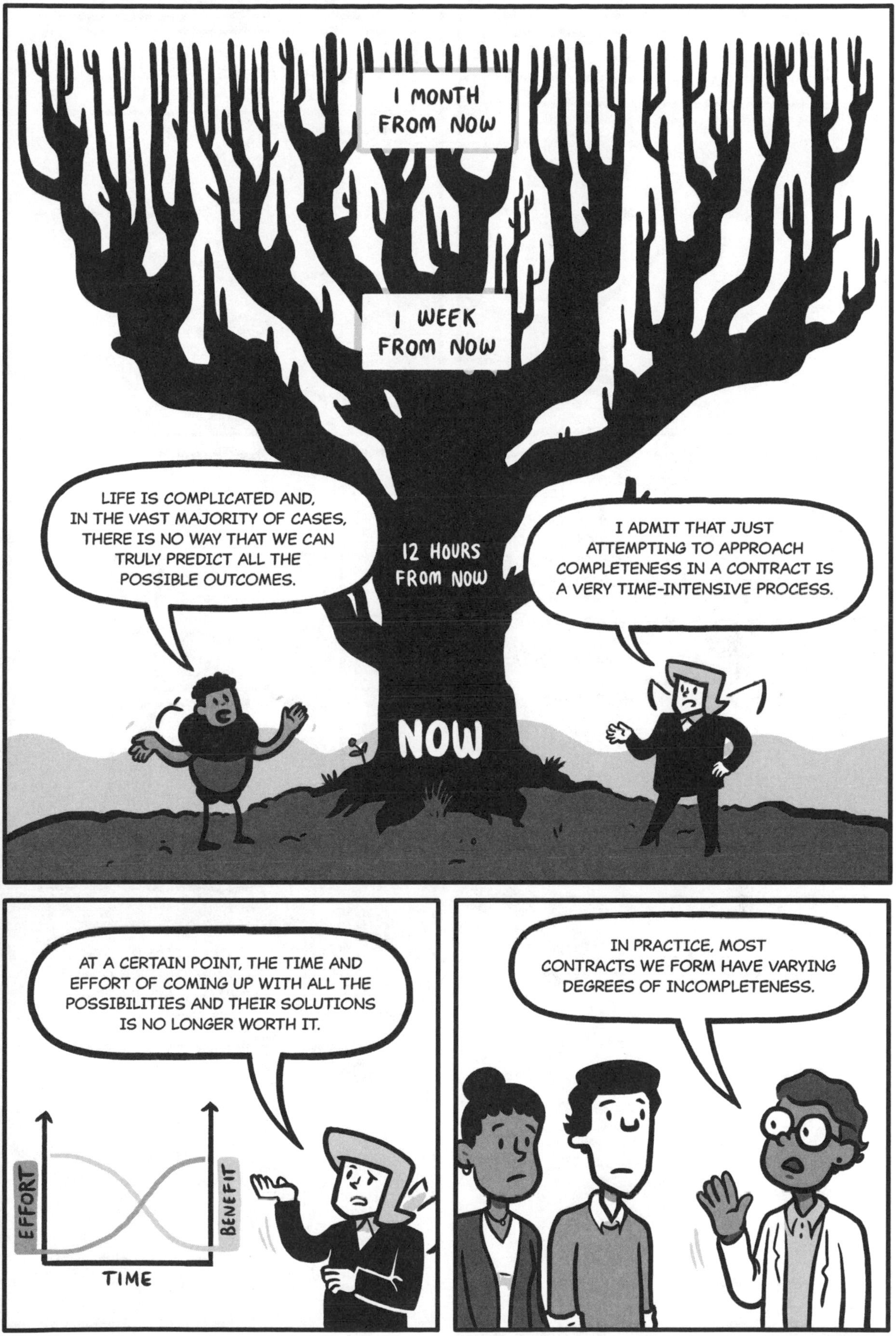
I MONTH FROM NOW
I WEEK FROM NOW
12 HOURS FROM NOW
NOW
LIFE IS COMPLICATED AND, IN THE VAST MAJORITY OF CASES, THERE IS NO WAY THAT WE CAN TRULY PREDICT ALL THE POSSIBLE OUTCOMES.
I ADMIT THAT JUST ATTEMPTING TO APPROACH COMPLETENESS IN A CONTRACT IS A VERY TIME-INTENSIVE PROCESS.
AT A CERTAIN POINT, THE TIME AND EFFORT OF COMING UP WITH ALL THE POSSIBILITIES AND THEIR SOLUTIONS IS NO LONGER WORTH IT.
EFFORT
BENEFIT
TIME
IN PRACTICE, MOST CONTRACTS WE FORM HAVE VARYING DEGREES OF INCOMPLETENESS.

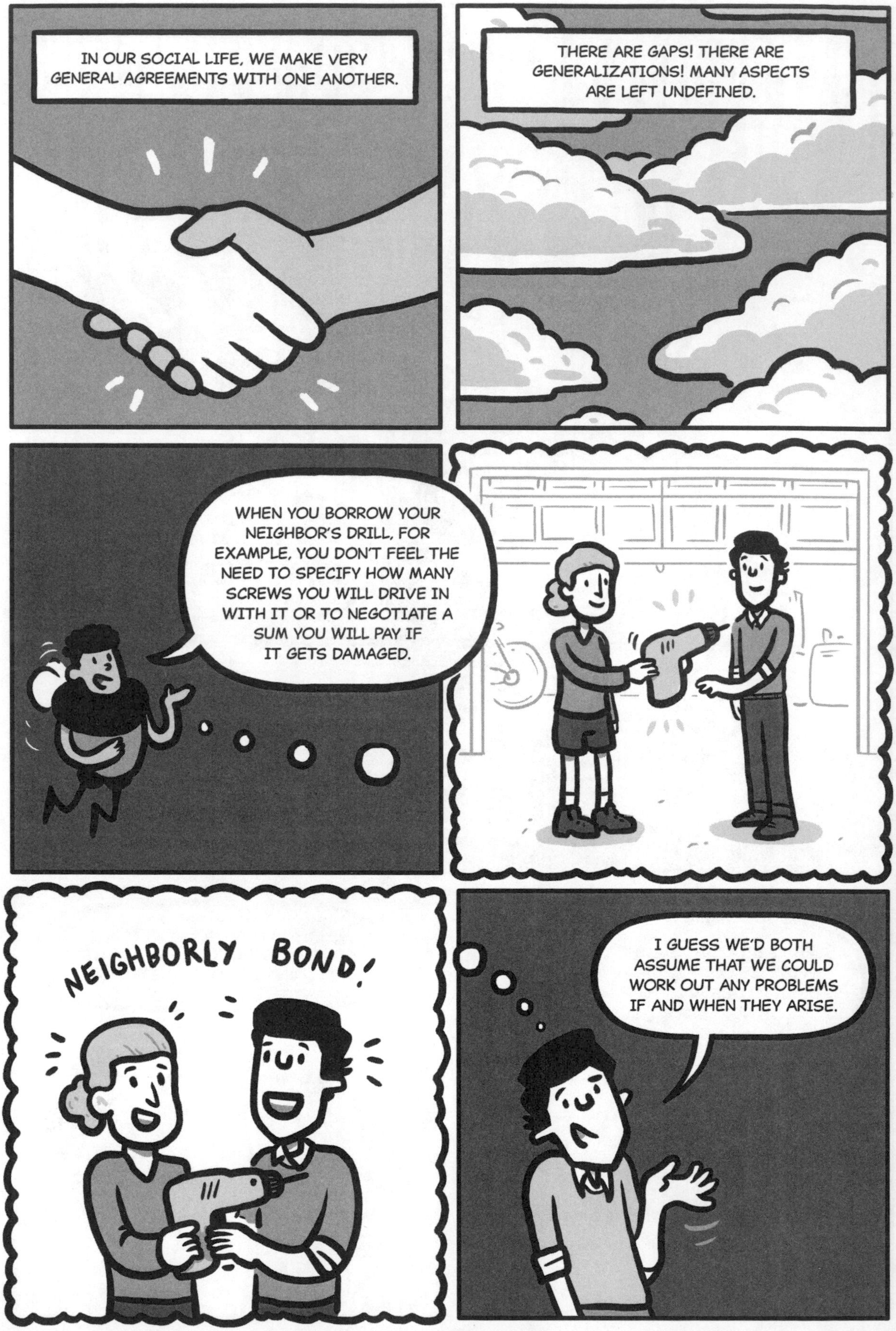
IN OUR SOCIAL LIFE, WE MAKE VERY GENERAL AGREEMENTS WITH ONE ANOTHER.
THERE ARE GAPS! THERE ARE GENERALIZATIONS! MANY ASPECTS ARE LEFT UNDEFINED.
WHEN YOU BORROW YOUR NEIGHBOR'S DRILL, FOR EXAMPLE, YOU DON'T FEEL THE NEED TO SPECIFY HOW MANY SCREWS YOU WILL DRIVE IN WITH IT OR TO NEGOTIATE A SUM YOU WILL PAY IF IT GETS DAMAGED.
NEIGHBORLY BOND!
I GUESS WE'D BOTH ASSUME THAT WE COULD WORK OUT ANY PROBLEMS IF AND WHEN THEY ARISE.

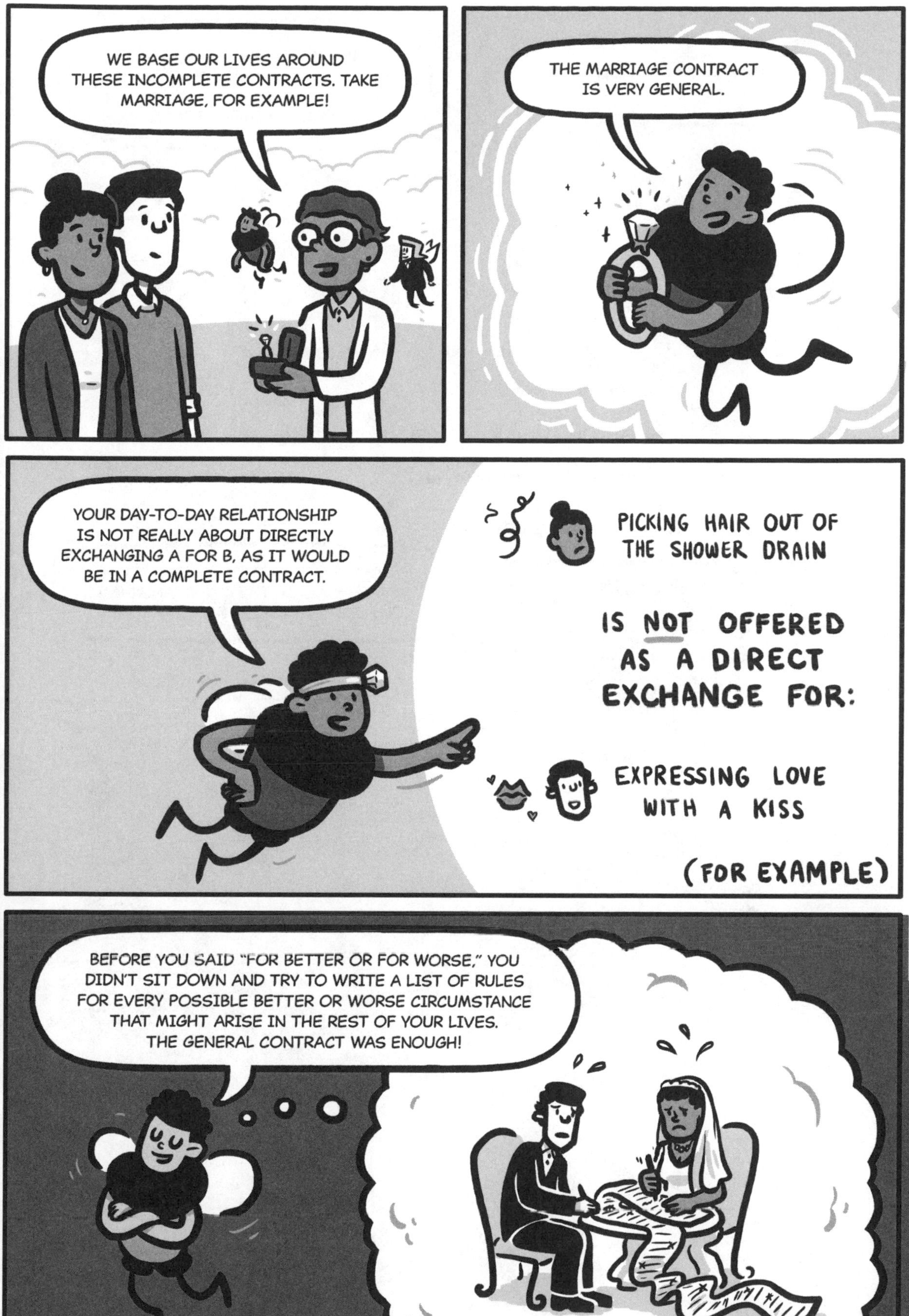

WE BASE OUR LIVES AROUND THESE INCOMPLETE CONTRACTS. TAKE MARRIAGE, FOR EXAMPLE!
THE MARRIAGE CONTRACT IS VERY GENERAL.
YOUR DAY-TO-DAY RELATIONSHIP IS NOT REALLY ABOUT DIRECTLY EXCHANGING A FOR B, AS IT WOULD BE IN A COMPLETE CONTRACT.
PICKING HAIR OUT OF THE SHOWER DRAIN
IS NOT OFFERED AS A DIRECT EXCHANGE FOR:
EXPRESSING LOVE WITH A KISS
(FOR EXAMPLE)
BEFORE YOU SAID "FOR BETTER OR FOR WORSE," YOU DIDN'T SIT DOWN AND TRY TO WRITE A LIST OF RULES FOR EVERY POSSIBLE BETTER OR WORSE CIRCUMSTANCE THAT MIGHT ARISE IN THE REST OF YOUR LIVES. THE GENERAL CONTRACT WAS ENOUGH!

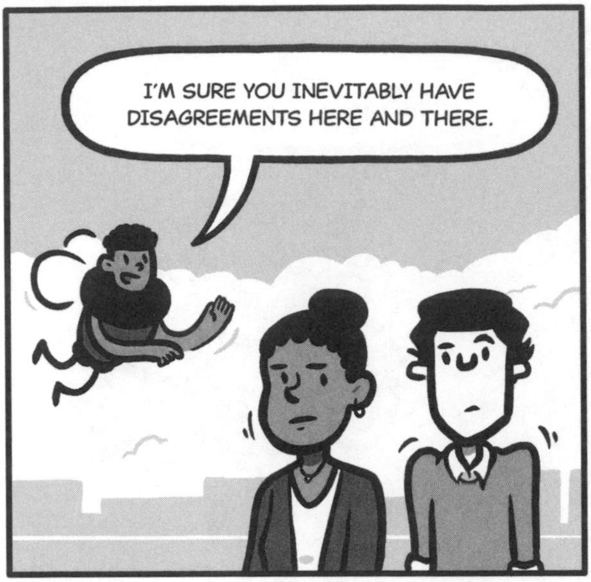
I'M SURE YOU INEVITABLY HAVE DISAGREEMENTS HERE AND THERE.

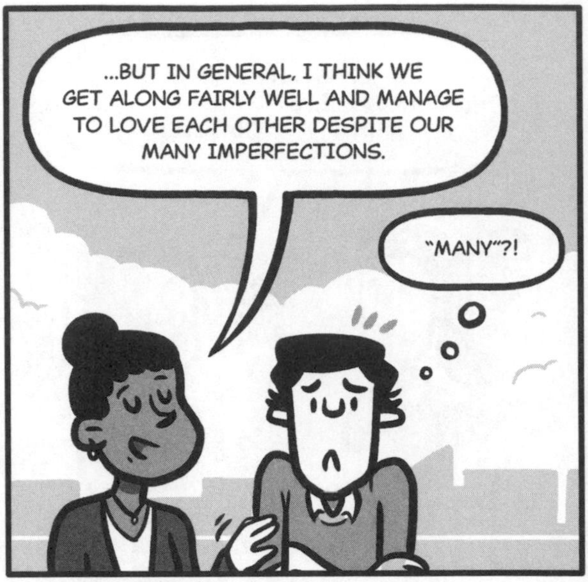
...BUT IN GENERAL, I THINK WE GET ALONG FAIRLY WELL AND MANAGE TO LOVE EACH OTHER DESPITE OUR MANY IMPERFECTIONS.
"MANY"?!

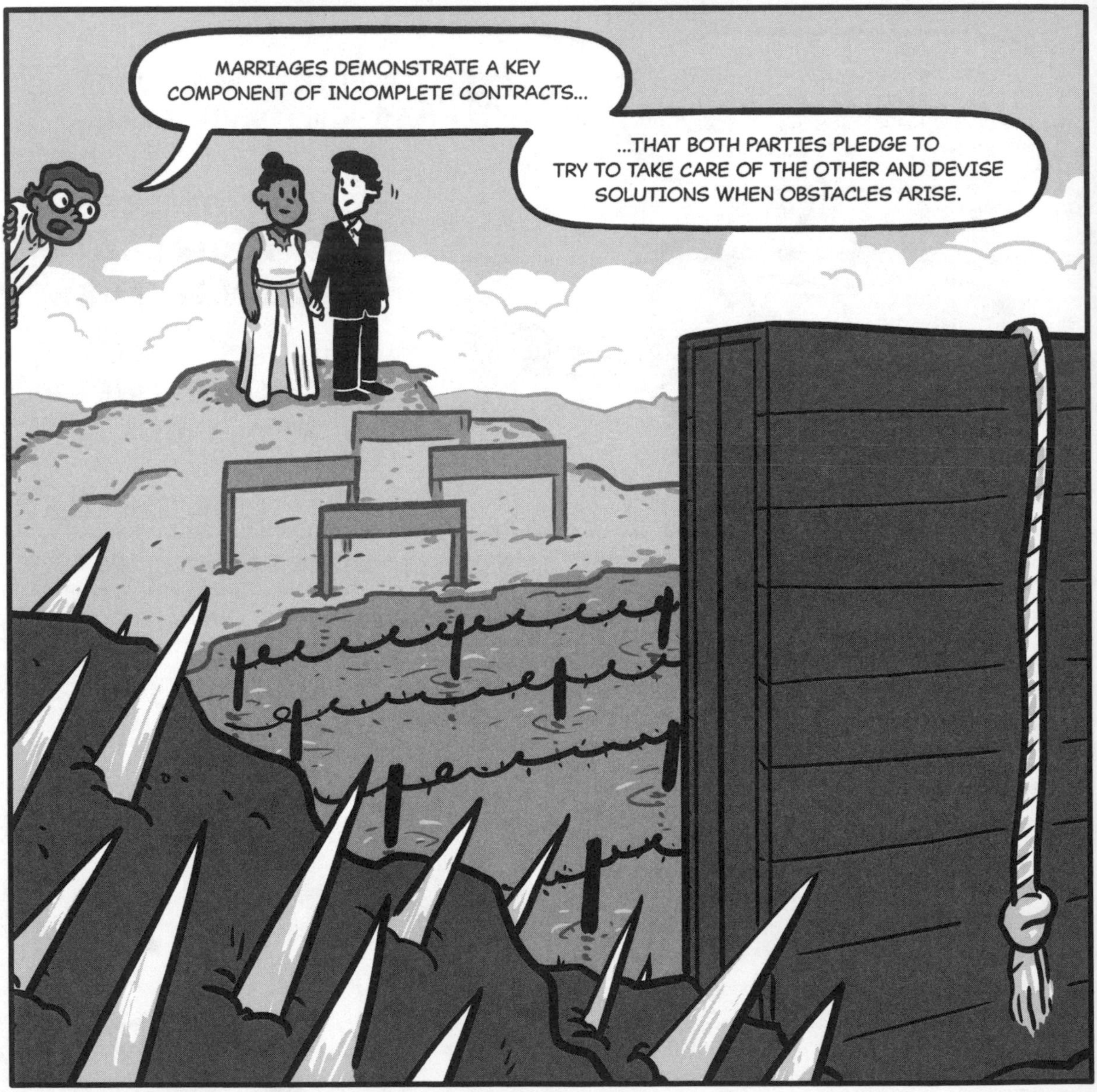
MARRIAGES DEMONSTRATE A KEY COMPONENT OF INCOMPLETE CONTRACTS...
...THAT BOTH PARTIES PLEDGE TO TRY TO TAKE CARE OF THE OTHER AND DEVISE SOLUTIONS WHEN OBSTACLES ARISE.

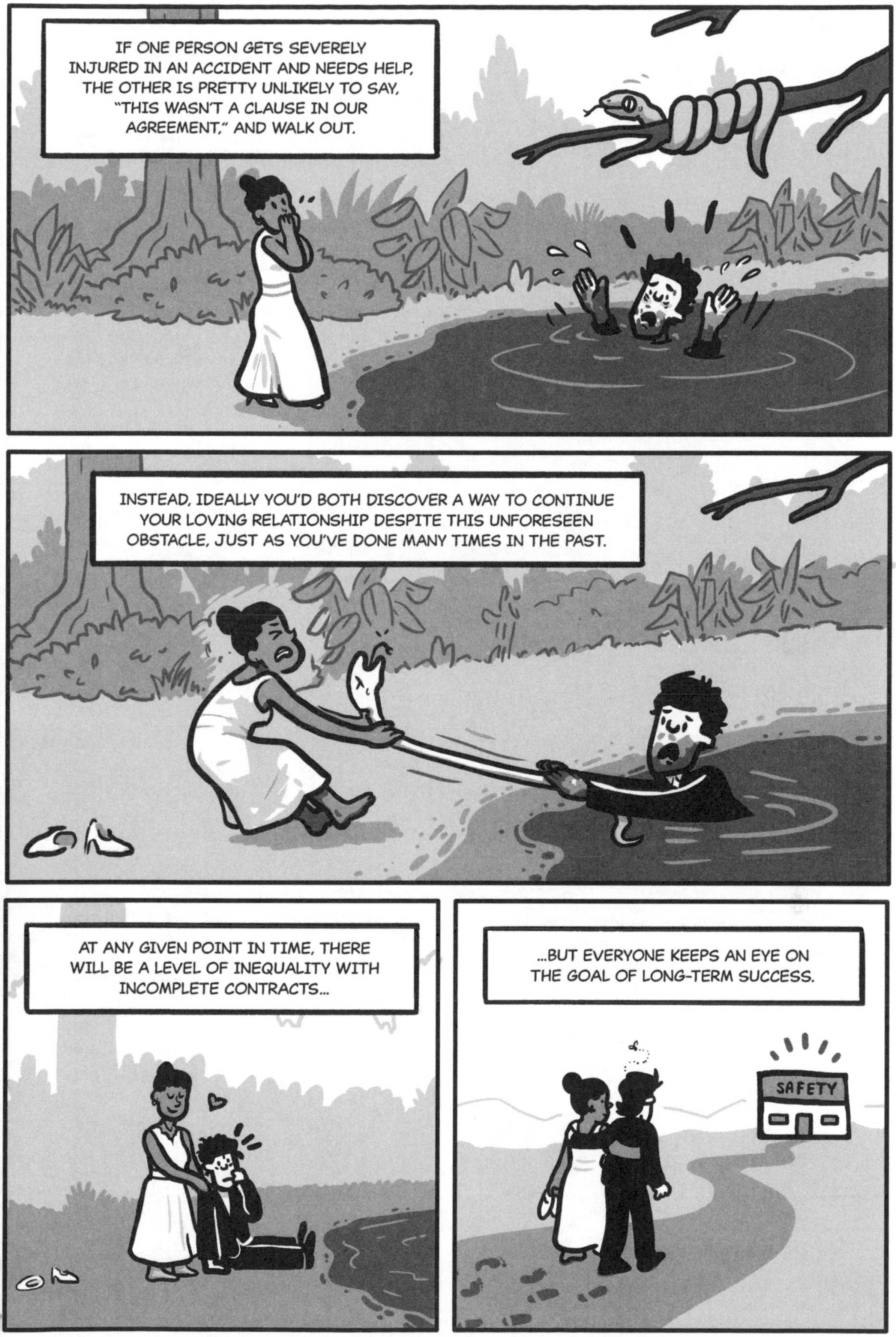
IF ONE PERSON GETS SEVERELY INJURED IN AN ACCIDENT AND NEEDS HELP, THE OTHER IS PRETTY UNLIKELY TO SAY, "THIS WASN'T A CLAUSE IN OUR AGREEMENT," AND WALK OUT.
INSTEAD, IDEALLY YOU'D BOTH DISCOVER A WAY TO CONTINUE YOUR LOVING RELATIONSHIP DESPITE THIS UNFORESEEN OBSTACLE, JUST AS YOU'VE DONE MANY TIMES IN THE PAST.
AT ANY GIVEN POINT IN TIME, THERE WILL BE A LEVEL OF INEQUALITY WITH INCOMPLETE CONTRACTS...
...BUT EVERYONE KEEPS AN EYE ON THE GOAL OF LONG-TERM SUCCESS.
SAFETY

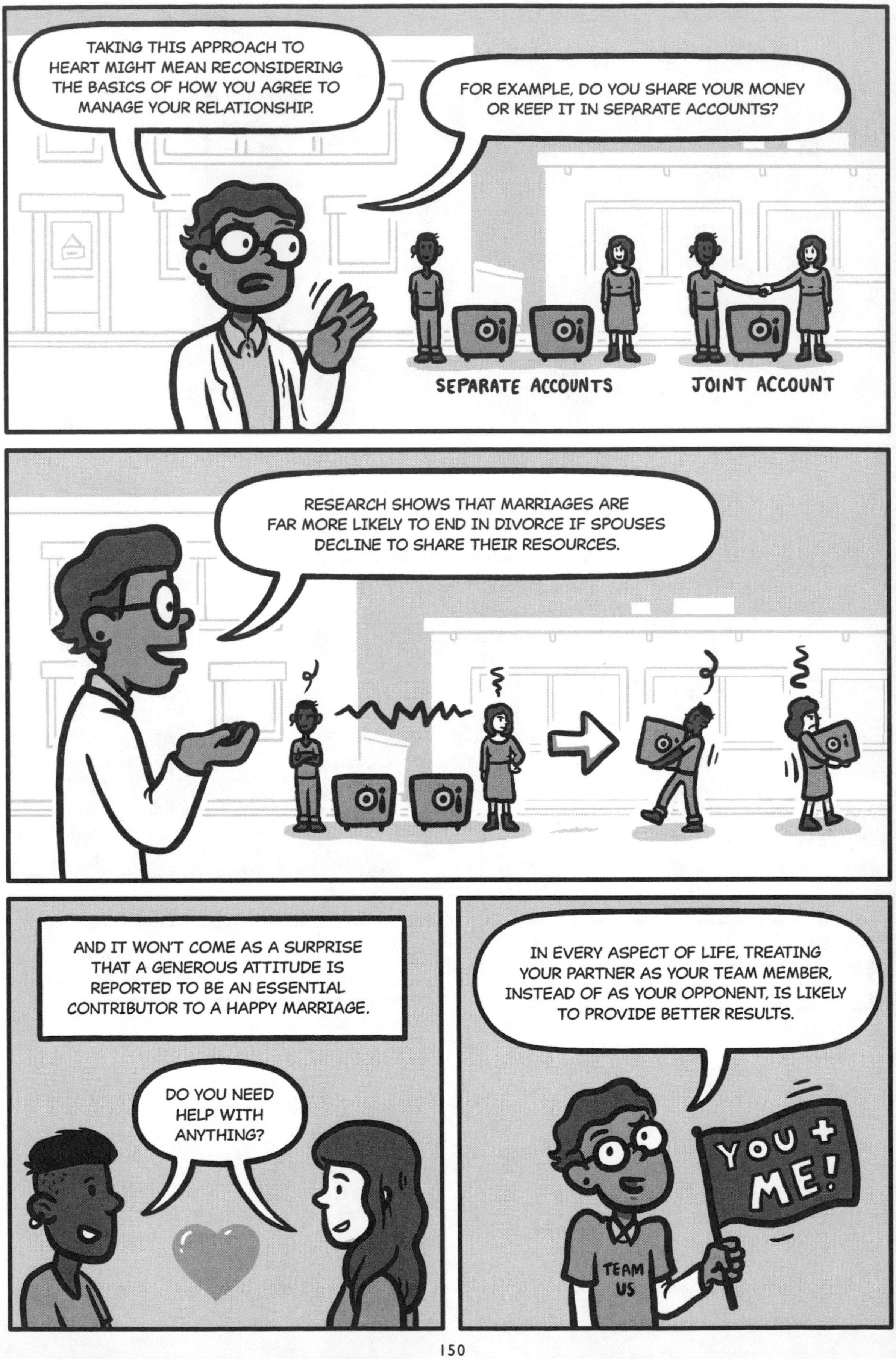
TAKING THIS APPROACH TO HEART MIGHT MEAN RECONSIDERING THE BASICS OF HOW YOU AGREE TO MANAGE YOUR RELATIONSHIP.
FOR EXAMPLE, DO YOU SHARE YOUR MONEY OR KEEP IT IN SEPARATE ACCOUNTS?
SEPARATE ACCOUNTS
JOINT ACCOUNT
RESEARCH SHOWS THAT MARRIAGES ARE FAR MORE LIKELY TO END IN DIVORCE IF SPOUSES DECLINE TO SHARE THEIR RESOURCES.
AND IT WON'T COME AS A SURPRISE THAT A GENEROUS ATTITUDE IS REPORTED TO BE AN ESSENTIAL CONTRIBUTOR TO A HAPPY MARRIAGE.
DO YOU NEED HELP WITH ANYTHING?
IN EVERY ASPECT OF LIFE, TREATING YOUR PARTNER AS YOUR TEAM MEMBER, INSTEAD OF AS YOUR OPPONENT, IS LIKELY TO PROVIDE BETTER RESULTS.
YOU + ME!
TEAM US

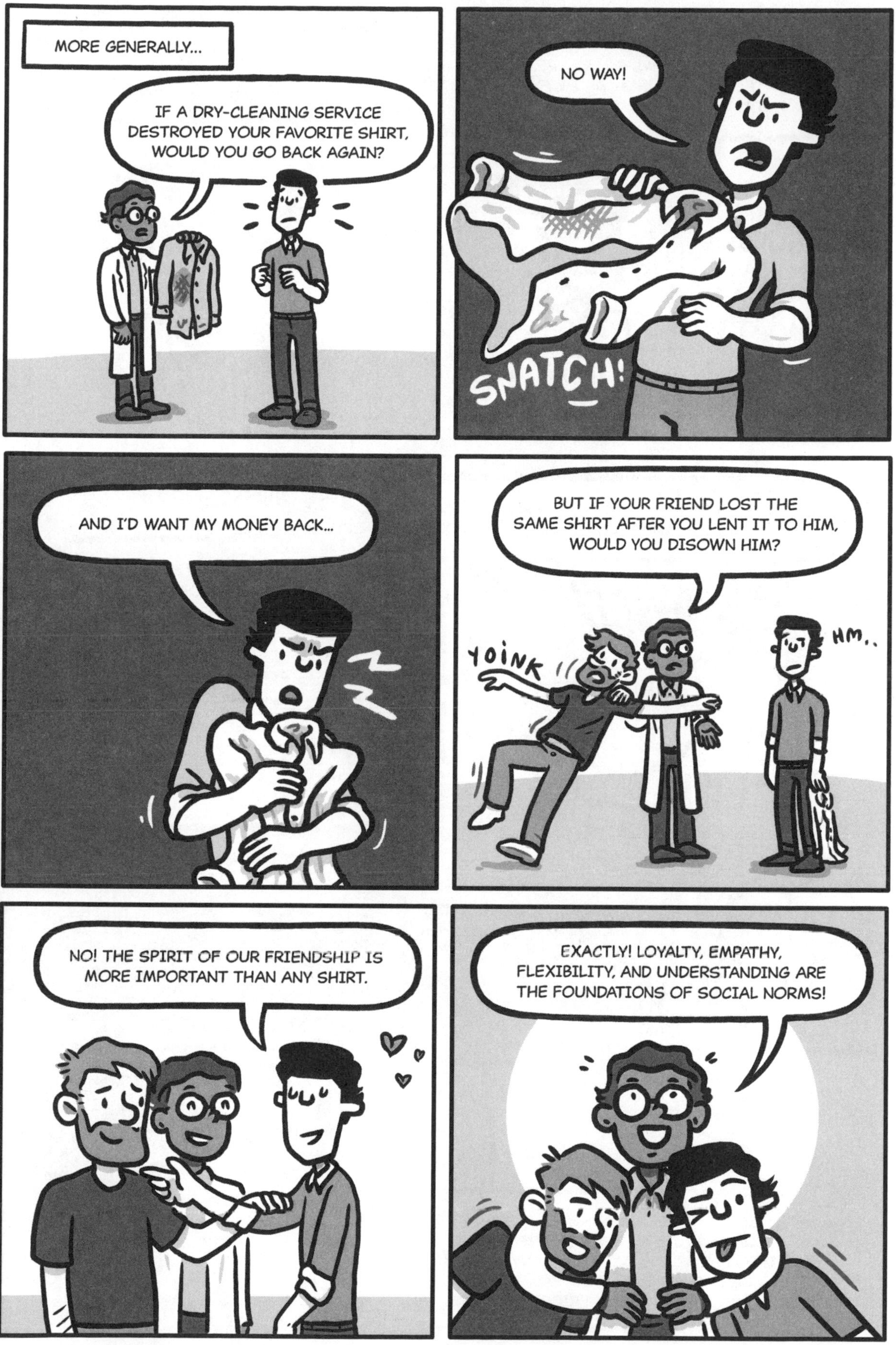
MORE GENERALLY...
IF A DRY-CLEANING SERVICE DESTROYED YOUR FAVORITE SHIRT, WOULD YOU GO BACK AGAIN?
NO WAY!
SNATCH!
AND I'D WANT MY MONEY BACK...
BUT IF YOUR FRIEND LOST THE SAME SHIRT AFTER YOU LENT IT TO HIM, WOULD YOU DISOWN HIM?
YOINK
HM..
NO! THE SPIRIT OF OUR FRIENDSHIP IS MORE IMPORTANT THAN ANY SHIRT.
EXACTLY! LOYALTY, EMPATHY, FLEXIBILITY, AND UNDERSTANDING ARE THE FOUNDATIONS OF SOCIAL NORMS!

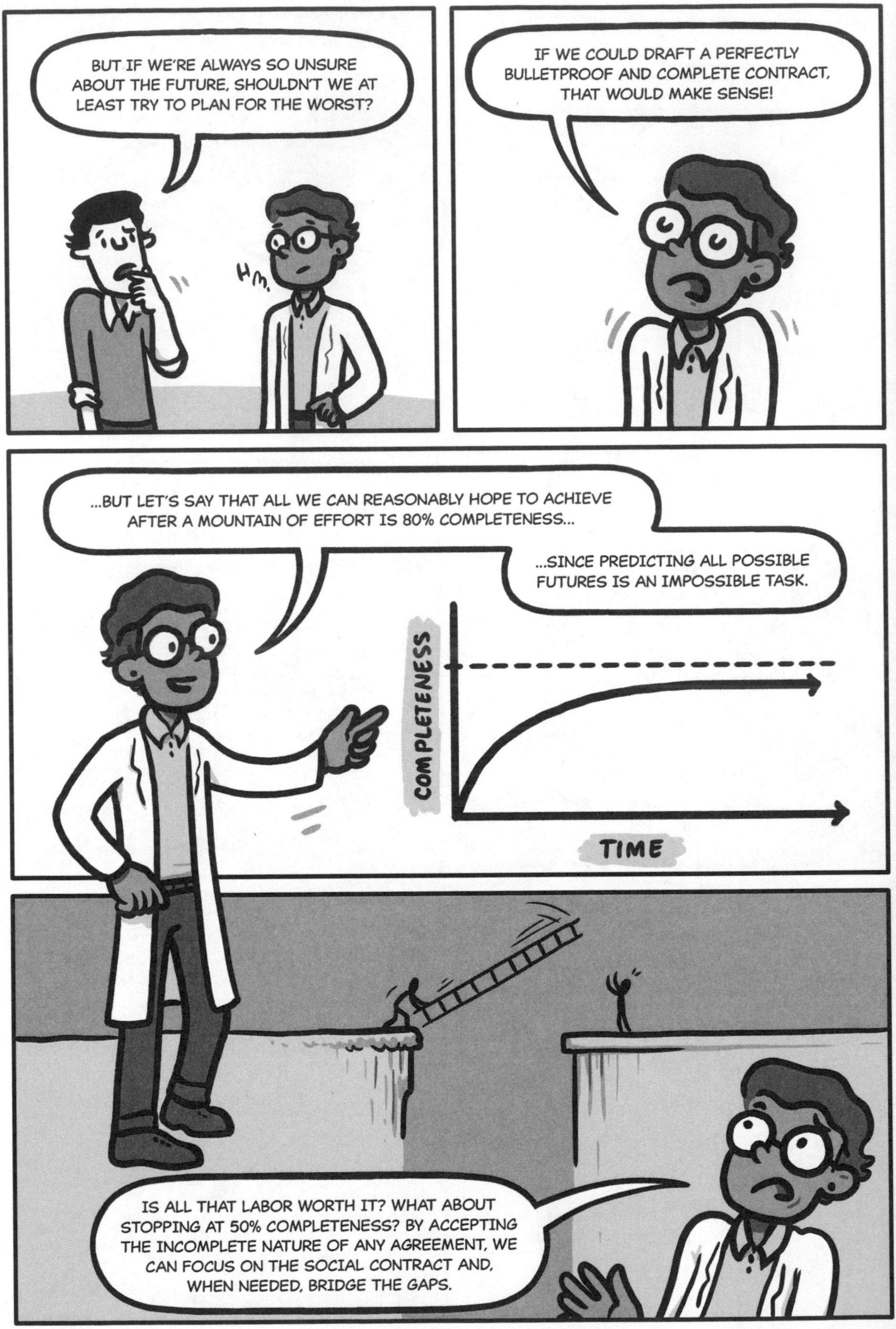
BUT IF WE'RE ALWAYS SO UNSURE ABOUT THE FUTURE, SHOULDN'T WE AT LEAST TRY TO PLAN FOR THE WORST?
HM.
IF WE COULD DRAFT A PERFECTLY BULLETPROOF AND COMPLETE CONTRACT, THAT WOULD MAKE SENSE!
...BUT LET'S SAY THAT ALL WE CAN REASONABLY HOPE TO ACHIEVE AFTER A MOUNTAIN OF EFFORT IS 80% COMPLETENESS...
...SINCE PREDICTING ALL POSSIBLE FUTURES IS AN IMPOSSIBLE TASK.
COMPLETENESS
TIME
IS ALL THAT LABOR WORTH IT? WHAT ABOUT STOPPING AT 50% COMPLETENESS? BY ACCEPTING THE INCOMPLETE NATURE OF ANY AGREEMENT, WE CAN FOCUS ON THE SOCIAL CONTRACT AND, WHEN NEEDED, BRIDGE THE GAPS.

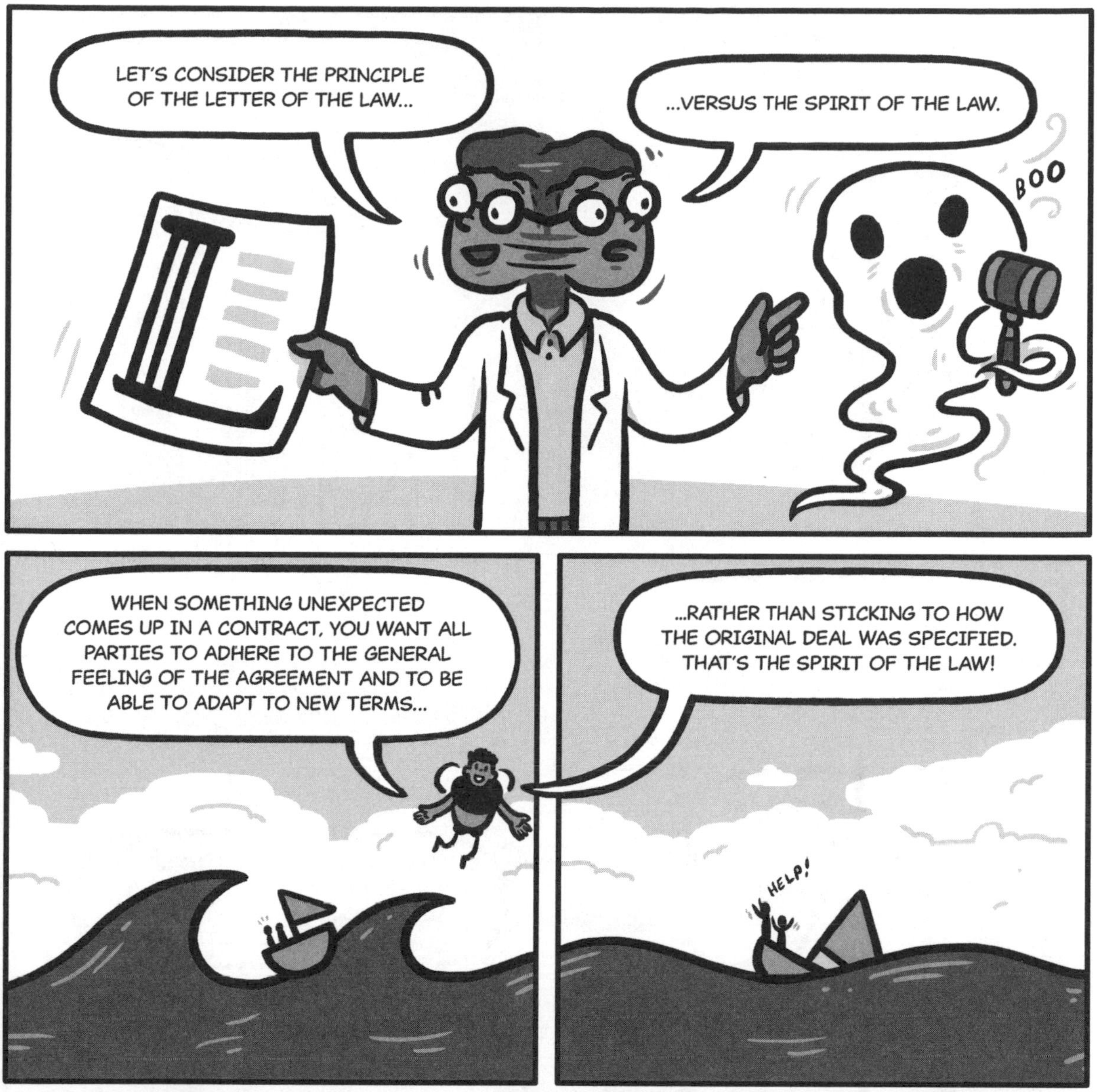
LET'S CONSIDER THE PRINCIPLE OF THE LETTER OF THE LAW...
...VERSUS THE SPIRIT OF THE LAW.
BOO
WHEN SOMETHING UNEXPECTED COMES UP IN A CONTRACT, YOU WANT ALL PARTIES TO ADHERE TO THE GENERAL FEELING OF THE AGREEMENT AND TO BE ABLE TO ADAPT TO NEW TERMS...
...RATHER THAN STICKING TO HOW THE ORIGINAL DEAL WAS SPECIFIED. THAT'S THE SPIRIT OF THE LAW!
HELP!
IF A CONTRACT IS OVERLY SPECIFIC, PEOPLE ARE MORE LIKELY TO SEE IT AS A MARKET TRANSACTION AND ONLY FOLLOW THE LETTER OF THE LAW AND NO MORE...
CONTRACT
...EVEN WHEN IT IS CLEAR THAT THIS WAS NOT THE ORIGINAL INTENTION.

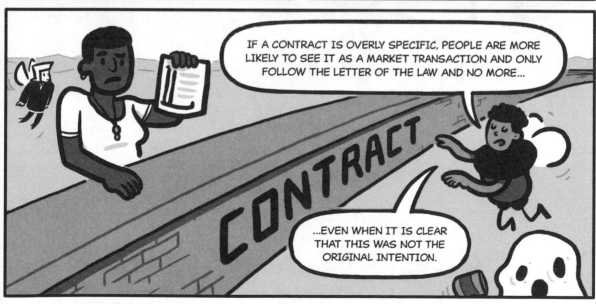

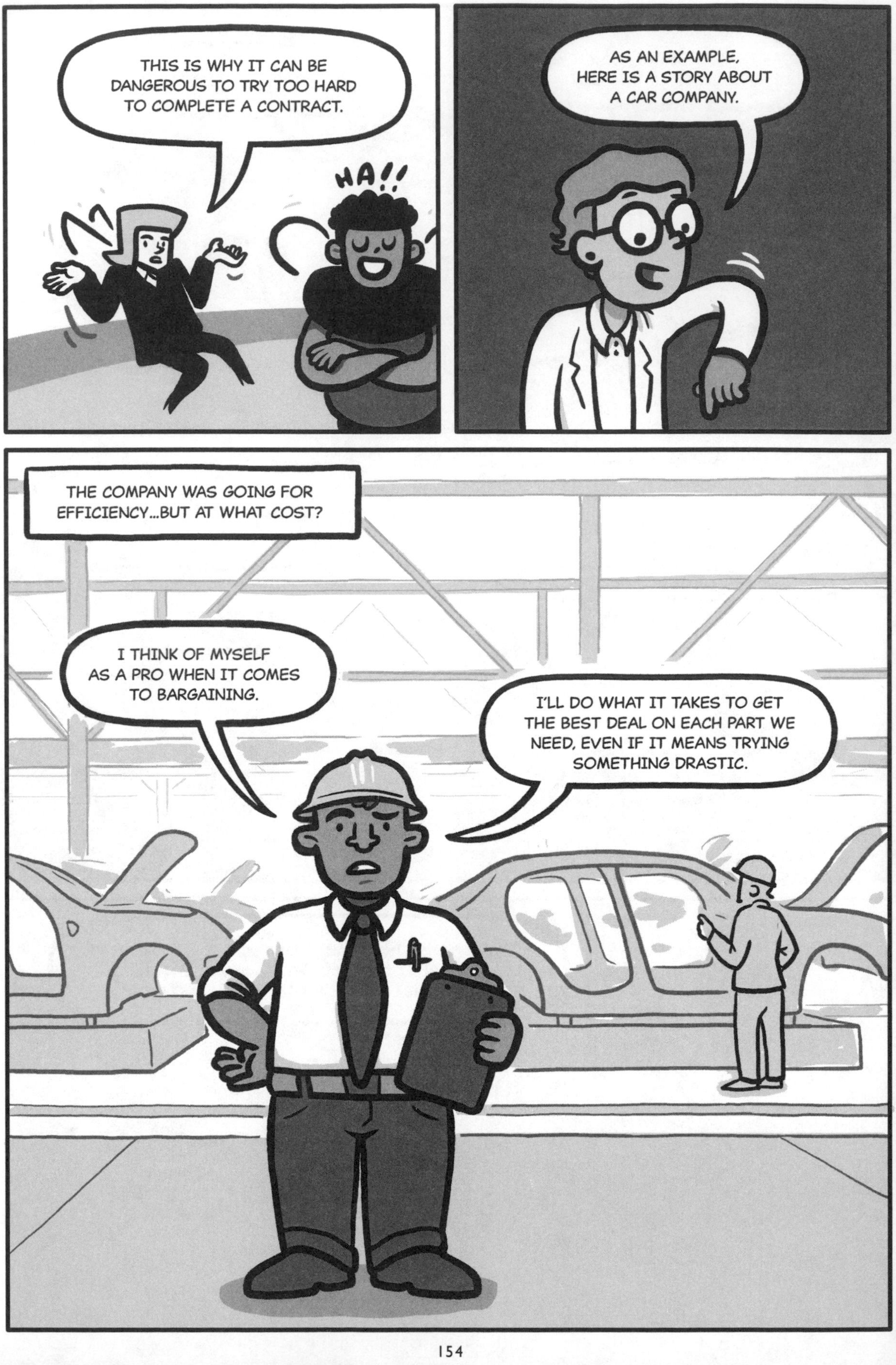
THIS IS WHY IT CAN BE DANGEROUS TO TRY TOO HARD TO COMPLETE A CONTRACT.
HA!!
AS AN EXAMPLE, HERE IS A STORY ABOUT A CAR COMPANY.
THE COMPANY WAS GOING FOR EFFICIENCY...BUT AT WHAT COST?
I THINK OF MYSELF AS A PRO WHEN IT COMES TO BARGAINING.
I'LL DO WHAT IT TAKES TO GET THE BEST DEAL ON EACH PART WE NEED, EVEN IF IT MEANS TRYING SOMETHING DRASTIC.

THE COMPANY ENDED UP CONDUCTING AN AUCTION WITH ITS PARTS SUPPLIERS TO GET THE LOWEST PRICES FOR EACH SPECIFIC COMPONENT.

ALL RIGHT, WHO CAN GIVE ME THE BEST DEAL ON 129 WHATSIT GENERATORS?

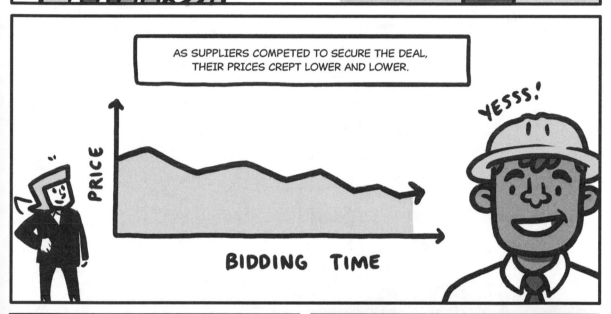

AS SUPPLIERS COMPETED TO SECURE THE DEAL, THEIR PRICES CREPT LOWER AND LOWER.

PRICE

BIDDING TIME

YESSS!

AT THE END OF THIS PROCESS, THE COMPANY DID MANAGE TO SQUEEZE ITS VARIOUS SUPPLIERS FOR THE VERY BEST DEALS ON EVERY SPECIFIC PART.

BUT...

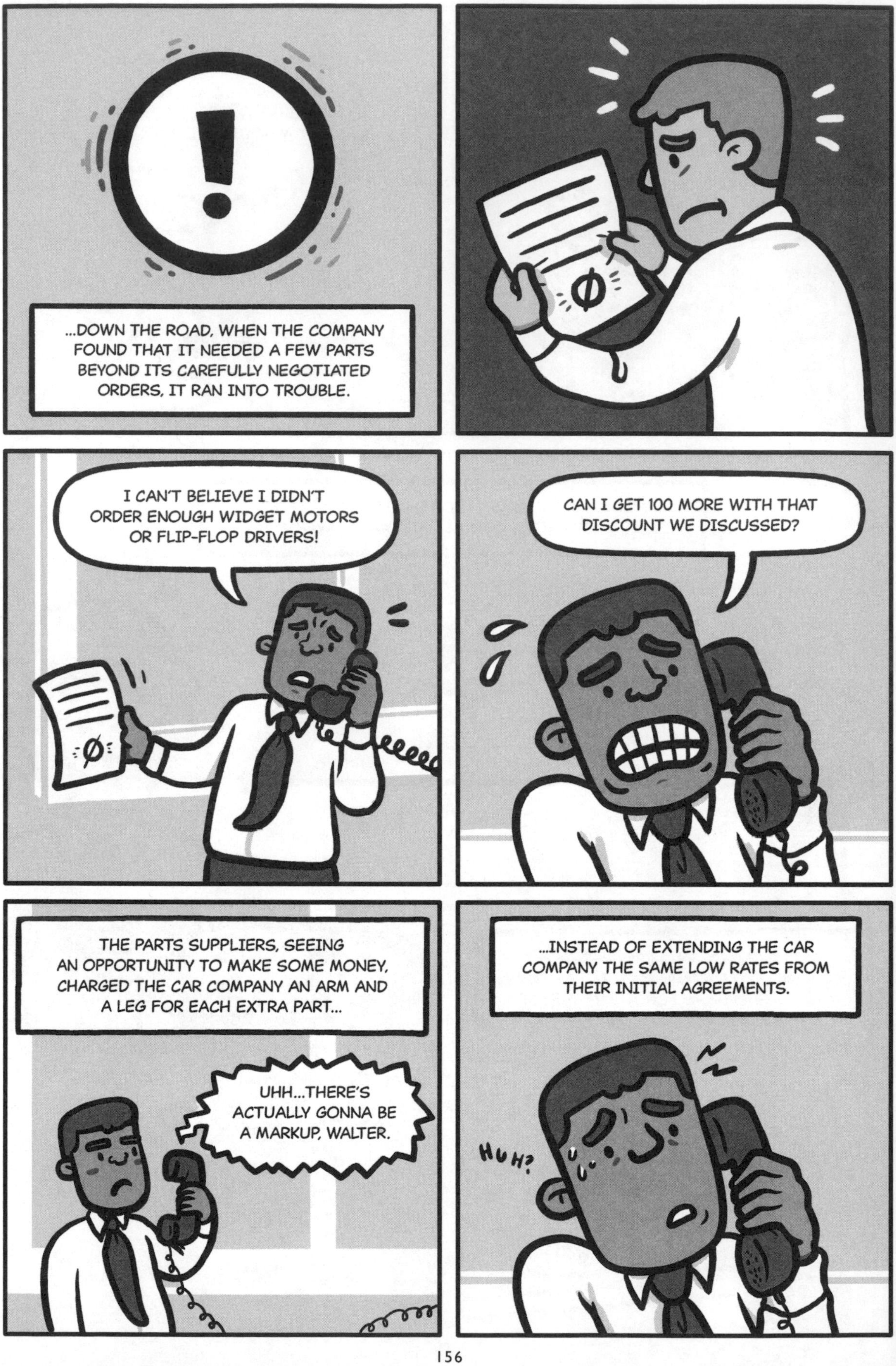
...DOWN THE ROAD, WHEN THE COMPANY FOUND THAT IT NEEDED A FEW PARTS BEYOND ITS CAREFULLY NEGOTIATED ORDERS, IT RAN INTO TROUBLE.
I CAN'T BELIEVE I DIDN'T ORDER ENOUGH WIDGET MOTORS OR FLIP-FLOP DRIVERS!
CAN I GET 100 MORE WITH THAT DISCOUNT WE DISCUSSED?
THE PARTS SUPPLIERS, SEEING AN OPPORTUNITY TO MAKE SOME MONEY, CHARGED THE CAR COMPANY AN ARM AND A LEG FOR EACH EXTRA PART...
UHH...THERE'S ACTUALLY GONNA BE A MARKUP, WALTER.
...INSTEAD OF EXTENDING THE CAR COMPANY THE SAME LOW RATES FROM THEIR INITIAL AGREEMENTS.
HUH?

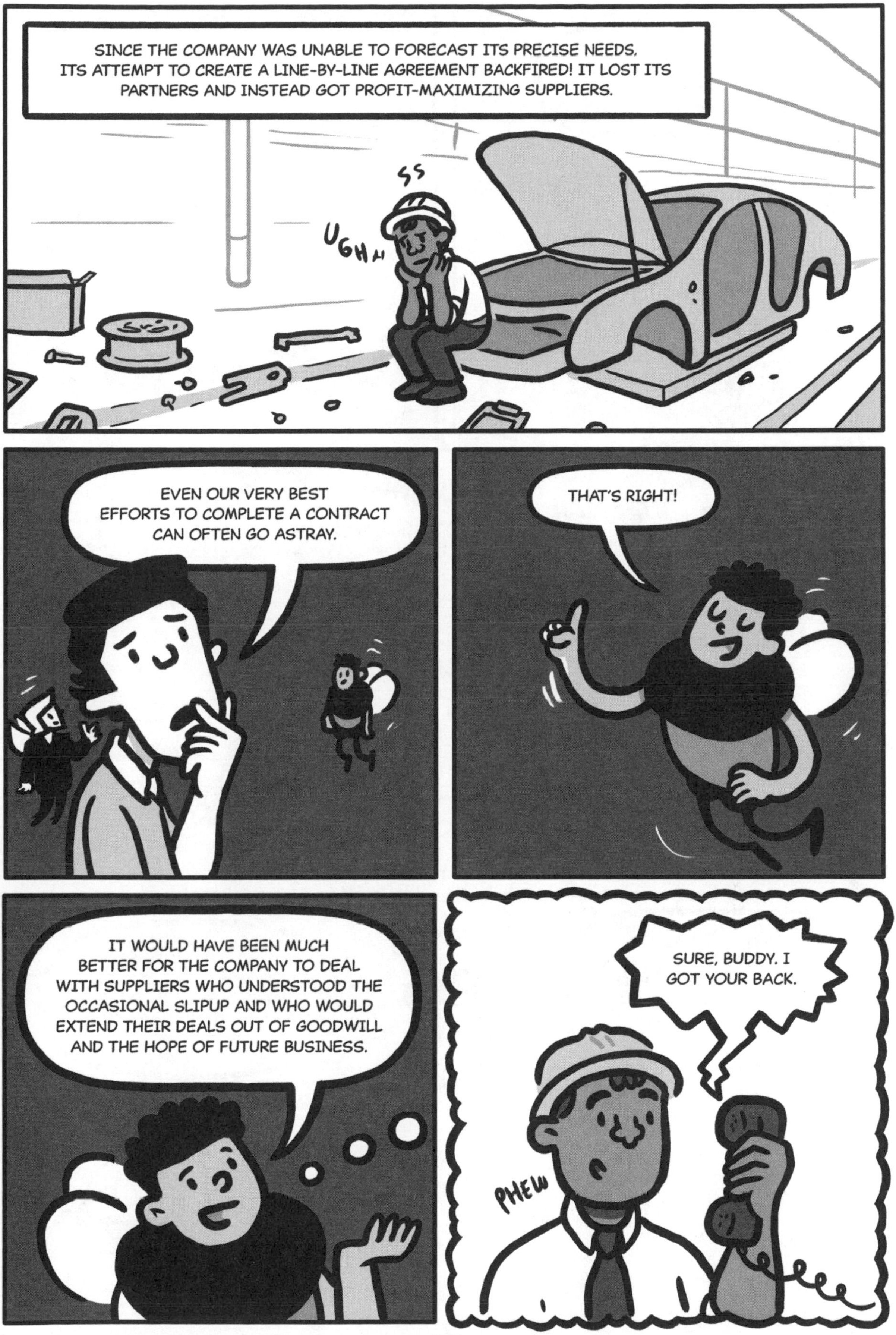
SINCE THE COMPANY WAS UNABLE TO FORECAST ITS PRECISE NEEDS, ITS ATTEMPT TO CREATE A LINE-BY-LINE AGREEMENT BACKFIRED! IT LOST ITS PARTNERS AND INSTEAD GOT PROFIT-MAXIMIZING SUPPLIERS.
SS
UGHH
EVEN OUR VERY BEST EFFORTS TO COMPLETE A CONTRACT CAN OFTEN GO ASTRAY.
THAT'S RIGHT!
IT WOULD HAVE BEEN MUCH BETTER FOR THE COMPANY TO DEAL WITH SUPPLIERS WHO UNDERSTOOD THE OCCASIONAL SLIPUP AND WHO WOULD EXTEND THEIR DEALS OUT OF GOODWILL AND THE HOPE OF FUTURE BUSINESS.
SURE, BUDDY. I GOT YOUR BACK.
PHEW

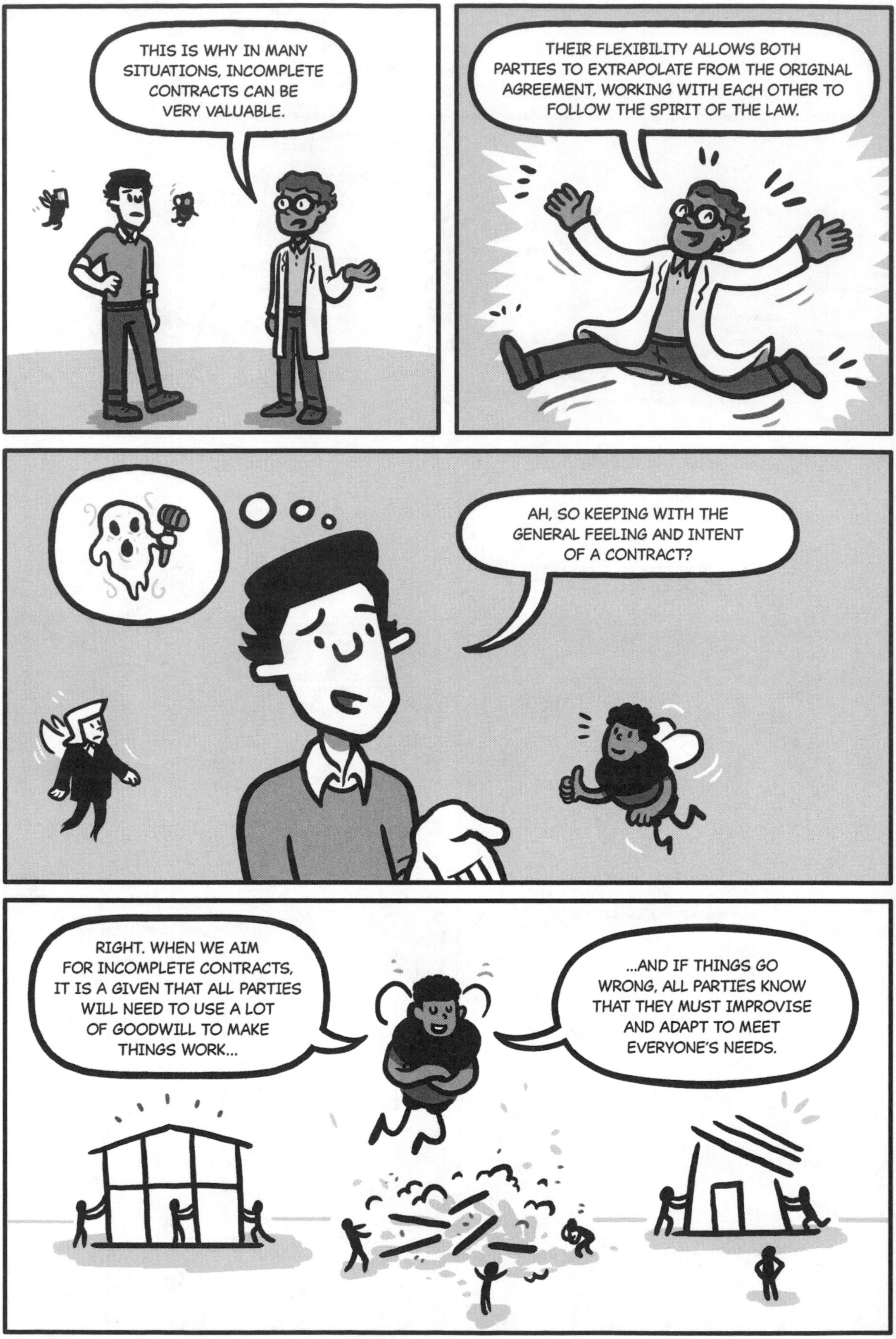
THIS IS WHY IN MANY SITUATIONS, INCOMPLETE CONTRACTS CAN BE VERY VALUABLE.
THEIR FLEXIBILITY ALLOWS BOTH PARTIES TO EXTRAPOLATE FROM THE ORIGINAL AGREEMENT, WORKING WITH EACH OTHER TO FOLLOW THE SPIRIT OF THE LAW.
AH, SO KEEPING WITH THE GENERAL FEELING AND INTENT OF A CONTRACT?
RIGHT. WHEN WE AIM FOR INCOMPLETE CONTRACTS, IT IS A GIVEN THAT ALL PARTIES WILL NEED TO USE A LOT OF GOODWILL TO MAKE THINGS WORK...
...AND IF THINGS GO WRONG, ALL PARTIES KNOW THAT THEY MUST IMPROVISE AND ADAPT TO MEET EVERYONE'S NEEDS.

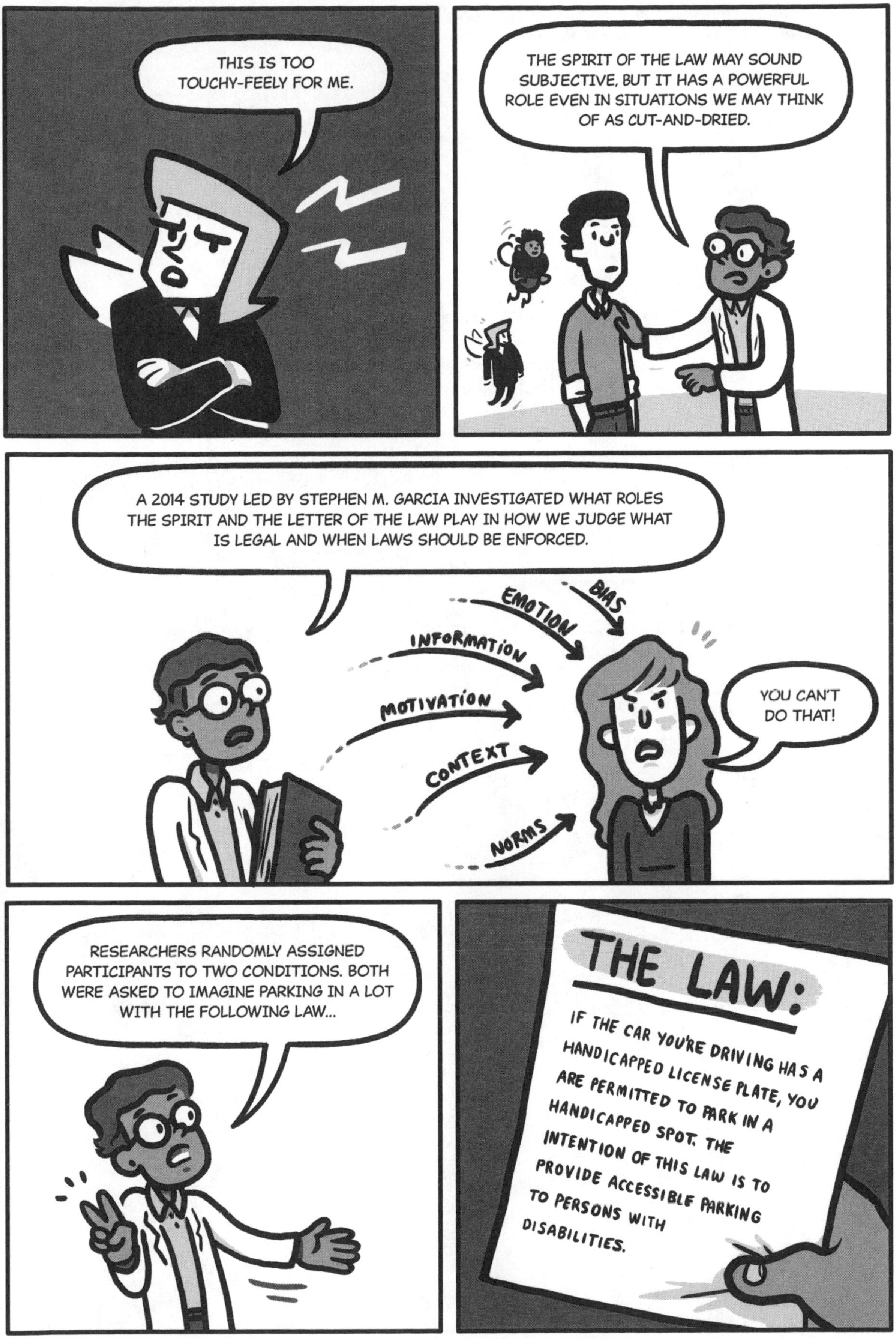
THIS IS TOO TOUCHY-FEELY FOR ME.
THE SPIRIT OF THE LAW MAY SOUND SUBJECTIVE, BUT IT HAS A POWERFUL ROLE EVEN IN SITUATIONS WE MAY THINK OF AS CUT-AND-DRIED.
A 2014 STUDY LED BY STEPHEN M. GARCIA INVESTIGATED WHAT ROLES THE SPIRIT AND THE LETTER OF THE LAW PLAY IN HOW WE JUDGE WHAT IS LEGAL AND WHEN LAWS SHOULD BE ENFORCED.
BIAS
EMOTION
INFORMATION
MOTIVATION
CONTEXT
NORMS
YOU CAN'T DO THAT!
RESEARCHERS RANDOMLY ASSIGNED PARTICIPANTS TO TWO CONDITIONS. BOTH WERE ASKED TO IMAGINE PARKING IN A LOT WITH THE FOLLOWING LAW...
THE LAW:
IF THE CAR YOU'RE DRIVING HAS A HANDICAPPED LICENSE PLATE, YOU ARE PERMITTED TO PARK IN A HANDICAPPED SPOT. THE INTENTION OF THIS LAW IS TO PROVIDE ACCESSIBLE PARKING TO PERSONS WITH DISABILITIES.

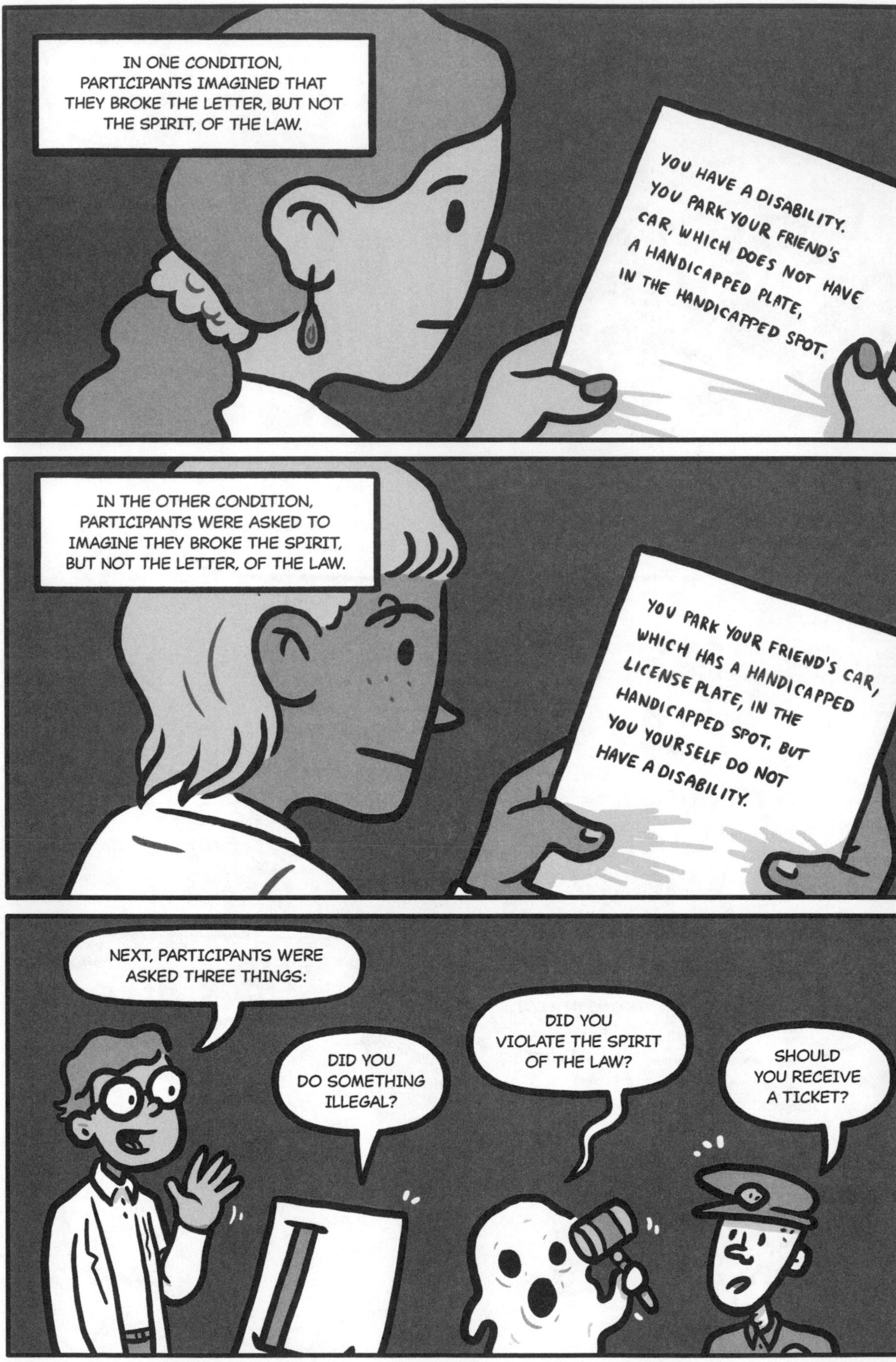
IN ONE CONDITION, PARTICIPANTS IMAGINED THAT THEY BROKE THE LETTER, BUT NOT THE SPIRIT, OF THE LAW.
YOU HAVE A DISABILITY. YOU PARK YOUR FRIEND'S CAR, WHICH DOES NOT HAVE A HANDICAPPED PLATE, IN THE HANDICAPPED SPOT.
IN THE OTHER CONDITION, PARTICIPANTS WERE ASKED TO IMAGINE THEY BROKE THE SPIRIT, BUT NOT THE LETTER, OF THE LAW.
YOU PARK YOUR FRIEND'S CAR, WHICH HAS A HANDICAPPED LICENSE PLATE, IN THE HANDICAPPED SPOT, BUT YOU YOURSELF DO NOT HAVE A DISABILITY.
NEXT, PARTICIPANTS WERE ASKED THREE THINGS:
DID YOU DO SOMETHING ILLEGAL?
DID YOU VIOLATE THE SPIRIT OF THE LAW?
SHOULD YOU RECEIVE A TICKET?

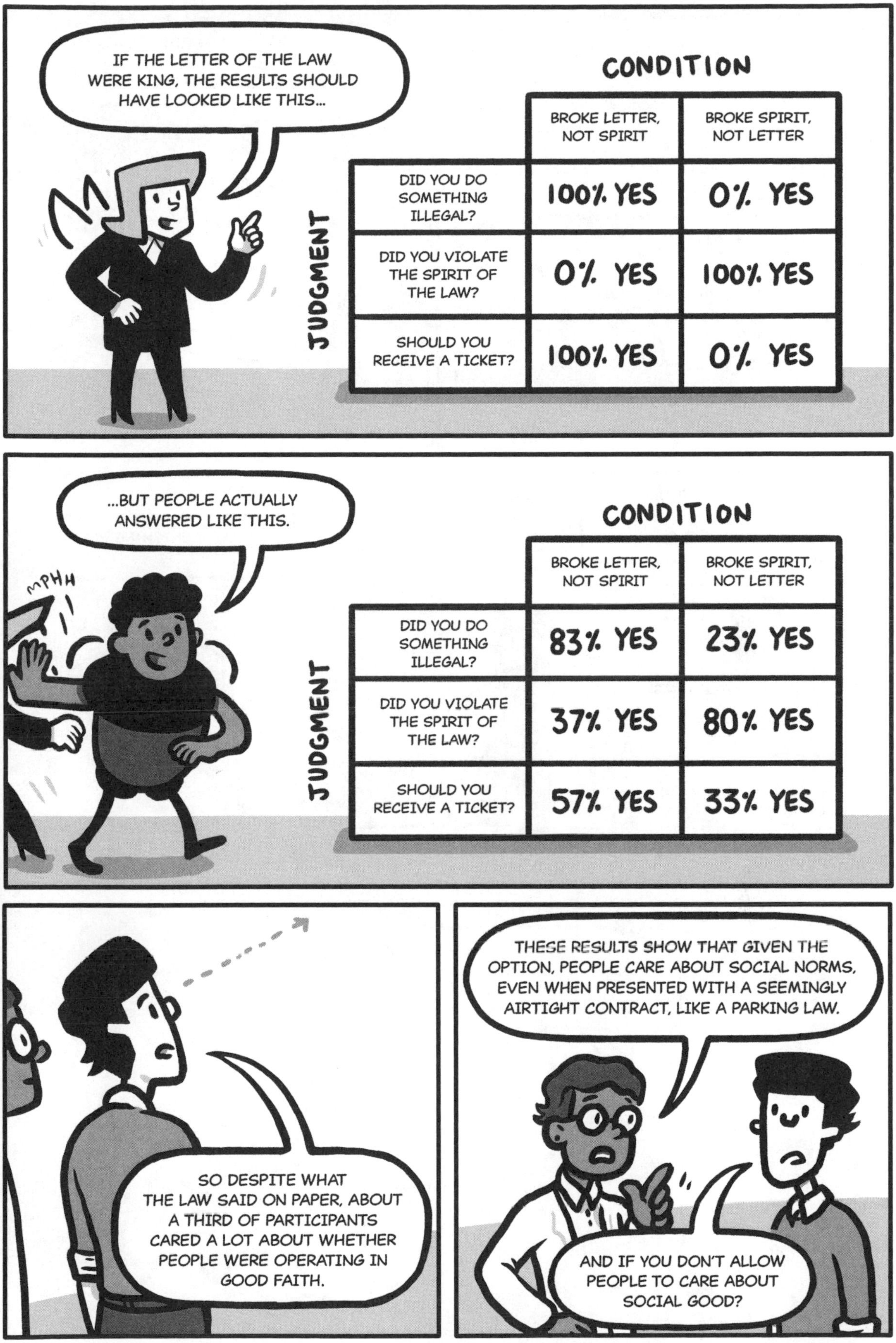

IF THE LETTER OF THE LAW WERE KING, THE RESULTS SHOULD HAVE LOOKED LIKE THIS...
CONDITION
JUDGMENT

	BROKE LETTER, NOT SPIRIT	BROKE SPIRIT, NOT LETTER
DID YOU DO SOMETHING ILLEGAL?	100% YES	0% YES
DID YOU VIOLATE THE SPIRIT OF THE LAW?	0% YES	100% YES
SHOULD YOU RECEIVE A TICKET?	100% YES	0% YES

...BUT PEOPLE ACTUALLY ANSWERED LIKE THIS.
MPHH
CONDITION
JUDGMENT

	BROKE LETTER, NOT SPIRIT	BROKE SPIRIT, NOT LETTER
DID YOU DO SOMETHING ILLEGAL?	83% YES	23% YES
DID YOU VIOLATE THE SPIRIT OF THE LAW?	37% YES	80% YES
SHOULD YOU RECEIVE A TICKET?	57% YES	33% YES

SO DESPITE WHAT THE LAW SAID ON PAPER, ABOUT A THIRD OF PARTICIPANTS CARED A LOT ABOUT WHETHER PEOPLE WERE OPERATING IN GOOD FAITH.
THESE RESULTS SHOW THAT GIVEN THE OPTION, PEOPLE CARE ABOUT SOCIAL NORMS, EVEN WHEN PRESENTED WITH A SEEMINGLY AIRTIGHT CONTRACT, LIKE A PARKING LAW.
AND IF YOU DON'T ALLOW PEOPLE TO CARE ABOUT SOCIAL GOOD?

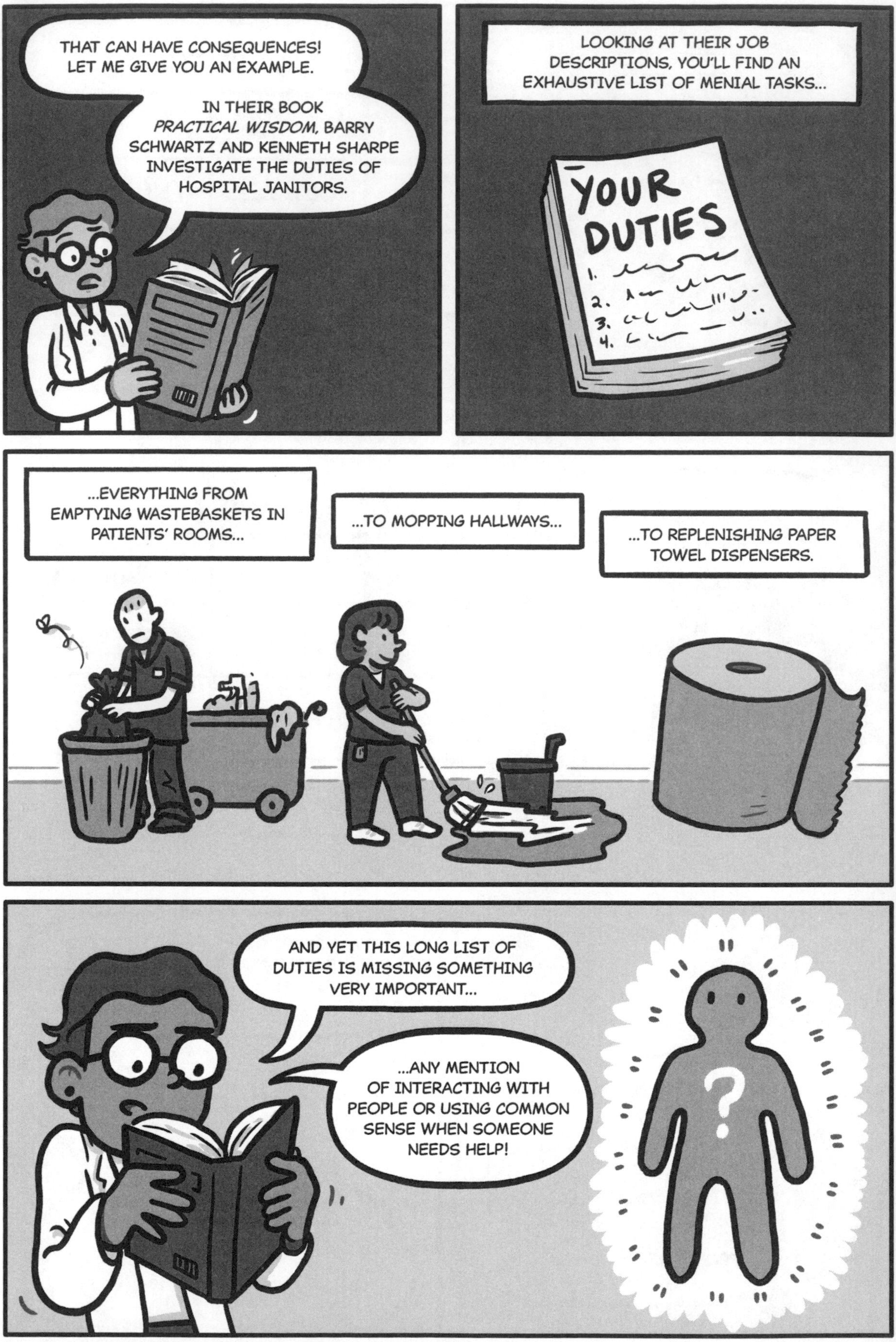
THAT CAN HAVE CONSEQUENCES! LET ME GIVE YOU AN EXAMPLE.
IN THEIR BOOK *PRACTICAL WISDOM*, BARRY SCHWARTZ AND KENNETH SHARPE INVESTIGATE THE DUTIES OF HOSPITAL JANITORS.
LOOKING AT THEIR JOB DESCRIPTIONS, YOU'LL FIND AN EXHAUSTIVE LIST OF MENIAL TASKS...
YOUR DUTIES
1.
2.
3.
4.
...EVERYTHING FROM EMPTYING WASTEBASKETS IN PATIENTS' ROOMS...
...TO MOPPING HALLWAYS...
...TO REPLENISHING PAPER TOWEL DISPENSERS.
AND YET THIS LONG LIST OF DUTIES IS MISSING SOMETHING VERY IMPORTANT...
...ANY MENTION OF INTERACTING WITH PEOPLE OR USING COMMON SENSE WHEN SOMEONE NEEDS HELP!
?

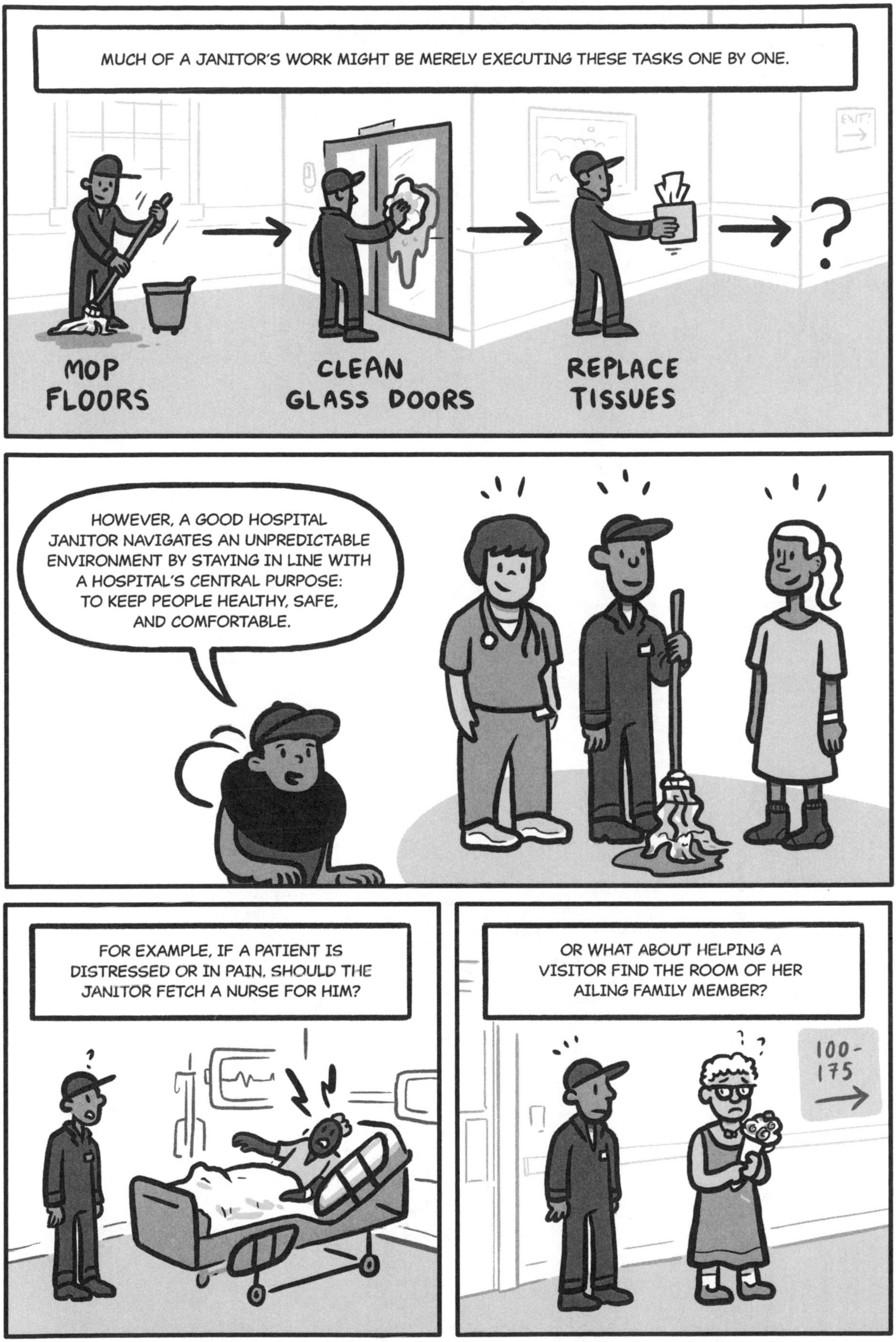
MUCH OF A JANITOR'S WORK MIGHT BE MERELY EXECUTING THESE TASKS ONE BY ONE.
MOP FLOORS
CLEAN GLASS DOORS
REPLACE TISSUES
?
HOWEVER, A GOOD HOSPITAL JANITOR NAVIGATES AN UNPREDICTABLE ENVIRONMENT BY STAYING IN LINE WITH A HOSPITAL'S CENTRAL PURPOSE: TO KEEP PEOPLE HEALTHY, SAFE, AND COMFORTABLE.
FOR EXAMPLE, IF A PATIENT IS DISTRESSED OR IN PAIN, SHOULD THE JANITOR FETCH A NURSE FOR HIM?
OR WHAT ABOUT HELPING A VISITOR FIND THE ROOM OF HER AILING FAMILY MEMBER?
100-175

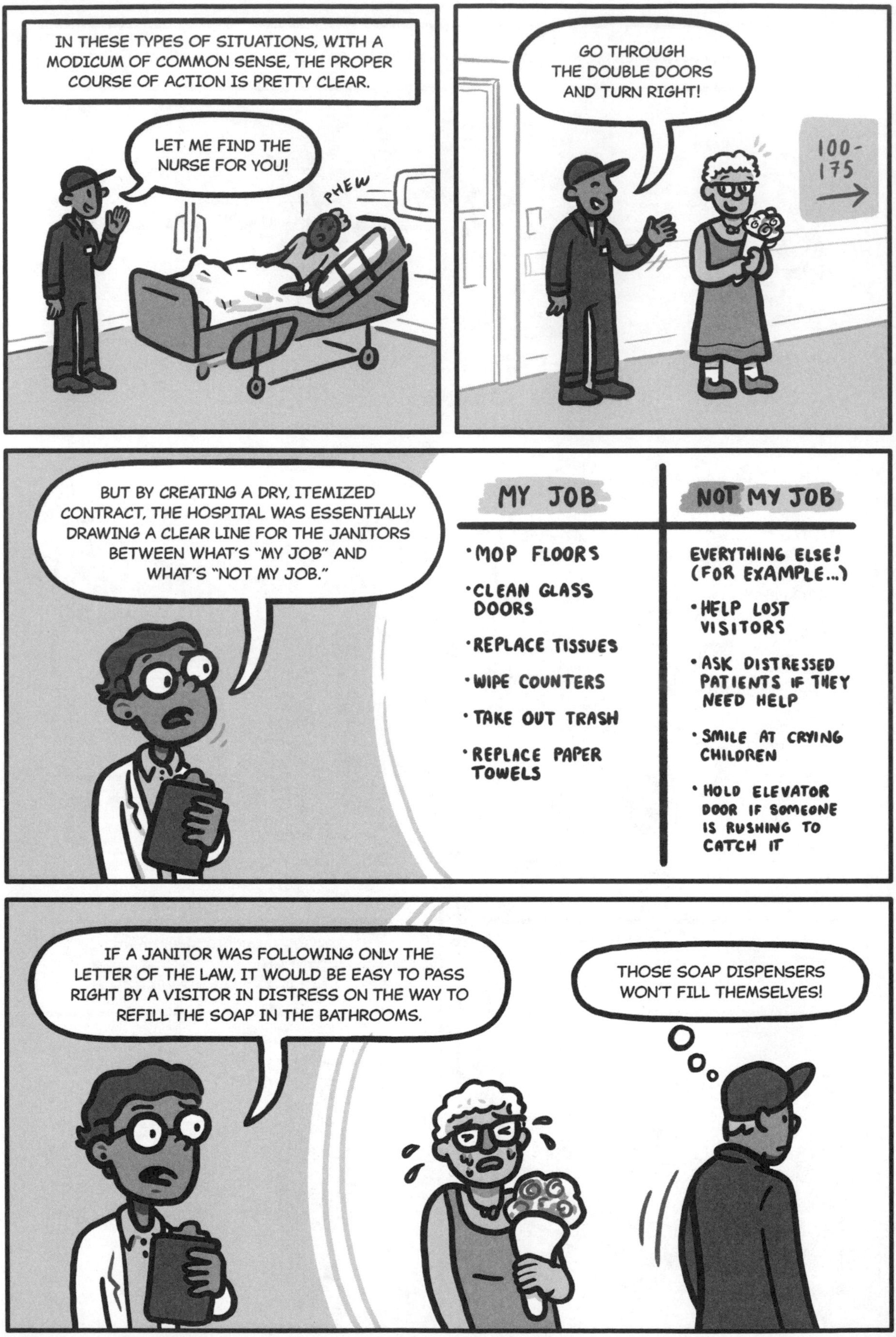
IN THESE TYPES OF SITUATIONS, WITH A MODICUM OF COMMON SENSE, THE PROPER COURSE OF ACTION IS PRETTY CLEAR.
LET ME FIND THE NURSE FOR YOU!
PHEW
GO THROUGH THE DOUBLE DOORS AND TURN RIGHT!
100-175
BUT BY CREATING A DRY, ITEMIZED CONTRACT, THE HOSPITAL WAS ESSENTIALLY DRAWING A CLEAR LINE FOR THE JANITORS BETWEEN WHAT'S "MY JOB" AND WHAT'S "NOT MY JOB."
MY JOB
• MOP FLOORS
• CLEAN GLASS DOORS
• REPLACE TISSUES
• WIPE COUNTERS
• TAKE OUT TRASH
• REPLACE PAPER TOWELS
NOT MY JOB
EVERYTHING ELSE! (FOR EXAMPLE...)
• HELP LOST VISITORS
• ASK DISTRESSED PATIENTS IF THEY NEED HELP
• SMILE AT CRYING CHILDREN
• HOLD ELEVATOR DOOR IF SOMEONE IS RUSHING TO CATCH IT
IF A JANITOR WAS FOLLOWING ONLY THE LETTER OF THE LAW, IT WOULD BE EASY TO PASS RIGHT BY A VISITOR IN DISTRESS ON THE WAY TO REFILL THE SOAP IN THE BATHROOMS.
THOSE SOAP DISPENSERS WON'T FILL THEMSELVES!

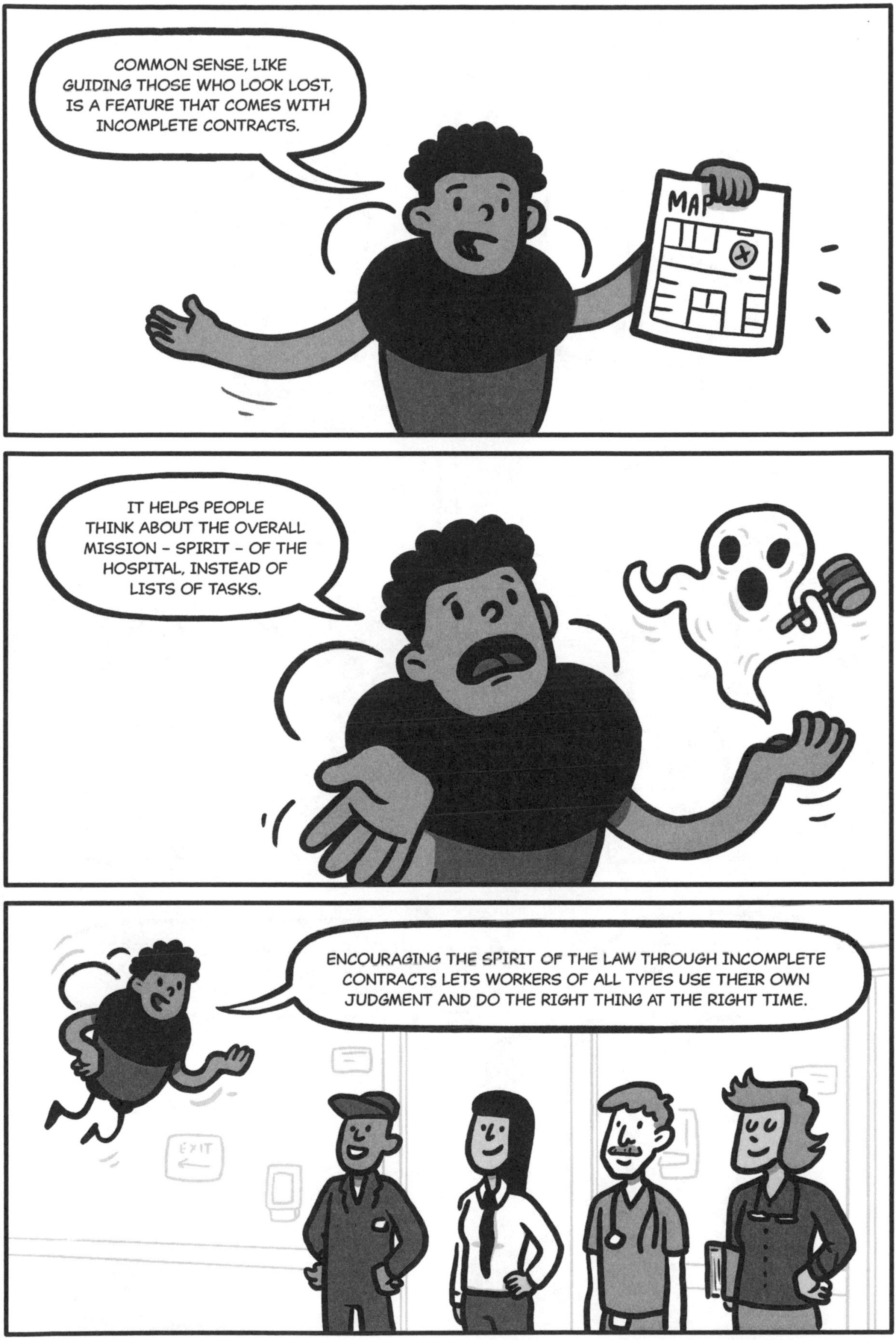
COMMON SENSE, LIKE GUIDING THOSE WHO LOOK LOST, IS A FEATURE THAT COMES WITH INCOMPLETE CONTRACTS.
MAP
IT HELPS PEOPLE THINK ABOUT THE OVERALL MISSION - SPIRIT - OF THE HOSPITAL, INSTEAD OF LISTS OF TASKS.
ENCOURAGING THE SPIRIT OF THE LAW THROUGH INCOMPLETE CONTRACTS LETS WORKERS OF ALL TYPES USE THEIR OWN JUDGMENT AND DO THE RIGHT THING AT THE RIGHT TIME.
EXIT

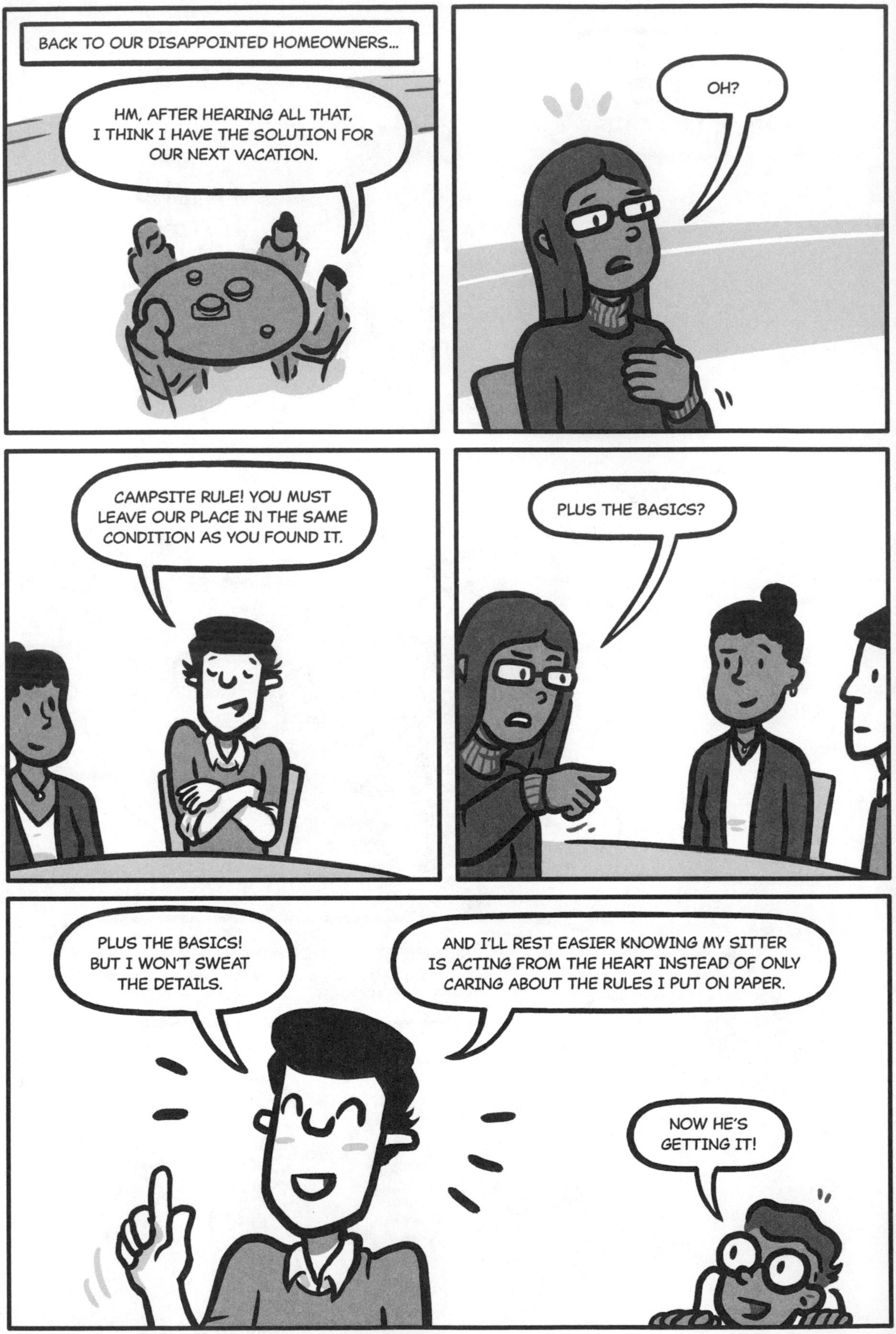
BACK TO OUR DISAPPOINTED HOMEOWNERS...
HM, AFTER HEARING ALL THAT, I THINK I HAVE THE SOLUTION FOR OUR NEXT VACATION.
OH?
CAMPSITE RULE! YOU MUST LEAVE OUR PLACE IN THE SAME CONDITION AS YOU FOUND IT.
PLUS THE BASICS?
PLUS THE BASICS! BUT I WON'T SWEAT THE DETAILS.
AND I'LL REST EASIER KNOWING MY SITTER IS ACTING FROM THE HEART INSTEAD OF ONLY CARING ABOUT THE RULES I PUT ON PAPER.
NOW HE'S GETTING IT!

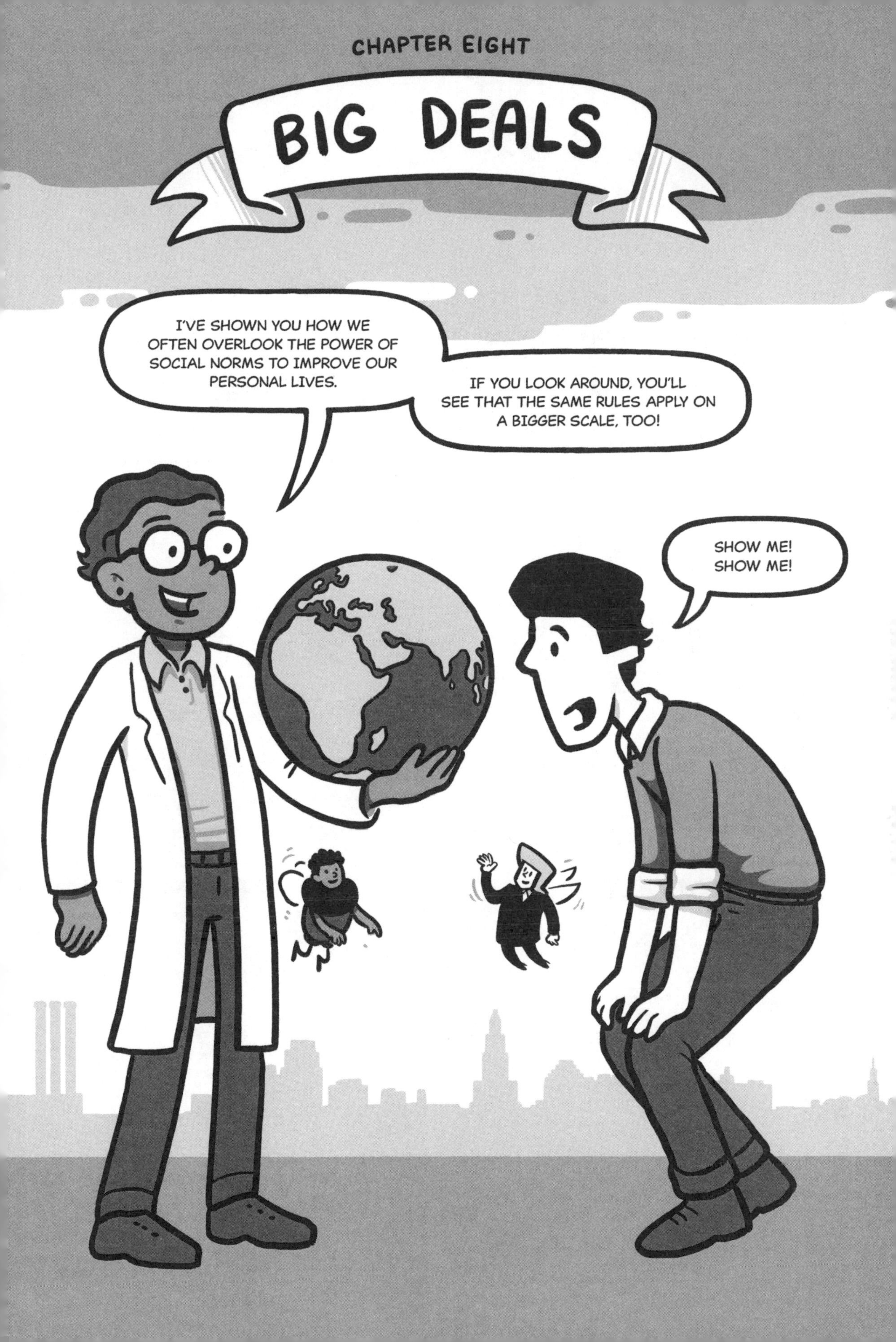
CHAPTER EIGHT
BIG DEALS
I'VE SHOWN YOU HOW WE OFTEN OVERLOOK THE POWER OF SOCIAL NORMS TO IMPROVE OUR PERSONAL LIVES.
IF YOU LOOK AROUND, YOU'LL SEE THAT THE SAME RULES APPLY ON A BIGGER SCALE, TOO!
SHOW ME! SHOW ME!

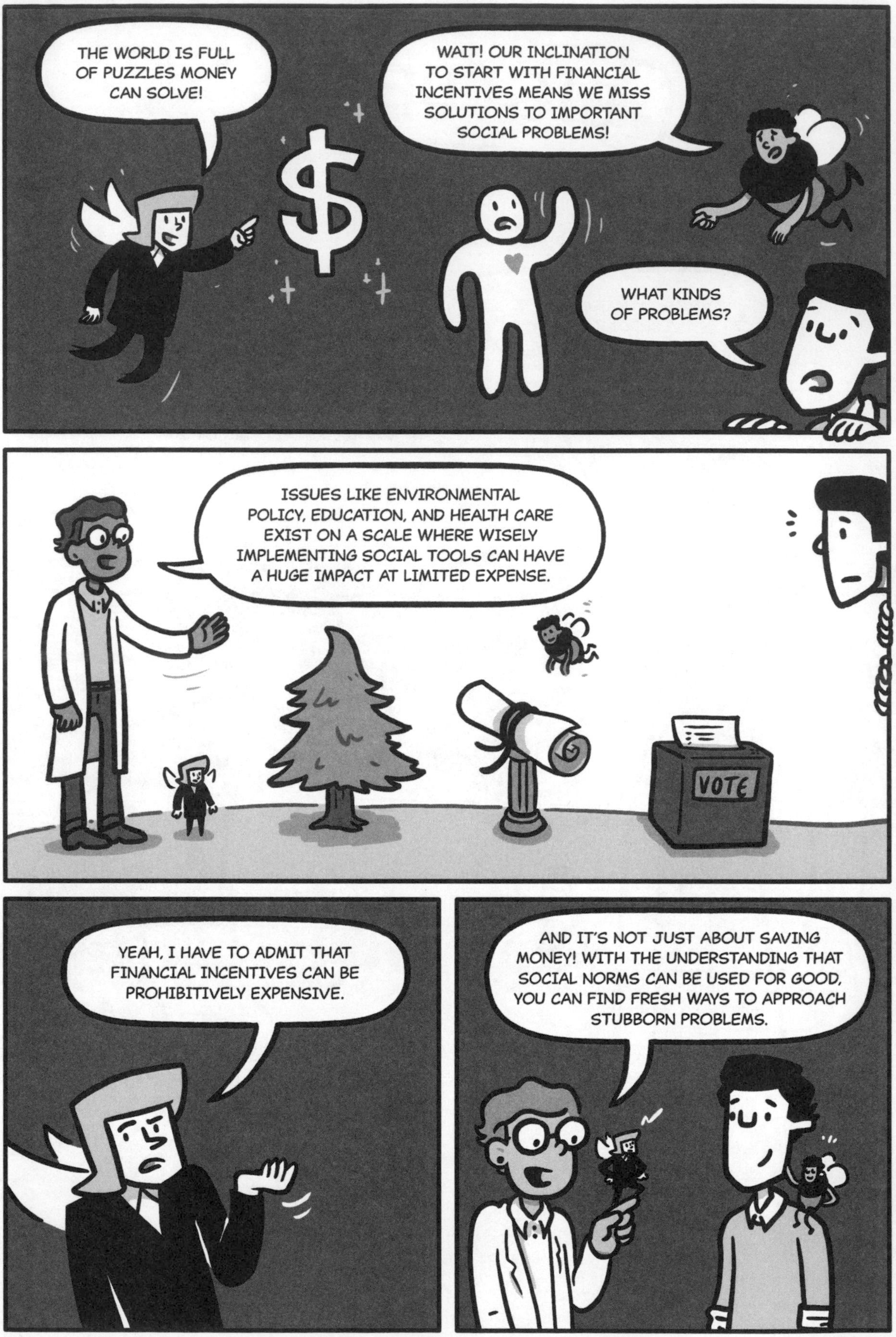
THE WORLD IS FULL OF PUZZLES MONEY CAN SOLVE!
WAIT! OUR INCLINATION TO START WITH FINANCIAL INCENTIVES MEANS WE MISS SOLUTIONS TO IMPORTANT SOCIAL PROBLEMS!
WHAT KINDS OF PROBLEMS?
ISSUES LIKE ENVIRONMENTAL POLICY, EDUCATION, AND HEALTH CARE EXIST ON A SCALE WHERE WISELY IMPLEMENTING SOCIAL TOOLS CAN HAVE A HUGE IMPACT AT LIMITED EXPENSE.
VOTE
YEAH, I HAVE TO ADMIT THAT FINANCIAL INCENTIVES CAN BE PROHIBITIVELY EXPENSIVE.
AND IT'S NOT JUST ABOUT SAVING MONEY! WITH THE UNDERSTANDING THAT SOCIAL NORMS CAN BE USED FOR GOOD, YOU CAN FIND FRESH WAYS TO APPROACH STUBBORN PROBLEMS.

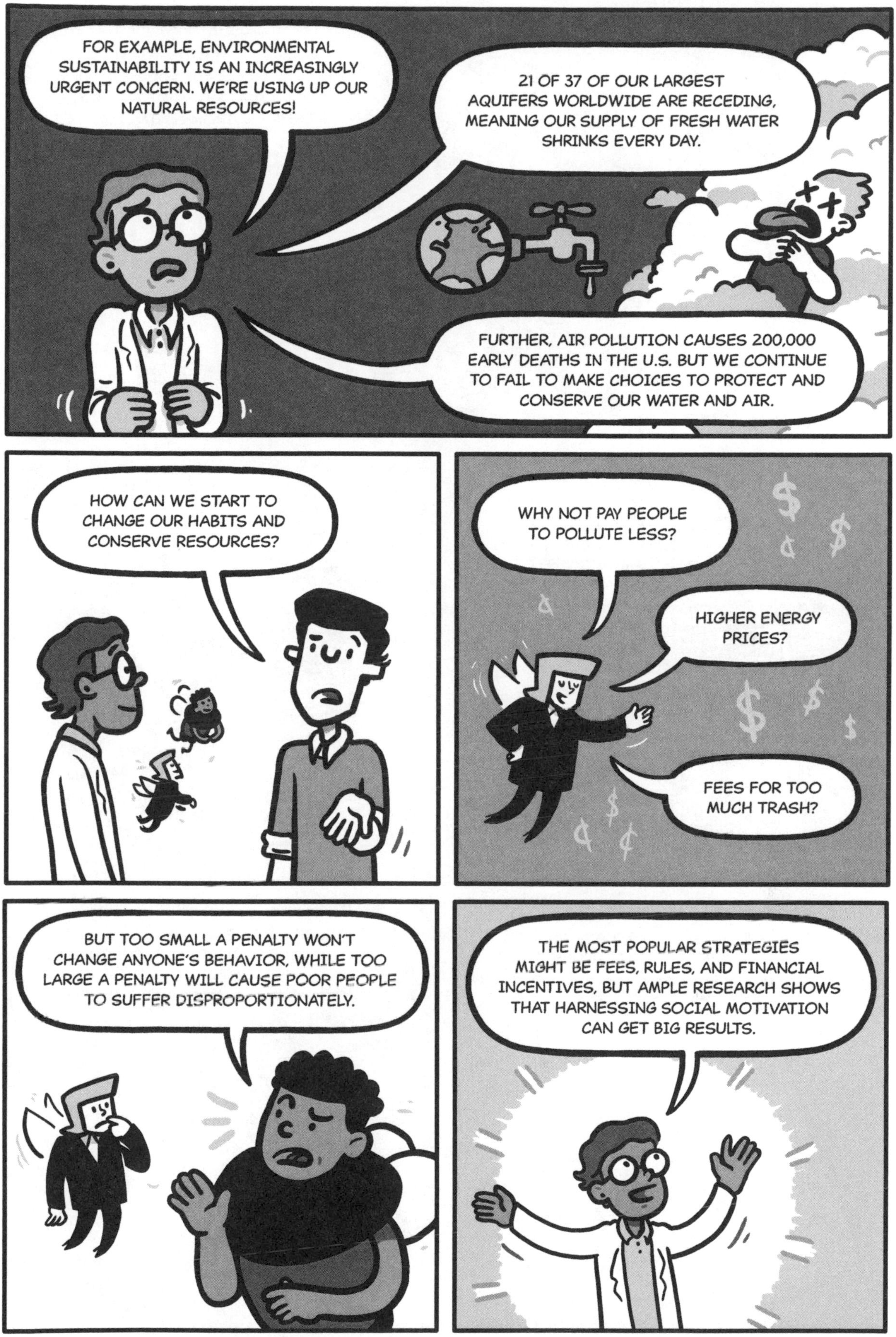
FOR EXAMPLE, ENVIRONMENTAL SUSTAINABILITY IS AN INCREASINGLY URGENT CONCERN. WE'RE USING UP OUR NATURAL RESOURCES!
21 OF 37 OF OUR LARGEST AQUIFERS WORLDWIDE ARE RECEDING, MEANING OUR SUPPLY OF FRESH WATER SHRINKS EVERY DAY.
FURTHER, AIR POLLUTION CAUSES 200,000 EARLY DEATHS IN THE U.S. BUT WE CONTINUE TO FAIL TO MAKE CHOICES TO PROTECT AND CONSERVE OUR WATER AND AIR.
HOW CAN WE START TO CHANGE OUR HABITS AND CONSERVE RESOURCES?
WHY NOT PAY PEOPLE TO POLLUTE LESS?
HIGHER ENERGY PRICES?
FEES FOR TOO MUCH TRASH?
BUT TOO SMALL A PENALTY WON'T CHANGE ANYONE'S BEHAVIOR, WHILE TOO LARGE A PENALTY WILL CAUSE POOR PEOPLE TO SUFFER DISPROPORTIONATELY.
THE MOST POPULAR STRATEGIES MIGHT BE FEES, RULES, AND FINANCIAL INCENTIVES, BUT AMPLE RESEARCH SHOWS THAT HARNESSING SOCIAL MOTIVATION CAN GET BIG RESULTS.

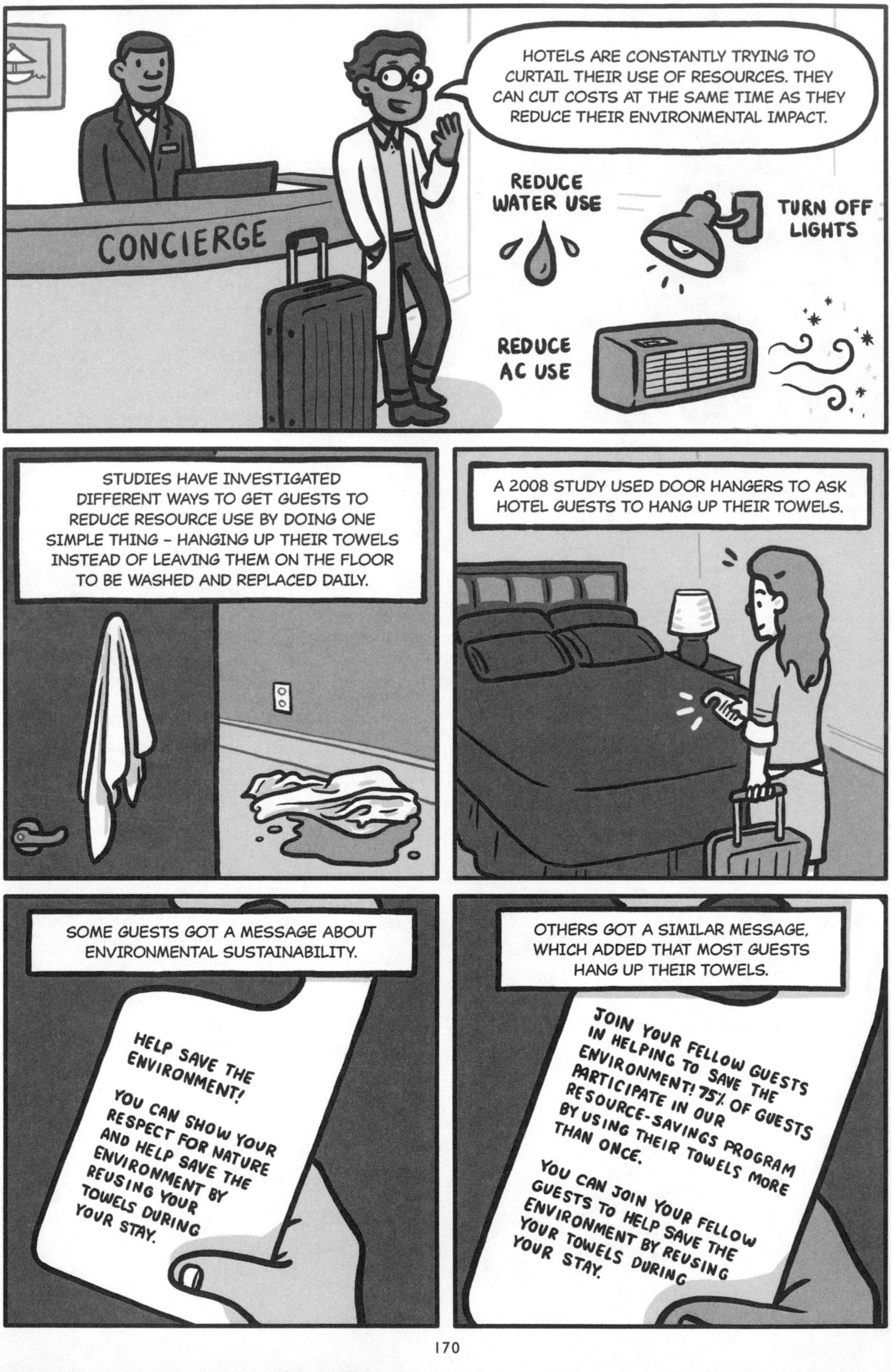
HOTELS ARE CONSTANTLY TRYING TO CURTAIL THEIR USE OF RESOURCES. THEY CAN CUT COSTS AT THE SAME TIME AS THEY REDUCE THEIR ENVIRONMENTAL IMPACT.
CONCIERGE
REDUCE WATER USE
TURN OFF LIGHTS
REDUCE AC USE
STUDIES HAVE INVESTIGATED DIFFERENT WAYS TO GET GUESTS TO REDUCE RESOURCE USE BY DOING ONE SIMPLE THING - HANGING UP THEIR TOWELS INSTEAD OF LEAVING THEM ON THE FLOOR TO BE WASHED AND REPLACED DAILY.
A 2008 STUDY USED DOOR HANGERS TO ASK HOTEL GUESTS TO HANG UP THEIR TOWELS.
SOME GUESTS GOT A MESSAGE ABOUT ENVIRONMENTAL SUSTAINABILITY.
HELP SAVE THE ENVIRONMENT!
YOU CAN SHOW YOUR RESPECT FOR NATURE AND HELP SAVE THE ENVIRONMENT BY REUSING YOUR TOWELS DURING YOUR STAY.
OTHERS GOT A SIMILAR MESSAGE, WHICH ADDED THAT MOST GUESTS HANG UP THEIR TOWELS.
JOIN YOUR FELLOW GUESTS IN HELPING TO SAVE THE ENVIRONMENT! 75% OF GUESTS PARTICIPATE IN OUR RESOURCE-SAVINGS PROGRAM BY USING THEIR TOWELS MORE THAN ONCE.
YOU CAN JOIN YOUR FELLOW GUESTS TO HELP SAVE THE ENVIRONMENT BY REUSING YOUR TOWELS DURING YOUR STAY.

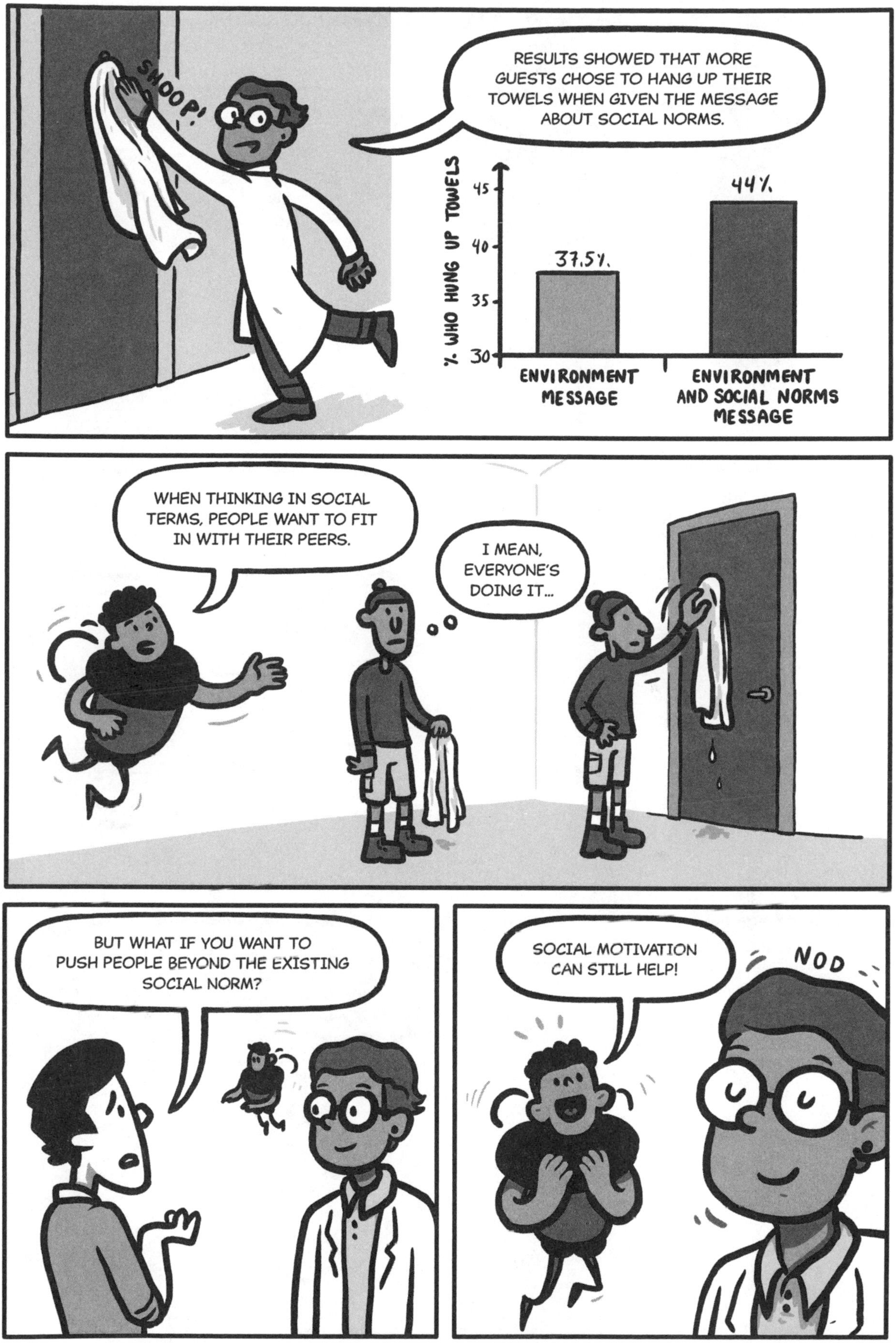
SHOOP!
RESULTS SHOWED THAT MORE GUESTS CHOSE TO HANG UP THEIR TOWELS WHEN GIVEN THE MESSAGE ABOUT SOCIAL NORMS.
% WHO HUNG UP TOWELS
45
40
35
30
37.5%
44%
ENVIRONMENT MESSAGE
ENVIRONMENT AND SOCIAL NORMS MESSAGE
WHEN THINKING IN SOCIAL TERMS, PEOPLE WANT TO FIT IN WITH THEIR PEERS.
I MEAN, EVERYONE'S DOING IT...
BUT WHAT IF YOU WANT TO PUSH PEOPLE BEYOND THE EXISTING SOCIAL NORM?
SOCIAL MOTIVATION CAN STILL HELP!
NOD

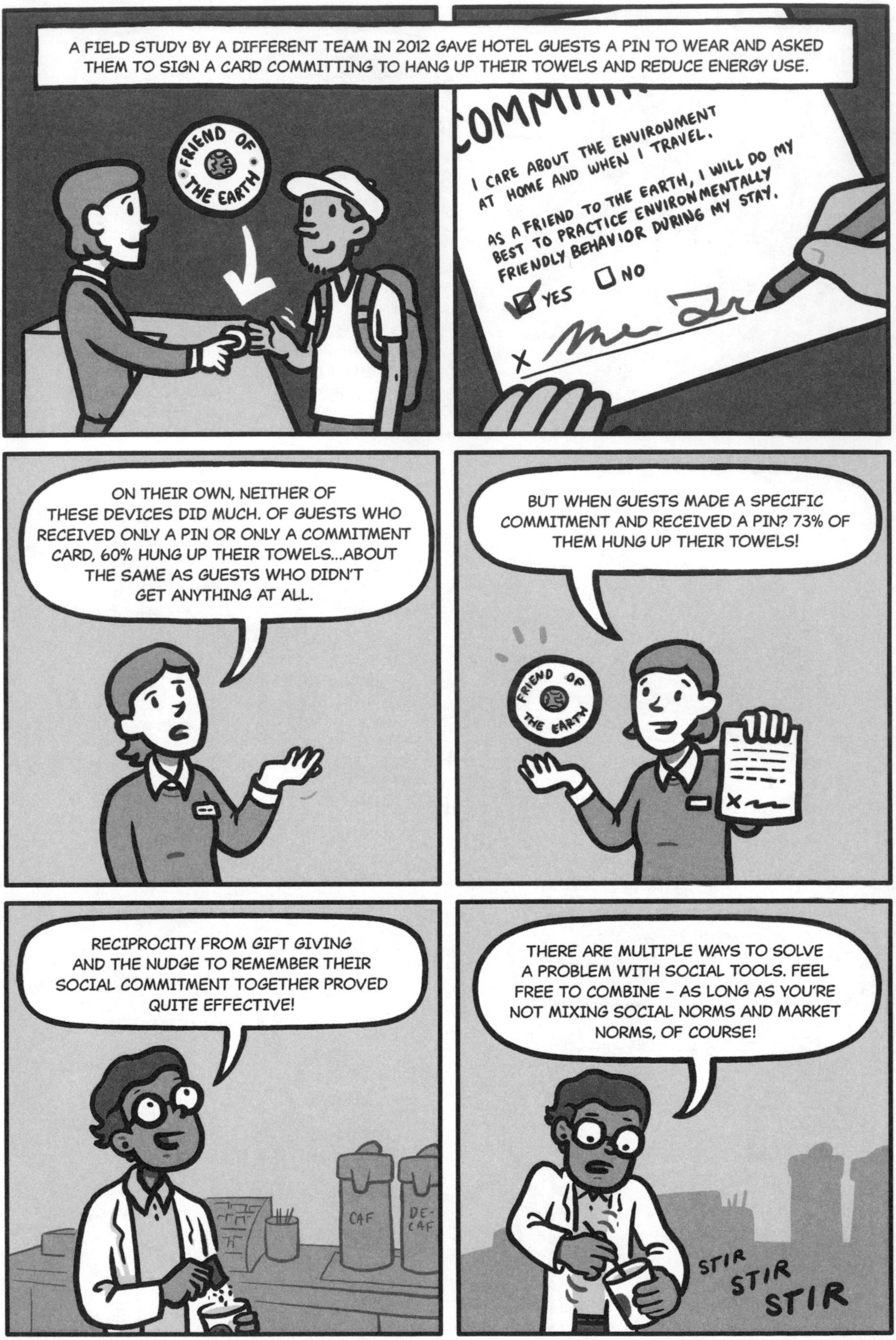
A FIELD STUDY BY A DIFFERENT TEAM IN 2012 GAVE HOTEL GUESTS A PIN TO WEAR AND ASKED THEM TO SIGN A CARD COMMITTING TO HANG UP THEIR TOWELS AND REDUCE ENERGY USE.
FRIEND OF THE EARTH
I CARE ABOUT THE ENVIRONMENT AT HOME AND WHEN I TRAVEL.
AS A FRIEND TO THE EARTH, I WILL DO MY BEST TO PRACTICE ENVIRONMENTALLY FRIENDLY BEHAVIOR DURING MY STAY.
YES
NO
X
ON THEIR OWN, NEITHER OF THESE DEVICES DID MUCH. OF GUESTS WHO RECEIVED ONLY A PIN OR ONLY A COMMITMENT CARD, 60% HUNG UP THEIR TOWELS...ABOUT THE SAME AS GUESTS WHO DIDN'T GET ANYTHING AT ALL.
BUT WHEN GUESTS MADE A SPECIFIC COMMITMENT AND RECEIVED A PIN? 73% OF THEM HUNG UP THEIR TOWELS!
FRIEND OF THE EARTH
RECIPROCITY FROM GIFT GIVING AND THE NUDGE TO REMEMBER THEIR SOCIAL COMMITMENT TOGETHER PROVED QUITE EFFECTIVE!
CAF
DE-CAF
THERE ARE MULTIPLE WAYS TO SOLVE A PROBLEM WITH SOCIAL TOOLS. FEEL FREE TO COMBINE – AS LONG AS YOU'RE NOT MIXING SOCIAL NORMS AND MARKET NORMS, OF COURSE!
STIR
STIR
STIR

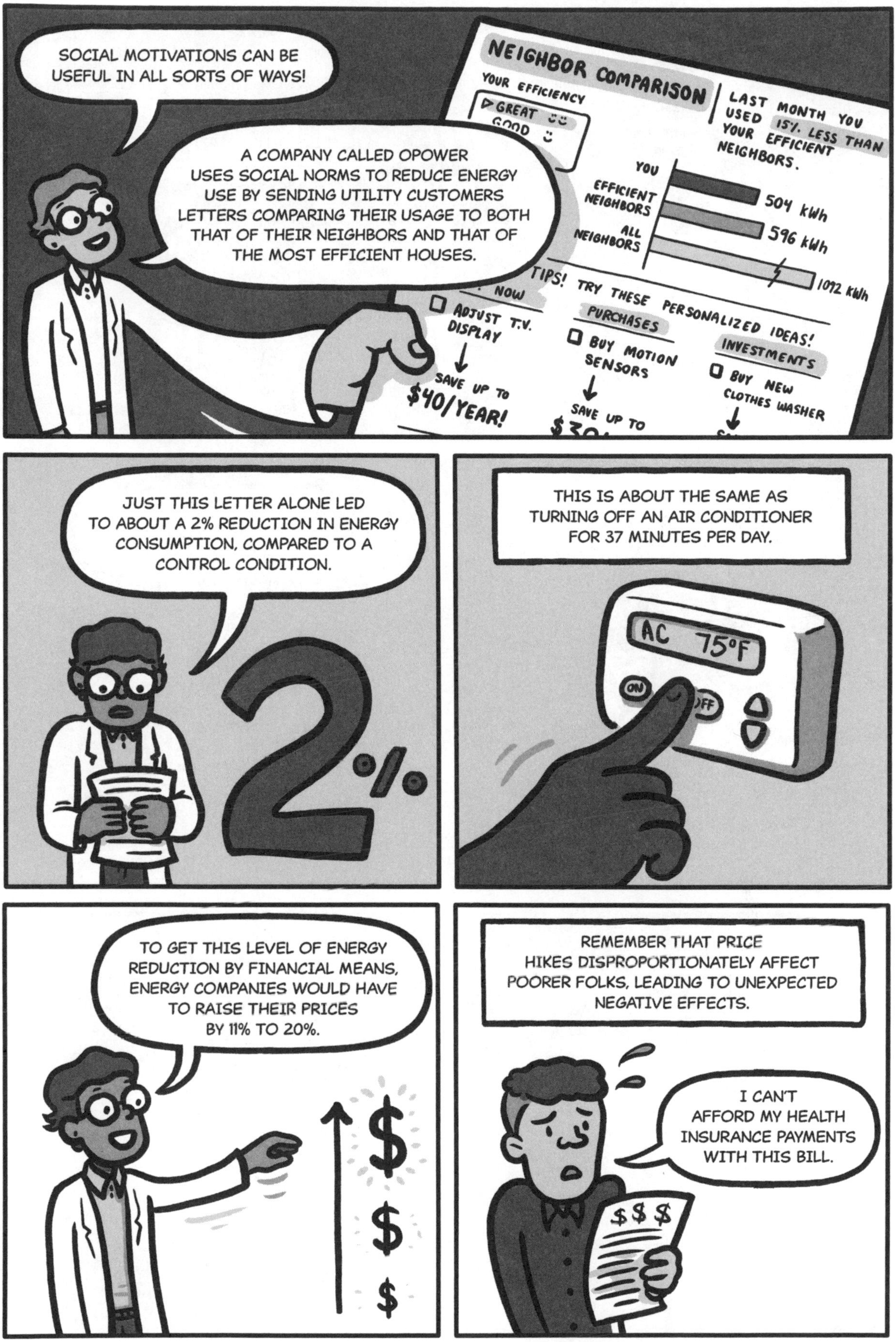
SOCIAL MOTIVATIONS CAN BE USEFUL IN ALL SORTS OF WAYS!
NEIGHBOR COMPARISON
YOUR EFFICIENCY
GREAT
GOOD
LAST MONTH YOU USED 15% LESS THAN YOUR EFFICIENT NEIGHBORS.
YOU
EFFICIENT NEIGHBORS
ALL NEIGHBORS
504 kWh
596 kWh
1092 kWh
A COMPANY CALLED OPOWER USES SOCIAL NORMS TO REDUCE ENERGY USE BY SENDING UTILITY CUSTOMERS LETTERS COMPARING THEIR USAGE TO BOTH THAT OF THEIR NEIGHBORS AND THAT OF THE MOST EFFICIENT HOUSES.
TIPS! TRY THESE PERSONALIZED IDEAS!
NOW
ADJUST T.V. DISPLAY
SAVE UP TO $40/YEAR!
PURCHASES
BUY MOTION SENSORS
SAVE UP TO
INVESTMENTS
BUY NEW CLOTHES WASHER
JUST THIS LETTER ALONE LED TO ABOUT A 2% REDUCTION IN ENERGY CONSUMPTION, COMPARED TO A CONTROL CONDITION.
2%
THIS IS ABOUT THE SAME AS TURNING OFF AN AIR CONDITIONER FOR 37 MINUTES PER DAY.
AC 75°F
ON
OFF
TO GET THIS LEVEL OF ENERGY REDUCTION BY FINANCIAL MEANS, ENERGY COMPANIES WOULD HAVE TO RAISE THEIR PRICES BY 11% TO 20%.
$
$
$
REMEMBER THAT PRICE HIKES DISPROPORTIONATELY AFFECT POORER FOLKS, LEADING TO UNEXPECTED NEGATIVE EFFECTS.
I CAN'T AFFORD MY HEALTH INSURANCE PAYMENTS WITH THIS BILL.
$$$

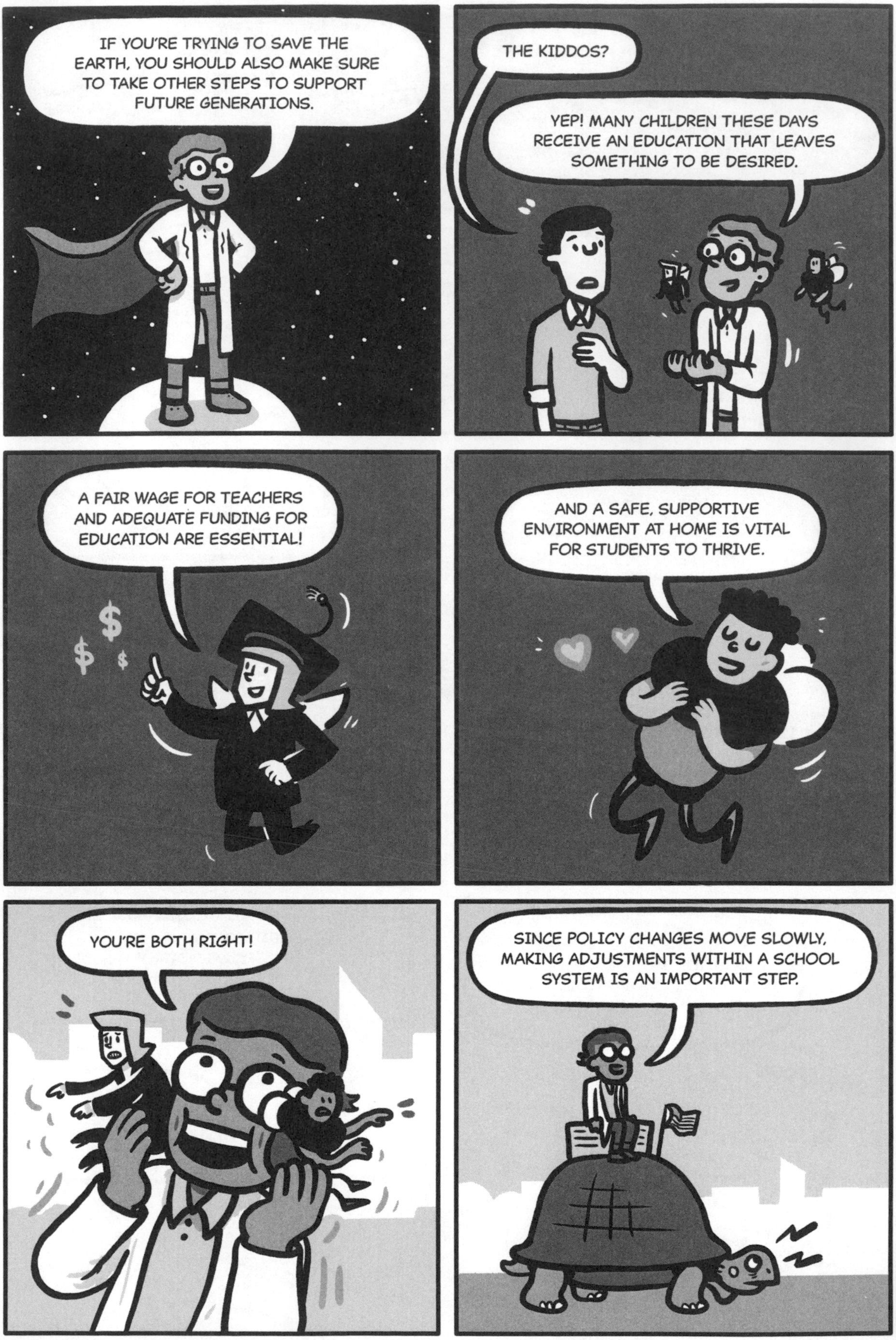

IF YOU'RE TRYING TO SAVE THE EARTH, YOU SHOULD ALSO MAKE SURE TO TAKE OTHER STEPS TO SUPPORT FUTURE GENERATIONS.
THE KIDDOS?
YEP! MANY CHILDREN THESE DAYS RECEIVE AN EDUCATION THAT LEAVES SOMETHING TO BE DESIRED.
A FAIR WAGE FOR TEACHERS AND ADEQUATE FUNDING FOR EDUCATION ARE ESSENTIAL!
AND A SAFE, SUPPORTIVE ENVIRONMENT AT HOME IS VITAL FOR STUDENTS TO THRIVE.
YOU'RE BOTH RIGHT!
SINCE POLICY CHANGES MOVE SLOWLY, MAKING ADJUSTMENTS WITHIN A SCHOOL SYSTEM IS AN IMPORTANT STEP.

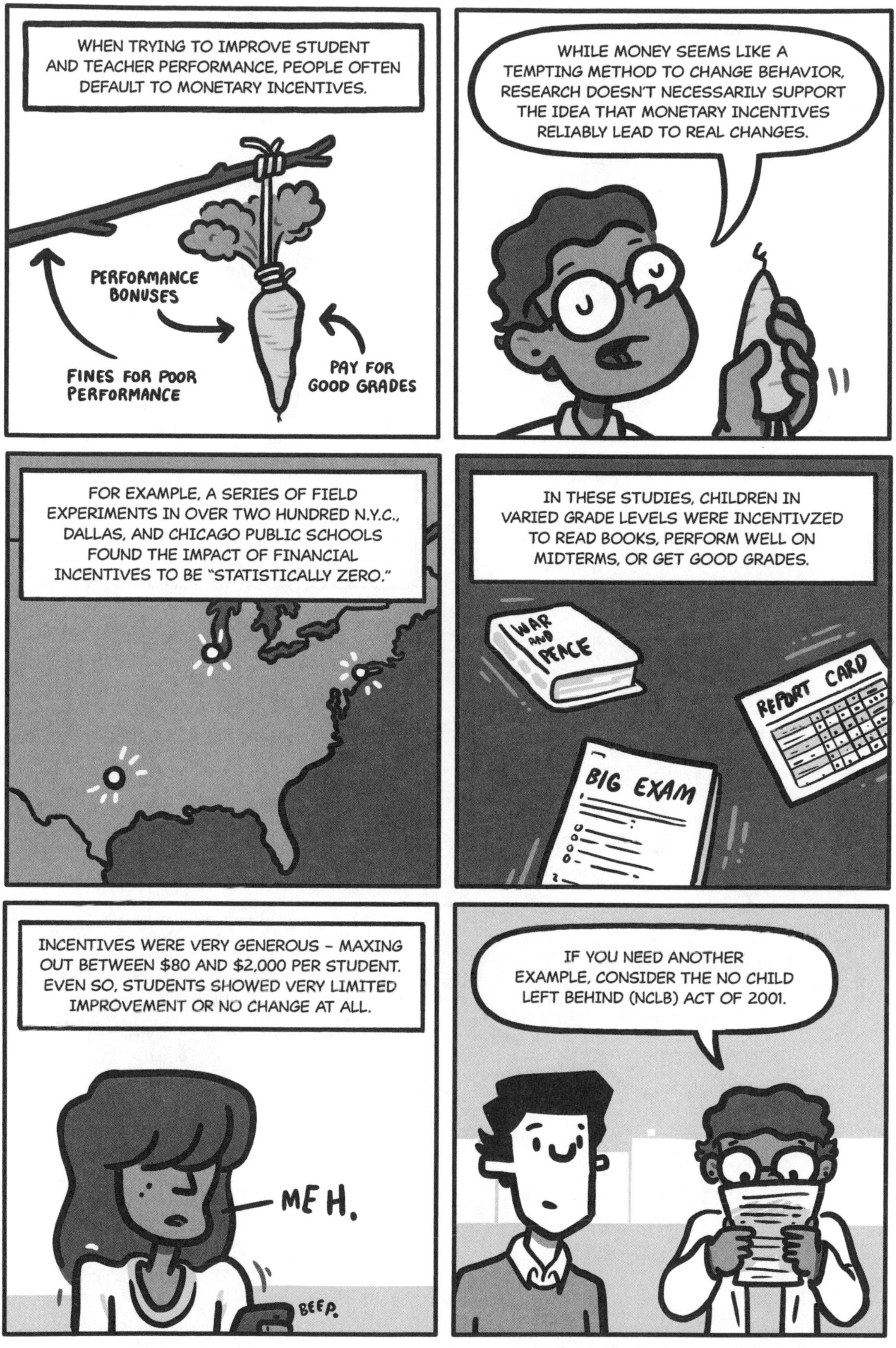
WHEN TRYING TO IMPROVE STUDENT AND TEACHER PERFORMANCE, PEOPLE OFTEN DEFAULT TO MONETARY INCENTIVES.
PERFORMANCE BONUSES
FINES FOR POOR PERFORMANCE
PAY FOR GOOD GRADES
WHILE MONEY SEEMS LIKE A TEMPTING METHOD TO CHANGE BEHAVIOR, RESEARCH DOESN'T NECESSARILY SUPPORT THE IDEA THAT MONETARY INCENTIVES RELIABLY LEAD TO REAL CHANGES.
FOR EXAMPLE, A SERIES OF FIELD EXPERIMENTS IN OVER TWO HUNDRED N.Y.C., DALLAS, AND CHICAGO PUBLIC SCHOOLS FOUND THE IMPACT OF FINANCIAL INCENTIVES TO BE "STATISTICALLY ZERO."
IN THESE STUDIES, CHILDREN IN VARIED GRADE LEVELS WERE INCENTIVZED TO READ BOOKS, PERFORM WELL ON MIDTERMS, OR GET GOOD GRADES.
WAR AND PEACE
REPORT CARD
BIG EXAM
INCENTIVES WERE VERY GENEROUS - MAXING OUT BETWEEN $80 AND $2,000 PER STUDENT. EVEN SO, STUDENTS SHOWED VERY LIMITED IMPROVEMENT OR NO CHANGE AT ALL.
MEH.
BEEP.
IF YOU NEED ANOTHER EXAMPLE, CONSIDER THE NO CHILD LEFT BEHIND (NCLB) ACT OF 2001.

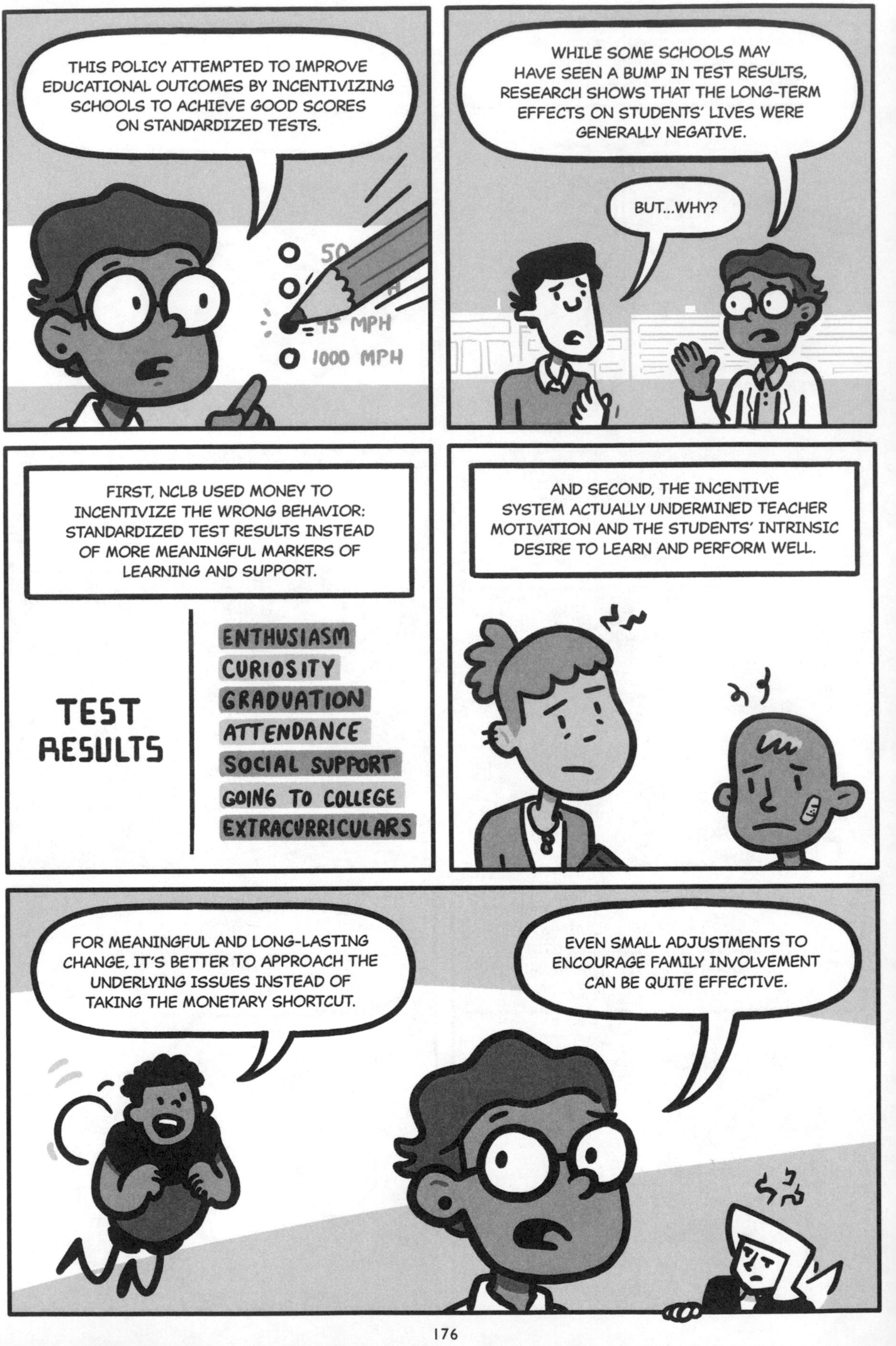

THIS POLICY ATTEMPTED TO IMPROVE EDUCATIONAL OUTCOMES BY INCENTIVIZING SCHOOLS TO ACHIEVE GOOD SCORES ON STANDARDIZED TESTS.
50
75 MPH
1000 MPH
WHILE SOME SCHOOLS MAY HAVE SEEN A BUMP IN TEST RESULTS, RESEARCH SHOWS THAT THE LONG-TERM EFFECTS ON STUDENTS' LIVES WERE GENERALLY NEGATIVE.
BUT...WHY?
FIRST, NCLB USED MONEY TO INCENTIVIZE THE WRONG BEHAVIOR: STANDARDIZED TEST RESULTS INSTEAD OF MORE MEANINGFUL MARKERS OF LEARNING AND SUPPORT.
TEST RESULTS
ENTHUSIASM
CURIOSITY
GRADUATION
ATTENDANCE
SOCIAL SUPPORT
GOING TO COLLEGE
EXTRACURRICULARS
AND SECOND, THE INCENTIVE SYSTEM ACTUALLY UNDERMINED TEACHER MOTIVATION AND THE STUDENTS' INTRINSIC DESIRE TO LEARN AND PERFORM WELL.
FOR MEANINGFUL AND LONG-LASTING CHANGE, IT'S BETTER TO APPROACH THE UNDERLYING ISSUES INSTEAD OF TAKING THE MONETARY SHORTCUT.
EVEN SMALL ADJUSTMENTS TO ENCOURAGE FAMILY INVOLVEMENT CAN BE QUITE EFFECTIVE.

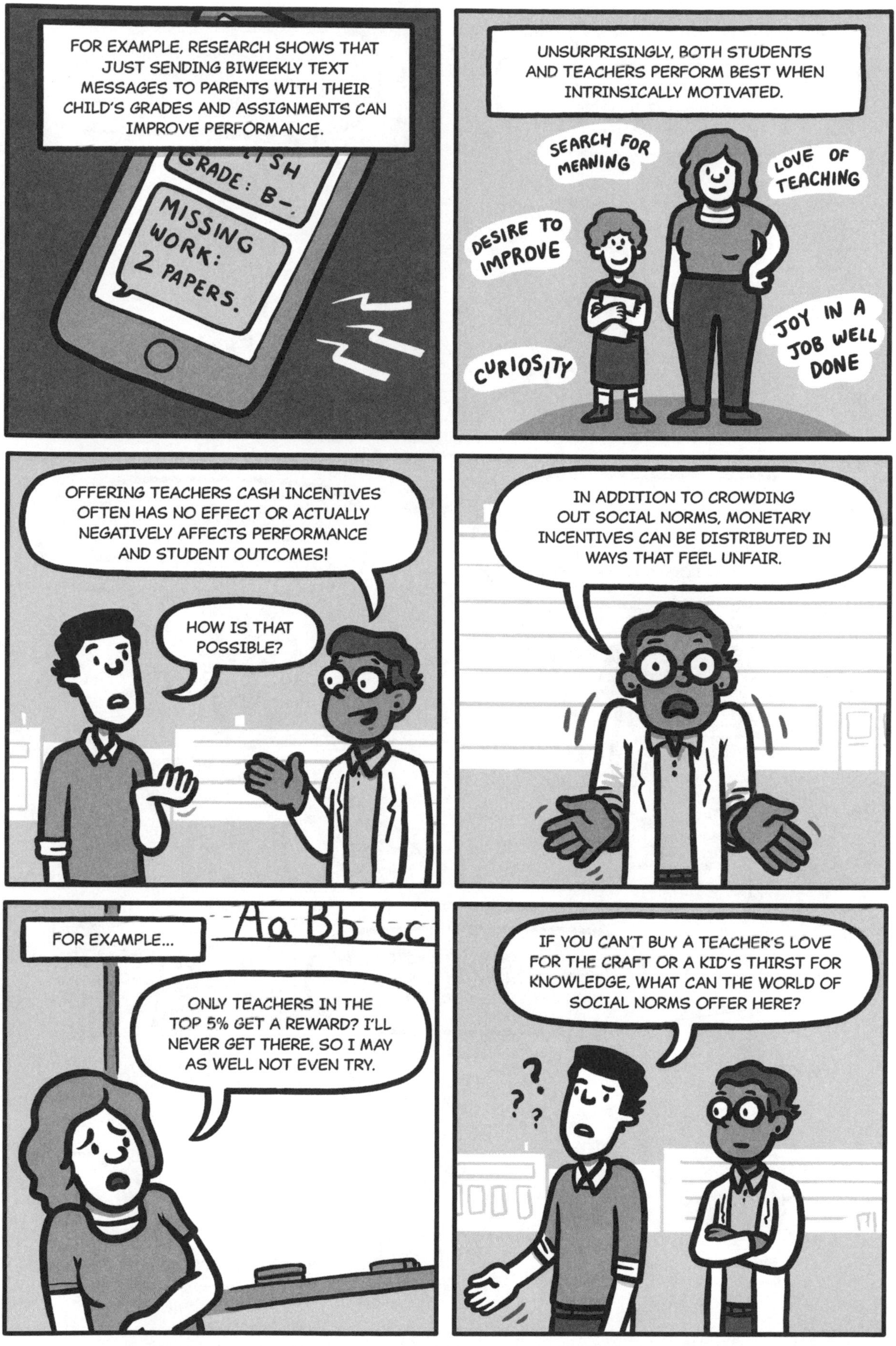
FOR EXAMPLE, RESEARCH SHOWS THAT JUST SENDING BIWEEKLY TEXT MESSAGES TO PARENTS WITH THEIR CHILD'S GRADES AND ASSIGNMENTS CAN IMPROVE PERFORMANCE.
GRADE: B-.
MISSING WORK: 2 PAPERS.
UNSURPRISINGLY, BOTH STUDENTS AND TEACHERS PERFORM BEST WHEN INTRINSICALLY MOTIVATED.
SEARCH FOR MEANING
LOVE OF TEACHING
DESIRE TO IMPROVE
JOY IN A JOB WELL DONE
CURIOSITY
OFFERING TEACHERS CASH INCENTIVES OFTEN HAS NO EFFECT OR ACTUALLY NEGATIVELY AFFECTS PERFORMANCE AND STUDENT OUTCOMES!
HOW IS THAT POSSIBLE?
IN ADDITION TO CROWDING OUT SOCIAL NORMS, MONETARY INCENTIVES CAN BE DISTRIBUTED IN WAYS THAT FEEL UNFAIR.
FOR EXAMPLE...
Aa Bb Cc
ONLY TEACHERS IN THE TOP 5% GET A REWARD? I'LL NEVER GET THERE, SO I MAY AS WELL NOT EVEN TRY.
IF YOU CAN'T BUY A TEACHER'S LOVE FOR THE CRAFT OR A KID'S THIRST FOR KNOWLEDGE, WHAT CAN THE WORLD OF SOCIAL NORMS OFFER HERE?

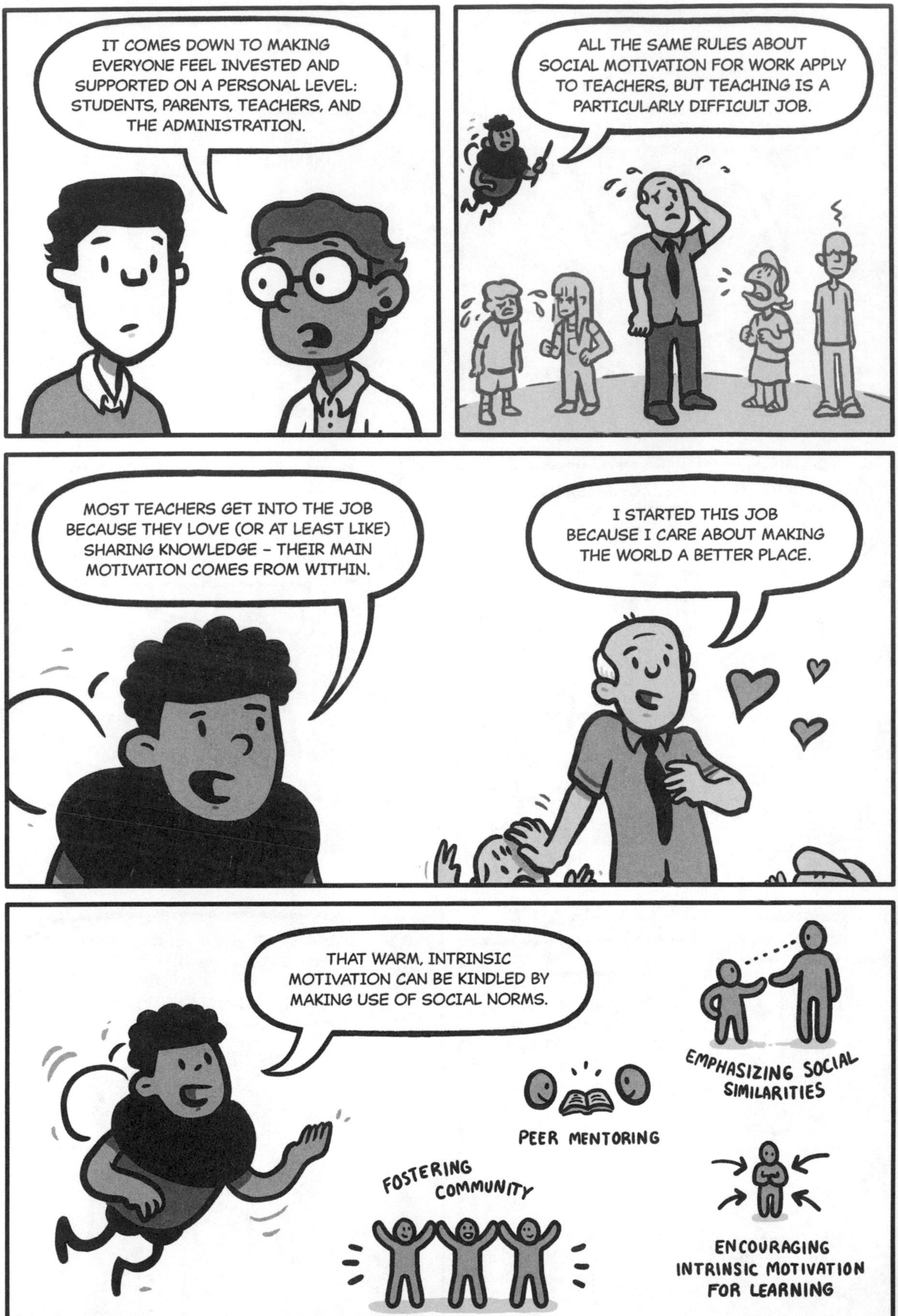
IT COMES DOWN TO MAKING EVERYONE FEEL INVESTED AND SUPPORTED ON A PERSONAL LEVEL: STUDENTS, PARENTS, TEACHERS, AND THE ADMINISTRATION.
ALL THE SAME RULES ABOUT SOCIAL MOTIVATION FOR WORK APPLY TO TEACHERS, BUT TEACHING IS A PARTICULARLY DIFFICULT JOB.
MOST TEACHERS GET INTO THE JOB BECAUSE THEY LOVE (OR AT LEAST LIKE) SHARING KNOWLEDGE - THEIR MAIN MOTIVATION COMES FROM WITHIN.
I STARTED THIS JOB BECAUSE I CARE ABOUT MAKING THE WORLD A BETTER PLACE.
THAT WARM, INTRINSIC MOTIVATION CAN BE KINDLED BY MAKING USE OF SOCIAL NORMS.
EMPHASIZING SOCIAL SIMILARITIES
PEER MENTORING
FOSTERING COMMUNITY
ENCOURAGING INTRINSIC MOTIVATION FOR LEARNING

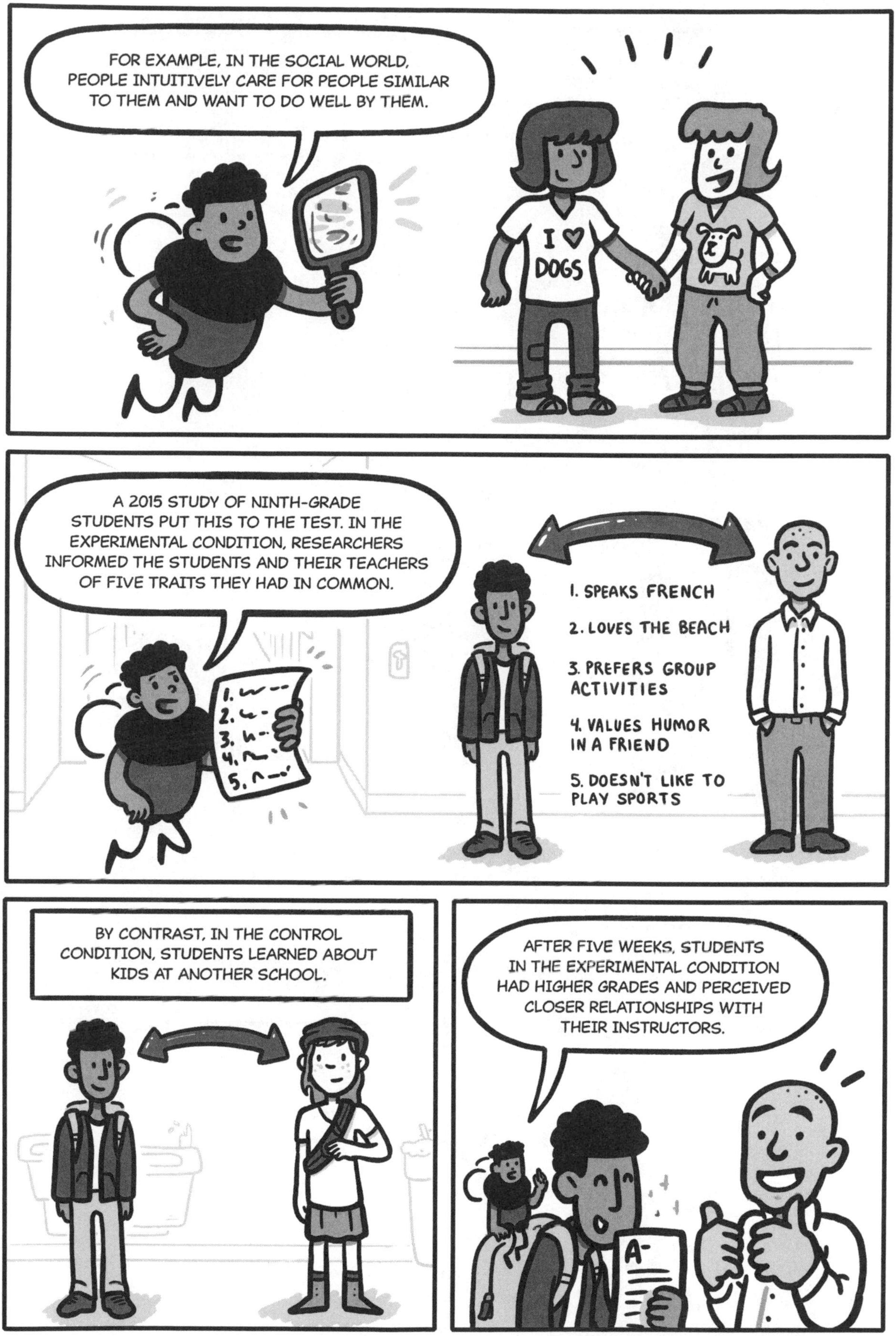
FOR EXAMPLE, IN THE SOCIAL WORLD, PEOPLE INTUITIVELY CARE FOR PEOPLE SIMILAR TO THEM AND WANT TO DO WELL BY THEM.
I ♥ DOGS
A 2015 STUDY OF NINTH-GRADE STUDENTS PUT THIS TO THE TEST. IN THE EXPERIMENTAL CONDITION, RESEARCHERS INFORMED THE STUDENTS AND THEIR TEACHERS OF FIVE TRAITS THEY HAD IN COMMON.
1. SPEAKS FRENCH
2. LOVES THE BEACH
3. PREFERS GROUP ACTIVITIES
4. VALUES HUMOR IN A FRIEND
5. DOESN'T LIKE TO PLAY SPORTS
BY CONTRAST, IN THE CONTROL CONDITION, STUDENTS LEARNED ABOUT KIDS AT ANOTHER SCHOOL.
AFTER FIVE WEEKS, STUDENTS IN THE EXPERIMENTAL CONDITION HAD HIGHER GRADES AND PERCEIVED CLOSER RELATIONSHIPS WITH THEIR INSTRUCTORS.
A-

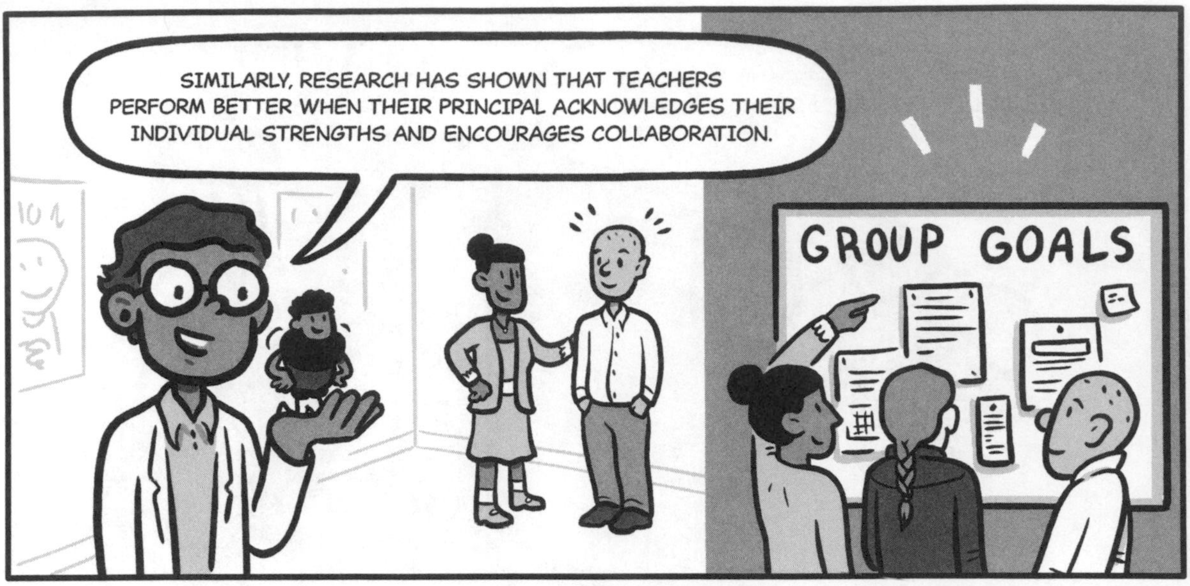
SIMILARLY, RESEARCH HAS SHOWN THAT TEACHERS PERFORM BETTER WHEN THEIR PRINCIPAL ACKNOWLEDGES THEIR INDIVIDUAL STRENGTHS AND ENCOURAGES COLLABORATION.
GROUP GOALS

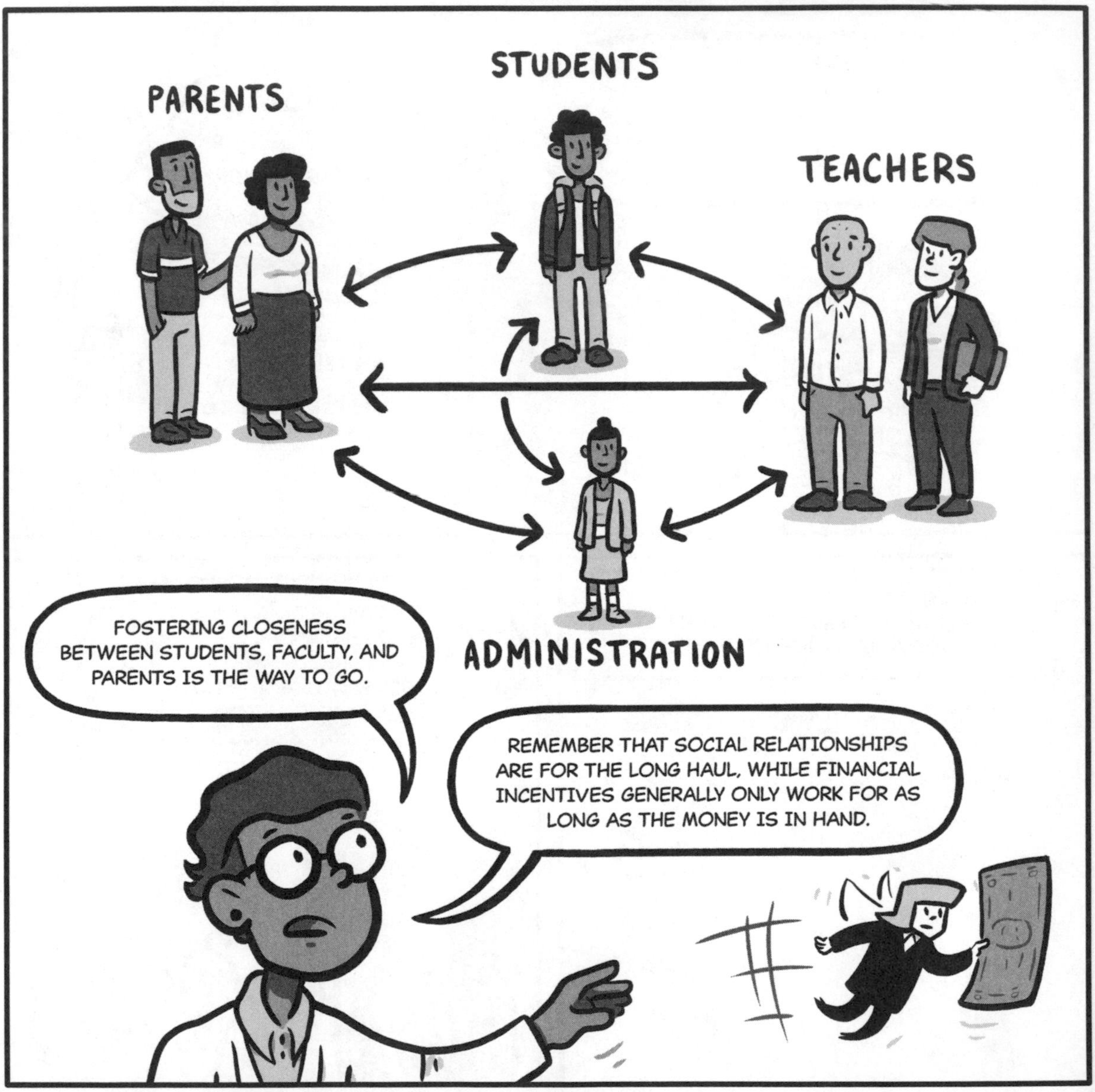
STUDENTS
PARENTS
TEACHERS
ADMINISTRATION
FOSTERING CLOSENESS BETWEEN STUDENTS, FACULTY, AND PARENTS IS THE WAY TO GO.
REMEMBER THAT SOCIAL RELATIONSHIPS ARE FOR THE LONG HAUL, WHILE FINANCIAL INCENTIVES GENERALLY ONLY WORK FOR AS LONG AS THE MONEY IS IN HAND.

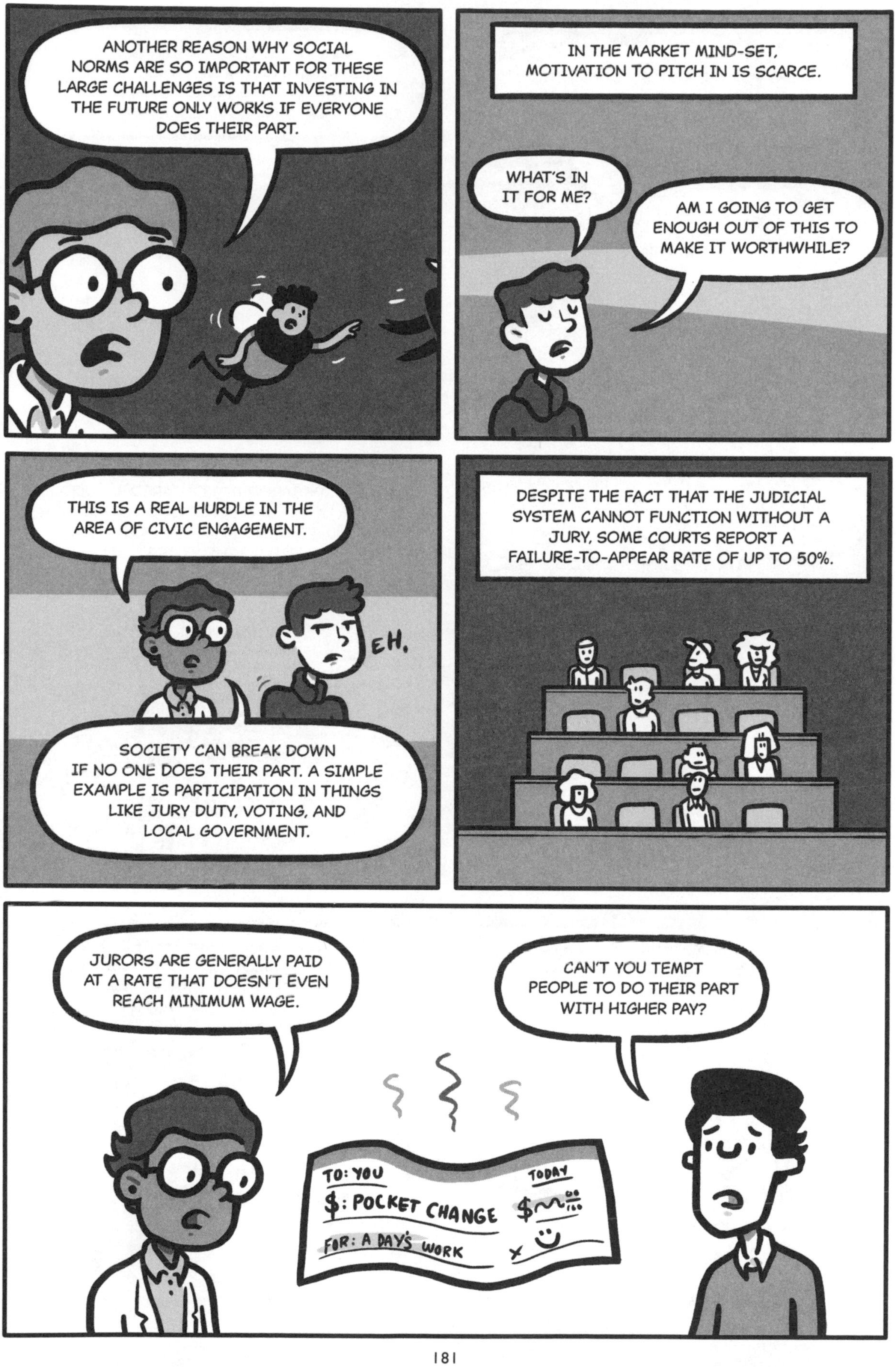
ANOTHER REASON WHY SOCIAL NORMS ARE SO IMPORTANT FOR THESE LARGE CHALLENGES IS THAT INVESTING IN THE FUTURE ONLY WORKS IF EVERYONE DOES THEIR PART.
IN THE MARKET MIND-SET, MOTIVATION TO PITCH IN IS SCARCE.
WHAT'S IN IT FOR ME?
AM I GOING TO GET ENOUGH OUT OF THIS TO MAKE IT WORTHWHILE?
THIS IS A REAL HURDLE IN THE AREA OF CIVIC ENGAGEMENT.
EH.
SOCIETY CAN BREAK DOWN IF NO ONE DOES THEIR PART. A SIMPLE EXAMPLE IS PARTICIPATION IN THINGS LIKE JURY DUTY, VOTING, AND LOCAL GOVERNMENT.
DESPITE THE FACT THAT THE JUDICIAL SYSTEM CANNOT FUNCTION WITHOUT A JURY, SOME COURTS REPORT A FAILURE-TO-APPEAR RATE OF UP TO 50%.
JURORS ARE GENERALLY PAID AT A RATE THAT DOESN'T EVEN REACH MINIMUM WAGE.
TO: YOU
TODAY
$: POCKET CHANGE
FOR: A DAY'S WORK
CAN'T YOU TEMPT PEOPLE TO DO THEIR PART WITH HIGHER PAY?

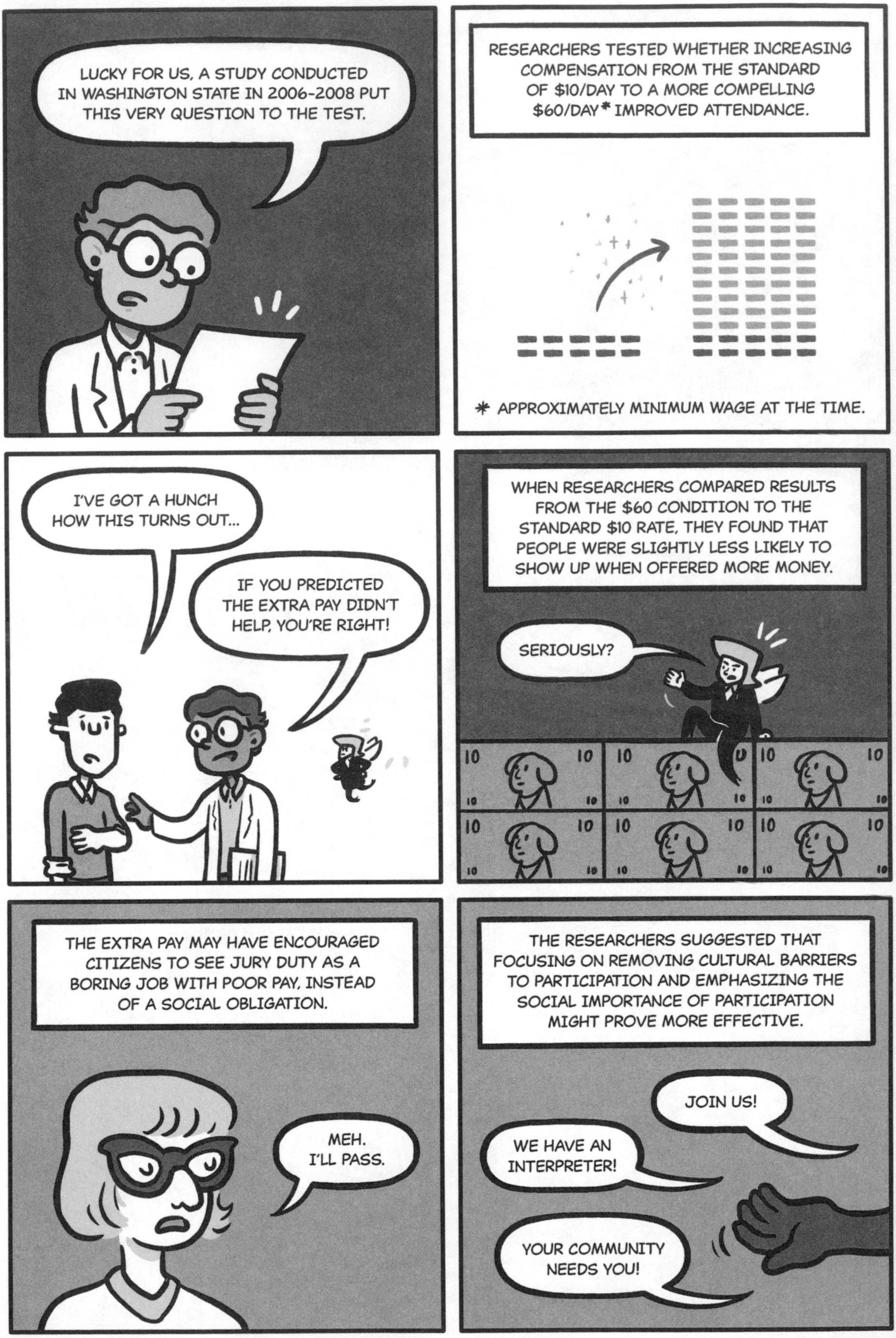
LUCKY FOR US, A STUDY CONDUCTED IN WASHINGTON STATE IN 2006-2008 PUT THIS VERY QUESTION TO THE TEST.
RESEARCHERS TESTED WHETHER INCREASING COMPENSATION FROM THE STANDARD OF $10/DAY TO A MORE COMPELLING $60/DAY* IMPROVED ATTENDANCE.
* APPROXIMATELY MINIMUM WAGE AT THE TIME.
I'VE GOT A HUNCH HOW THIS TURNS OUT...
IF YOU PREDICTED THE EXTRA PAY DIDN'T HELP, YOU'RE RIGHT!
WHEN RESEARCHERS COMPARED RESULTS FROM THE $60 CONDITION TO THE STANDARD $10 RATE, THEY FOUND THAT PEOPLE WERE SLIGHTLY LESS LIKELY TO SHOW UP WHEN OFFERED MORE MONEY.
SERIOUSLY?
THE EXTRA PAY MAY HAVE ENCOURAGED CITIZENS TO SEE JURY DUTY AS A BORING JOB WITH POOR PAY, INSTEAD OF A SOCIAL OBLIGATION.
MEH. I'LL PASS.
THE RESEARCHERS SUGGESTED THAT FOCUSING ON REMOVING CULTURAL BARRIERS TO PARTICIPATION AND EMPHASIZING THE SOCIAL IMPORTANCE OF PARTICIPATION MIGHT PROVE MORE EFFECTIVE.
JOIN US!
WE HAVE AN INTERPRETER!
YOUR COMMUNITY NEEDS YOU!

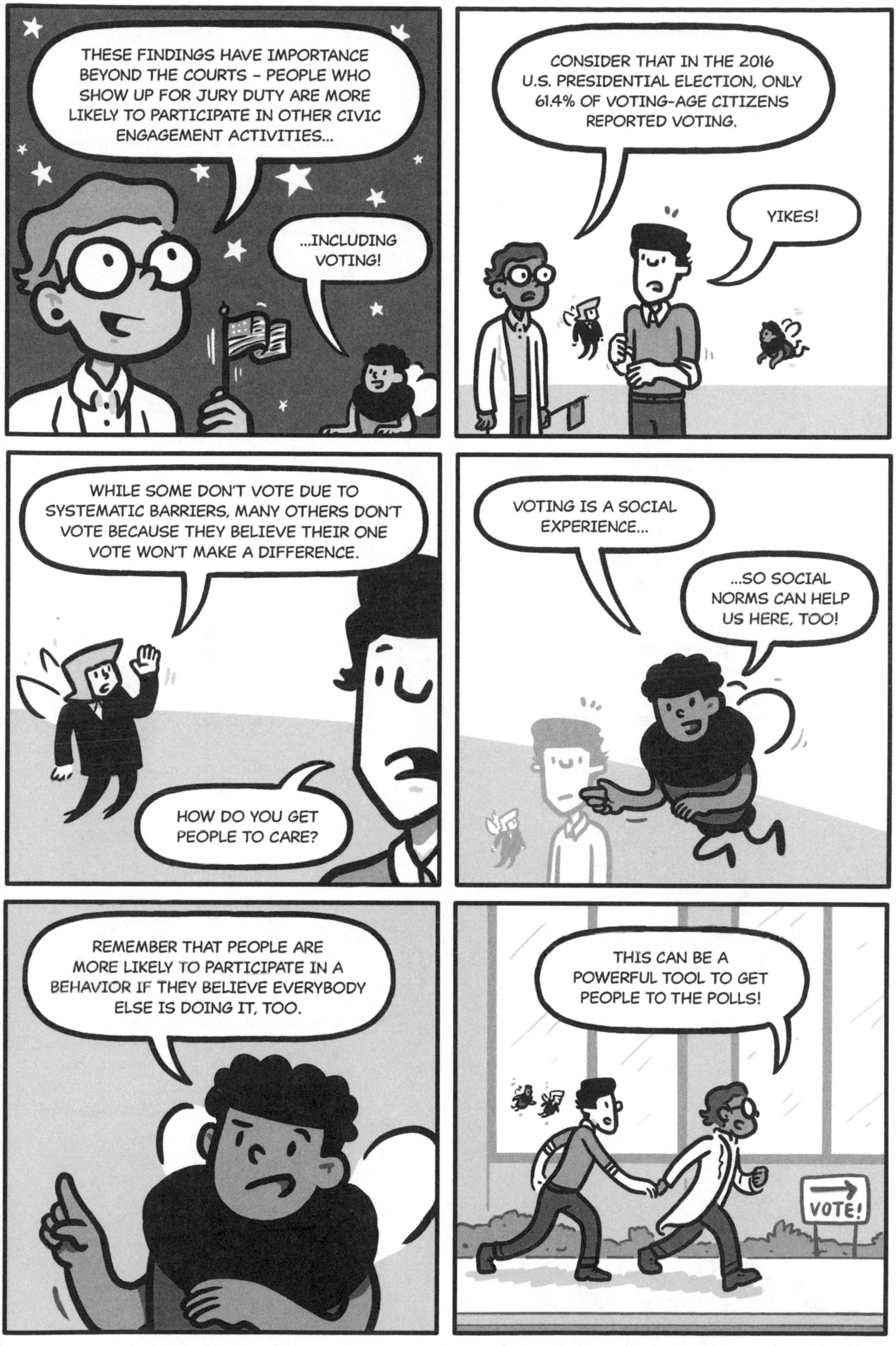
THESE FINDINGS HAVE IMPORTANCE BEYOND THE COURTS – PEOPLE WHO SHOW UP FOR JURY DUTY ARE MORE LIKELY TO PARTICIPATE IN OTHER CIVIC ENGAGEMENT ACTIVITIES...
...INCLUDING VOTING!
CONSIDER THAT IN THE 2016 U.S. PRESIDENTIAL ELECTION, ONLY 61.4% OF VOTING-AGE CITIZENS REPORTED VOTING.
YIKES!
WHILE SOME DON'T VOTE DUE TO SYSTEMATIC BARRIERS, MANY OTHERS DON'T VOTE BECAUSE THEY BELIEVE THEIR ONE VOTE WON'T MAKE A DIFFERENCE.
HOW DO YOU GET PEOPLE TO CARE?
VOTING IS A SOCIAL EXPERIENCE...
...SO SOCIAL NORMS CAN HELP US HERE, TOO!
REMEMBER THAT PEOPLE ARE MORE LIKELY TO PARTICIPATE IN A BEHAVIOR IF THEY BELIEVE EVERYBODY ELSE IS DOING IT, TOO.
THIS CAN BE A POWERFUL TOOL TO GET PEOPLE TO THE POLLS!
VOTE!

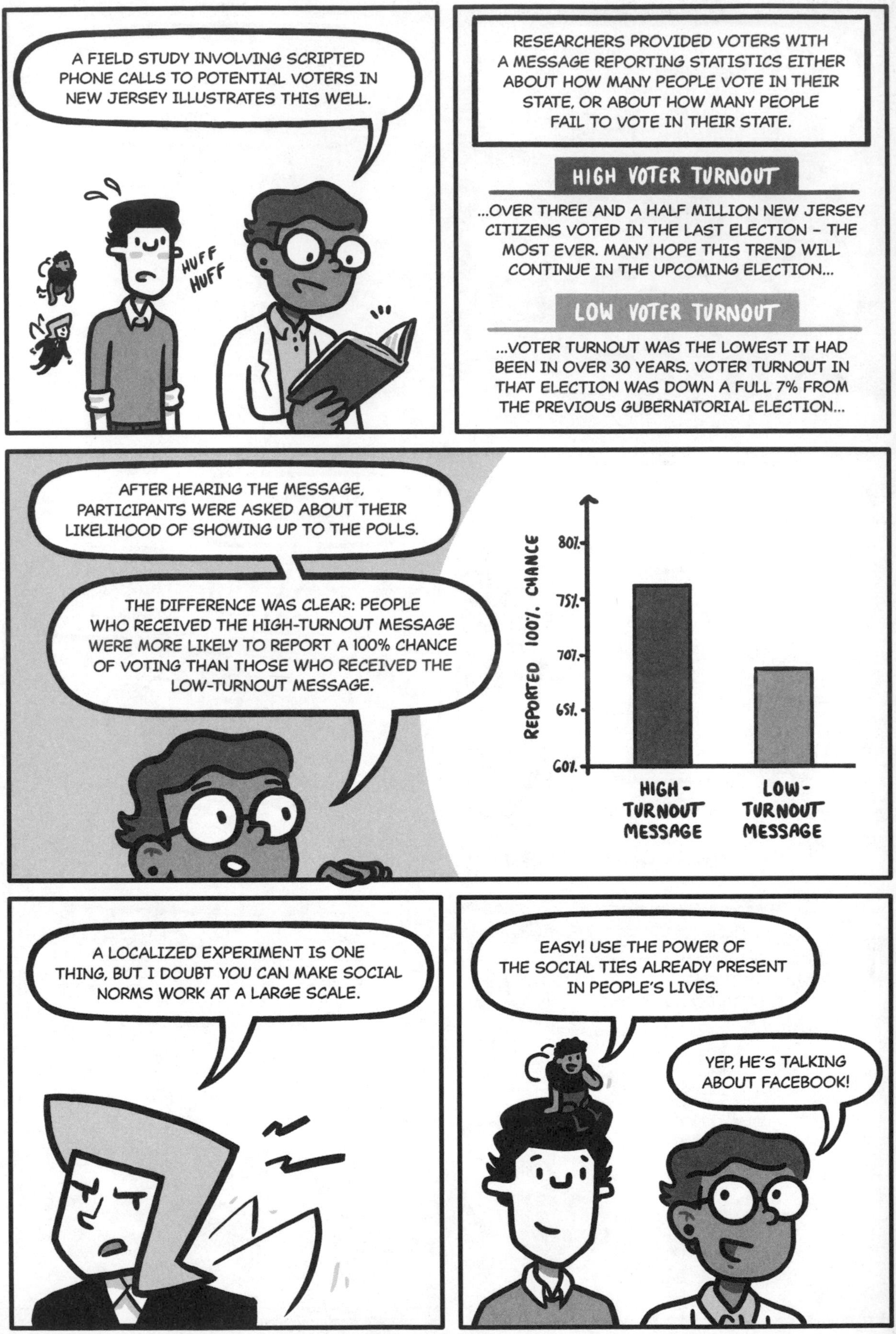
A FIELD STUDY INVOLVING SCRIPTED PHONE CALLS TO POTENTIAL VOTERS IN NEW JERSEY ILLUSTRATES THIS WELL.
HUFF HUFF
RESEARCHERS PROVIDED VOTERS WITH A MESSAGE REPORTING STATISTICS EITHER ABOUT HOW MANY PEOPLE VOTE IN THEIR STATE, OR ABOUT HOW MANY PEOPLE FAIL TO VOTE IN THEIR STATE.
HIGH VOTER TURNOUT
...OVER THREE AND A HALF MILLION NEW JERSEY CITIZENS VOTED IN THE LAST ELECTION – THE MOST EVER. MANY HOPE THIS TREND WILL CONTINUE IN THE UPCOMING ELECTION...
LOW VOTER TURNOUT
...VOTER TURNOUT WAS THE LOWEST IT HAD BEEN IN OVER 30 YEARS. VOTER TURNOUT IN THAT ELECTION WAS DOWN A FULL 7% FROM THE PREVIOUS GUBERNATORIAL ELECTION...
AFTER HEARING THE MESSAGE, PARTICIPANTS WERE ASKED ABOUT THEIR LIKELIHOOD OF SHOWING UP TO THE POLLS.
THE DIFFERENCE WAS CLEAR: PEOPLE WHO RECEIVED THE HIGH-TURNOUT MESSAGE WERE MORE LIKELY TO REPORT A 100% CHANCE OF VOTING THAN THOSE WHO RECEIVED THE LOW-TURNOUT MESSAGE.
REPORTED 100% CHANCE
80%
75%
70%
65%
60%
HIGH-TURNOUT MESSAGE
LOW-TURNOUT MESSAGE
A LOCALIZED EXPERIMENT IS ONE THING, BUT I DOUBT YOU CAN MAKE SOCIAL NORMS WORK AT A LARGE SCALE.
EASY! USE THE POWER OF THE SOCIAL TIES ALREADY PRESENT IN PEOPLE'S LIVES.
YEP, HE'S TALKING ABOUT FACEBOOK!

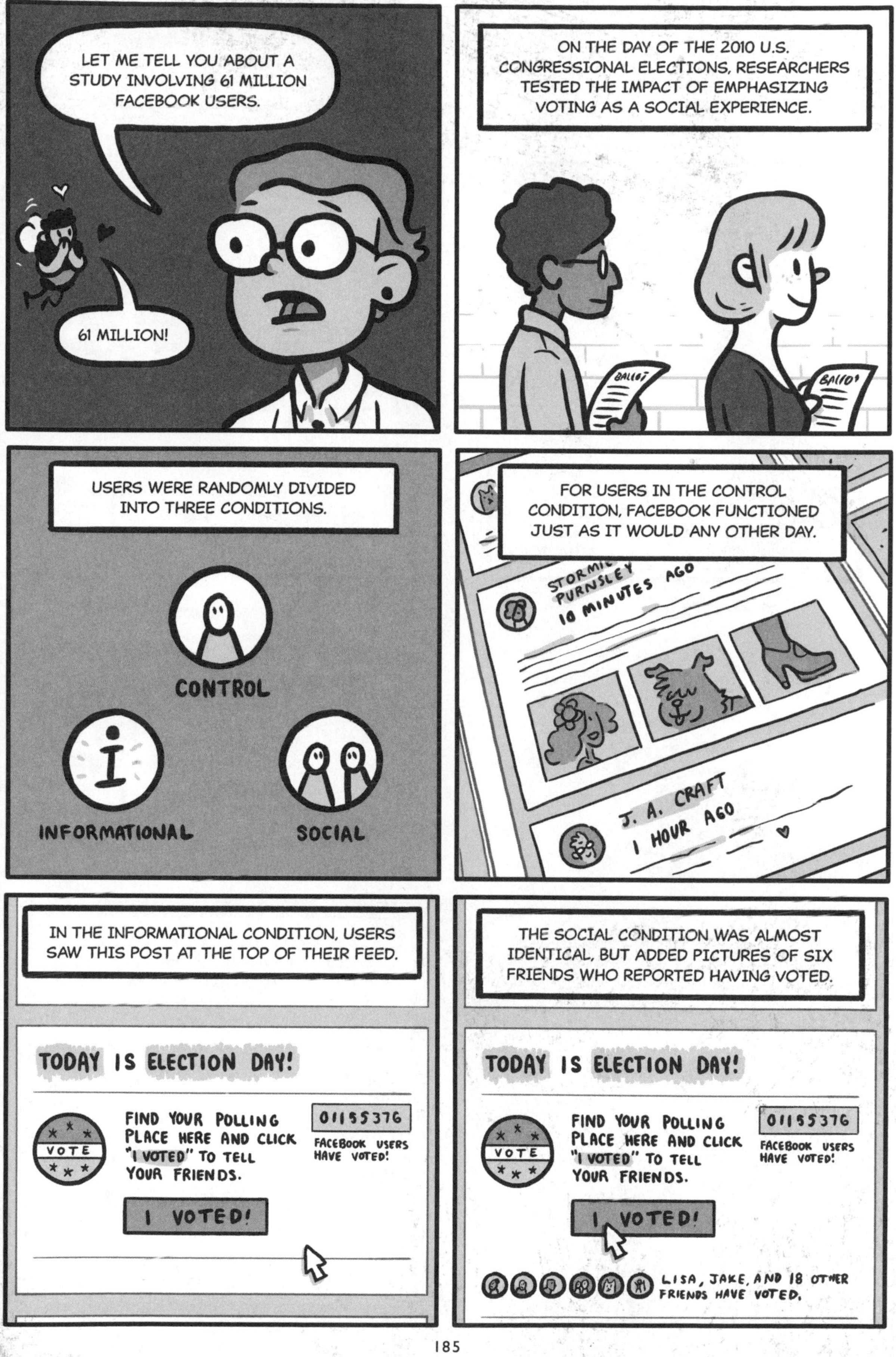
LET ME TELL YOU ABOUT A STUDY INVOLVING 61 MILLION FACEBOOK USERS.
61 MILLION!
ON THE DAY OF THE 2010 U.S. CONGRESSIONAL ELECTIONS, RESEARCHERS TESTED THE IMPACT OF EMPHASIZING VOTING AS A SOCIAL EXPERIENCE.
USERS WERE RANDOMLY DIVIDED INTO THREE CONDITIONS.
CONTROL
INFORMATIONAL
SOCIAL
FOR USERS IN THE CONTROL CONDITION, FACEBOOK FUNCTIONED JUST AS IT WOULD ANY OTHER DAY.
10 MINUTES AGO
J. A. CRAFT
1 HOUR AGO
IN THE INFORMATIONAL CONDITION, USERS SAW THIS POST AT THE TOP OF THEIR FEED.
TODAY IS ELECTION DAY!
FIND YOUR POLLING PLACE HERE AND CLICK "I VOTED" TO TELL YOUR FRIENDS.
VOTE
01155376
FACEBOOK USERS HAVE VOTED!
I VOTED!
THE SOCIAL CONDITION WAS ALMOST IDENTICAL, BUT ADDED PICTURES OF SIX FRIENDS WHO REPORTED HAVING VOTED.
TODAY IS ELECTION DAY!
FIND YOUR POLLING PLACE HERE AND CLICK "I VOTED" TO TELL YOUR FRIENDS.
VOTE
01155376
FACEBOOK USERS HAVE VOTED!
I VOTED!
LISA, JAKE, AND 18 OTHER FRIENDS HAVE VOTED.

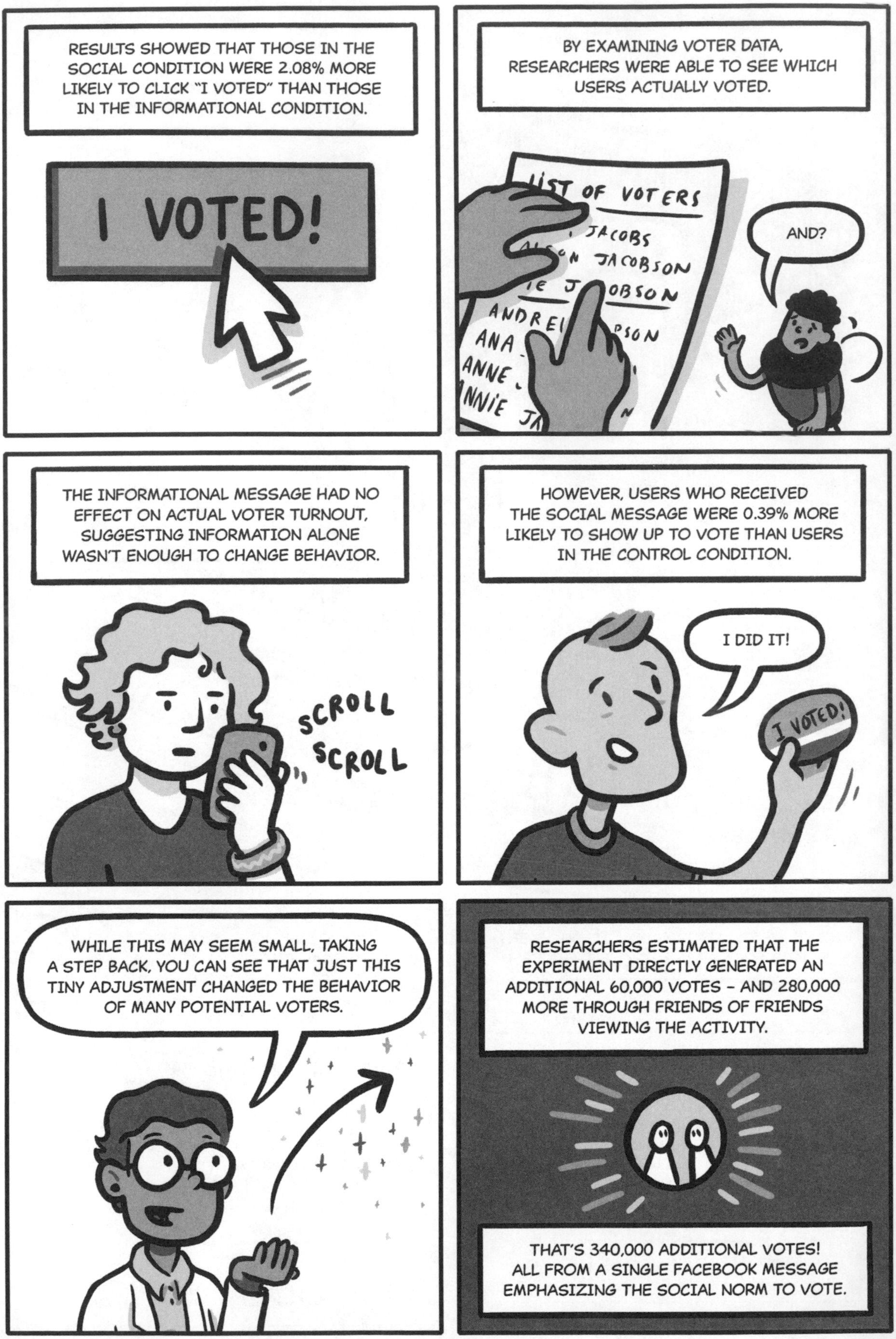
RESULTS SHOWED THAT THOSE IN THE SOCIAL CONDITION WERE 2.08% MORE LIKELY TO CLICK "I VOTED" THAN THOSE IN THE INFORMATIONAL CONDITION.
I VOTED!
BY EXAMINING VOTER DATA, RESEARCHERS WERE ABLE TO SEE WHICH USERS ACTUALLY VOTED.
AND?
THE INFORMATIONAL MESSAGE HAD NO EFFECT ON ACTUAL VOTER TURNOUT, SUGGESTING INFORMATION ALONE WASN'T ENOUGH TO CHANGE BEHAVIOR.
SCROLL
SCROLL
HOWEVER, USERS WHO RECEIVED THE SOCIAL MESSAGE WERE 0.39% MORE LIKELY TO SHOW UP TO VOTE THAN USERS IN THE CONTROL CONDITION.
I DID IT!
I VOTED!
WHILE THIS MAY SEEM SMALL, TAKING A STEP BACK, YOU CAN SEE THAT JUST THIS TINY ADJUSTMENT CHANGED THE BEHAVIOR OF MANY POTENTIAL VOTERS.
RESEARCHERS ESTIMATED THAT THE EXPERIMENT DIRECTLY GENERATED AN ADDITIONAL 60,000 VOTES – AND 280,000 MORE THROUGH FRIENDS OF FRIENDS VIEWING THE ACTIVITY.
THAT'S 340,000 ADDITIONAL VOTES! ALL FROM A SINGLE FACEBOOK MESSAGE EMPHASIZING THE SOCIAL NORM TO VOTE.

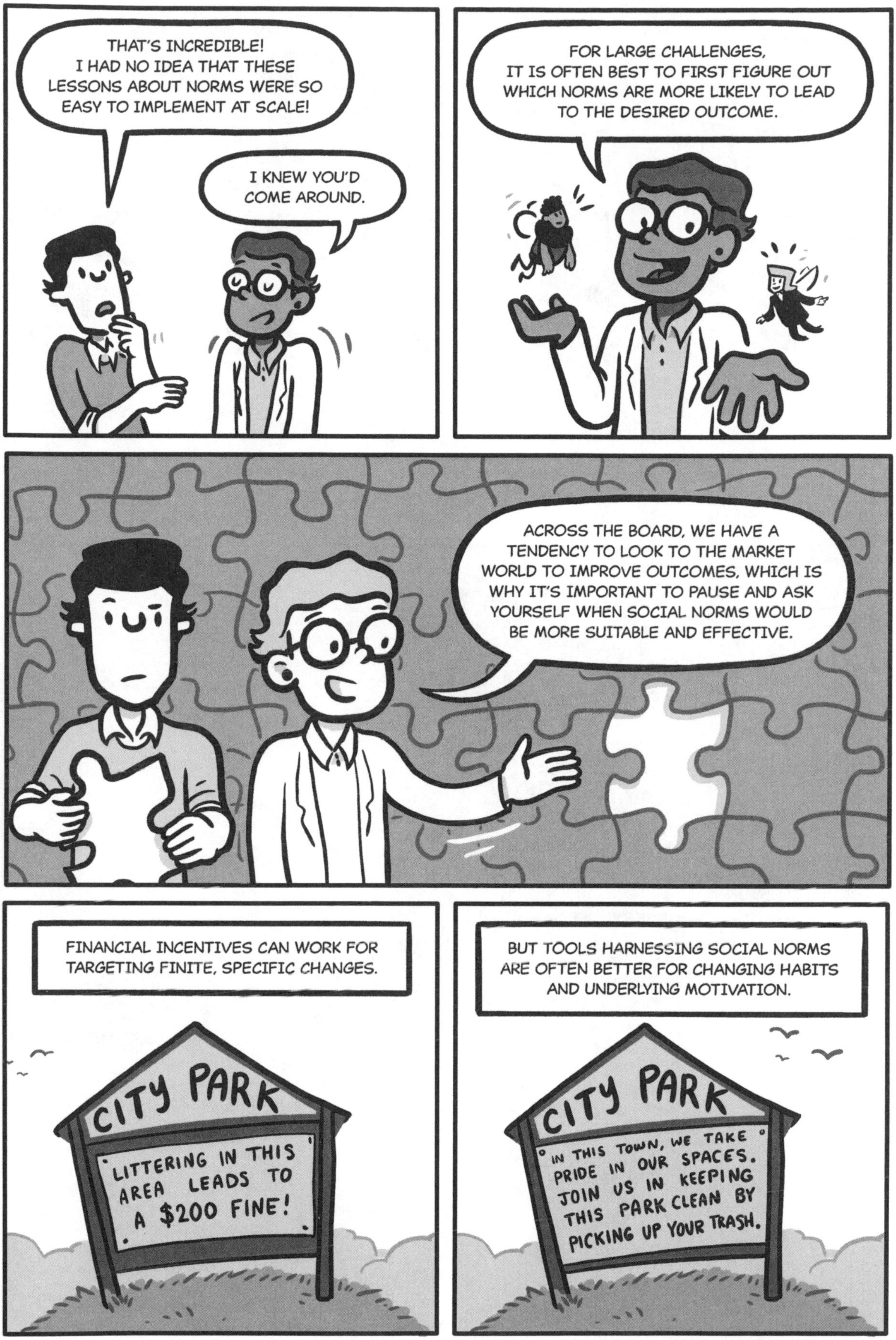
THAT'S INCREDIBLE! I HAD NO IDEA THAT THESE LESSONS ABOUT NORMS WERE SO EASY TO IMPLEMENT AT SCALE!
I KNEW YOU'D COME AROUND.
FOR LARGE CHALLENGES, IT IS OFTEN BEST TO FIRST FIGURE OUT WHICH NORMS ARE MORE LIKELY TO LEAD TO THE DESIRED OUTCOME.
ACROSS THE BOARD, WE HAVE A TENDENCY TO LOOK TO THE MARKET WORLD TO IMPROVE OUTCOMES, WHICH IS WHY IT'S IMPORTANT TO PAUSE AND ASK YOURSELF WHEN SOCIAL NORMS WOULD BE MORE SUITABLE AND EFFECTIVE.
FINANCIAL INCENTIVES CAN WORK FOR TARGETING FINITE, SPECIFIC CHANGES.
CITY PARK
LITTERING IN THIS AREA LEADS TO A $200 FINE!
BUT TOOLS HARNESSING SOCIAL NORMS ARE OFTEN BETTER FOR CHANGING HABITS AND UNDERLYING MOTIVATION.
CITY PARK
IN THIS TOWN, WE TAKE PRIDE IN OUR SPACES. JOIN US IN KEEPING THIS PARK CLEAN BY PICKING UP YOUR TRASH.

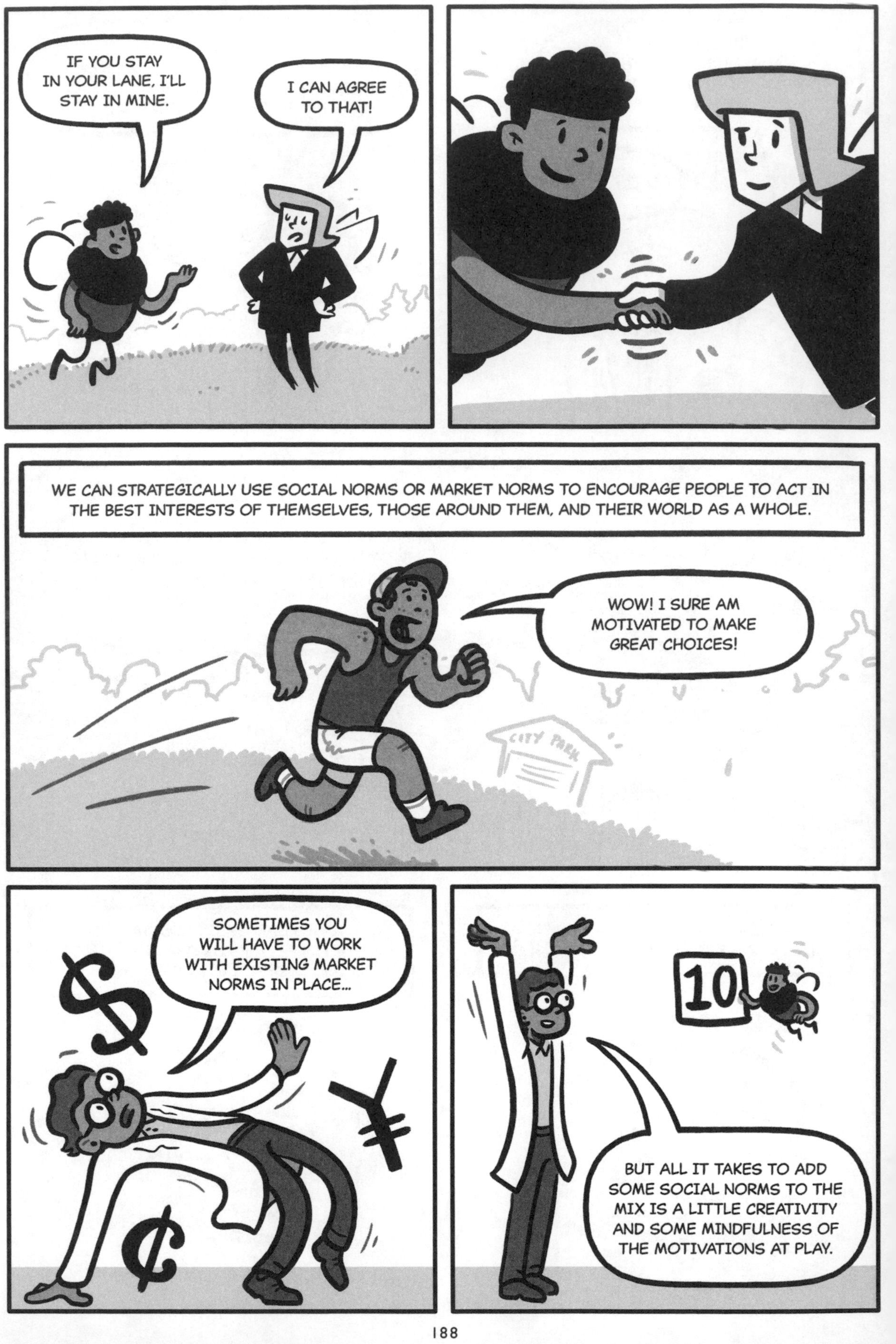
IF YOU STAY IN YOUR LANE, I'LL STAY IN MINE.
I CAN AGREE TO THAT!
WE CAN STRATEGICALLY USE SOCIAL NORMS OR MARKET NORMS TO ENCOURAGE PEOPLE TO ACT IN THE BEST INTERESTS OF THEMSELVES, THOSE AROUND THEM, AND THEIR WORLD AS A WHOLE.
WOW! I SURE AM MOTIVATED TO MAKE GREAT CHOICES!
CITY PARK
SOMETIMES YOU WILL HAVE TO WORK WITH EXISTING MARKET NORMS IN PLACE...
10
BUT ALL IT TAKES TO ADD SOME SOCIAL NORMS TO THE MIX IS A LITTLE CREATIVITY AND SOME MINDFULNESS OF THE MOTIVATIONS AT PLAY.

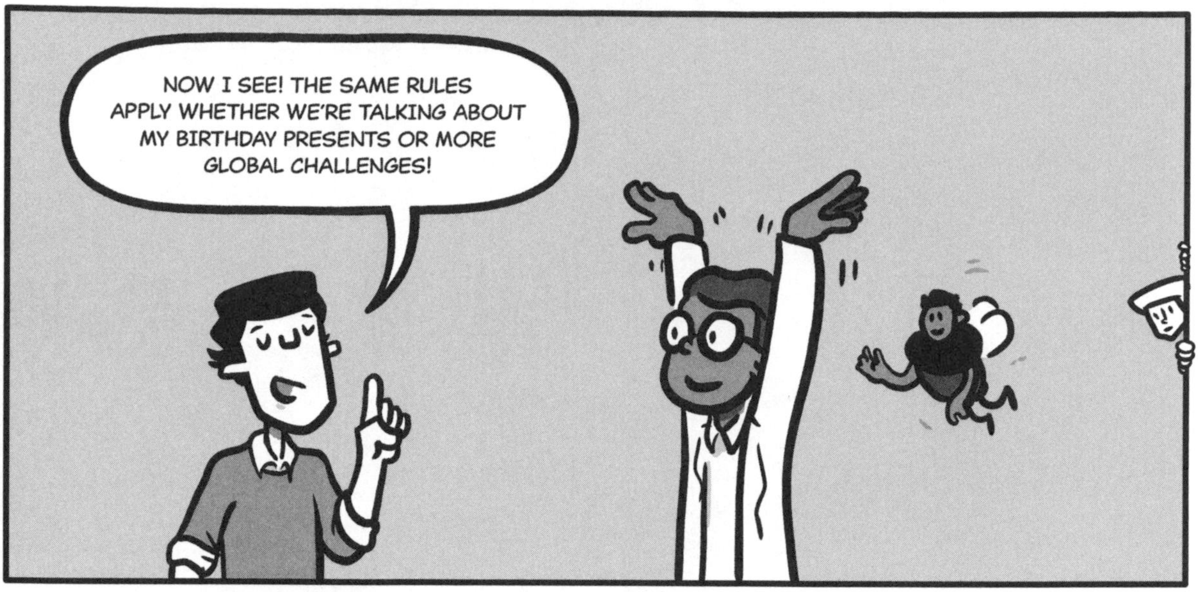
NOW I SEE! THE SAME RULES APPLY WHETHER WE'RE TALKING ABOUT MY BIRTHDAY PRESENTS OR MORE GLOBAL CHALLENGES!

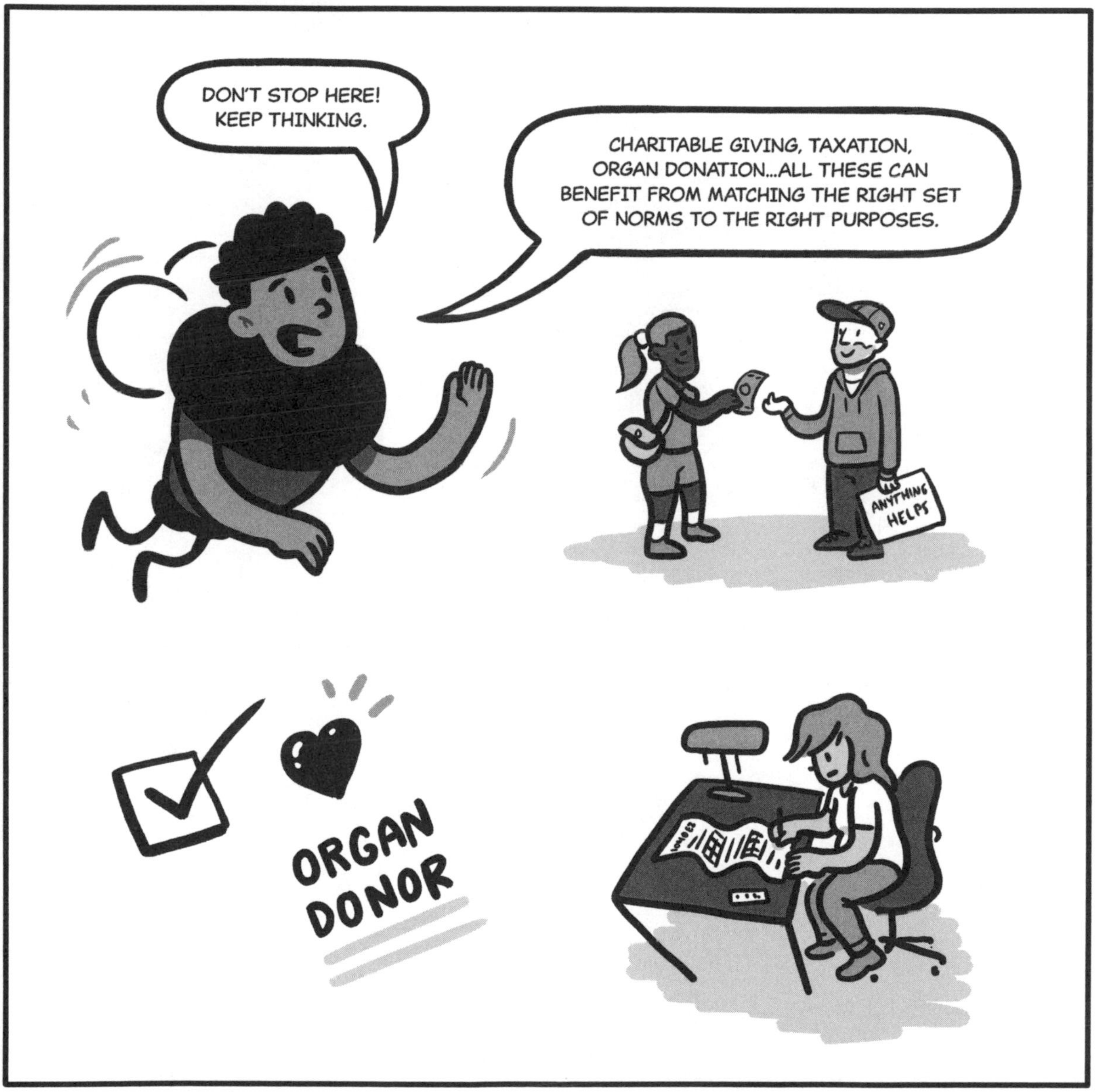
DON'T STOP HERE! KEEP THINKING.
CHARITABLE GIVING, TAXATION, ORGAN DONATION...ALL THESE CAN BENEFIT FROM MATCHING THE RIGHT SET OF NORMS TO THE RIGHT PURPOSES.
ANYTHING HELPS
ORGAN DONOR

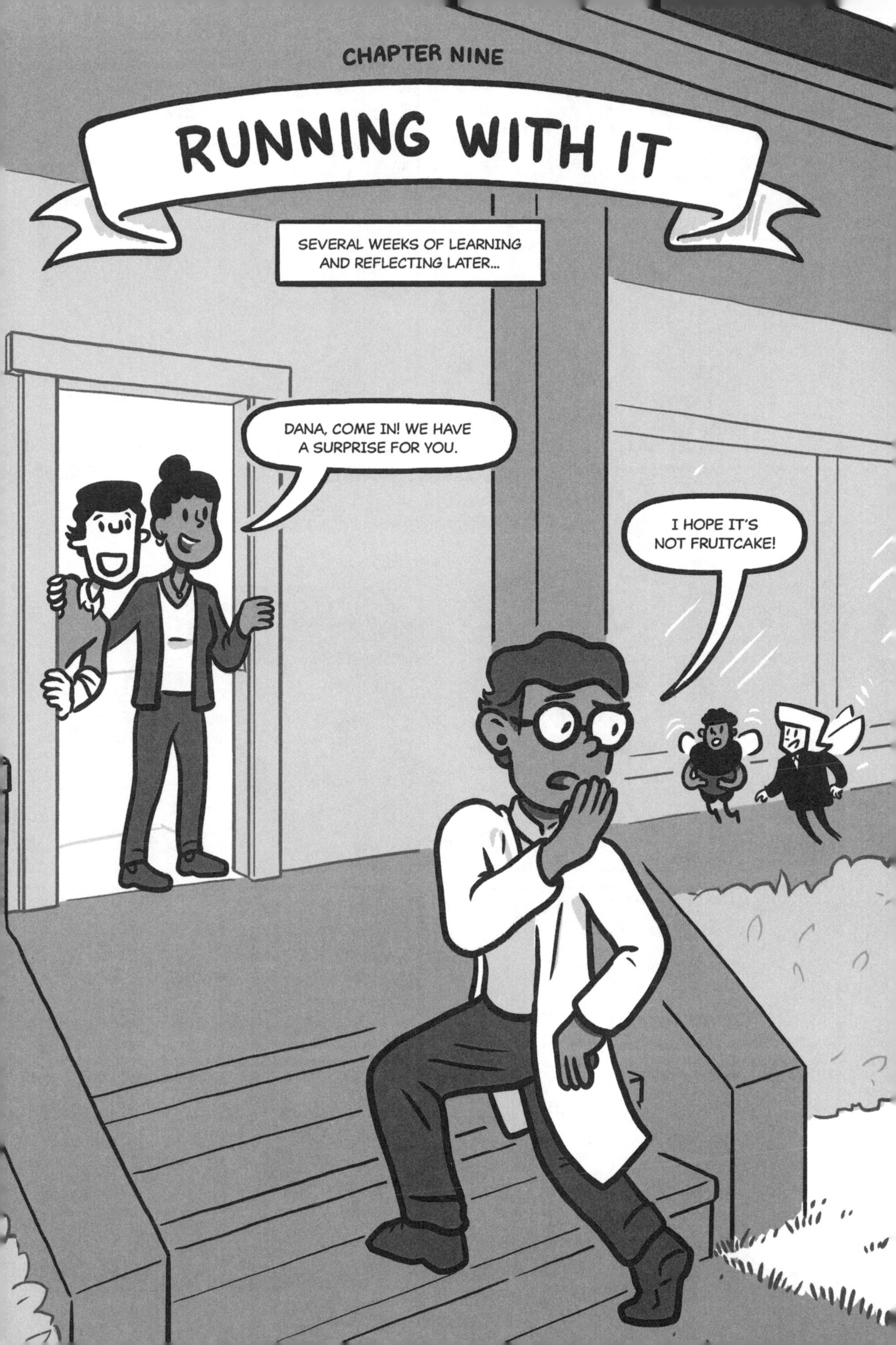
CHAPTER NINE
RUNNING WITH IT
SEVERAL WEEKS OF LEARNING AND REFLECTING LATER...
DANA, COME IN! WE HAVE A SURPRISE FOR YOU.
I HOPE IT'S NOT FRUITCAKE!

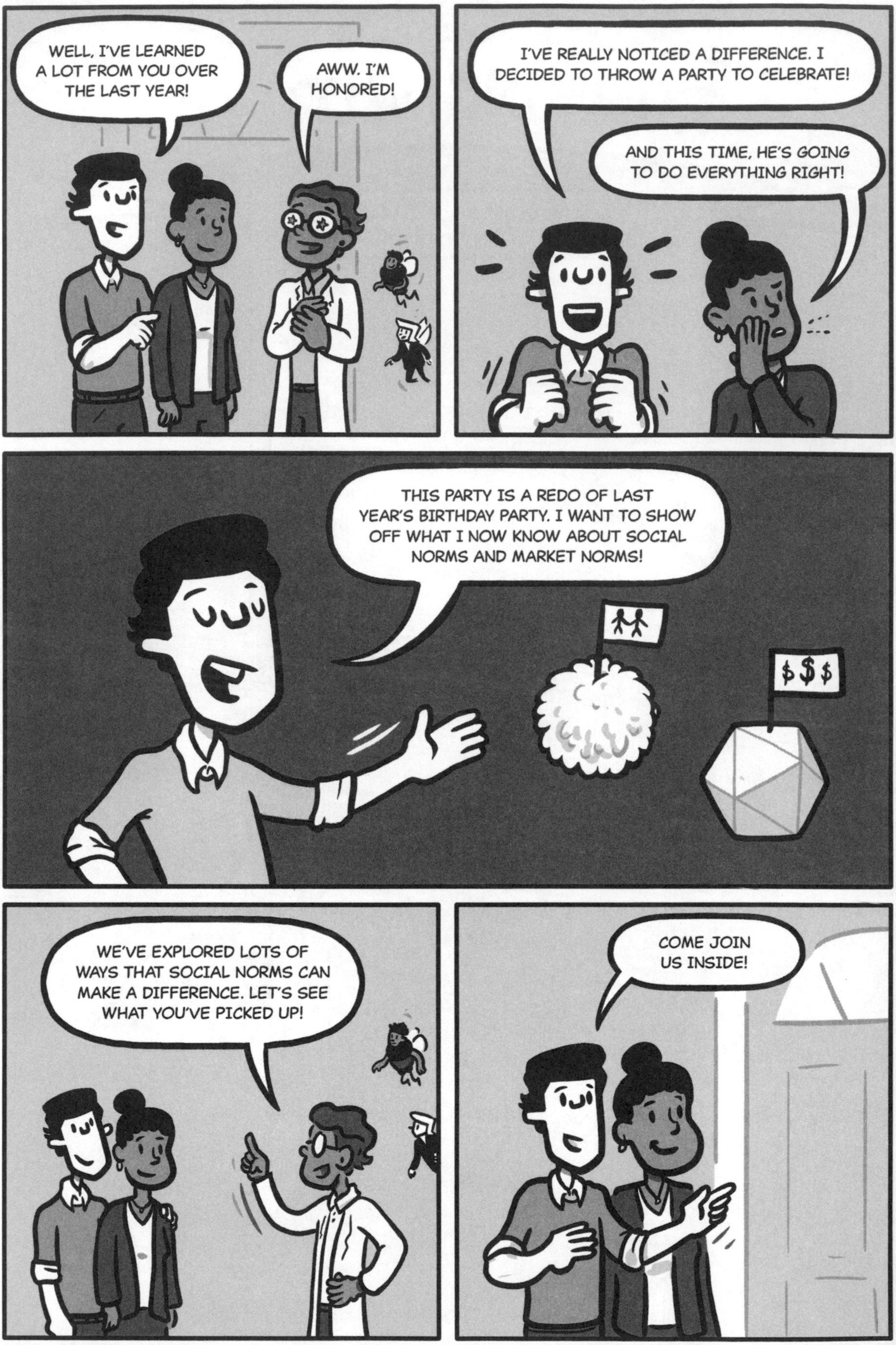
WELL, I'VE LEARNED A LOT FROM YOU OVER THE LAST YEAR!
AWW. I'M HONORED!
I'VE REALLY NOTICED A DIFFERENCE. I DECIDED TO THROW A PARTY TO CELEBRATE!
AND THIS TIME, HE'S GOING TO DO EVERYTHING RIGHT!
THIS PARTY IS A REDO OF LAST YEAR'S BIRTHDAY PARTY. I WANT TO SHOW OFF WHAT I NOW KNOW ABOUT SOCIAL NORMS AND MARKET NORMS!
$$$
WE'VE EXPLORED LOTS OF WAYS THAT SOCIAL NORMS CAN MAKE A DIFFERENCE. LET'S SEE WHAT YOU'VE PICKED UP!
COME JOIN US INSIDE!

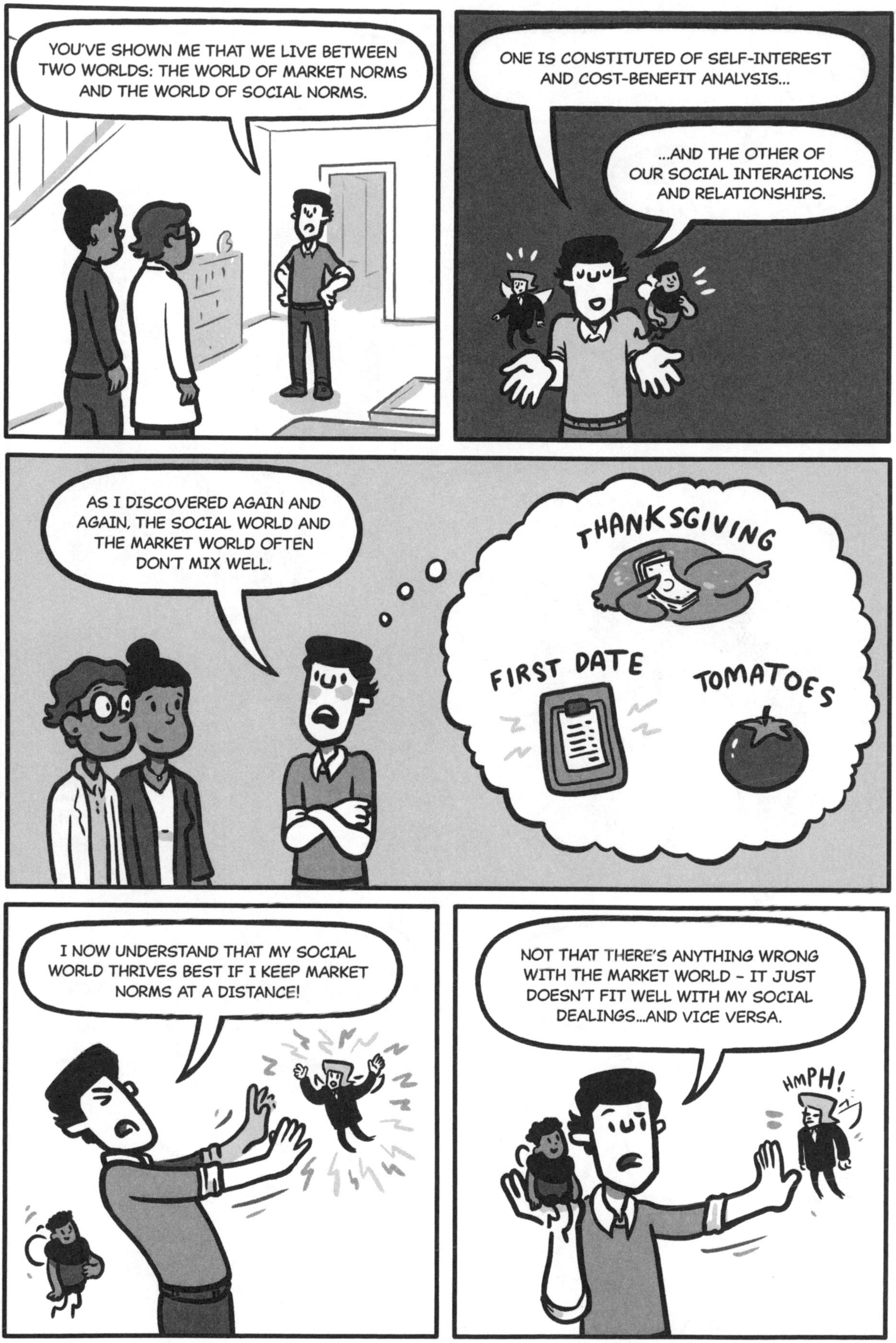
YOU'VE SHOWN ME THAT WE LIVE BETWEEN TWO WORLDS: THE WORLD OF MARKET NORMS AND THE WORLD OF SOCIAL NORMS.
ONE IS CONSTITUTED OF SELF-INTEREST AND COST-BENEFIT ANALYSIS...
...AND THE OTHER OF OUR SOCIAL INTERACTIONS AND RELATIONSHIPS.
AS I DISCOVERED AGAIN AND AGAIN, THE SOCIAL WORLD AND THE MARKET WORLD OFTEN DON'T MIX WELL.
THANKSGIVING
FIRST DATE
TOMATOES
I NOW UNDERSTAND THAT MY SOCIAL WORLD THRIVES BEST IF I KEEP MARKET NORMS AT A DISTANCE!
NOT THAT THERE'S ANYTHING WRONG WITH THE MARKET WORLD – IT JUST DOESN'T FIT WELL WITH MY SOCIAL DEALINGS...AND VICE VERSA.
HMPH!

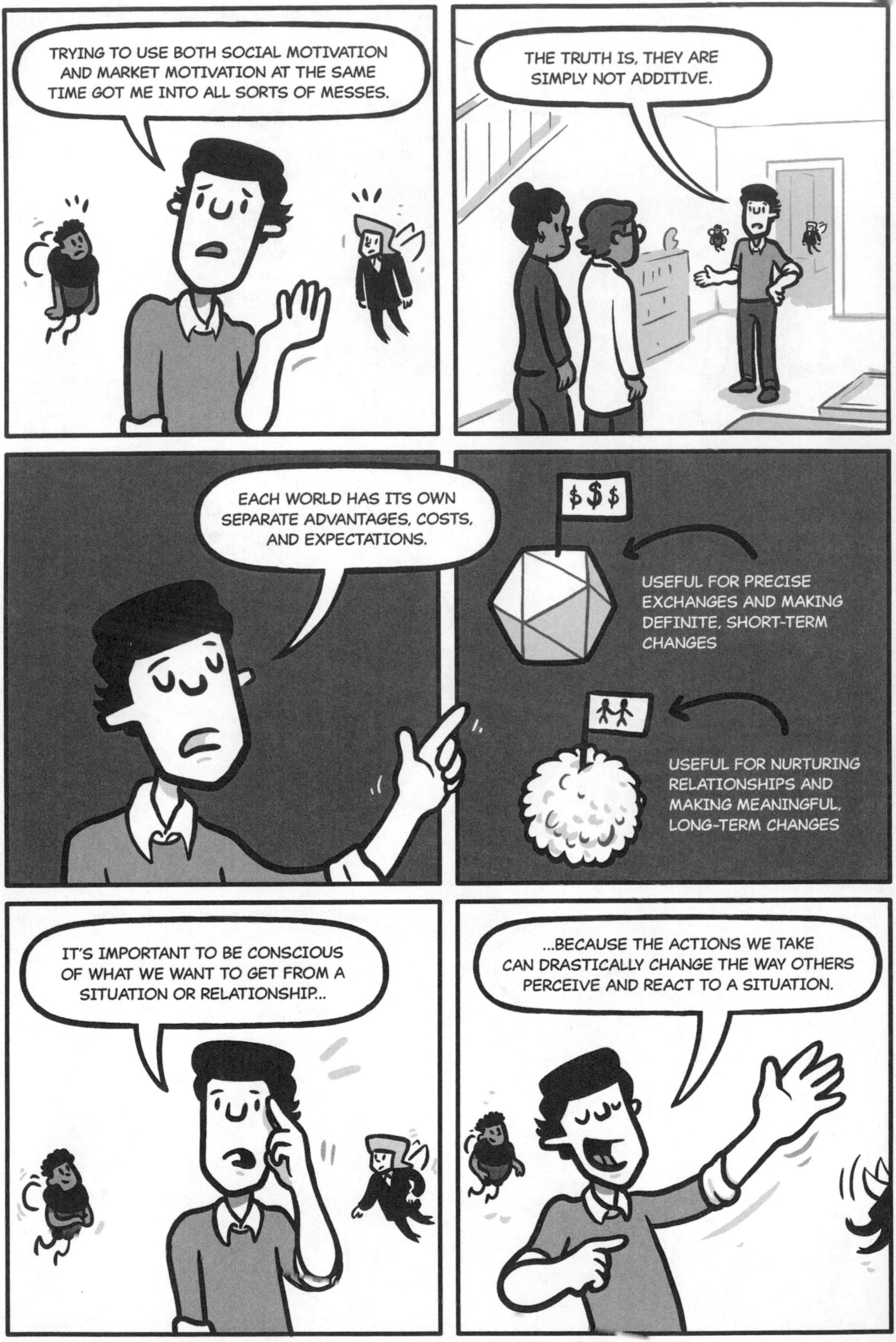
TRYING TO USE BOTH SOCIAL MOTIVATION AND MARKET MOTIVATION AT THE SAME TIME GOT ME INTO ALL SORTS OF MESSES.
THE TRUTH IS, THEY ARE SIMPLY NOT ADDITIVE.
EACH WORLD HAS ITS OWN SEPARATE ADVANTAGES, COSTS, AND EXPECTATIONS.
$$$
USEFUL FOR PRECISE EXCHANGES AND MAKING DEFINITE, SHORT-TERM CHANGES
USEFUL FOR NURTURING RELATIONSHIPS AND MAKING MEANINGFUL, LONG-TERM CHANGES
IT'S IMPORTANT TO BE CONSCIOUS OF WHAT WE WANT TO GET FROM A SITUATION OR RELATIONSHIP...
...BECAUSE THE ACTIONS WE TAKE CAN DRASTICALLY CHANGE THE WAY OTHERS PERCEIVE AND REACT TO A SITUATION.

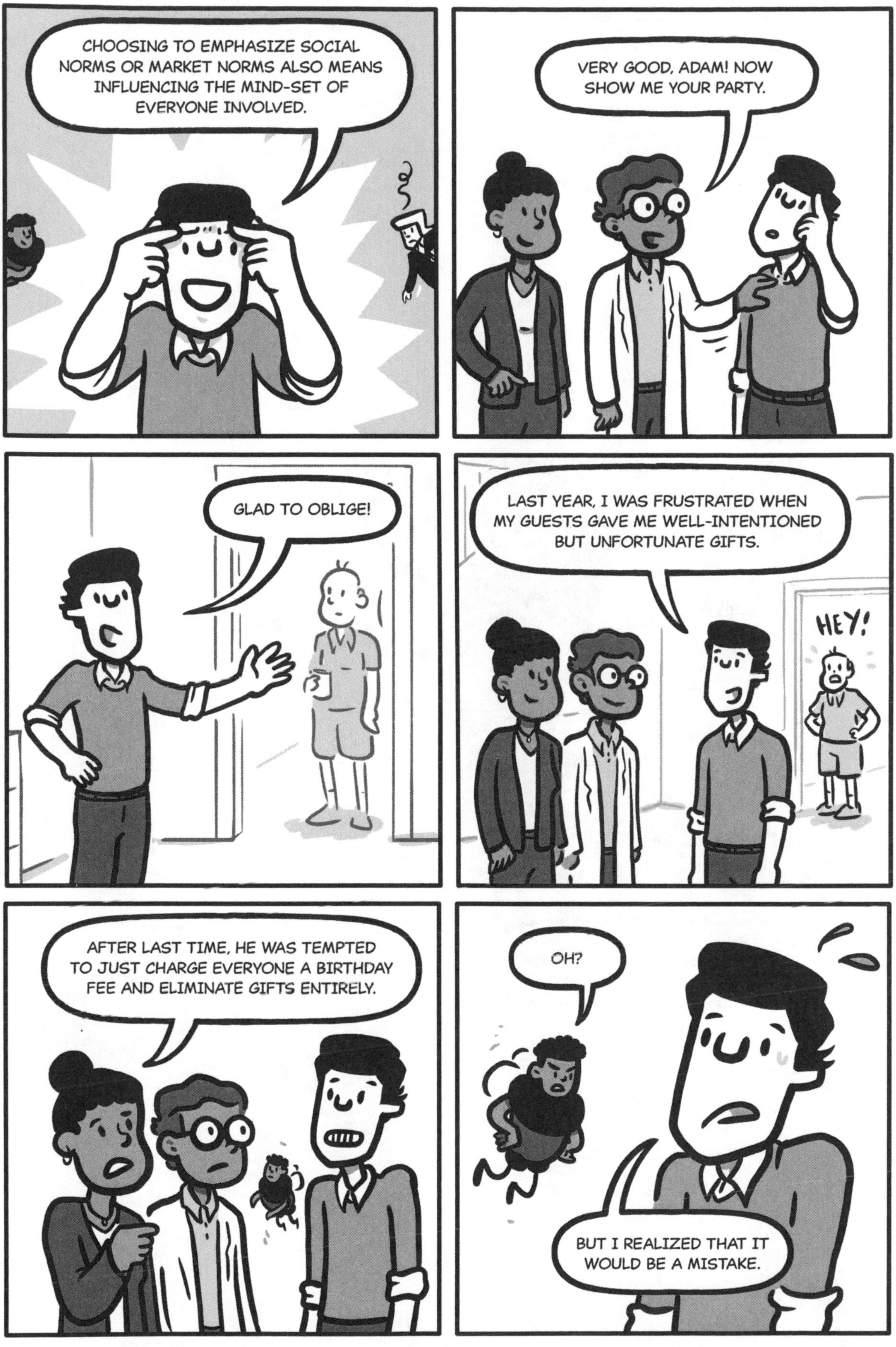
CHOOSING TO EMPHASIZE SOCIAL NORMS OR MARKET NORMS ALSO MEANS INFLUENCING THE MIND-SET OF EVERYONE INVOLVED.
VERY GOOD, ADAM! NOW SHOW ME YOUR PARTY.
GLAD TO OBLIGE!
LAST YEAR, I WAS FRUSTRATED WHEN MY GUESTS GAVE ME WELL-INTENTIONED BUT UNFORTUNATE GIFTS.
HEY!
AFTER LAST TIME, HE WAS TEMPTED TO JUST CHARGE EVERYONE A BIRTHDAY FEE AND ELIMINATE GIFTS ENTIRELY.
OH?
BUT I REALIZED THAT IT WOULD BE A MISTAKE.

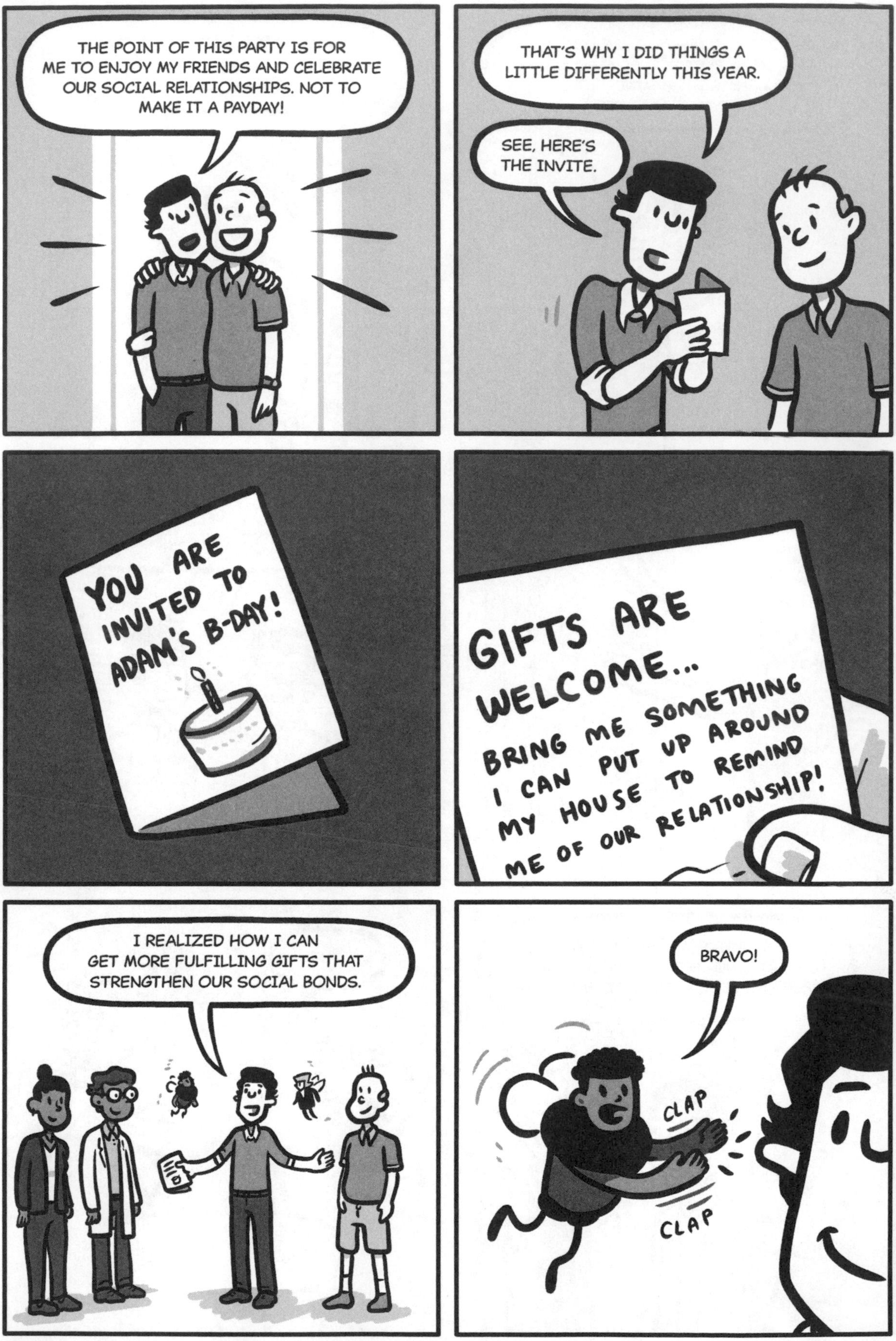
THE POINT OF THIS PARTY IS FOR ME TO ENJOY MY FRIENDS AND CELEBRATE OUR SOCIAL RELATIONSHIPS. NOT TO MAKE IT A PAYDAY!
THAT'S WHY I DID THINGS A LITTLE DIFFERENTLY THIS YEAR.
SEE, HERE'S THE INVITE.
YOU ARE INVITED TO ADAM'S B-DAY!
GIFTS ARE WELCOME...
BRING ME SOMETHING I CAN PUT UP AROUND MY HOUSE TO REMIND ME OF OUR RELATIONSHIP!
I REALIZED HOW I CAN GET MORE FULFILLING GIFTS THAT STRENGTHEN OUR SOCIAL BONDS.
BRAVO!
CLAP
CLAP

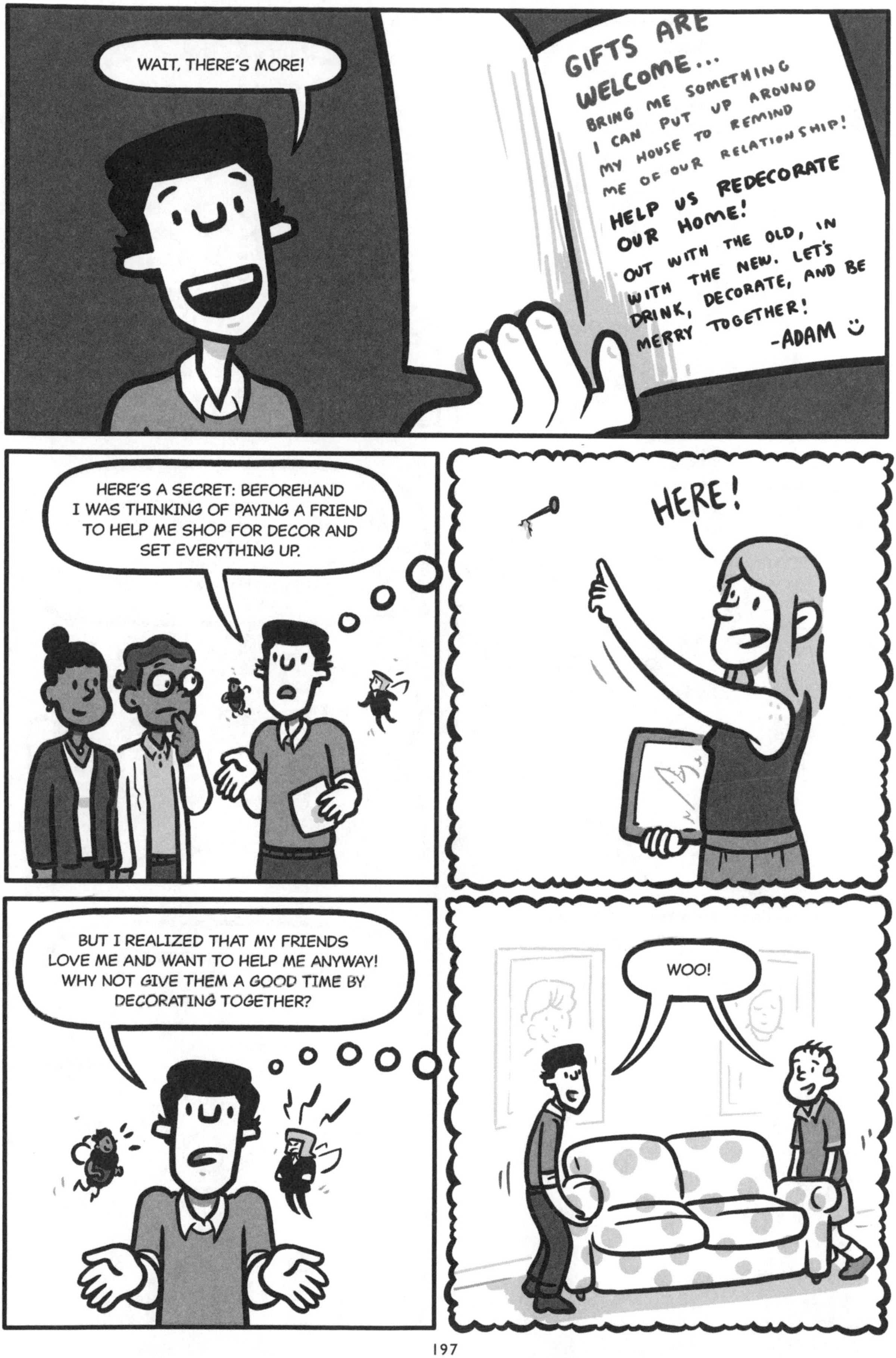
WAIT, THERE'S MORE!
GIFTS ARE WELCOME...
BRING ME SOMETHING I CAN PUT UP AROUND MY HOUSE TO REMIND ME OF OUR RELATIONSHIP!
HELP US REDECORATE OUR HOME!
OUT WITH THE OLD, IN WITH THE NEW. LET'S DRINK, DECORATE, AND BE MERRY TOGETHER!
-ADAM
HERE'S A SECRET: BEFOREHAND I WAS THINKING OF PAYING A FRIEND TO HELP ME SHOP FOR DECOR AND SET EVERYTHING UP.
HERE!
BUT I REALIZED THAT MY FRIENDS LOVE ME AND WANT TO HELP ME ANYWAY! WHY NOT GIVE THEM A GOOD TIME BY DECORATING TOGETHER?
WOO!

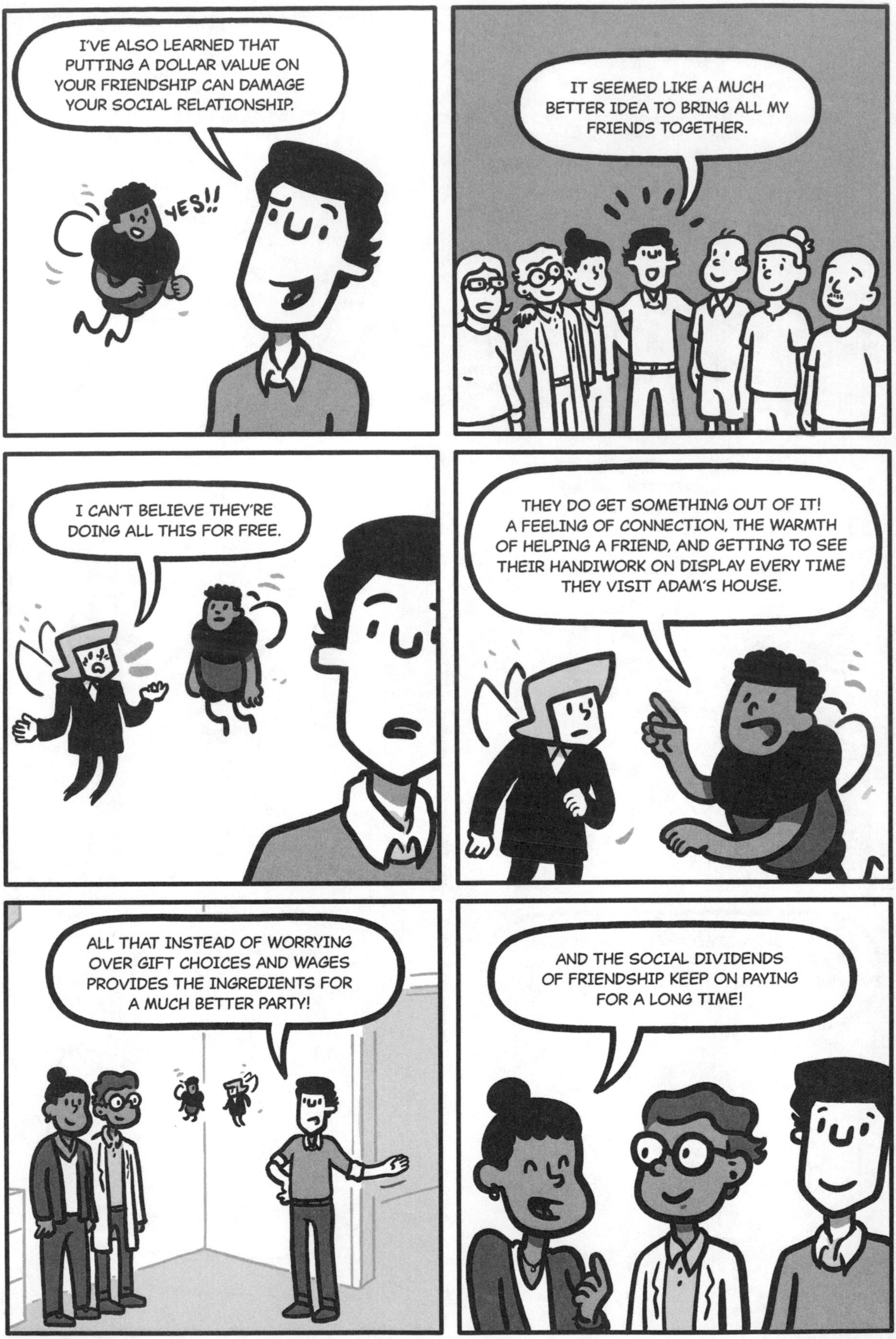
I'VE ALSO LEARNED THAT PUTTING A DOLLAR VALUE ON YOUR FRIENDSHIP CAN DAMAGE YOUR SOCIAL RELATIONSHIP.
YES!!
IT SEEMED LIKE A MUCH BETTER IDEA TO BRING ALL MY FRIENDS TOGETHER.
I CAN'T BELIEVE THEY'RE DOING ALL THIS FOR FREE.
THEY DO GET SOMETHING OUT OF IT! A FEELING OF CONNECTION, THE WARMTH OF HELPING A FRIEND, AND GETTING TO SEE THEIR HANDIWORK ON DISPLAY EVERY TIME THEY VISIT ADAM'S HOUSE.
ALL THAT INSTEAD OF WORRYING OVER GIFT CHOICES AND WAGES PROVIDES THE INGREDIENTS FOR A MUCH BETTER PARTY!
AND THE SOCIAL DIVIDENDS OF FRIENDSHIP KEEP ON PAYING FOR A LONG TIME!

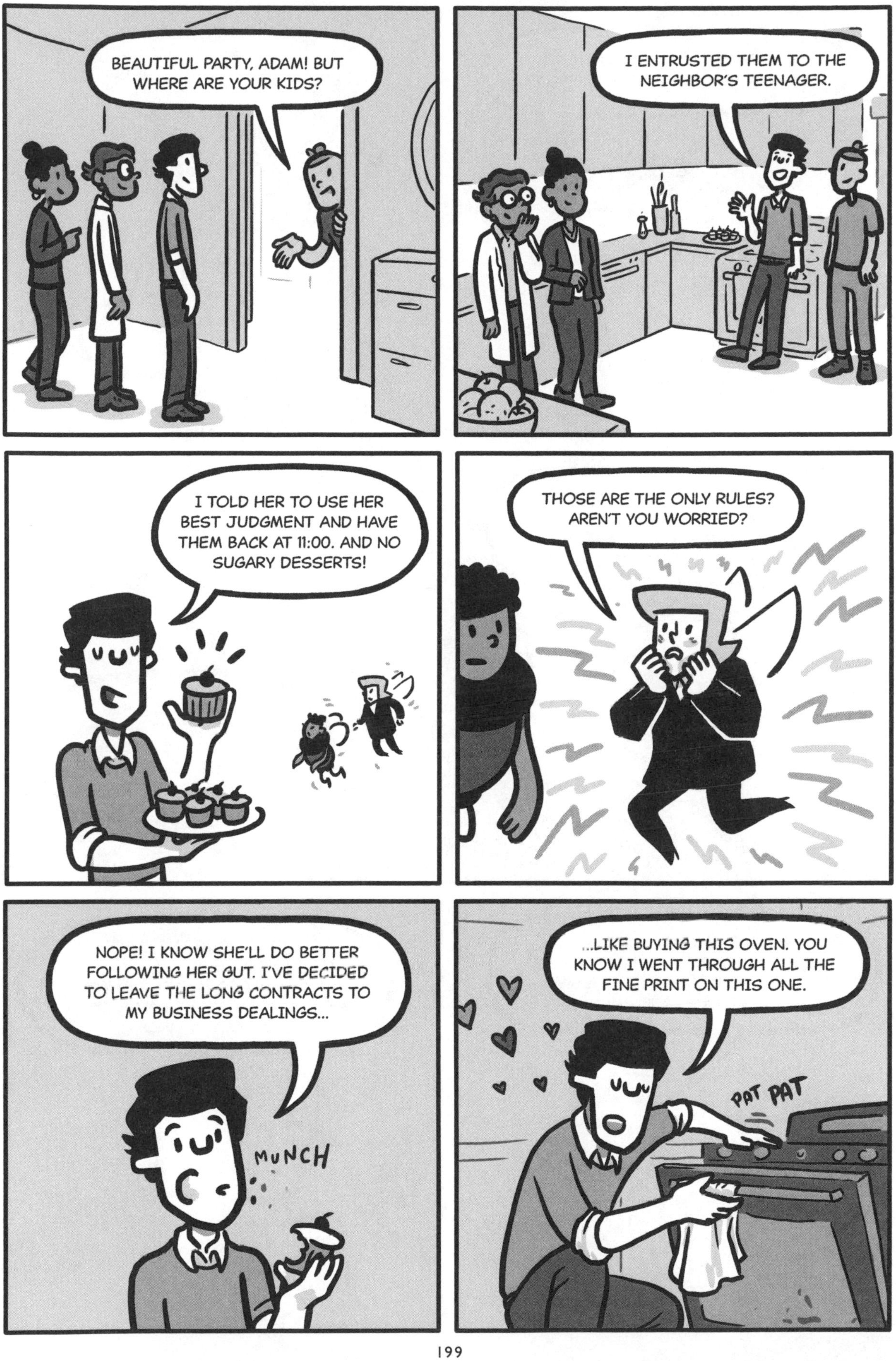
BEAUTIFUL PARTY, ADAM! BUT WHERE ARE YOUR KIDS?
I ENTRUSTED THEM TO THE NEIGHBOR'S TEENAGER.
I TOLD HER TO USE HER BEST JUDGMENT AND HAVE THEM BACK AT 11:00. AND NO SUGARY DESSERTS!
THOSE ARE THE ONLY RULES? AREN'T YOU WORRIED?
NOPE! I KNOW SHE'LL DO BETTER FOLLOWING HER GUT. I'VE DECIDED TO LEAVE THE LONG CONTRACTS TO MY BUSINESS DEALINGS...
MUNCH
...LIKE BUYING THIS OVEN. YOU KNOW I WENT THROUGH ALL THE FINE PRINT ON THIS ONE.
PAT PAT

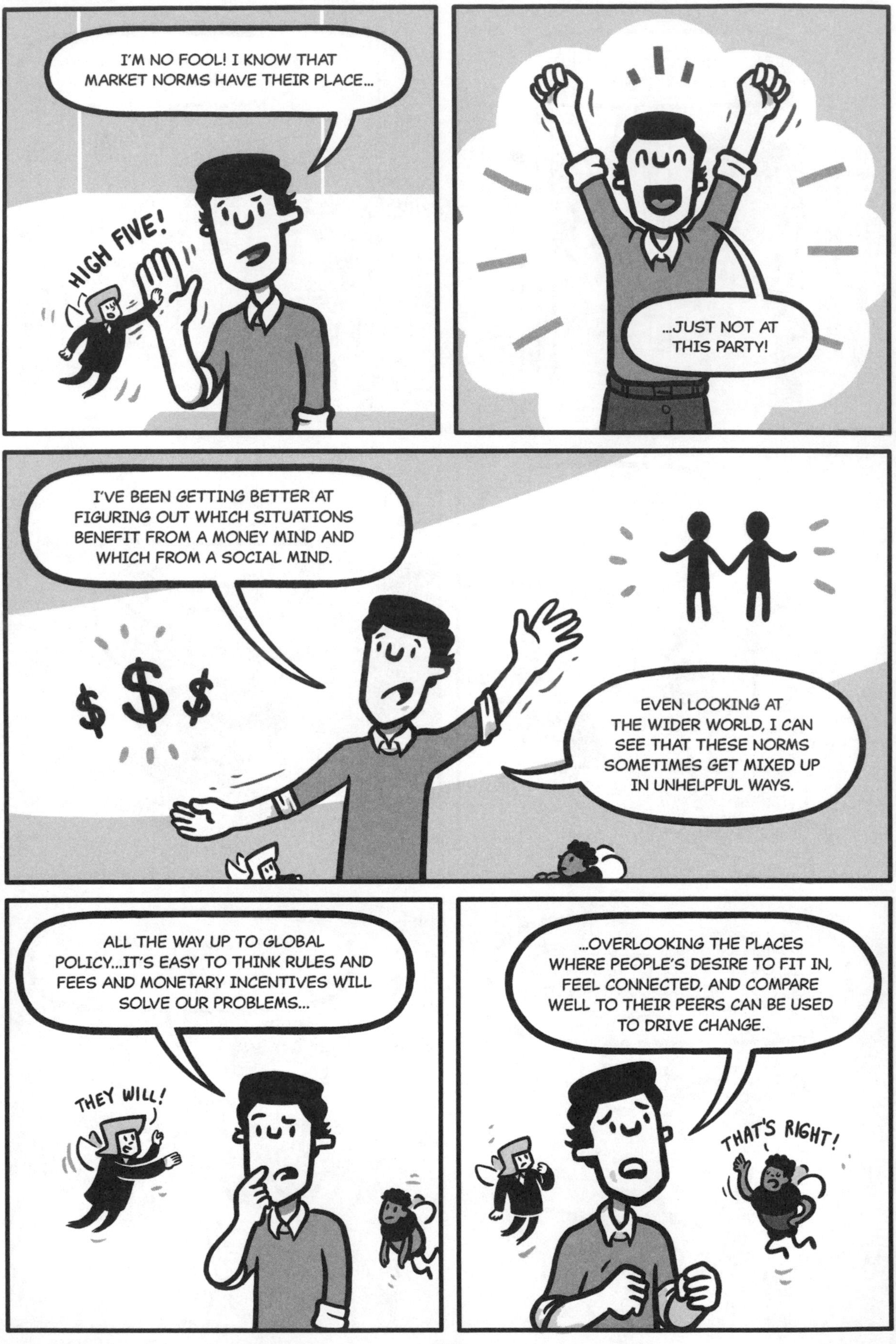
I'M NO FOOL! I KNOW THAT MARKET NORMS HAVE THEIR PLACE...
HIGH FIVE!
...JUST NOT AT THIS PARTY!
I'VE BEEN GETTING BETTER AT FIGURING OUT WHICH SITUATIONS BENEFIT FROM A MONEY MIND AND WHICH FROM A SOCIAL MIND.
$ $ $
EVEN LOOKING AT THE WIDER WORLD, I CAN SEE THAT THESE NORMS SOMETIMES GET MIXED UP IN UNHELPFUL WAYS.
ALL THE WAY UP TO GLOBAL POLICY...IT'S EASY TO THINK RULES AND FEES AND MONETARY INCENTIVES WILL SOLVE OUR PROBLEMS...
THEY WILL!
...OVERLOOKING THE PLACES WHERE PEOPLE'S DESIRE TO FIT IN, FEEL CONNECTED, AND COMPARE WELL TO THEIR PEERS CAN BE USED TO DRIVE CHANGE.
THAT'S RIGHT!

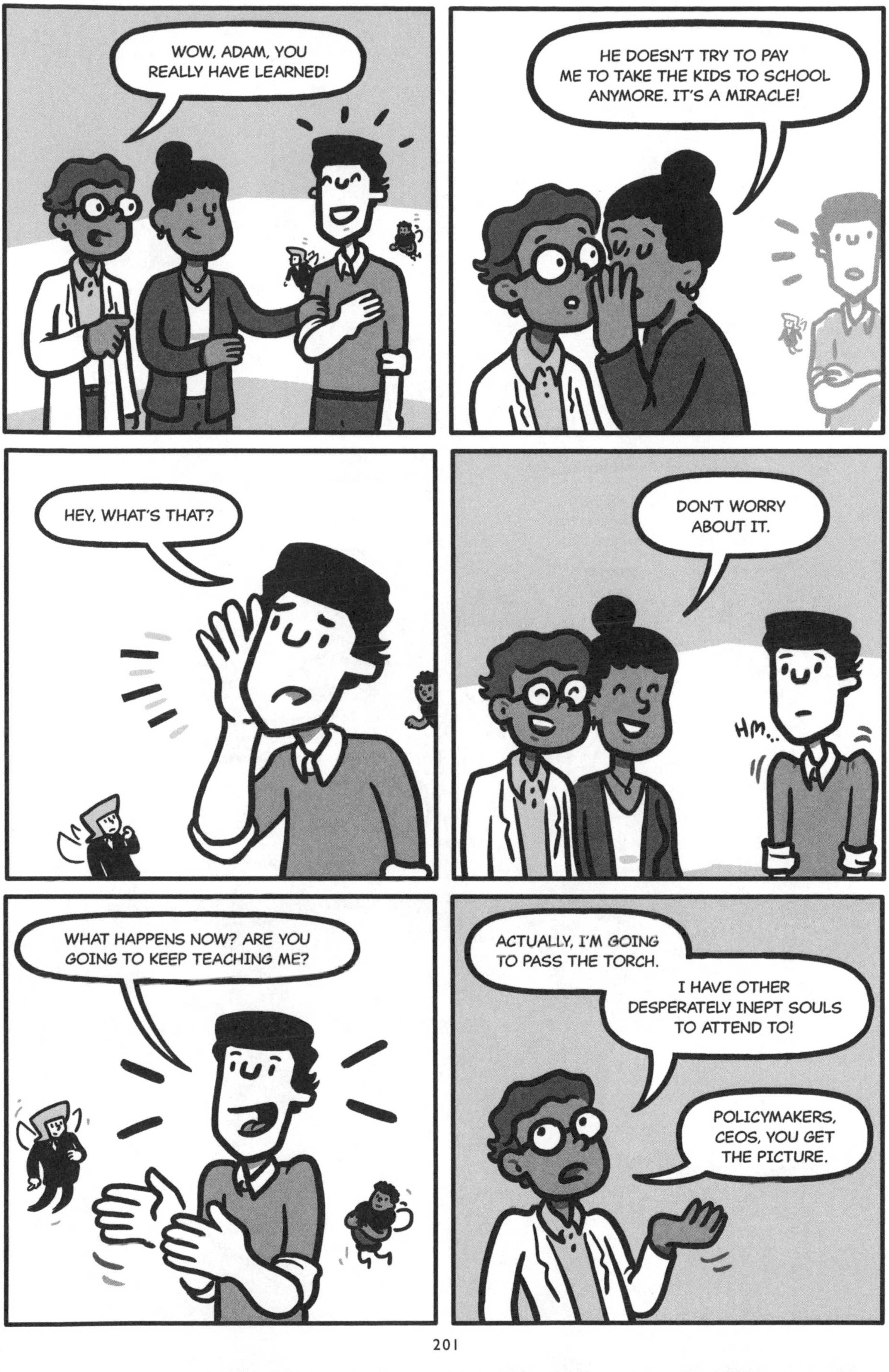
WOW, ADAM, YOU REALLY HAVE LEARNED!
HE DOESN'T TRY TO PAY ME TO TAKE THE KIDS TO SCHOOL ANYMORE. IT'S A MIRACLE!
HEY, WHAT'S THAT?
DON'T WORRY ABOUT IT.
HM...
WHAT HAPPENS NOW? ARE YOU GOING TO KEEP TEACHING ME?
ACTUALLY, I'M GOING TO PASS THE TORCH.
I HAVE OTHER DESPERATELY INEPT SOULS TO ATTEND TO!
POLICYMAKERS, CEOS, YOU GET THE PICTURE.

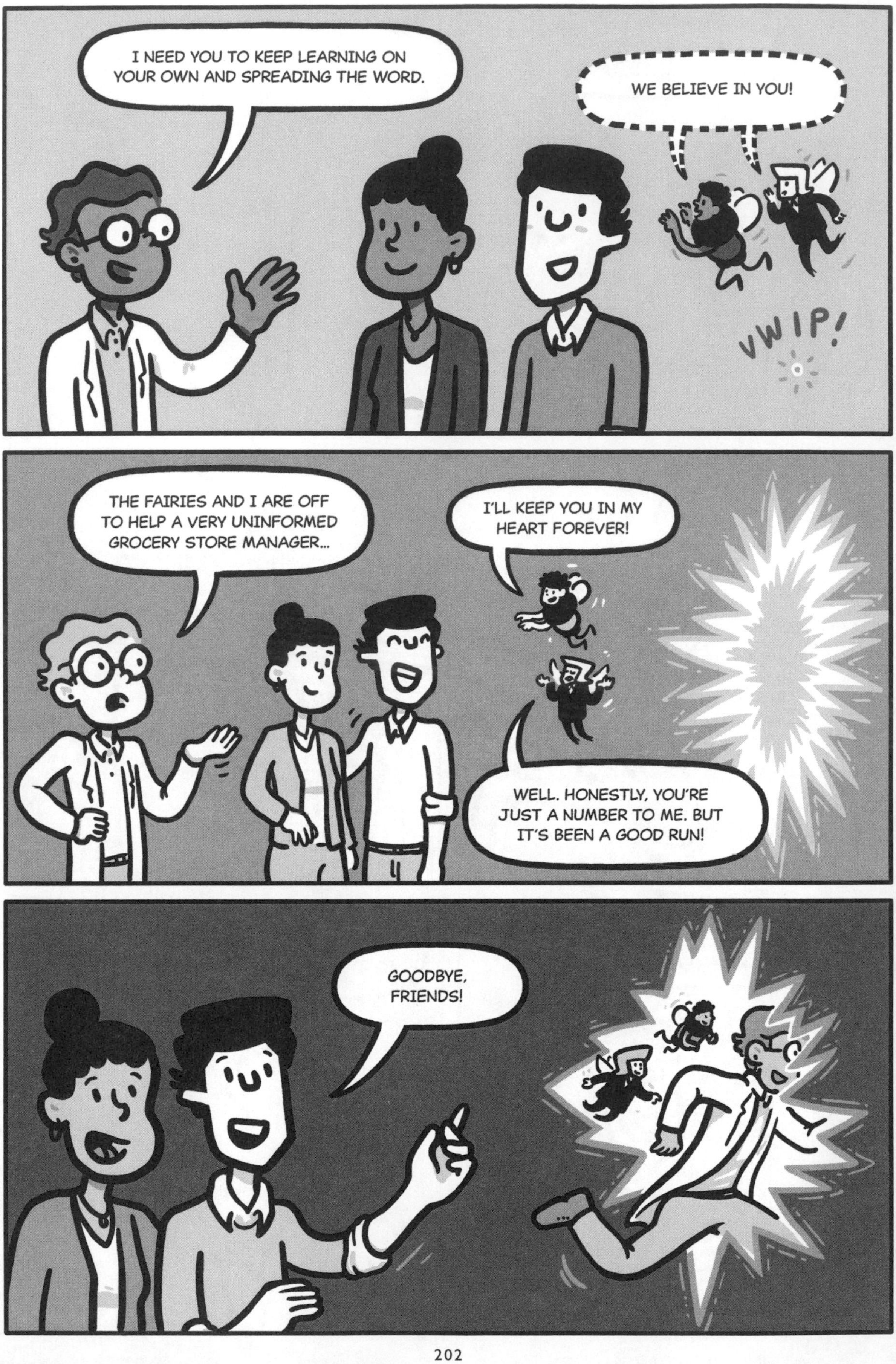
I NEED YOU TO KEEP LEARNING ON YOUR OWN AND SPREADING THE WORD.
WE BELIEVE IN YOU!
VWIP!
THE FAIRIES AND I ARE OFF TO HELP A VERY UNINFORMED GROCERY STORE MANAGER...
I'LL KEEP YOU IN MY HEART FOREVER!
WELL. HONESTLY, YOU'RE JUST A NUMBER TO ME. BUT IT'S BEEN A GOOD RUN!
GOODBYE, FRIENDS!

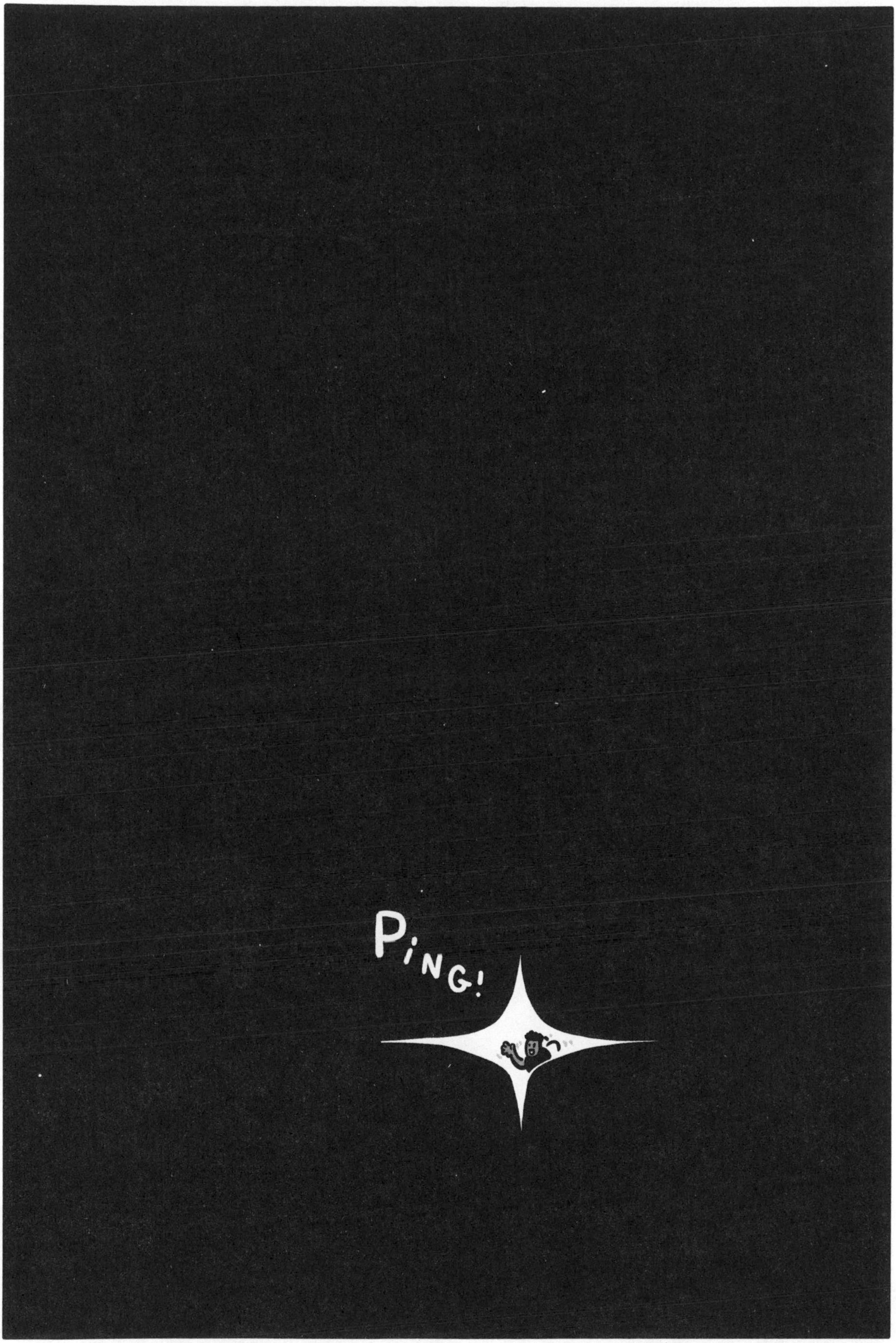
PING!

NOTES

1. TWO DIFFERENT WORLDS

27 *We asked participants to drag a circle*: James Heyman and Dan Ariely, "Effort for Payment: A Tale of Two Markets," *Psychological Science* 15, no. 11 (November 2004): 787–93.

2. GETTING PERSONAL

46 *"pain of paying"*: Dan Ariely, *Predictably Irrational: The Hidden Forces That Shape Our Decisions*, revised and expanded ed. (New York: HarperCollins, 2009).

3. THE GIFT THAT GIVES

54 *the circle-dragging experiment*: James Heyman and Dan Ariely, "Effort for Payment: A Tale of Two Markets," *Psychological Science* 15, no. 11 (November 2004): 787–93.

59 *Cycle of giving*: Lalin Anik, Lara B. Aknin, Michael I. Norton, and Elizabeth W. Dunn, "Feeling Good About Giving: The Benefits (and Costs) of Self-Interested Charitable Behavior," Working Paper 10-012, Harvard Business School, 2009.

66 *how often they gave gifts from different categories*: Guy Hochman, "Gift Giving Survey" (working paper, Duke University, 2013).

4. PUTTING IDEAS TO WORK

79 *In 2008, researchers Nina Mazar, On Amir, and Dan Ariely*: Nina Mazar, On Amir, and Dan Ariely, "The Dishonesty of Honest People: A Theory of Self-Concept Maintenance," *Journal of Marketing Research* 45, no. 4 (December 2008): 633–44.

5. WILLINGNESS TO WORK AND MARKETPLACE MOTIVATION

86 *people generally prefer to receive the money*: Victoria A. Shaffer and Hal R. Arkes, "Preference Reversals in Evaluations of Cash Versus Non-Cash Incentives," *Journal of Economic Psychology* 30, no. 6 (December 2009): 859–72.

91 *In 2009, researchers ran a study in a poor village in India*: Dan Ariely, Uri Gneezy, George Loewenstein, and Nina Mazar, "Large Stakes and Big Mistakes," *Review of Economic Studies* 76, no. 2 (2009): 451–69.

93 *experiment conducted by the Goodyear Tire and Rubber Company*: John M. Jack and Tom K. Gravalos, "The Trouble with Money," *Business Insider Worldwide* (Minneapolis: BI Performance Services, 1995).

96 *looked at how different short-term bonuses affected productivity*: Liad Bareket-Bojmel, Guy Hochman, and Dan Ariely, "It's (Not) All About the Jacksons: Testing Different Types of Short-Term Bonuses in the Field," *Journal of Management* 45, no. 2 (February 2017): 534–54. (Pub. online, 2014.)

99 *recruited participants at a German university to enter data into computers*: Sebastian Kube, Michel André Maréchal, and Clemens Puppe, "The Currency of Reciprocity: Gift Exchange in the Workplace," *American Economic Review* 102, no. 4 (2012): 1644–62.

102 *Intrinsic motivation works from the inside*: Richard M. Ryan and Edward L. Deci, "Self-Determination Theory and the Facilitation of Intrinsic Motivation, Social Development, and Well-Being," *American Psychologist* 55, no. 1 (January 2000): 68–78.

104 *In 1973, Mark Lepper and David Greene conducted a study involving preschoolers drawing pictures*: Mark R. Lepper, David Greene, and Richard E. Nisbett, "Undermining Children's Intrinsic Interest with Extrinsic Reward: A Test of the 'Overjustification' Hypothesis," *Journal of Personality and Social Psychology* 28, no. 1 (1973): 129–37.

6. GOING TO THE MARKET AND BACK AGAIN

123 *A 2001 study of day cares*: Uri Gneezy and Aldo Rustichini, "A Fine Is a Price," *Journal of Legal Studies* 29, no. 1 (January 2000): 1–17.

128 *Just ask Netflix!*: Nick Wingfield and Brian Stelter, "How Netflix Lost 800,000 Members, and Good Will," *New York Times*, October 24, 2011.

131 *Stephan Meier's study at the University of Zurich*: Stephan Meier, "Do Subsidies Increase Charitable Giving in the Long Run? Matching Donations in a Field Experiment," *Journal of the European Economic Association* 5, no. 6 (December 2007): 1203–22.

7. FEELING COMPLETE

145 *At a certain point, the time and effort*: Keith J. Crocker and Kenneth J. Reynolds, "The Efficiency of Incomplete Contracts: An Empirical Analysis of Air Force Engine Procurement," *Rand Journal of Economics* 24, no. 1 (Spring 1993): 126–46.

150 *marriages are far more likely to end in divorce*: Catherine Kenney and Ryan Bogle, "Money, Honey If You Want to Get Along with Me: Money Management and Union Dissolution in Marriage and Cohabitation," Working Paper no. 25, Princeton University, Woodrow Wilson School of Public and International Affairs, Center for Research on Child Wellbeing, May 2010.

150 *a generous attitude is reported to be an essential contributor*: Tara Parker-Pope, "Is Generosity Better Than Sex?" *New York Times*, December 11, 2011, https://archive.nytimes.com/query.nytimes.com/gst/fullpage-9F04E5DA1139F932A25751C1A9679D8B63.html.

159 *A 2014 study led by Stephen M. Garcia*: Stephen M. Garcia, Patricia Chen, and Matthew T. Gordon, "The

Letter Versus the Spirit of the Law: A Lay Perspective on Culpability," *Judgment and Decision Making* 9, no. 5 (September 2014): 479–90.

162 *Barry Schwartz and Kenneth Sharpe investigate the duties of hospital janitors*: Barry Schwartz and Kenneth E. Sharpe, "Practical Wisdom: Aristotle Meets Positive Psychology," *Journal of Happiness Studies* 7, no. 3 (2006): 377–95; Barry Schwartz and Kenneth E. Sharpe, *Practical Wisdom: The Right Way to Do the Right Thing* (New York: Riverhead Books, 2010).

8. BIG DEALS

169 *21 of 37 of our largest aquifers*: Alexandra S. Richey, Brian F. Thomas, Min-Hui Lo, John T. Reager, James S. Famiglietti, Katalyn Voss, Sean Swenson, and Matthew Rodell, "Quantifying Renewable Groundwater Stress with GRACE," *Water Resources Research* 51, no. 7 (2015): 5217–38.

169 *air pollution causes 200,000 early deaths in the U.S.*: Fabio Caiazzo, Akshay Ashok, Ian A. Waitz, Steve H. L. Yim, and Steven R. H. Barrett, "Air Pollution and Early Deaths in the United States, Part I: Quantifying the Impact of Major Sectors in 2005," *Atmospheric Environment* 79 (2013): 198–208.

170 *A 2008 study used door hangers*: Noah J. Goldstein, Robert B. Cialdini, and Vladas Griskevicius, "A Room with a Viewpoint: Using Social Norms to Motivate Environmental Conservation in Hotels," *Journal of Consumer Research* 35, no. 3 (2008): 472–82.

172 *A field study by a different team*: Katie Baca-Motes, Amber Brown, Ayelet Gneezy, Elizabeth A. Keenan, and Leif D. Nelson, "Commitment and Behavior Change: Evidence from the Field," *Journal of Consumer Research* 39, no. 5 (2012): 1070–84.

173 *A company called Opower uses social norms*: Hunt Allcott, "Social Norms and Energy Conservation," *Journal of Public Economics* 95, nos. 9–10 (October 2011): 1082–95.

175 *a series of field experiments in over two hundred N.Y.C., Dallas, and Chicago public schools*: Roland G. Fryer, Jr., "Financial Incentives and Student Achievement: Evidence from Randomized Trials," *Quarterly Journal of Economics* 126, no. 4 (May 2011): 1755–98.

176 *While some schools may have seen a bump in test results*: Marianne Perie and David P. Baker, "Job Satisfaction Among America's Teachers: Effects of Workplace Conditions, Background Characteristics, and Teacher Compensation," Statistical Analysis Report, National Center for Education Statistics, July 1997.

176 *the incentive system actually undermined teacher motivation*: Lisa Guisbond, Monty Neill, and Bob Schaeffer, "NCLB's Lost Decade for Educational Progress: What Can We Learn from This Policy Failure?" *Educação & Sociedade* 33, no. 119 (2012): 405–30.

176 *it's better to approach the underlying issues*: Valerie Strauss, "No Child Left Behind's Test-Based Policies Failed. Will Congress Keep Them Anyway?" *Washington Post*, February 13, 2015.

177 *Just sending biweekly text messages*: Peter Bergman, "Parent-Child Information Frictions and Human Capital Investment: Evidence from a Field Experiment," CESifo Working Paper Series no. 5391, June 24, 2015.

177 *both students and teachers perform best when instrinisically motivated*: Ronald D. Sylvia and Tony Hutchison, "What Makes Ms. Johnson Teach? A Study of Teacher Motivation," *Human Relations* 38, no. 9 (September 1985): 841–56.

179 *informed the students and their teachers of five traits*: Hunter Gehlbach, Maureen E. Brinkworth, Aaron M. King, Laura M. Hsu, Joseph McIntyre, and Todd Rogers, "Creating Birds of Similar Feathers: Leveraging Similarity to Improve Teacher-Student Relationships and Academic Achievement," *Journal of Educational Psychology* 108, no. 3 (2016): 342–52.

181 *some courts report a failure-to-appear rate of up to 50%*: Maxine Bernstein, "Judges Cracking Down on

People Who Snub Jury Duty," Associated Press, May 21, 2017, https://apnews.com/62b279c38615469 fb9bee505c9c66ff5.

182 *people were slightly less likely to show up when offered more money*: Andrew J. Bloeser, Carl McCurley, and Jeffery J. Mondak, "Jury Service as Civic Engagement: Determinants of Jury Summons Compliance," *American Politics Research* 40, no. 2 (2012): 179–204.

183 *in the 2016 U.S. presidential election*: Thom File, *Characteristics of Voters in the Presidential Election of 2016*, United States Census Bureau, September 2018, https://www.census.gov/content/dam/Census/library/publications/2018/demo/P20-582.pdf.

184 *people who received the high-turnout message were more likely to report a 100% chance of voting*: Alan S. Gerber and Todd Rogers, "Descriptive Social Norms and Motivation to Vote: Everybody's Voting and so Should You," *Journal of Politics* 71, no. 1 (2009): 178–91.

186 *users who received the social message*: Robert M. Bond, Christopher J. Fariss, Jason J. Jones, Adam D. I. Kramer, Cameron Marlow, Jaime E. Settle, and James H. Fowler, "A 61-Million-Person Experiment in Social Influence and Political Mobilization," *Nature* 489, no. 7415 (2012): 295.

ACKNOWLEDGMENTS

This book would not be possible without the support of many lab members at the Center for Advanced Hindsight at Duke University. Your insight, humor, and patience bridged all the right gaps. Thank you for joining our grand experiment.

Our gratitude also goes out to everyone who has helped this project come to fruition, especially Jim Levine, Amanda Moon, Laird Gallagher, and Benjamin Rosenstock.

A NOTE ABOUT THE AUTHORS

DAN ARIELY is the James B. Duke Professor of Psychology and Behavioral Economics at Duke University. He is the founder and director of the Center for Advanced Hindsight, cocreator of the film documentary *(Dis)Honesty: The Truth About Lies*, and a three-time *New York Times* bestselling author. His books include *Predictably Irrational*, *The Upside of Irrationality*, *The (Honest) Truth About Dishonesty*, and *Irrationally Yours*.

MATT R. TROWER is a comic artist and illustrator living in Durham, North Carolina. They work as the resident artist for the Center for Advanced Hindsight at Duke University. When they aren't translating research into art, they spend their time petting dogs and zipping up drag queens.